Managing Local Governments

Designing management control systems that deliver value

Emanuele Padovani and David W. Young

Routledge
Taylor & Francis Group

LONDON AND NEW YORK

First published 2012
by Routledge
2 Park Square, Milton Park, Abingdon, Oxon OX14 4RN

Simultaneously published in the USA and Canada
by Routledge
711 Third Avenue, New York, NY 10017

Routledge is an imprint of the Taylor & Francis Group, an informa business

British Library Cataloguing in Publication Data
A catalogue record for this book is available from the British Library

Library of Congress Cataloging in Publication Data
Padovani, Emanuele.
  Managing local governments: designing management control systems
  that deliver value/Emanuele Padovani and David W. Young.
     p. cm. – (Routledge masters in public management)
  Includes bibliographical references and index.
  1. Local government. 2. Public administration.
  3. Cost control. 4. Strategic planning.
  I. Young, David W. II. Title. JS78.P29 2012
352.14–dc23   2011024459

ISBN: 978-0-415-78329-3 (hbk)
ISBN: 978-0-415-78330-9 (pbk)
ISBN: 978-0-203-14998-0 (ebk)

Typeset in Perpetua by Sunrise Setting Ltd

MIX
Paper from
responsible sources
FSC
www.fsc.org   FSC® C004839

Printed and bound in Great Britain by
TJ International Ltd, Padstow, Cornwall

Managing Local Governments

Local go
political
complex

This
enhance
putting
the-box

- Inc
- Bu
- Ex
- Ass
- Us
  for

This
senior a
are con
and serv

Emanue
lic Sect
consultan
control, ou
managemen

David W. You
Boston Univers
agement Progra
a visiting professo
Pisa, and the Unive

ROUTLEDGE MASTERS IN PUBLIC MANAGEMENT

Edited by Stephen P. Osborne, Owen Hughes, and Walter Kickert

Routledge Masters in Public Management series is an integrated set of texts. It is intended to form the backbone for the holistic study of the theory and practice of public management as part of

- a taught Masters, MBA or MPA course at a university or college
- a work-based, in-service, programme of education and training, or
- a programme of self-guided study

Each volume stands alone in its treatment of its topic, whether it be strategic management, marketing or procurement, and is co-authored by leading specialists in their field. However, all volumes in the series share both a common pedagogy and a common approach to the structure of the text. Key features of all volumes in the series include:

- A critical approach to combining theory with practice which educates its reader, rather than solely teaching him/her a set of skills
- Clear learning objectives for each chapter
- The use of figures, tables and boxes to highlight key ideas, concepts and skill
- An annotated bibliography, guiding students in their further reading
- A dedicated case study in the topic of each volume, to serve as a focus for discussion and learning

Managing Change and Innovation in Public Service Organizations
Stephen P. Osborne and Kerry Brown

Risk and Crisis Management in the Public Sector
Lynn T. Drennan and Allan McConnell

Contracting for Public Services
Carsten Greve

Performance Management in the Public Sector
Wouter van Dooren, Geert Bouckaert, and John Halligan

Financial Management and Accounting in the Public Sector
Gary Bandy

Strategic Leadership in the Public Sector
Paul Joyce

Managing Local Governments: Designing Management Control Systems That Deliver Value
Emanuele Padovani and David W. Young

Dedication

This is book is dedicated to Professor Giuseppe Farneti.

A teacher, mentor, colleague, and friend who has had a profound influence on our professional lives.

Contents

List of figures, tables, and boxes

FIGURES

TABLES

BOXES

Preface

This book has been written for both students of public management and managers of local governments. It will also be helpful to managers of county, state, regional, and perhaps even national governments. And it likely will be of interest to managers of semiautonomous public entities, such as water and sewer authorities or public utilities. It should be of special interest to elected officials of cities, towns, municipalities, and other local government entities, as well as to the citizens who elect those officials to office.

The book does not purport to describe, or even support, business as usual. Instead, we argue that local governments (LGs) in general are poorly managed and do not provide anywhere near as much value to their citizens as they could by making some (often relatively minor) changes in how they conduct their affairs.

Most LG managers will resist the sorts of changes we propose – these changes will take them well outside their comfort zones. But, in an era of constrained resources for all public sector entities, including LGs, and with taxpayer resistance to providing increased funding without some evidence of value for their money, it is time for LG managers to make the move.

Middle managers cannot be expected to make these changes on their own – many have been doing the same job for years, if not decades, and the changes we propose will entail new ways of doing their jobs. For very valid reasons, they can be expected to resist these changes. Therefore, senior managers will need to support and encourage the changes, which means that senior managers will be moving outside *their* comfort zones. Thus, if senior managers are to be encouraged to rethink the way their LGs conduct their activities, elected officials will need to insist that the changes be made. Perhaps citizens, as members of citizen boards, or simply as vocal taxpayers, will need to make it clear to these elected officials that remaining in office is contingent upon making some of the changes that we discuss herein.

This book, then, is a call to arms. It proposes new ways of thinking about how LGs can be managed, and it provides enough examples to demonstrate that the changes we propose are not academic "pie in the sky" thinking. They have taken place in some locales, and can take place in others. What is needed is the will to forge ahead.

Acknowledgments

We are grateful to several people for their assistance in preparing this book. David owes a major intellectual debt to the late Robert N. Anthony, with whom he co-authored five editions of *Management Control in Nonprofit Organizations*. Emanuele owes a similar debt to Professor Giuseppe Farneti, who has been his mentor and collaborator for many years.

We both are also grateful to the students and faculty who were with us in three editions of the Summer School on Public Management, which was held at the Forlì Campus of the University of Bologna in Italy. We learned a great deal from these groups. In this regard, we would like to single out two of our teaching colleagues, Leslie Breitner and Janelle Heineke.

Emanuele is especially appreciative to the several local governments where he has conducted his research over the past seven years. They have provided him with examples – some good and some perhaps not so good – that have helped him develop his thinking about the matters we discuss in this book.

Finally, we are both grateful to our families. David's sons (Christian and Tony) spent several months without their father's presence while he was in Italy working on the book (although it is not clear that they suffered much as a result of their greater freedom to cavort!). Emanuele's wife (Valentina) and son (Giovanni) occasionally found him working on the book when they hoped he would be available for some family fun.

Abbreviations

BSC	Balanced scorecard
CF	Cash flow
CVP	Cost-volume-profit (analysis)
I	Investment
IRR	Internal rate of return
LG	Local government
MCS	Management control system
NPM	New Public Management
NPV	Net present value
PVF	Present value factor
R&D	Research and development
ROA	Return on assets
ROE	Return on equity
WCC	Weighted cost of capital
WRA	Weighted return on assets

Introduction

The book is designed so that the chapters build on each other, but each also can stand on its own reasonably well. The book is not a novel, so it is fine, perhaps even desirable, for a reader who is interested in a particular topic to head directly to the chapter focusing on that topic. To assist readers in that decision, we briefly describe the contents of each chapter.[1]

CHAPTER 1: THE CONTEXT FOR MANAGEMENT CONTROL SYSTEMS IN LOCAL GOVERNMENTS (EP)

We begin the book with a discussion of the size and nature of local governments (LGs) across the globe. There are many different types of LGs, and we discuss them briefly, including a description of the kinds of services they provide. We also identify the general characteristics of LGs that affect their ability to develop good management control systems, such as the absence of a profit measure, and, more generally, the difficulty they face in measuring performance.

Readers who are familiar with LGs – or at least with their own LG – may wish to skip Chapter 1, and begin with Chapter 2, where the "meat" of the book begins.

CHAPTER 2: MANAGEMENT CONTROL SYSTEMS: AN OVERVIEW (DY)

In this chapter we put management control into its context as the bridge between strategic planning and task control, and then discuss its various elements. We briefly describe the structure and process of a management control system (akin to describing the anatomy and physiology of a human body). Subsequent chapters expand upon the ideas in this chapter.

CHAPTER 3: BARRIERS TO EFFECTIVE MANAGEMENT CONTROL IN LOCAL GOVERNMENTS (DY)

Here we discuss the many barriers that LGs face in their efforts to implement improved management control systems, and hence to move toward what has been called the New Public Management (NPM) Paradigm. These barriers are multifaceted. They include the fact that a typical LG provides a heterogeneous mix of programs, ranging from street cleaning to social welfare. They include conceptual barriers such the need for generational and consumer equity. They are related to the difficulty of identifying and measuring positive externalities for some services, and for developing pricing units for others.

The barriers also include a variety of more practical matters that face an LG, such as the lack of a control culture, highly centralized decision making, an absence of market forces for many services and programs, and the existence of restrictive personnel policies. In designing its management control system, an LG's senior managers must take all of these factors into account – a daunting task, indeed.

CHAPTER 4: THE STRUCTURE FOR MANAGEMENT CONTROL (EP)

In this chapter, we argue that an LG comprises a network of "responsibility centers," i.e., organizational units that have some sort of financial responsibility (as well, often, as some important *non-financial* or programmatic responsibilities). We argue that the concept of profit centers, while perhaps having a distasteful connotation to many LG managers, can be a powerful element in an LG's management control structure. We also introduce the idea of shadow profit centers – profit centers that use an external vendor's prices as a source of surrogate revenue, so that their performance can be compared with the private sector. And we talk about the difficulty that many LGs have in finding the right balance between a program structure and a departmental structure.

CHAPTER 5: PROGRAMMING (DY)

With this chapter, we begin our discussion of the management control process. The first phase of the process – programming – is where an LG makes decisions that have a long-term impact. Such decisions include initiating a new program or purchasing a new fixed asset. New fixed assets can range from a bridge or tunnel to a fire truck, or even to a desktop computer. We discuss a technique called "net present value" that is used in the private sector for such decisions and that could easily be used by an LG. Finally, we discuss two matters that are unique to all public sector organizations, including LGs: assessing benefits when bottom line performance is not the only consideration, and valuing a human life. The latter is important for projects that are intended to save lives, such as improved traffic safety or cancer screening.

CHAPTER 6: BUDGETING (EP)

Budgeting is the second phase of the management control process. In this chapter, we talk about the general nature of the operating budget, as well as the strategic context in which it sits. We identify some important behavioral aspects of budgeting, and take up the several steps that are involved in the "mechanical" side of the process. Here, we stress the importance of a "revenue-first" policy. We also contrast a line item budget with a program budget, and discuss the importance of including output and other performance measures in the budgeting phase of the process. We conclude the chapter by identifying some of what we call "budgeting misfits" – areas where the budget does not coincide with, or reinforce, certain other aspects of the LG's strategy or operations.

CHAPTER 7: MEASURING FULL COSTS AND SETTING PRICES (DY)

Here we address the topic of measuring full costs and discuss their role in setting prices. We talk about the two stages of cost accounting, and point out that few LGs have done a serious job of Stage 1 (the easier stage) and almost none has engaged in Stage 2 activities (attaching a mission center's costs to its outputs). We also discuss the difficulty of setting prices in an LG, pointing out the importance of unbundling prices whenever possible, but also identifying areas where prices based on full costs may not be appropriate. These areas include those where an LG's senior management team believes that some services (such as public safety or traffic lights) should be funded with general tax dollars, largely because there is no easy way to price them but also because they are, for all intents and purposes, "public goods."

CHAPTER 8: MEASURING DIFFERENTIAL COSTS AND ASSESSING OUTSOURCING OPPORTUNITIES (EP)

In this chapter, we emphasize the idea that different costs are used for different purposes, and that assessing cost behavior is important for many "alternative choice" decisions that are made in an LG. We discuss cost-volume-profit analysis, and argue that it is as important for an LG as it is for a for-profit company. We spend considerable time on the topic of outsourcing, pointing out that there are different degrees of risk when outsourcing a program or service, and that high-risk outsourcing needs to be managed differently from low-risk outsourcing.

CHAPTER 9: MEASURING PERFORMANCE (EP)

Measuring performance is a tricky matter in any nonprofit, but especially in an LG where much of the revenue is derived from general taxes and government grants, and hence there is no "sales revenue," as such, for many of an LG's services. In addition, performance can be measured along four dimensions, which we discuss in this chapter: inputs, processes, outputs, and outcomes. As one moves along this scale, there is an increase in the value of the information but a corresponding increase in the difficulty of obtaining reliable data. Nevertheless, LGs are in a unique position of being able to coordinate the outputs of several different departments toward an outcome that will benefit its citizenry. We use an example of "clean and safe streets" – an outcome whose achievement requires contributions of outputs from several different departments, such as public safety, road maintenance, and trash collection.

CHAPTER 10: REPORTING AND ACTION (DY)

Although reporting is classified as the final phase of the management control process, it is important to keep in mind that the "action" portion of the phase makes the process a closed loop, linking this phase back to all the others. Reports provide information that can help managers take action with regard to ongoing operations, the budget, or the LG's programs.

The chapter discusses two very powerful accounting techniques that can assist in taking action: flexible budgeting and variance analysis. Both have been used extensively in the private sector but have seen little application in LGs. We provide some examples of how their use could improve an LG's ability to provide more cost-effective services to its citizens. We also discuss some of the criteria for a good set of management control reports.

CHAPTER 11: THE ORGANIZATIONAL CONTEXT FOR A LOCAL GOVERNMENT'S MANAGEMENT CONTROL SYSTEM (DY)

We use this chapter to pull together a number of concepts that have been discussed in previous chapters, and that can provide the broad context for an LG's management control system. We begin by summarizing the characteristics of a well-managed local government. LG managers can use this as a sort of "scorecard" to assess where they might best begin to think about areas for improvement. We then position the management control process as one of seven activities that must be integrated and managed in concert if an LG is to be successful in achieving its objectives. We conclude with some thoughts on the change process. It is fine for senior managers to know what kind of management control system they want, but it often is difficult to make the needed changes a reality. These thoughts can be helpful to an LG's senior management in designing a change effort.

CASE STUDIES

Some of the book's chapters are followed by appendices. These either provide additional depth to the material in the chapter, or illustrate how some of the chapter's ideas actually were used in an LG setting. We also provide a variety of examples (in boxes) throughout each chapter to illustrate how one or more of the chapter's concepts were put to work. Since there is no such thing as a "typical" LG, the examples no doubt cannot be transferred from one LG setting to another without some tweaking. Nevertheless, they should be helpful to get the creative juices flowing.

If the book is used in an academic setting, the instructor may wish to supplement some of the chapters with one or more case studies. A case study generally has a manager as its focal point, who is required to make a decision concerning some aspect of the organization. Students are expected to use the chapter's concepts (as well as concepts from other courses or books) to analyze the problem presented in the case, and to recommend a course of action.

Case studies on LGs are available from several sources:

- *John F. Kennedy School of Government Case Program:* Cases on government organizations of all kinds and sizes can be found here. Go to: http://www.ksgcase.harvard.edu
- *Harvard Business School Publishing:* Cases on government organizations also can be found at Harvard Business School Publishing. Go to: http://hbsp.harvard.edu
- *The Crimson Press Curriculum Center:* Go to: www.thecrimsongroup.org and click on Curriculum Center. Search on "government." This Web site also contains a portal to the Kennedy Schools Case Program.
- *Case books:* There are several case-books that instructors may wish to consider. These can be found most easily by going to www.Amazon.com, and searching on "Local Government Management and Cases."

NOTE

1 While the work has been written jointly, the lead author of each chapter is specified with the initials (EP or DY).

Chapter 1

The context for management control systems in local governments

LEARNING OBJECTIVES

At the end of this chapter you should:

- Be able to recognize the many different types of local governments (LGs) that can exist across the globe.
- Understand the general characteristics of LGs that affect their ability to develop good management control systems, such as the absence of a profit measure and the difficulty they face in measuring performance.
- Know the boundaries of a management control system in an LG, and understand why it will never provide as good a basis for planning or measuring performance as a comparable system does in a for-profit organization.

KEY POINTS

- LGs function at one of three levels: (1) basic (e.g., municipality, borough, city, urban district), (2) intermediate (e.g., province, county, metropolitan district), and (3) regional or state. In general, the number of levels in a given country varies depending on the country's size and political structure.
- Pure LGs have (1) jurisdiction over a given local territory, (2) decision-making bodies elected by citizens, (3) a mandate to provide for multiple public services, and (4) a degree of autonomy in imposing their taxes and policies. Municipalities and similar forms of LGs in both Europe and the United States fall into this category.
- Ten percent of the countries in the world have over 83 percent of the LGs. In 20 countries, LG expenditures are 20 percent or more of GDP.

- LG programs and services can include urban planning, housing, road construction and maintenance, transportation, education, vocational training, cultural activities, museums, libraries, leisure services, health care, welfare and social services, public safety (police and fire protection), economic development, water provision, sewage disposal, natural gas distribution, electricity, tourism, and environmental protection.
- Regardless of the form they take, or the country in which they exist, LGs typically face a similar set of constraints: (1) absence of a profit measure, (2) difficulty in measuring performance, (3) political influences in decision making, (4) restricted sources of financial support, (5) dominance of professionals in some services (e.g., health and education), and (6) external influences on decision-making.
- LGs have played, and continue to play, a key role in the provision of services to citizens in almost all countries As Table 1.1 indicates, there are over 700,000 LGs in the world, over half of which are in the Asia Pacific region. Of these some 250,000 (35 percent of the total) are in India.

An LG is an entity that provides services to meet a variety of needs in a specific community. According to one view, an LG provides services "that households and enterprises cannot as economically provide by themselves" (Asian Development Bank and Ministry of Finance, China, March 2000). In Latin America, where they often are called "sub-national," LGs' expenditures as a percentage of total national public expenditures have increased over the past decade from 13 to 19 percent (Bliss and DeShazo, 2009). Globally, as Table 1.2 shows, this percentage ranges from a low of about 4 percent (in Nicaragua and Panama) to 81 percent (in China). As Table 1.2 also shows, the average percentage for those regions with available data ranges from about 23 percent in North America to 33 percent in Eurasia.

Table 1.1 Distribution of local governments by region of the world

	Number	% of Total
Africa	15,565	2.2
Middle East-Western Asia	42,533	6.0
Europe	95,524	13.4
Asia Pacific	373,697	52.3
Eurasia	78,438	11.0
Latin America	16,641	2.3
North America	91,455	12.8
Total	713,853	100.0

Source: Adapted from World Bank and United Cities and Local Government, 2008.

Table 1.2 "*Pure*" *local governments by country and region and their expenditures as percents of GDP and total public expenditures*

Region/country	Number	Expenditures as % of GDP	Expenditures as % total public expenditures
AFRICA			
Algeria	1,589	n.a.	n.a.
Egypt	4,860	n.a.	n.a.
Benin	77	0.5	n.a.
Cameroon	340	n.a.	n.a.
Côte d'Ivoire	257	0.9	n.a.
Gabon	97	n.a.	n.a.
Ghana	166	0.3	n.a.
Guinea	342	n.a.	n.a.
Kenya	186	n.a.	n.a.
Madagascar	1,557	n.a.	n.a.
Mali	752	0.3	n.a.
Morocco	1,559	n.a.	n.a.
Mozambique	1,085	n.a.	n.a.
Niger	305	0.3	n.a.
Nigeria	774	n.a.	n.a.
Senegal	433	1.1	n.a.
South Africa	287	1.3	n.a.
Tanzania	209	n.a.	n.a.
Togo	60	0.4	n.a.
Tunisia	264	n.a.	n.a.
Uganda	180	0.7	n.a.
Zambia	72	n.a.	n.a.
Zimbabwe	114	0.8	n.a.
Total/Average	15,565	0.6	n.a.
MIDDLE EAST – WESTERN ASIA			
Bahrain	12	n.a.	n.a.
Iran, Isl. Rep	1,273	n.a.	n.a.
Iraq	n.a.	n.a.	n.a.
Jordan	111	n.a.	n.a.
Kuwait	n.a.	n.a.	n.a.
Lebanon	936	n.a.	n.a.
Oman	43	n.a.	n.a.
Palestine	88	n.a.	n.a.
Qatar	10	n.a.	n.a.
Saudi Arabia	196	n.a.	n.a.
Syria	576	n.a.	n.a.
Turkey	38,616	n.a.	n.a.
United Arab Emirates	n.a.	n.a.	n.a.
Yemen	672	n.a.	n.a.
Total/Average	42,533		

Table 1.2 *Continued*

Region/country	Number	Expenditures as % of GDP	Expenditures as % total public expenditures
EUROPE			
Austria	2,301	7.9	15.9
Belgium	599	6.1	13.8
Bulgaria	236	6.5	n.a.
Czech Republic	6,306	12.1	28.5
Denmark	289	33.0	60.4
Finland	452	20.1	38.5
France	36,655	11.1	20.3
Germany	15,359	7.3	15.4
Greece	1,085	3.1	6.0
Hungary	3,147	13.0	25.9
Ireland	185	6.8	42.4
Italy	8,206	15.4	32.5
Luxembourg	118	5.4	13.0
Netherlands	659	15.5	35.1
Norway	454	13.1	n.a.
Poland	2,862	13.5	30.3
Portugal	4,579	6.3	12.8
Slovenia	192	8.4	11.2
Spain	8,140	5.9	52.1
Sweden	313	25.0	44.3
Switzerland	2,919	25.2	n.a.
United Kingdom	468	13.2	29.0
Total/Average	95,524	12.5	27.8
ASIA-PACIFIC			
Australia	703	2.0	7.0
China	44,267	22.0	81.0
India	250,671	2.9	18.5
Indonesia	483	6.0	33.0
Japan	3,687	12.3	53.6
Malaysia	288	4.0	13.0
New Zealand	90	3.9	9.4
Pakistan	6,632	2.6	14.0
Philippines	43,656	n.a.	n.a.
Republic of Korea	3,769	16.0	44.0
Thailand	7,949	2.0	9.0
Vietnam	11,502	11.0	48.0
Total/Average	373,697	7.7	30.0

Table 1.2 Continued

Region/country	Number	Expenditures as % of GDP	Expenditures as % total public expenditures
EURASIA			
Armenia	930	1.3	n.a.
Azerbaijan	2,827	0.2	27.5
Belarus	1,665	19.3	40.1
Georgia	1,017	4.6	n.a.
Kazakhstan	2,523	10.8	48.0
Kyrgyz Republic	526	3.4	12.0
Moldova	942	7.2	29.0
Russia	23,972	5.3	18.0
Tajikistan	3,187	n.a.	n.a.
Turkmenistan	50	n.a.	n.a.
Ukraine	30,402	11.0	n.a.
Uzbekistan	10,397	23.0	55.0
Total/Average	78,438	8.6	32.8
LATIN AMERICA			
Argentina	2,223	25.2	41.8
Bolivia	336	30.0	29.5
Brazil	5,562	24.6	42.1
Chile	360	34.2	15.0
Colombia	1,131	35.2	29.8
Costa Rica	88	25.5	6.0
Cuba	183	n.a.	n.a.
Dominican Republic	184	19.3	7.0
Ecuador	241	24.5	22.1
El Salvador	276	17.5	8.7
Guatemala	354	11.7	13.0
Honduras	316	34.1	5.6
Mexico	2,439	23.3	31.9
Nicaragua	167	30.3	3.8
Panama	84	24.8	3.8
Paraguay	248	33.3	7.0
Peru	2,095	19.2	26.8
Uruguay	19	29.6	13.2
Venezuela	335	32.2	n.a.
Total/Average	16,641	26.4	18.1

Table 1.2 *Continued*

Region/ country	Number	Expenditures as of GDP	Expenditures as % total public expenditures
NORTH AMERICA			
Canada	3,930	7.5	17.8
United States	87,525	9.6	27.4
Total/Average	91,455	8.6	22.6
Total number of local governments	713,853		
Total number of countries	104		

High in solid box			Low in thin box

n.a. = not available.

Sources: Computations from World Bank, and United Cities and Local Government 2008; for the number of provincial, municipal, and other pure local governments of European countries, L. Bobbio, 2002: 68; for local public expenditure/total public expenditure (%) of European countries, Dexia 2004.

The importance of good LG management is a topic of growing interest. In countries such as China, where urbanization is expanding rapidly, the capacity of LGs to deal with the pressures of citizen demands has reached near crisis proportions. Indeed, 47 percent of the Chinese population lived in urban municipalities in 2010, creating serious infrastructure and social welfare spending needs (Central Intelligence Agency of the United States, 2011; Asian Development Bank and Ministry of Finance, China, March 2000). Similarly, in most Latin American countries, where LG expenditures average over 25 percent of GDP (about double that of Europe, and three times the average of Eurasia and North America), the managerial issues have moved beyond corruption (a hot topic in the early 2000s) to matters of the "socioeconomic wellbeing" of the citizenry (Bliss and DeShazo 2009).

In the United States and Europe, the measurement of LG performance has become a regular topic in the public administration and public management literature. Various approaches to improving the management of LG expenditures are being discussed with some frequency, including matters of strategic planning, output measurement, efficiency, programmatic outcomes, and citizen satisfaction (for example, see: Watson and Hassett 2003; Rivenbark and Kelly 2003).

This book addresses the above matters from the perspective of an LG's management control system – a topic that has been addressed only peripherally in discussions about improving LG performance. An LG's management control system includes

11

both its *structure*, i.e., its responsibility centers (such as enterprise funds, which are, in effect, profit centers) and a four-phase *process* that comprises programming, budgeting, measuring, and reporting. In many LGs, in line with contemporary trends, the management control process has begun to focus on non-financial as well as financial performance.

TYPES OF LOCAL GOVERNMENTS

For the purposes of this book, LGs comprise a wide variety of entities, including cities, towns, provinces, counties, prefectures, boroughs, municipalities, and metropolitan districts. The terminology varies among countries and is related, in part, to administrative traditions. From the perspective of an LG's management control system, however, the specific nature of the entity is relatively unimportant. The concepts we discuss can be applied to almost any type of LG.

There are many types of LGs. They vary across countries and sometimes even within a given country – such as in the United States (Kemp 2007). These entities tend to fall into two broad categories: pure and hybrid (sometimes called "first tier" and "second tier" or "first level" and "second level").

Pure local governments

Pure LGs have (1) jurisdiction over a given local territory, (2) decision-making bodies elected by citizens, (3) a mandate to provide for multiple public services, and (4) a certain degree of autonomy in imposing their taxes and policies (Cole and Boyne 1995). Municipalities and similar forms of LGs in both Europe and the United States fall into this category.

The number of pure LGs varies substantially among the countries shown in Table 1.2, from a low of 10 in Qatar to a high of 250,000 in India, with an average of just under 7,000 per country. This number is somewhat misleading, however, as it is biased by the Asia Pacific region (which has an average of about 31,000 LGs per country) and North America (where the average is over 45,000 per country). Table 1.3 shows the 11 countries that have 10,000 or more LGs. As it indicates, although these countries comprise only about 10 percent of the countries in Table 1.2, they have over 83 percent of the LGs.

Despite the imbalance shown in Table 1.3, LGs have varying economic significance in different countries. Their expenditures range from less than 1 percent of GDP in countries such as Azerbaijan, Mali, Ghana, and Niger, to over 35 percent in Colombia. Table 1.4 lists the 20 countries with LG expenditures in excess of 20 percent of GDP. As it indicates, most of these countries are in Latin America.

Finally, in terms of total public sector expenditures, LGs also rank high in many countries. Table 1.5 lists the 18 countries where LG expenditures are at least

Table 1.3 *Countries with 10,000 or more local governments*

	Number
India	250,671
United States	87,525
China	44,267
Philippines	43,656
Turkey	38,616
France	36,655
Ukraine	30,402
Russia	23,972
Germany	15,359
Vietnam	11,502
Uzbekistan	10,397
Total	593,022
Percent of Total LGs	83.1%

Source: Adapted from World Bank and United Cities and Local Government 2008.

30 percent of total public expenditures. In five of these countries (Spain, Japan, Uzbekistan, Denmark, and China) more than half of all public expenditures take place at the LG level.

While it may not be readily apparent, it should be noted that only a handful of countries appear on more than one of these lists. Only China and Uzbekistan appear on all three lists. Seven countries (Argentina, Brazil, Denmark, Finland, Mexico, Sweden, Vietnam) appear on two lists. A total of 29 countries appear on only one list, each of which is a different measure of the importance of LGs in an economy. Overall, 38 countries, or about 36 percent of the total in Table 1.2, rely on LGs in a significant way to provide services to their citizens. Lowering the threshold for inclusion on a list would raise this total even higher. For example, using 20 percent as the cutoff for Table 1.5 would add another 7 countries to the list, bringing the overall total to 45 countries.

Given the significance of LGs in many economies, the way they are managed has become a global concern. Less obviously, and perhaps somewhat counter-intuitively, the concern is not one that is confined solely to the industrialized world.

Hybrid local governments

In hybrid LGs, the governing bodies are elected or appointed by higher-level governments. Also in this group are collections of small entities that aim to carry out general governance functions for wide areas. Inter-municipal entities, such as those in Hungary, are examples of this kind of territorial government, as are consortia among small municipalities, such as one finds in several European countries.

Table 1.4 *Countries with LG expenditures that are 20 percent or more of GDP*

Colombia	35.2
Chile	34.2
Honduras	34.1
Paraguay	33.3
Denmark	33.0
Venezuela	32.2
Nicaragua	30.3
Bolivia	30.0
Uruguay	29.6
Costa Rica	25.5
Argentina	25.2
Switzerland	25.2
Sweden	25.0
Panama	24.8
Brazil	24.6
Ecuador	24.5
Mexico	23.3
Uzbekistan	23.0
China	22.0
Finland	20.1

Source: Adapted from World Bank and United Cities and Local Government 2008.

BOX 1.1 FORMING CONSORTIA

Many small municipal governments in France and Italy have formed consortia in order to manage services such as waste collection, water and sewer provision, or public transportation. Their goal, of course, is to reach a level of operations that achieves some reasonable economies of scale.

Depending on administrative and regulatory contexts, hybrid LGs may have legal and administrative arrangements that conceal their true nature. For example, in countries, such as Germany, New Zealand, Sweden, and Italy the process of "corporatization" has contributed to a blurring of the line between the LG and one or more local agencies. In these countries, many services have been outsourced to public-owned corporations. Outsourcing has taken place for both public utilities and a variety of other LG functions and activities, such as cultural events, recreational activities, and internal administrative operations. The latter include planning, accounting, and data-processing (for example, see: Grossi and Mussari 2008; Wollmann 2008).

Table 1.5 *Countries with LG expenditures that are 30 percent or more of total public expenditures*

China	81.0
Denmark	60.4
Uzbekistan	55.0
Japan	53.6
Spain	52.1
Kazakhstan	48.0
Vietnam	48.0
Sweden	44.3
Republic of Korea	44.0
Ireland	42.4
Brazil	42.1
Argentina	41.8
Finland	38.5
Netherlands	35.1
Indonesia	33.0
Italy	32.5
Mexico	31.9
Poland	30.3

Source: Adapted from World Bank and United Cities and Local Government 2008.

In many instances, hybrid LGs operate at a local level but depend on funding from the federal, state, or regional level. In addition, many of the specific policies they carry out are determined at a higher level. This type of entity is particularly common in countries with a Napoleonic tradition, such as prefectures in France (Peters 2008). Similarly, local healthcare agencies in Italy are funded by, and their general operating policies are determined at, the regional level. Within the parameters of these policies, they operate autonomously.

INTERGOVERNMENTAL RELATIONSHIPS

In addition to being classified in terms of their relationships to other layers of government, LGs can be classified by the areas and local communities they serve. In this regard, they function at one of three levels: (1) basic (e.g., municipality, borough, city, urban district), (2) intermediate (e.g., province, county, metropolitan district), and (3) regional or state. In general, the number of levels in a given country varies depending on the country's size and political structure (Delcamp 1990). Indeed, some LGs are more like central governments in terms of their operation and functions.

15

In many Central Asian countries, for example, services such as health care, education, social welfare, communal property, local finances, and territorial development are managed by national entities integrated in a hierarchically centralized system with different functions taking place at different levels of the vertical structure. Regulatory functions belong to the country's central administration, while LGs simply enforce national laws or provide nationally mandated services.

A similar approach exists in the European Union, where an individual country's policies in certain areas are subordinated to the EU's policies. Under this type of arrangement, an LG wields its power within a network of other governments, an approach that often is termed "vertical" intergovernmental relations (Wright 1988).

There also can be "horizontal relationships" among several LGs, which can include cross-border cooperation. The municipal consortia in France and Italy, mentioned earlier, are examples. In addition, there may be a variety of "outsourcing" arrangements that involve cooperation between a small LG and a larger one. Such relationships exist in Italy for social welfare, transportation, schools, and recreation.

Regardless of the vertical/horizontal distinction, LGs play a vital role in many countries, sometimes providing services at the behest of national governments and sometimes doing so relatively autonomously. Regardless of the distinction, in all LGs, except perhaps the tiniest, there is a need for a strong management control system to help manage the LG's programs and services.

KINDS OF SERVICES

Although differences exist due to administrative traditions, culture, history, and stage of economic development, an LG's functions can span a wide array of programs and services. The possibilities include urban planning, housing, road construction and maintenance, transportation, education, vocational training, cultural activities, museums, libraries, leisure services, health care, welfare and social services, public safety (police and fire protection), economic development, water provision, sewage disposal, natural gas distribution, electricity, tourism, and environmental protection (Norton 1994). Table 1.6 contrasts the service responsibilities in Australia, Canada, New Zealand, and the United States.

As Table 1.6 indicates, an LG can have a vast, and frequently complex, set of managerial responsibilities concerning not only so-called "public goods" (such as public safety, street lighting, parks, and road maintenance) but also a wide range of services that fall into the "merit goods" category (education, water and sewer services, energy, social welfare, health care, and support for business development).[1] With regard to these four countries, it is evident that LGs in the United States provide, or assist in the provision of, the highest percentage of functions (29 out of 36 listed), while in New Zealand LG responsibilities are limited to agriculture land planning and fire protection.

16

Table 1.6 *Governmental functions in Australia, Canada, New Zealand, and the United States*

Functions	Australia	Canada	New Zealand	United States
Planning				
Housing	S, L	P, L *	C, T *	F, L *
Town planning	L	P *, L	R	L
Agriculture land planning	S, L	P, L*	L	S *, L *
Regional planning	L		R	S *, L *
Education				
Preschool	S	P	C	L *
Primary	S	P	C	L
Secondary	S	P	C	L
Vocational and technical	S	P	C	S, L
Higher education	F, S	F	C	S
Adult education	S	P	C	S, L
Other	S		C	
Social services				
Kindergarten and nursery	S	P	C	S, L *
Family welfare services	S	P	C	F, S, L
Welfare housing	S, L *	P, L *	C	
Social security	F	P	C	F
Other			T *	
Health services				
Primary care	F	P	C	Private*
Hospital	S	P	C	F, L *
Health protection	F, S, L	F, P	C, T	F, S, L *
Mental hospital	S	P	C	S
Water supply				
Water and sanitation	S, L	L	T	L *
Water supply	S, L *	P, L	T	L *
Energy supply				
Gas services	S	P	C, R	L *
Electricity	S	P	T *	L *
Public transport				
Roads	S	L	C, T	F
Transport	S	L	C, R, T	S, L
Urban roads	S, L	L	T	S, L
Urban public transport	L	L	T	S, L *
Ports	S	F, P, L	T *	L *
Airports	S	F, P, L	C *, T *	F, L *
Other transportation				F, L *

Table 1.6 *Continued*

Functions	Australia	Canada	New Zealand	United States
Business development support				
Agriculture, forests, and fisheries	F, P, L *	F, P	C, T *	F, S
Economic promotion	F, P, L *	P, L	C *, T *	S, L *
Trade and industry	F, P, L *	F, P	C *	F, S, L *
Tourism	F, P, L *	F, P, L	C*, R*, T*	S, L *
Other economic services	F, P, L *		C *, T *	L *
Security				
Police	S	L (generally)	C, R	S, L
Fire	S	P, L	R, L	L

Key: C = Central; F = Federal; S = State; R = Regional; P = Province; T = Territorial; L = Local; * = discretionary service.
Source: Adapted from World Bank and United Cities and Local Government 2008: 239–40.

CHARACTERISTICS OF LOCAL GOVERNMENTS THAT AFFECT MANAGEMENT CONTROL

Regardless of the form they take, or the country where they operate, LGs typically face a similar set of constraints:

- Absence of a profit measure
- Difficulty in measuring performance
- Political influences in decision making
- Restricted sources of financial support
- Dominance of professionals (in some services, such as health and education)
- External influences on decision making

Each of these is discussed below.

Absence of a profit measure

All organizations use resources to produce goods and services; that is, they use inputs to produce outputs. An organization's *effectiveness* is measured by the extent to which its outputs help it to attain its goals; its *efficiency* is measured by the relationship between its outputs and inputs. In a for-profit organization, profit provides an overall measure of both effectiveness and efficiency. The absence of a single, satisfactory, overall measure of performance comparable to the profit measure is one of the most serious problems LG managers face in developing an effective management control system.

To appreciate the significance of this statement, one needs to consider the usefulness and limitations of the profit measure in for-profit organizations.

The profit measure has five advantages: It (1) provides a single criterion that can be used to evaluate proposed courses of action, (2) permits a quantitative analysis of proposals where benefits can be directly compared with costs, (3) is a single, broad measure of performance, (4) facilitates decentralization, and (5) permits comparisons of performance among entities that carry out dissimilar functions. Each of these points is discussed below, and contrasted with the situation in an LG.

Single criterion

In a for-profit company, profit provides a way of focusing the considerations involved in choosing among alternative courses of action. A decision maker can address such questions as: Is the proposal likely to produce a satisfactory level of profits? Is Alternative A likely to add more to profits than Alternative B?

Of course, an analysis is rarely as simple and straightforward as this. Most proposals cannot be assessed exclusively in terms of their impact on profits, since almost all proposals involve considerations that cannot be measured solely in monetary terms. Nevertheless, profit provides a focus for decision making.

In an LG, there often is no clear-cut objective criterion that can be used to analyze alternative courses of action. Indeed, members of the management team of an LG often will not even agree on the relative importance of various objectives.

BOX 1.2 THE DIFFICULTY OF MAKING COMPARISONS OF EFFECTIVENESS ACROSS PROGRAMS

All members of an LG's management team may agree that the addition of a new firehouse would add to the effectiveness of the fire department. However, some likely would disagree on the importance of an expenditure to increase the effectiveness of the fire department versus a comparable expenditure on schools, parks, streets, or welfare.

Quantitative analysis

The easiest type of proposal to analyze is one in which estimated costs can be compared directly with estimated benefits. Such an analysis is possible when the objective is profitability. However, for most important decisions in an LG, managers have no accurate way to estimate the relationship between costs and benefits. Indeed, they frequently have difficulty judging the impact that a given expenditure will have on achieving the LG's goals. For example, would the addition of another police officer increase the protection that the police force provides by an amount that exceeds his or her salary? Would the amount an LG spends on, say, a program to retrain unemployed persons result in a benefit that exceeds the cost?

Issues of this sort are difficult to analyze in quantitative terms because there is no good way to estimate the benefits of a given increment in spending. Moreover, since it often is difficult to express benefits in monetary terms, the choice among several alternatives depends on criteria other than profit.

Performance measurement

Profit provides a measure that incorporates a great many separate aspects of performance. The best manager is not the one who generates the most sales volume, considered by itself; nor the one who uses labor, material, or capital most efficiently; nor the one who best controls overhead costs. Rather, the best manager is the one who, on balance, does the best job of combining all of these separate activities. Profit incorporates all of them. The key consideration is not who improved different items on a company's operating statement, but who improved the *bottom line*. This measure provides managers with an easily understood signal as to how well they are doing, and it provides others with an objective basis for judging a given manager's performance.

By contrast, financial performance is only a secondary goal in an LG. Yet, its importance is often overemphasized. This can happen when individuals with managerial experience in for-profit companies become involved in an LG, perhaps as members of citizen review boards. Accustomed to the primacy of profits, they frequently find it difficult to adjust their thinking, failing to recognize that the principal goal of an LG is to render service. They also may not understand that the amount and quality of services rendered often cannot be quantified easily, and that trying to assess performance is not only difficult but sometimes impossible.

BOX 1.3   MEASURING ADEQUACY

What is "adequate" fire protection? Measures such as response time (from call to arrival on site), dollar loss per fire, number of persons killed or injured by a fire in a given year, and other similar statistics might be used, but none of them directly addresses the question of the adequacy of fire protection.

Decentralization

For-profit organizations have a well-understood goal: profitability (usually measured in terms of return on assets or return on equity). The performance of individual managers can be measured in terms of their contribution to that goal. Because of this, senior management can safely delegate many decisions to lower levels in the organization.

Most LGs have multiple goals and no good way of measuring their performance in attaining them. They therefore cannot delegate as many important decisions to lower-level managers as they otherwise might. For this reason, many problems in an LG, especially a hybrid one, must be resolved at higher government levels. The paperwork and related procedures involved in sending problems up the hierarchy, and in transmitting the resulting decisions back to the field, can be quite elaborate, giving rise, in part, to frequent criticisms that are levied against the *bureaucracy*. Such criticisms generally are unwarranted, however, because, in the absence of something corresponding to the profit measure, there is no easy way for an LG to decentralize decision-making.

BOX 1.4 MEASURING BENEFITS

Social and healthcare services represent an important area of activity for many LGs, but their benefits are not easily measurable. Therefore a country's central government may create a set of legal and professional procedures in an attempt to guarantee consistent performance by lower-level governmental units, including LGs. Doing so limits the decision-making latitude of the managers of those units.

Comparison of unlike units

The profit measure permits a comparison of the performance of entities that engage in heterogeneous operations. The performance of a department store can be compared with that of a paper mill in terms of a single criterion: which had a higher return on assets?

Profitability therefore provides a mechanism that combines the various elements of performance within a company, and that can assist in making comparisons among organizations. All organizations that have a goal of profitability can be compared, at least roughly, in terms of return on assets or equity. This is true even though their size, technology, products, and markets are quite different from one another.

By contrast, one LG program can be compared with another only if the two have similar functions. A fire department can be compared with other fire departments, and a trash collection department with other trash collection departments, but there is no way to compare the effectiveness of a fire department with that of a trash collection department.

Difficulty in measuring performance

As the above discussion suggests, the goals of LGs are usually complex and often intangible, and their outputs often are difficult or impossible to measure. As a result, the performance measurement challenges faced by LGs are far greater than those faced by for-profit organizations.

In general, output information is needed to measure both effectiveness and efficiency. In a for-profit organization, revenue can be used as the measure. In an LG, no such monetary measure exists because revenues do not approximate true output as they usually do in a for-profit company.

Similarly, without a profit measure, analyses of effectiveness and efficiency require substitute measures of output. Despite the importance of devising such alternative measures, the management control systems in many LGs tend to be deficient in this respect.

Ironically, the problem of measuring output in non-monetary terms is not unique to LGs. The same problem exists in departments or units of for-profit organizations where discretionary costs predominate (e.g., research, accounting, human resources). Conversely, the output of many individual activities in LGs, such as vehicle maintenance and clerical work, can be measured as easily as the corresponding activities in a for-profit entity.

Political influences in decision making

Clearly, LGs are political in nature – they are responsible to the electorate or to a legislative body that presumably represents the electorate. There are several consequences of this status.

Necessity for re-election

In almost all LGs, decisions result from multiple, often conflicting, pressures. In part, these political pressures are inevitable, and, up to a point, desirable. Indeed, since elected officials are accountable to voters, the pressures presumably represent appropriate forces. Elected officials cannot function if they are not re-elected, and in order to be re-elected they must advance the needs of their constituents. But, in an effort to gain support for programs important to their constituents, they often must support the programs of some of their colleagues, even though they personally do not favor them.

Public visibility

In some instances, the need for improved management arises not because an LG is large and complex, but because its activities are highly visible. More generally, the press and the public in many locales feel they have a right to know everything about a government organization, but the channels for distributing this information are not always unbiased. Although some media stories describing mismanagement are fully justified, others tend to be exaggerated or to give inadequate recognition to the inevitability of mistakes by managers in any organization. To reduce the potential for unfavorable media stories, LG managers may take steps to reduce the amount of sensitive information that flows through the formal management control system. Unfortunately, this also lessens the usefulness of the system.

Multiple external pressures

The electoral process, with public review through the media and opposing political parties, results in a wider variety of pressures on managers of LGs than on managers of private entities. In general, elected public officials generate more controversy about their decisions than do business managers. In the absence of profit as a clear-cut measure of performance, these pressures may be erratic, illogical, or even influenced by momentary fads. Frequently, they may lead to an emphasis on short-term goals or to programmatic decisions devoid of careful analysis. Shareholders demand satisfactory earnings, whereas the public and governing bodies of LGs do not always channel their pressures toward good resource utilization.

Legislative restrictions

LGs, especially hybrid ones, often operate within statutes enacted by a higher-level authority. These statutes can be more restrictive than the charter and bylaws of a for-profit entity, and they often prescribe detailed practices, which, in many instances are relatively difficult to change.

Civil service

There is widespread belief that civil service regulations inhibit good management control. It is by no means clear, though, that they are as important as some people believe. Indeed, civil service regulations in many LGs may be no more restrictive than union regulations and norms in for-profit organizations.

BOX 1.5   UNION CONSTRAINTS

Union rules regarding work assignments, such as the number of engineers and other personnel aboard trains, or the roles of electricians and plumbers on a repair job, can constrain a for-profit manager's decision-making latitude.

23

An important difference, though, is that union rules generally affect individuals near the bottom of the organization, whereas civil service rules often affect individuals throughout the LG, including many middle managers. As a result, civil service laws tend to create a "civil service mentality" – you need not produce success; you only need to avoid making major mistakes. This attitude is a significant barrier to managers who wish to improve an LG's effectiveness.

Restricted sources of financial support

A for-profit company obtains resources by selling its goods and services. If the flow of this revenue is inadequate – if, for example, the company makes a product that the market does not want – the company does not survive. Moreover, a company cannot sell products unless their quality is acceptable and their price is in line with what the market is willing to pay. Thus, the market dictates the nature of a for-profit company's operations.

Some LGs obtain a portion of their financial resources from "sales" revenue. This is the case with public transportation, water and sewer services, and off-track betting, to name a few. Essentially, these "client-supported" programs and services are subject to many of the same market forces as their for-profit counterparts.

Unlike for-profit companies, however, LGs receive considerable financial support from sources other than revenue for services rendered. With, say, property taxes or regional grants, there is no direct connection between the amount of resources provided to the LG and the amount of services received by citizens. Individuals receive essentially the same services (such as snow removal, road repair, or street lighting) whether they pay high or low taxes. Moreover, appropriations made to an LG by a higher-level legislative body usually are not related directly to the services received by that body's taxpayers.

Contrast between client-supported and public-supported organizations

For-profit organizations want more clients. More clients imply more revenues, and more revenues imply greater success. In LGs, there is no such relationship. Indeed, additional clients may place a strain on resources. This is especially true when an LG's available resources are fixed by appropriations. Thus, while in most for-profit organizations, a new client is an opportunity to be pursued vigorously, a new LG client may be only a burden – someone to be avoided or accepted with misgivings.

This negative or ambivalent attitude toward clients gives rise to complaints about the poor service and surly attitude of some LG employees. Clients of for-profit organizations tend to hear "please" and "thank you" more often than an LG's clients.

BOX 1.6 RESPONDING TO CUSTOMERS

A study in New York City found that 63.9 percent of the time, individuals calling food stamp dispensing centers could not get through to a staff person because of busy signals or a failure to answer within 15 rings. Moreover, 84.4 percent of the callers who reached a staff person were given incorrect and incomplete information (City of New York 1988).

The impact of competition

Competition provides a powerful incentive to use resources wisely. Profits decline if a for-profit firm lets its costs get out of control, its product lines become obsolete, or its quality decreases. An LG has no such automatic danger signal. As a substitute for the market mechanism for allocating resources, LG managers compete with one another for available funds. The police department, the parks department, and the road maintenance department all try to get as large a slice as possible of the LG's budget pie. In responding to their requests, senior management tries to judge what services clients should have, or what best promotes the public interest, rather than what the market wants, but this is a tricky proposition.

BOX 1.7 IMPORTANCE OF SATISFYING RESOURCE PROVIDERS

Just as the success of a for-profit organization depends on its ability to satisfy its clients, the success of an LG depends on its ability to satisfy its resource providers. As a result, a public works department is likely to place more emphasis on repairing the road in front of the mayor's house than in doing so in a low-income neighborhood.

Dominance of professionals

In many LG departments, the individuals who are the keys to success are professionals: physicians, engineers, librarians, social workers, teachers, and so forth. Professionals often have goals that are inconsistent with good resource utilization. This creates a dilemma that has important implications for senior management.

Professionals are motivated by at least two sets of standards: those of the LG and those of their profession. Although the former are related to the LG's objectives, the latter may be inconsistent with them. In fact, the rewards for helping to achieve the LG's objectives may be much less significant than those for achieving professional recognition. The reluctance of teachers to serve on school or department committees is a direct reflection of this reward structure.

In addition, many professionals prefer to work independently. However, because the essence of management is getting things done through people, professionals with such a temperament are not naturally suited to a managerial role.

Finally, a professional's education typically does not include a management component. Most professional schools believe that training in the skills of the profession is far more important than training in the skills needed to manage organizations employing members of the profession. For example, most police officers believe that "policing skills" are more important than managerial ones. This has often led professionals to underestimate the importance of the management function. While education and external pressures for better organizational performance may help to change this perception, the culture of many professions reinforces the tendency to disparage managers.

One result of this cultural difference is that professionals tend to give inadequate weight to the financial implication of their decisions. Many physicians, for example, feel that no limit should be placed on the amount spent to save a human life. Unfortunately, in a world of limited resources, such an attitude is unrealistic.

External influences on decision making

In LGs, external influences tend to come from a number of sources, leading to a diffusion of power. Consequently, there often are conflicting judgments about objectives and the appropriate means to attain them. By contrast, in a for-profit company, the board of directors and the chief executive officer usually have similar objectives.

As discussed previously, there may be a vertical division of authority among levels of government in some countries. As a result, each level is responsible for different facets of the same problem. In addition, agencies (or units within agencies) may have their own special-interest clienteles (such as a housing authority and building tenants). Moreover, a group of citizens often can have political power that is stronger than that of the head of the agency. Similarly, senior-management authority may be divided, especially in LGs where spending authority is vested in committees of independently elected officials, or where government is in the hands of commissions, each of whose members administers a particular segment of the organization, such as streets or public health.

BOX 1.8 DIVISION OF RESPONSIBILITIES BETWEEN NATIONAL AND LOCAL GOVERNMENTS

A national government may finance the construction and maintenance of major highways and perhaps some minor ones as well, but an LG may be responsible for constructing and maintaining local highways and roads.

A manager's latitude also may be determined by political boundaries that are structural or geographic in nature. For example, the mayor of Los Angeles, California, has much narrower responsibility than the mayor of New York City because county government in California is responsible for many services that in New York fall under the city organization.

Often, too, an LG's employees may be insulated from senior management by virtue of civil service rules. Career civil servants may know that they will outlast the term of office of the elected or appointed chief executive. If a particular project cannot be sold to the current boss, the project's sponsors may bide their time and hope to sell it to the next one. Conversely, if they dislike a new policy, they may drag their heels long enough to allow new management to take over and possibly rescind the policy.

This fragmentation of authority complicates management control. One consequence is that an LG manager comes to depend on political power to influence those individuals who cannot be controlled directly. Consequently, managers tend to focus on both their political and financial objectives; that is, they tend to measure the political costs and benefits of alternatives, as well as the related financial costs and benefits.

BOUNDARIES OF THE MANAGEMENT CONTROL SYSTEM

Management control is an important activity, but it is by no means the whole of management. LG managers must make judgments about people: their integrity, their ability, their potential, their fitness for a given job, and their compatibility with colleagues. Senior management is responsible for building an effective organization and for motivating its employees to work toward its goals.

Of course, managers also have functions that are not "managerial" as such. As an example, the following list shows some of the external agencies and persons on which the mayor of a large city must depend (Kotter and Lawrence 1974):

- Unions or employee associations that could call a strike or work stoppage
- The civil service, which could make it easy or impossible to get competent employees
- The city council, which could call hearings that could take up the mayor's time, and be a source of embarrassment
- A higher-level government, which could constrain the mayor's activities in a number of ways, and which provides partial funding for some of the city's programs
- The local press, which could embarrass the mayor
- Adjoining cities and towns, whose actions could have a positive or negative impact on the mayor's programmatic decision-making
- The local community, which, if organized, could constrain the mayor's actions through the press or the city council

SUMMARY

The characteristics of LGs described in this chapter can be grouped into two broad categories – technical and behavioral. Both are important to the management control system. Technical characteristics relate to the difficulty of measuring outputs and assessing the relationship between inputs and outputs. This difficulty is unique to non-profit organizations in general and to LGs in particular. Improvements in performance measurement are possible, however, and managers need to spend considerable efforts to make them. Nevertheless, it must be recognized that the resulting management control system will never provide as good a basis for planning or measuring performance as a comparable system would do in a for-profit organization.

Behavioral characteristics encompass all the other topics in this book. The significance of these characteristics is twofold. First, most behavioral factors that impede good management control can be overcome by improved understanding and education. Second, unless these problems are overcome, any improvement in the technical area is likely to have little real impact on an LG's overall performance.

DISCUSSION QUESTIONS

1   Which of the general characteristics of an LG is the most serious impediment to performance measurement? Why?
2   What changes to its management control system might an LG make to move the system closer to the kind of system used in a for-profit organization? How hard will it be to make these changes?

NOTE

1 Public goods are items (goods or services) where one individual's consumption does not lead to a reduction in the item's availability to any other individual (called "non-rivalry") and where it is impossible to exclude anyone from consuming the item (called "non-excludability"). An example is street lighting. Merit goods do not have these characteristics. They are provided by the public sector to individuals on the basis of some concept of need, and their consumption is based, in part, on a person's ability and willingness to pay for them. For a closer analysis of the difference between public goods and merit goods, please refer to any microeconomics textbook (e.g., Varian 2009).

REFERENCES

Asian Development Bank and Ministry of Finance, China (March 2000) *Managing Urban Change: Strategic Options for Municipal Governance and Finance in China (PRC: TA 2924 — Study of Municipal Public Finance)*. Available http://www.adb.org/Documents/Reports/Consultant/TA2924_PRC_Final_Report.pdf (accessed April 20, 2011).

Bliss, K. and DeShazo, P. (2009) "Controlling Corruption in Local Government in Latin America: A Report of the CSIS [Center for Strategic and International Studies] Americas Program," *Policy Papers on the Americas*, Vol. XX, Study 1. Available: http://csis.org/files/media/csis/pubs/090127_bliss_contolcorruption_web.pdf (accessed April 20, 2011).

Bobbio, L. (2002) *I governi locali nelle democratie contemporanee*, Bari, Italy: Edition Laterza.

Central Intelligence Agency of the United States (2011) *The World Factbook*. Washington, DC: Central Intelligence Agency. Available HTTP: https://www.cia.gov/library/publications/the-world-factbook/index.html (accessed April, 20 2011).

City of New York, The (1988) *Comptroller's Report*, Vol. 12, No. 6, February.

Cole, M. and Boyne, G. (1995) "So You Think You Know What Local Government Is?," *Local Government Studies*, 21(2): 191–205.

Delcamp, A. (1990) *Les Institutions Locales en Europe*, Paris, France: Presses Universitaires de France.

Dexia (2004) *Local Finance in the Twenty Five Countries of the European Union*, Paris, France: Dexia.

Grossi, G. and Mussari, R. (2008) "Effects of Outsourcing on Performance Measurement and Reporting: The Experience of Italian Local Governments," *Public Budgeting and Finance*, 28(1): 22–38.

Kemp, R.L. (ed.) (2007) *Forms of Local Government. A Handbook on City, County and Regional Options*, Jefferson, North Carolina: McFarland.

Kotter, J.P. and Lawrence, P.R. (1974) *Mayors in Action: 5 Approaches to Urban Governance*, New York: John Wiley and Sons.

Norton, A. (1994) *International Handbook of Local and Regional Government. A Comparative Analysis of Advanced Democracies*, Aldershot, United Kingdom: Edward Elgar.

Peters, B.G. (2008) "The Napoleonic Tradition," *The International Journal of Public Sector Management*, 21(2): 118–32.

Rivenbark, W.C. and Kelly, J.M. (2003) "Management Innovation in Smaller Municipal Government," *State and Local Government Review*, 35(2): 196–205.

Varian, H.R. (2009) *Intermediate Microeconomics: A Modern* Approach, 8th edn, New York: W.W. Norton and Company.

Watson, D.J. and Hassett W.L. (2003) *Local Government Management: Current Issues and Best Practices*, New York: M.E. Sharpe.

Wollmann, H. (2008) *Comparing Local Government Reforms in England, Sweden, France and Germany*. Berlin, Germany: Humboldt-Universität zu Berlin,

29

Institute of Social Science. Available www.wuestenrot-stiftung.de/download/ local-government (accessed September 16, 2011).

World Bank and United Cities and Local Governments (2008) Decentralization and Local Democracy in the Word: First Global Report by United Cities and Local Governments. Available: www.cities_localgovernments.org/gold/gold_report.asp (accessed September 16, 2011).

Wright, D.S. (1988) *Understanding Intergovernmental Relations*, Monterey, California: Brooks-Cole.

FURTHER READING

A good read to understand the variety of types, different magnitude of resources used, and services provided by LGs within the different regions of the world, is the report *Decentralization and Local Democracy in the World* by the World Bank and United Cities and Local Governments (United Cities and Local Governments 2008). Pollitt's *The Essential Public Manager* (Open University Press 2003) is a popular book which is useful for beginners to locate LGs into the wider context of public management, presenting the key themes and problems that public management faces. *Reinventing Government* by Osborne and Gaebler (Plume, Penguin Group 1992) offers the reader the basic ideas of the New Public Management paradigm, i.e., the "entrepreneurial spirit" which is transforming the public sector within which management control plays a key role.

Chapter 2

Management control systems: an overview

LEARNING OBJECTIVES

At the end of this chapter you should:

- Recognize that a management control system sits between strategic planning and task control.
- Understand the structure and process of a management control system (akin to anatomy and physiology of a human body).
- Know about the management control structure options, and the four phases of the management control process (programming, budgeting, measuring, and reporting).
- Recognize that the way the management control system is designed and used in a given local government (LG) is influenced by the LG's external and internal environments.
- Understand the distinction between full costs, differential costs, and responsibility costs.
- Begin to appreciate the difficulty of measuring non-financial performance (including outputs and outcomes) in an LG.

KEY POINTS

- The management control system attempts to measure revenues (which are resource inflows) and expenses (which are resource outflows).
- Because most LGs have cash accounting systems, the information used by their management control systems tends to be deficient – it fails to account

properly for resource inflows and outflows. To correct this deficiency, an LG needs to convert to accrual accounting.

- A good management control system will measure non-monetary information on outputs in an effort to show what its programs are accomplishing.
- Since management control assists managers to decide on the optimum allocation of resources, it is governed, in part, by the principles of economics. But, since it looks at the influence of measurement and reporting systems on the behavior of managers, professionals, and others, it also is governed by the principles of social psychology.
- An LG's external environment is important because management control must be concerned with matters such as the actions of citizens, the constraints imposed by funding providers and legislative bodies, and the customs and norms of the LG's society.
- An LG's internal environment is important because management control affects, and is affected by, the LG's organizational structure, its members' behavior, its information systems, and its culture.
- When there is both a responsibility center structure and a program structure, the management control system must identify their interactions. In many LGs, the result is the need for a matrix structure.

All LGs, even the smallest, engage in some form of management control. In large LGs, the management control system (MCS) tends to be formal, whereas in smaller ones it often is quite informal. Management control has existed as long as organizations have been in existence, and both managers and academics have contributed to the evolution and definition of principles for designing MCSs.

As with most principles of management, management control principles are incomplete, inconclusive, tentative, vague, contradictory, and inadequately supported by experimental or other evidence. Some initial "truths" have been proven wrong. Other principles, however, have shown considerable validity in terms of managerial and organizational performance, leading managers to take them into account.

Most studies of management control have been conducted in for-profit businesses. As a result, descriptions of management control tend to assume a profit orientation. This book, by contrast, looks at management control in the context of LGs. The underlying thesis is that the basic concepts of management control are the same in both for-profit organizations and LGs, but that, because of the special characteristics of LGs, the way managers apply these concepts will differ in some important respects.

PLANNING AND CONTROL ACTIVITIES

Managers engage in a wide variety of activities. They lead, teach, organize, influence, plan, and control. This book focuses on the latter two activities. In the planning activity, managers decide what should be done and how to do it. In the control activity, they attempt to obtain the desired results.

There are three different types of planning and control activities: strategic planning, management control, and task control. Since our focus in this book is management control, we will describe the other two types of activities only briefly. The purpose in doing so is to clarify the boundaries of management control (Anthony 1988).

Strategic planning

Senior management generally determines an organization's goals and the general nature of the activities needed to achieve them, or what Michael Porter has called the organization's *strategy* (Porter 1996). *Strategic planning* is the process of deciding on these goals and activities. While goals tend to change slowly, the activities needed to attain them may change frequently, usually whenever senior management perceives an opportunity for improvement. Since these sorts of opportunities do not arise in orderly, predictable ways, strategic decisions are not made according to a prescribed timetable. The strategic planning process (or what sometimes is called the *strategy formulation process*) therefore is essentially irregular and in many respects unsystematic.

In LGs, unlike in many for-profit businesses, the strategic planning process takes place in the context of a broader political process. Citizens' needs and wants are more diverse and unfocused than a for-profit entity's customers, for example. In addition, many members of an LG's senior management team must be certain that these needs are met in a way that helps to assure their re-election. Indeed, in many respects, the "bottom line" of an LG is *votes*, not profits. In this context, a typical strategic decision an LG faces is the need to select and prioritize activities that are designed to improve its community's quality of life. Usually these decisions are made by the mayor or the town council (to whom voters have delegated the task). They cover a set of general goals and the broad activities needed to attain them.

BOX 2.1 EXAMPLE OF AN LG STRATEGY

The City of Tampa, Florida, has the stated vision: "Tampa will be recognized as a diverse, progressive city, celebrated as the most desirable place to live, learn, work, and play." Tampa's mission is "to deliver outstanding services to enhance the quality of life within [its] community." Its values are "integrity, excellence, teamwork, respect." Its strategic areas are: "Invest in Tampa's Neighborhoods,

---

33

Economic Development in Our Most Challenged Areas, Downtown as a Residential Community, Efficient City Government Focused on Customer Service, City of the Arts, Making Regional Mass Transit a Reality."

For details on each strategic area, see www.tampagov.net/dept_mayor/strategic_areas (accessed April 20, 2011).

Task control

At the other extreme are those activities used to carry out the day-to-day administrative operations of the organization. *Task control* is the process of assuring that these activities are carried out effectively and efficiently. They vary with the nature of the organization's operations. In LGs, as in other public sector organizations, compliance with regulations and laws is an important aspect of task control.

BOX 2.2 TASK CONTROL ACTIVITIES

In a public works department, assuring that traffic lights are functioning properly is task control. So is the timely preparation of paychecks for employees, the collection of tax revenues that are due from residents, and the issuance of commercial and building permits under the LG's laws and regulations.

Many task control activities do not involve managers. If they are automated, they do not even involve human beings, except to assure that the task control activity is functioning properly.

Management control

Management control sits between strategic planning and task control. It accepts the goals determined in the strategic planning process as given, and focuses on the activities needed to attain them. As such, it attempts to assure that the organization's programs are effective and efficient. An effective program is one that moves the organization toward its goals. An efficient program is one that accomplishes its purposes at the lowest possible cost.

Unlike strategic planning, management control is regular and systematic, with steps repeated in a predictable way. And, unlike task control, which may not involve human beings, management control is fundamentally behavioral. It involves managers interacting with other managers, and, in many LG departments, with members of a professional staff, such as engineers, physicians, social workers, police officers, educators, and firefighters. Moreover, because the managers themselves sometimes are professionals, there can be difficulties in decision making since professional and organizational goals are not always aligned.

Since management control assists managers to decide on the optimum allocation of resources, it is governed, in part, by the principles of economics. But management control also looks at the influence of measurement and reporting systems on the behavior of managers, professionals, and others; in this respect, it is governed by the principles of social psychology. Not only are the principles found in these two disciplines quite different, but their relative importance to the management control activity varies greatly in different situations. One of the goals of this book is to help readers develop an ability to incorporate the optimal mix of economic and behavioral factors into their management control efforts.

Getting the optimal mix of these two factors is important because most LGs do not have a choice as to whether they will implement an MCS. In several European countries, such as Italy and France, LGs are required by law to develop an MCS. In these countries and others, the challenge is not to *have* an MCS, but to design one that assists the LG to achieve its objectives as efficiently as possible.

THE CONTEXT FOR MANAGEMENT CONTROL

The way the MCS is designed and used in a given LG is influenced by the LG's external and internal environments. The external environment is important because management control must be concerned with matters such as the actions of citizens, the constraints imposed by funding providers and legislative bodies, and the customs and norms of the LG's society. The internal environment is important because management control affects, and is affected by, the LG's structure, its members' behavior, its information systems, and its organizational culture. Some of these internal aspects are discussed briefly here. They will be discussed more fully in subsequent chapters, and especially in Chapter 11.

Organizational structure

An LG can be structured in a variety of ways, generally determined by the tasks that it needs to carry out. Most LGs have a structure in which employees and managers are grouped into some fairly traditional departments, such as water and sewer, public works, public safety, and education. Some also have a program structure, in which employees and managers from different departments work together to accomplish some programmatic goals.

35

BOX 2.3   PROGRAM STRUCTURE VERSUS ORGANIZATIONAL STRUCTURE

A program for clean and safe streets would require contributions from, among others, the departments of public safety, road maintenance, and trash removal. These departments may also contribute to such programs as ecology improvement and public health improvement.

The management control activity takes the existing organizational structure as given, and overlays it with a network of responsibility centers. A responsibility center is a group of people working toward some financial objectives, and, with increasing frequency, toward some non-financial objectives as well. It is headed by a manager who is responsible for the actions of its members. The network of responsibility centers – called the management control structure – is discussed briefly later in this chapter and in considerable detail in Chapter 4.

Organizational relationships and members' behavior

An LG's responsibility centers can be classified as either line or staff. Line units carry out the work of the organization, and are the focal points of the MCS. One task of the MCS is to measure their performance. Staff units, by contrast, provide advice and assistance to the line units. The people in these units collect, summarize, and present information that is useful for management control. Although a staff unit may consist of many people, line managers make the significant operational decisions.

BOX 2.4   STAFF MEMBERS DO ANALYSES, LINE MANAGERS MAKE DECISIONS

The staff of a public works department may help the department's manager with the legal and economic analyses for an outsourcing decision, but the manager, not the staff, makes the final decision.

The person responsible for the design and operation of the MCS is the controller. In practice, the controller may have other titles, such as chief financial officer or chief accountant. It is important to keep in mind, however, that the controller is a staff member, whose job is to work with department or program managers to determine their information needs, and to provide that information to them in ways they find helpful.

Information

An important part of management control is information. As with any resource, the information resource involves both costs and benefits. An important task for the controller is to work with line managers to help assure that the value of the information provided by the MCS exceeds the cost of collecting and disseminating it.

The accounting system

A typical LG's accounting system provides *historical* information about revenues and expenses. By contrast, budgetary accounting, which also is part of an LG's accounting system, refers to the *upcoming fiscal year*. Budgetary choices often are constrained by legal obligations, one of which, in many LGs, is that total expenses should not exceed total revenues. Revenues are financial inflows that come from sources such as local taxes, service fees, fines, and grants from other government entities; they sometimes are restricted to certain uses (such as for social welfare, housing, or roads). Expenses are financial outflows.

In general, although revenues and expenses should be accounted for on an *accrual* basis, many LGs use *cash accounting* systems. Such a system is not able to account properly for revenues when they were *earned* and expenses when they were *incurred* (regardless of when the corresponding cash inflows and cash outflows took place). As a result, these LGs cannot provide accurate financial information to either their citizens or their managers.

Accrual accounting generally is considered to be the preferred method for recording revenues and expenses, and is used in almost all private sector organizations throughout the world. In recent years it has been proposed for LGs in several countries (Caperchione and Mussari 2000). While the idea of accrual accounting has received considerable support from both practitioners and academics, most LGs are still a long way from using it. Yet, until an LG converts to accrual accounting, it will have a difficult time developing an effective MCS.

In addition to measuring resources received and consumed for management control purposes, an LG's accounting system is used for two other basic purposes: reporting to outside parties and special analyses. Since our focus in this book is on management control, we discuss the two other uses only briefly.

Reporting to outside parties

Accounting information is prepared for outside agencies according to reporting requirements that they specify. Ideally, the information contained in these special-purpose reports simply summarizes information that is already contained in the accounting system. This is because the information needs of outside agencies presumably do not vary greatly from those of the LG's managers. The ideal is not always the case, however.

BOX 2.5   REPORTING TO FUNDERS

An LG that accepts funds from its central government, or from a regional government, usually must prepare reports on its use of these funds. The content (and often the format) of these reports is specified by the outside entity that provides the funds. In the European Union, for instance, grants to LGs are designated for specific purposes (such as for a program, a service, or an infrastructure project). The LG must account to the EU for its use of the funds.

Special analyses

Special analyses include reports used in connection with one-time studies, such as those done in conjunction with strategic planning. Strategic decisions are made only occasionally, however, and each decision requires tailor-made information. This information cannot ordinarily be collected in any routine, recurring fashion. Rather, it must be assembled when the need arises and in the form required for the specific decision being made.

BOX 2.6   NON-ROUTINE ANALYSES

An LG considering outsourcing its waste collection service would need to compare the cost of the contract with the cost savings in the department of public works. While the department of public works no doubt will have cost information available, the analysis of which costs would be eliminated if waste collection were outsourced would require a special analysis.

INFORMATION USED IN THE MANAGEMENT CONTROL SYSTEM

Information for management control purposes usually is classified in two ways: by responsibility centers and by programs. The accounting system must be able to integrate these two. In addition, the MCS contains two types of information not found in the accounting system: estimates of what will happen in the future and estimates of what should happen. The former are called forecasts; the latter are called standards or budgets. Budgets are discussed briefly later in this chapter, and in considerable detail in Chapter 6.

Measuring inputs and outputs

In measuring what might happen, what should happen, and what did happen, the MCS must contain information on both inputs and outputs. Inputs are the resources the LG used (or plans to use) during any given period, structured into both programs and responsibility centers. Outputs are the results it attained (or expects to attain) from the use of those resources. Both inputs and outputs can be either monetary or non-monetary, and a good MCS will contain information on both.

Non-monetary inputs are usually expressed as physical quantities, such as hours of labor, reams of paper, or kilowatt-hours of electricity. When non-monetary information is converted to monetary information, the result is called cost. Monetary information provides a common denominator that permits the quantities of individual resources to be combined. For example, labor cost can be combined with material cost.

Cost information

Cost is a measure of the amount of resources used for a purpose. In accounting terms, this purpose is called a cost object. The education of a student, the extinguishing of a fire, the completion of a special study, and the development of a museum exhibit are all examples of cost objects. Ordinarily, responsibility centers work on cost objects.

Inputs are resources used by a responsibility center in working on a cost object. The visitors to a museum or the students in a school are not the inputs of a responsibility center. Rather, its inputs are the resources it uses in operating the museum (such as acquisitions and curators) or educating the students (such as workbooks and teachers).

Input information consists of three basic types of cost construction: full costs, differential costs, and responsibility costs. Each is used for a different purpose, and considerable misunderstanding can arise if the cost construction for one purpose is used inappropriately for another. Full costs and responsibility costs are ordinarily collected in the accounts. For reasons discussed below, differential costs are not collected in the accounts.

Full cost: Full cost is the total amount of resources used for a cost object. It is the sum of the cost object's direct costs plus a fair share of the LG's indirect (or overhead) costs.

Direct costs can be traced to a single cost object. For example, the salaries and fringe benefits of persons who work exclusively on a single cost object (such as a cultural event) are direct costs of that cost object. By contrast, indirect costs are incurred jointly for two or more cost objects, and a fair share of them must be allocated to each cost object to obtain full cost. Full costs are discussed in greater detail in Chapter 7.

Differential costs: Costs that change under one set of conditions from what they would be under another are differential. They are useful in many decisions involving a choice among alternative courses of action, where the costs would differ depending

39

on the alternative under consideration. Since the costs that are relevant for a given decision depend on the nature the situation, there is no general way of labeling a given item of cost as differential or non-differential, and therefore no way of recording differential costs in the formal accounts. An analyst assessing differential costs would use information from the accounting system to estimate the costs that are relevant for each of the proposed alternatives, and thus how they would differ from one to the next.

In many alternative choice decisions, an important classification of costs is whether they are variable or fixed. Variable costs are those that change proportionally with changes in the volume of activity. Since twice as many workbooks are required to teach two students than to teach one, workbook costs are variable. By contrast, the salary of a school's principal does not change with the number of students, so it is a fixed cost. Other costs, such as teachers' salaries, share features of both, changing as volume increases or decreases but not in direct proportion. Differential costs are discussed in Chapter 8.

Responsibility costs: Costs incurred by or on behalf of a responsibility center are responsibility costs. They are classified as either controllable or non-controllable. An item of cost is controllable if it is influenced in a significant way by the actions of the manager of the responsibility center in which it was incurred. Since all items of cost are ultimately controllable by someone in the organization, the term "controllable" always refers to a specific responsibility center. Importantly, the definition refers to a significant amount of influence, rather than complete influence. Few managers have complete influence over any item of cost.

BOX 2.7 PURCHASING RESPONSIBILITY VERSUS USAGE RESPONSIBILITY

An LG's purchasing department (a responsibility center) buys toner cartridges, which are used by other responsibility centers, such as the legal department, the social welfare department, and the preschool program. The purchasing department is expected to control the cost per toner cartridge but not the number of cartridges used. The other responsibility centers are expected to do this.

Output information

Inputs almost always can be measured in terms of cost, but outputs are more difficult to measure. In a for-profit organization, revenue is often a surrogate for output, although even there it rarely is a complete expression of output, since it does not encompass everything that the organization does. For example, it excludes such activities as pollution control and environmental cleanup, which may be important outputs from a societal perspective.

Many LGs do not have good quantitative measures of output. A school can easily measure the number of students graduated, but it is much more difficult – usually impossible – to measure how much education each of them acquired.

The degree to which outputs can be measured quantitatively varies greatly with circumstances. If the quantity of output is relatively homogeneous, such as attendees at a cultural event, it often can be measured precisely. If, however, the goods or services are heterogeneous, such as different types of social welfare services, an LG has difficulty in summarizing the separate output units into a meaningful measure of total output.

Converting dissimilar physical goods to monetary equivalents – by computing revenue – is one way to solve this problem. Indeed, if the fees of an LG's client-serving departments are structured properly, based on a full cost analysis, the total quantity of output of those departments is reliably measured by revenues. This is true even though the services rendered consist of dissimilar activities such as the use of water and sewer services, ice-skating rinks, parking lots, and swimming pools.

As we discuss in Chapter 7, there are many possible exceptions to this rule in an LG, such as when a service is deliberately priced below its full cost to create an incentive to encourage its use. An example is the collection of recyclable trash.

Quality of output

At best, revenue measures the quantity of output. Measurement of the *quality* of output is much more difficult, and often cannot be made at all. In many situations, quality is determined strictly on a judgmental basis. In some instances there is simply a go/no-go measurement – either the output is of satisfactory quality or it is not.

BOX 2.8 PROXIES FOR OUTPUT QUALITY

It is always difficult, and often not feasible, to measure, or even estimate, the outputs of a school. Instead, graduates, courses completed successfully, and similar measures are used as surrogates. Measuring the outputs of police departments, fire departments, or recreation departments is similarly problematic.

Part of the difficulty in measuring output arises because, in addition to producing goods and services, responsibility centers produce *intangible benefits*. They may prepare employees for advancement, for example, or instill attitudes of loyalty and pride of accomplishment or, alternatively, attitudes of disloyalty and indolence. They may also affect the image of the LG as perceived by the outside world (including its taxpayers). Some of these outputs, such as better-trained employees, are investments – they are created to benefit operations in future periods, and will become inputs at some future time. Because of inherent obstacles to measurement, however, investments in intangible outputs are rarely recorded in the formal accounting system. Output measures are discussed more fully in Chapter 9.

Efficiency and effectiveness

Efficiency and effectiveness are the two criteria for judging the performance of a responsibility center. As discussed in Chapter 1, the amount of profit in a for-profit organization is a measure of both effectiveness and efficiency. Since, by definition, an LG does not have a goal to earn a profit, the difference between revenue and expense says nothing about either criterion.

Efficiency

Efficiency is the ratio of a responsibility center's outputs to its inputs. It is almost always used in a relative, rather than absolute, sense. For example, one does not ordinarily say that Unit A in an organization is 80 percent efficient. Rather, one says that Unit A is more or less efficient than Unit B, or that it is more or less efficient now than it was in the past, or that it is more or less efficient than planned or budgeted.

Unit A is more efficient than Unit B if it uses either fewer resources than Unit B but has the same output or uses the same resources as Unit B but has more output. Note that the first measure does not require us to quantify output; it only requires a reasonable judgment that the outputs of the two units are approximately equal. If management is satisfied that Units A and B are both doing a satisfactory job, and if their jobs are of comparable magnitude, then the unit with fewer inputs (that is, lower costs) is more efficient.

BOX 2.9   COMPARING EFFICIENCY

If two preschools are judged to be furnishing adequate education, the one with a lower cost per student is more efficient. If one the two preschools provides the service at a lower cost per pupil but it does not satisfy the minimum standards of quality, it is not more efficient.

The second type of efficiency measure, which contrasts different levels of output given approximately equal levels of input, requires some quantitative indication of output. It is therefore more difficult to use in many situations. If two elementary schools have the same cost per student, for example, one can be said to be more efficient than the other only if it provides more education, but this is extremely difficult to measure.

> ## BOX 2.10 COMPARING ACTUAL COSTS TO STANDARD COSTS AS MEASURE OF EFFICIENCY
>
> In many responsibility centers, measures of efficiency can be developed that relate actual costs to some standard. The standard expresses the costs that management has determined should be incurred for a given level of output. For example, an LG might develop a standard cost per cubic meter of water provided by its water department. Assuming there is no deterioration in the quality of water, the actual cost per cubic meter compared to the standard would be a measure of the department's efficiency.

Effectiveness

The effectiveness of a responsibility center is measured in terms of how its outputs contribute to its objectives. Since outputs (and success in meeting them) may be difficult to quantify, however, measures of effectiveness often are difficult to obtain. Effectiveness, therefore, is often expressed in qualitative, judgmental terms, such as "The metropolitan bus service is doing a good job," or "the reliability of the bus service has slipped somewhat in recent years."

Combining efficiency and effectiveness

An organizational unit should attempt to be both efficient and effective; it is not a matter of being one or the other. A manager who uses the resources specified in the budget may be efficient; but if the center's output is inadequate, it is ineffective.

> ## BOX 2.11 EFFECTIVENESS VERSUS EFFICIENCY
>
> The employees in a welfare office may process claims and applications with little wasted motion, making the office efficient. If the personnel have the attitude that their function is to ensure the perfect completion of every form, however, rather than to help clients obtain welfare services, the office is ineffective.

The role of outcomes

In addition to a focus on *outputs*, an LG must concern itself with a variety of *outcomes* (or what some have called "social indicators"). It is not enough just to measure outputs — an LG also must be concerned with the impact of its programs and departments on its citizenry.

BOX 2.12   OUTCOME AS THE FINAL GOAL OF LGs' ACTIVITIES

An LG might have a very good mass transportation system as measured by revenues or a customer satisfaction survey (i.e., its outputs), but if the system is not available in certain areas, it may not have much of an impact on meeting the transportation needs of the citizens who live and/or work in those areas. If that is the case, it also may not have much of an impact on the LG's desired outcome of reducing air pollution. Also, mass transportation may have other intended societal impacts, such as the improvement of declining urban areas, and even side effects, such as an influence on the real estate market (e.g., the increase of market value of houses and shops located near transit stations).

THE MANAGEMENT CONTROL STRUCTURE

As discussed previously, the management control structure is an organization's network of responsibility centers. Many large LGs have complicated hierarchies of responsibility centers: divisions, branches, departments, sections, and units. With the exception of those at the bottom of the organization, each responsibility center consists of aggregations of smaller responsibility centers, and the entire organization is itself a responsibility center. Senior management must plan and control the work of all these responsibility centers.

BOX 2.13   THE BREAKDOWN OF RESPONSIBILITY CENTERS

A public school system consists of a number of responsibility centers, such as its elementary, middle, and high schools. Each school, in turn, comprises separate responsibility centers, such as a language department or a physics department. These departments may, in turn, be divided into separate responsibility centers; the language department may be composed of sections for each language, for example.

A responsibility center should help an LG to achieve the goals that were determined in its strategic planning process. A responsibility center also has inputs of labor, material, and services. The language department in Box 2.13 has inputs of faculty, staff, educational materials, and maintenance services. It uses these inputs to produce its outputs. If the responsibility center is effective, its outputs (such as the knowledge and skill that its students acquire in language) will be closely related to its objectives, and presumably will help to satisfy one or more of the school system's goals.

Types of responsibility centers

There are five principal types of responsibility centers: revenue centers, discretionary expense centers, standard expense centers, profit centers, and investment centers. Senior management's objective in choosing a given type of responsibility center is to hold the center's manager accountable for those inputs and/or outputs over which he or she can exercise a reasonable amount of control. We will look more closely at the nature of an LG's responsibility centers in Chapter 4.

Mission centers and support centers

Regardless of type, a responsibility center can be classified as either a mission or a support center. The output of a mission center contributes directly to the objectives of the organization. The output of a support center contributes to the work of other responsibility centers, which may be either mission centers or support centers. A support center is often called a service center.

BOX 2.14 MISSION CENTERS VERSUS SUPPORT CENTERS

An LG's recreation department ordinarily would be designated as a mission center – it contributes directly to the LG's objectives. Usually, finance and personnel departments are designated as support centers – they contribute to the work of other responsibility centers but do not contribute directly to the LG's objectives.

Responsibility centers and programs

Some LGs distinguish between responsibility centers and programs. They thus have both a responsibility center structure and a program structure in their MCS. The responsibility center structure, which usually contains information classified by department, is used for planning each responsibility center's activities, coordinating its work with other responsibility centers, and measuring its performance. The program structure, by contrast, contains information that relates more directly to the LG's desired outcomes.

BOX 2.15   THE CONTRIBUTION OF RESPONSIBILITY CENTERS TO PROGRAMS

An LG may have a public safety *program*, with certain goals, such as reducing crime, minimizing property damage from fires, and decreasing the number of traffic accidents. Several different *responsibility centers* – the police department, the fire department, and the traffic or public works department – all contribute to this program, each with its own set of goals. The various goals might include increasing the hours spent on surveillance of specific areas, increasing the number of hours spent on building inspections for fire prevention activities, and reducing the malfunctioning rate of traffic signals and public lights.

When there is both a responsibility center structure and a program structure, the MCS must identify their interactions. In some instances, a responsibility center may work solely on one program, and it may be the only responsibility center working on that program. If so, the responsibility center structure corresponds to the program structure. In some LGs, for example, one responsibility center is charged with providing police protection, another for education, a third for solid waste disposal, and so on.

One-to-one correspondence between responsibility centers and programs does not always exist, however. When this happens, as in the public safety program example in Box 2.15, the MCS must identify the relationships between the two.

Table 2.1 depicts a possible relationship between responsibility centers and programs. It divides responsibility centers between mission centers and support centers. A given mission center, such as the Public Safety Department, can work for several programs. Here, it issues fines for unsafe driving in support of the Clean and Safe Streets Program, levies fines for littering and violation of pollution standards in support of the Ecological Improvement Program, and conducts building inspections in support of the Public Health Improvement Program. As the exhibit indicates, other mission centers also contribute in various ways to these three programs.

At the same time, a given program can receive services from several mission and support centers. Here, the Ecological Improvement Program receives not only the services discussed above from the Public Safety Department, but also services from the Road Maintenance Department (to synchronize traffic lights to improve the flow of traffic), and the Trash Removal Department to recycle trash.

THE MANAGEMENT CONTROL PROCESS

The management control process takes place in the context of an LG's goals and the activities that senior management has chosen for achieving them. As discussed previously, decisions about goals and activities are made in the strategic planning process, which is largely unsystematic and informal.

Table 2.1 *Relationship between responsibility centers and programs*

Responsibility centers	City programs		
	Clean and safe streets	Ecology improvement	Public health improvement
Mission centers:			
Public safety	Levy fines for unsafe driving	Levy fines for littering/polluting	Make building inspections
Road maintenance	Repair potholes	Synchronize traffic lights	Maintain streets
Trash removal	Make two pickups per week in densely populated neighborhoods	Recycle 50 percent trash	Minimize spillage of trash
Support centers:			
Human resources	Support centers' costs are allocated to mission centers in order		
City administration	to determine the full cost of each mission center. The full cost		
Legal department	of each program can then be determined by adding the full cost		
Mail distribution	of the services provided by each mission center		

Much of the management control process also is informal. It occurs by means of memoranda, meetings, hallway conversations, and even such signals as facial expressions – control devices not amenable to systematic description. Most LGs also have a formal, more systematic, process, however, which has four phases: programming, budgeting, measuring, and reporting. These usually are well defined and well understood by an LG's program and responsibility center managers.

The four phases occur in a regular cycle. Together they constitute a closed loop, as indicated in Figure 2.1.

Programming

In the programming phase, senior management determines the major programs the organization will initiate during the coming period, and the approximate revenues and expenses that will be associated with each. These decisions ordinarily are made within the context of the goals and activities that emerged from the strategy formulation (or strategic planning) process, although they frequently have political overtones. Strategic planning and management control merge in the programming phase.

Some LGs state their programs in the form of a long-range plan that forecasts outputs and inputs for several years ahead – perhaps five or ten years (or perhaps the same length as a legislative period). Some may do so for only two or three years. By contrast, in the case of public utilities, the plan may be for as long as 20 years. Other

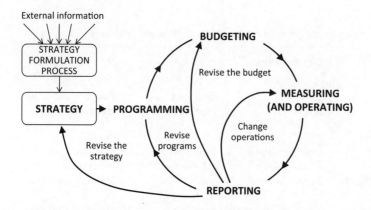

External information

STRATEGY
FORMULATION
PROCESS

STRATEGY → PROGRAMMING

BUDGETING

Revise the budget

MEASURING
(AND OPERATING)

Revise the
strategy

Revise
programs

Change
operations

REPORTING

Figure 2.1 *The management control process*
Source: Adapted from Young 2008: 14.

LGs do not have a formal mechanism for describing their future programs. They rely instead on proposals for new programs that emerge during the budgeting phase of the management control process.

Programs in industrial companies are usually products or product lines. In an LG, programs define the types of services the organization has decided to provide. Sometimes, as shown in Table 2.1, programs involve collaboration among several mission centers; in other instances, a program is provided exclusively by a single mission center. An example of the latter would be a recycling program run by the public works department (a mission center), and not requiring assistance from any other departments.

To the extent feasible, a decision about a new program should be based on an economic analysis that compares its estimated revenues or other benefits with its estimated costs. Reliable estimates of a program's benefits often are very difficult to make, however. As a result, decisions about new programs tend to rest on the ability of the LG's senior managers and elected officials to exercise sound judgment in the face of some persuasive program advocates, political pressures, and the interests of external constituencies.

BOX 2.16 SELECTION OF PROGRAMS BASED ON PERSUASION

A proposal to construct a statue of a famous local personality in a town square may have considerable support from a vocal group of citizens. As a result it may be given greater priority than the construction of a municipal parking garage, even though the parking garage would earn revenue.

Budgeting

A budget is a plan, expressed in quantitative (usually monetary) terms, that covers a specified period, usually a year. In the budgeting phase of the management control process, each program's objectives are translated into terms that correspond to the spheres of responsibility of the managers charged with implementing them.

BOX 2.17 BUDGETING COMPLEXITIES

A public school program on Renaissance art may have several objectives: train a certain number of students, provide some cross-cultural experiences, raise a designated amount of support from the community, and so forth. During the budgeting phase, the school determines the faculty and staff resources that are to be committed to the program, the necessary operating expenses (such as travel) for the program, and, perhaps, some program objectives (for example, to have a certain number of international visitors to the school). The manager of the program assumes responsibility for accomplishing these objectives within some specified amount of resources (the budget), and various department chairs assume responsibility for providing the requisite faculty to teach in the program.

The process of arriving at the budget is essentially one of negotiation between responsibility center managers and their superiors. The end product of these negotiations is a statement of the outputs expected during the budget year and the resources (inputs) that will be used to achieve them. As such, the agreed-upon budget is a bilateral commitment. Responsibility center managers commit to producing the planned output with the agreed amount of resources, and their superiors commit to agreeing that such performance is satisfactory. Both commitments are subject to the qualification "unless circumstances change significantly."

Measuring

During the period of actual operations, managers supervise what is going on, and the accounting staff keeps records of actual resources consumed and actual outputs achieved. If an LG has the sort of matrix structure shown in Table 2.1, the records must be maintained so as to reflect the costs incurred by both programs and responsibility centers. Program cost records are used as a basis for future programming; responsibility cost records are used to measure the performance of responsibility center managers.

49

BOX 2.18   COST VERSUS EXPENSE

The terms "cost" and "expense" sometimes are used interchangeably but they are not necessarily the same. If salaries for a month total $100,000, this is both a cost and an expense, and the two are identical.

By contrast, a new fire truck may *cost*, say, $100,000 but, if it is expected to last for ten years, the annual *expense* (depreciation) is $10,000. In computing the full cost of the fire department for a year, an analyst would use the $10,000 depreciation expense, not the $100,000 cost. A similar approach is used for inventory. If an LG buys ten toner cartridges for a total of $1,000, it has incurred a *cost* of $1,000. When it uses up one toner cartridge, it has had an expense of $100. Unless an LG uses accrual accounting, it can confuse cost and expense, thereby misleading readers of its financial statements.

Reporting

Accounting information, along with other information, is summarized, analyzed, and reported to those individuals who are responsible for knowing what is happening in the LG, as well as those charged with attaining agreed-upon levels of performance. The reports, which enable managers to compare planned with actual outputs and inputs, are used for three purposes: operational control, performance assessment, and program evaluation.

- ■ *Operational control:* The reports help program, department, and other line managers to identify situations that may be "out of control." These managers then are expected to investigate them, and initiate corrective action where necessary and feasible.
- ■ *Performance assessment:* The reports also are used by senior management to assess operating managers' performance. Such assessments lead to actions such as praise for a job well done, constructive criticism, promotion, reassignment, or, in extreme cases, termination.
- ■ *Program evaluation:* For any of a number of reasons, the plan for a program may be sub-optimal, or the program may not be meeting its objectives. If so, the reports may indicate that it needs to be revised, or that a more formal program evaluation needs to be initiated.

The reporting phase thus closes the loop of the management control process. It can lead back to the first phase (a reconsideration of the program), the second phase (a revision of the budget), or the third phase (a modification of operations). It can also lead senior management to reconsider the organization's approaches to achieving its goals, or even to a revision of the goals – i.e., a revision of the strategy.

CHARACTERISTICS OF A GOOD MANAGEMENT CONTROL SYSTEM

Management control systems differ considerably from one LG to the next. In some LGs they work well; in others, they are in need of considerable redesign if they are to help the LG achieve its goals. The absence of one or more of the following is an indication that the system needs redesign.

A total system

Properly designed, an MCS embraces all aspects of an LG's operations. This is because senior management must have access to information about all parts of the LG's operations.

Goal congruence

A basic principle of social psychology is that persons act according to their perceived best interests. Because of this, one characteristic of a good MCS is that it encourages managers to act in accordance with both their own best interests and the best interests of the LG as a whole. In the language of social psychology, the system should encourage *goal congruence* – it should be structured so that the goals of individual managers are consistent with the goals of the LG as a whole.

Perfect congruence between individual and organizational goals rarely exists. As a minimum, however, the system should not include evaluation and reward criteria that make the individual's best interests inconsistent with, or contrary to, the best interests of the LG. For example, a lack of goal congruence exists if the MCS emphasizes reduced costs and, in doing so, encourages managers to sacrifice quality, provide inadequate service, or engage in activities that reduce costs in one department but cause a more than offsetting increase in another.

Financial framework

With rare exceptions, an MCS should be built around a financial structure. This does not mean that accounting information is the sole, or even the most important, part of the MCS; it means only that the accounting system provides a unifying core to which managers can relate other types of information. Although the financial structure is usually the central focus, non-monetary measures, such as minutes per task, number of persons served, or cubic meters of water provided, are also important parts of the system.

51

Rhythm

The management control process tends to be rhythmic: it follows a definite pattern and timetable, month after month, year after year. In budget preparation, certain steps are taken in a prescribed sequence and at certain times each year: dissemination of guidelines, preparation of estimates, transmission of these estimates up through the several echelons of the organization, review of these estimates, final approval by senior management, and dissemination back through the organization.

Integration

An MCS should be a coordinated, integrated system. Although data collected for one purpose may differ from those collected for another, these data should be reconcilable. Although the MCS is a single system, in some LGs it also consists of two interlocking subsystems – one focused on programs and one on responsibility centers.

SUMMARY

Management control systems sit between strategic planning and task control, and they include both programs and responsibility centers. Their information comes from the accounting system, which measures what *has* happened in terms of resource inflows and outflows, and from the programming and budgeting phases of the management control process, which measures what *should* happen. Because most LGs use cash accounting, the information used by their MCSs tends to be deficient – it fails to account properly for resource inflows and outflows. An LG's MCS will continue to have this deficiency until there is a conversion to accrual accounting.

Despite this limitation, the MCS attempts to measure revenues (which are resource inflows) and expenses (which are resource outflows). In addition, a good MCS also will measure non-monetary information on outputs in an effort to show what its programs are accomplishing. To accomplish these tasks, the MCS contains both a structure and a process (akin to anatomy and physiology in the human body). This chapter discussed both briefly. We will discuss these topics in greater detail in subsequent chapters.

DISCUSSION QUESTIONS

1   Which of the general characteristics of an LG is the most serious impediment to performance measurement? Why?

2   What changes to its MCS might an LG make to move the system closer to the kind of system used in a for-profit organization? How hard will it be to make these changes?

REFERENCES

Anthony, R.N. (1988) *The Management Control Function,* Boston: Harvard Business School Press.

Caperchione, E. and Mussari, R. (eds) (2000) *Comparative Issues in Local Government Accounting,* Norwell, Massachusetts: Kluwer Academic Publishers.

Porter, M.E. (1996) "What Is Strategy," *Harvard Business Review,* 74(6): 61–78.

FURTHER READING

A management control system is one of several levers of control in management's hands. Simons' publication *Levers of Organization Design: How Managers Use Accountability Systems for Greater Performance and Commitment* (Harvard Business School Press, 2005) helps to position an MCS within the other available levers. A very popular read on this topic is *Management Control Systems* by Anthony and Govindarajan (12th edn, McGraw-Hill/Irwin 2006). While this latter book has an all-encompassing motivation, Young's book *Management Control in Nonprofit Organizations* (Crimson Press Curriculum Center 2008) has a specific focus on nonprofits, the broad category of organizations where LGs sit.

Chapter 3

Barriers to effective management control in local governments

LEARNING OBJECTIVES

At the end of this chapter you should:

- Appreciate the many barriers that local governments (LGs) face in their efforts to implement improved management control systems, and hence to move toward what has been called the New Public Management (NPM) paradigm.
- Understand the distinction between bureaucratic control and managerial control.
- Recognize that a typical LG provides a heterogeneous mix of programs and services, ranging from street cleaning to social welfare, and that these programs and services can differ in terms of (a) the formality of the relationship to clients, (b) the degree of customization and professional judgment, (c) the nature of demand in relation to supply, (d) the method of service delivery, and (e) the capital-labor mix in service delivery.
- Understand how the principles of generational equity and consumer equity influence whether and how much an LG charges for some of its services.
- Be able to address the conceptual issues involved in deciding whether a program or service should receive a subsidy from general tax revenue.

KEY POINTS

- The principles of generational and consumer equity are related to the difficulty that an LG faces in developing pricing units for its services.

- According to the principle of generational equity, the current year's taxpayers should pay only for the expenses of the current year's programs and services, and not for the expenses incurred in operating those programs or services in a prior year, or to fund any expenses that might be incurred in future years.
- According to the principle of consumer equity, user fees should support a program or service when there is an easily measurable unit of output and when consumption is a matter of choice.
- Applying the principles of generational and consumer equity can be particularly tricky in areas such as education, water and sewer services, trash pickup and disposal, public transit, and fire protection. Part of the difficulty lies in determining if there is (a) an appropriate pricing unit, and (b) the presence (or absence) of positive externalities.
- If a program or service is to be subsidized, determining the size of the subsidy can be tricky. An LG must answer two questions. First, is the department that receives the subsidy operating as efficiently as possible? Second, could the funds being used for the subsidy be put to better use for some other purpose? The first is a question of efficiency. The second is a question of priorities.

A central focus of public management over the last several decades has been to minimize waste and ensure efficient and effective public services (Nolan 2001: Introduction). Efforts to do so have resulted in four trends: (1) an attempt to slow down or reverse government growth, (2) a shift toward privatization and quasi-privatization in service provision, (3) an increase in the use of information technology, and (4) a focus on improved policy design, decision styles, and inter-government cooperation (Hood 1991).

These trends are part of what has been called the *New Public Management (NPM) paradigm* (Hood 1991; 1995). This paradigm depicts governments as leaner, more effective entities – ones that can do "more with less" (Osborne and Gaebler 1992; Koppenjan and Klijn 2004). To accomplish this, the NPM paradigm comprises restructured organizational units that have improved definitions of responsibilities and increased managerial autonomy. It envisions the elimination of unneeded bureaucratic procedures, and an emphasis on frugal behavior so as to minimize waste. It expects public officials to adopt managerial approaches that have proven successful in the private sector, and, when appropriate, to use private-sector contractors to deliver services so as to both decrease costs and improve quality. And its emphasis on quality improvement includes efforts to measure outputs, results, and performance. Whenever possible, it benchmarks these measures against external standards.

More recently, in response to the increasingly complex nature of public policy implementation and service delivery, the New Public Governance (NPG) concept has emerged. The NPG concept emphasizes collaboration among governments and between public and private sector organizations in the provision of services. Despite this emphasis, the NPG concept retains several of the NPM paradigm's principal ideas, especially the need for effective intra-organizational collaboration and cost-effective service management (Osborne 2010: 7).

BARRIERS TO IMPLEMENTING THE NPM PARADIGM

Unfortunately, for most LGs, the NPM paradigm – as well as some elements of the NPG concept – are not at all descriptive. Rather, they constitute an economic "ideal type" – a state of affairs, akin to a purely competitive market, that is sought in the abstract but never actually attained. Some of the barriers to success are historical precedents, some are structural, and some are a matter of uninformed or poor choices by LG managers. Nevertheless, the reality is that most LGs have not emphasized or measured outputs, results, or performance, and those that have done so rarely have benchmarked their data against external standards. Moreover, if an LG has developed contracts with private entities in an effort to decrease costs and increase quality, it most likely has not incorporated its vendors into its management control system in any meaningful way.

In part, these difficulties are a result of some unusual, and tricky, issues an LG faces in designing its management control system. For instance, many members of an LG's senior management team consist of elected officials who must contend with a variety of external forces and political influences that inhibit the implementation of a good MCS (Kotter and Lawrence 1974). Moreover, because new programs often are political, they may not receive a rigorous financial feasibility analysis prior to implementation. At the same time, many programmatic objectives – such as "adequate" police protection or "appropriate" fire response time – are difficult to define and measure, let alone benchmark.

Even from a financial perspective, the traditional territory of management control, an LG's efforts to measure performance are impeded by the fact that much of its revenue comes from property or other general taxes that are unrelated to the services it provides to its citizens. Additionally, the restricted use of some revenues for specific purposes in some LGs limits senior management's flexibility to shift resources from one activity or program to another, thereby constraining mid-year programmatic adjustments when circumstances change or unforeseen needs emerge.[1] Finally, some LGs still keep their accounts on a cash basis, a practice that makes it difficult to account for the true generation or consumption of resources.[2]

One question that surfaces as a result of this gap between the NPM paradigm and the current state of affairs is: "What are the *true* barriers to good local government

Table 3.1 *Bureaucratic control versus managerial control*

	Type of control	
Dimension	Bureaucratic	Managerial
Managerial focus	Norms	Results
Breadth of orientation	Narrow	Wide
Managerial latitude	Rigid	Flexible
Budgetary orientation	Spend completely	Spend efficiently
Adaptation to change in environment	Little	Much

Source: Borgonovi and Rondo-Brovetto (1988).

management?" More specifically, since examples can be found in many industrialized countries of efficient and effective private sector management, are there any helpful lessons that can be transferred from the private sector to an LG?

In part, the difference between the two forms of management lies in the concept of a bureaucracy, where there is a sizable body of literature, beginning over 60 years ago with Max Weber (1947), and including several classic works (Gouldner 1954; Blau 1955; Parsons 1960; Crozier 1964). One recurring theme in this literature that relates to improved management control systems in LGs is the distinction between bureaucratic and managerial control. The distinction can be described along the five dimensions shown in Table 3.1.

In light of these distinctions, most observers would agree that a change from bureaucratic to managerial control would be highly desirable in any LG in any sort of economic or social system. The question, then, is what prevents such a move? The purpose of this chapter is to discuss the barriers to such a move, and to suggest some ways to overcome them.

BOX 3.1 SIX ESSENTIAL CHARACTERISTICS OF MANAGERIAL CONTROL

In making the distinction between bureaucratic and managerial control, Farneti (1995) has expanded on the ideas shown in Table 3.1. In his view good managerial control has six fundamental characteristics:

- *Integration:* Financial measures are combined with non-financial measures.
- *Commitment:* Managerial control is embedded in the organizations' life.

- *Dynamism:* The different phases of the management control process allow senior management to shift the organization's priorities in response to environment changes.
- *Flexibility:* Managers are not held responsible for differences between actual and budget that arise because of increases or decreases in volume that are outside their control (e.g., meters of snow to be plowed).[3]
- *Personal responsibility:* Targets (which represent the LG's objectives) are related to the managers who control them.
- *Planning:* Ex-post evaluations are made possible by establishing ex-ante specifications of targets.

To fully understand the barriers to achieving the NPM paradigm, and to put them in an appropriate context for assessing ways to eliminate them, one first must recognize that an LG can comprise an extremely heterogeneous group of programs and services. As Table 3.2 shows, these programs and services can differ in terms of (1) the formality of the relationship to clients, (2) the degree of customization and professional judgment, (3) the nature of demand in relation to supply, (4) the method of service delivery, and (5) the capital–labor mix in service delivery.

As a result of these distinctions, LG managers must be careful to assess the conclusions about barriers and steps to overcome them in the context of their own situations. What works to overcome a barrier for one LG, or for one program or department within a given LG, may not work for another.

BARRIERS TO EFFECTIVE MANAGERIAL CONTROL

Despite the heterogeneity shown in Table 3.2, there are several important conceptual and practical barriers to effective management control in most LGs. Many of these can be overcome with some creative thinking on the part of an LG's senior management team.

Conceptual barriers

The design and implementation of a good management control system in an LG is impeded by four conceptual barriers, each of which can help to explain the slow progress toward the NPM paradigm: (1) the principle of generational (or inter-year) equity, (2) the principle of consumer equity, (3) the juxtaposition of positive externalities and pricing units, and (4) the pricing of programs and services without positive externalities.

Table 3.2 Differences among local governments departments, programs, and services

Relationship to clients		
Nature of service delivery	Formal relationship	No formal relationship
Continuous delivery	Water and sewer service	Police department
Discrete transactions	Credit union	Public hospital

Customization in service delivery		
Professional judgment required	High	Low
High	Legal aid services	Preventive health programs
Low	Welfare office	Food stamp program

Demand fluctuations during a year		
Demand/capacity relationship	Wide	Narrow
Peak demand usually can be met	Electric utility	Public school
Peak demand regularly exceeds capacity	Museum	Public housing authority

Availability of service sites		
Method of service delivery	Single Site	Multiple Sites
Client goes to organization	Welfare office	Public transit
Organization comes to client	Social work agency	Fire department

Importance of people-based attributes			
Importance of asset-based attributes	High	Medium	Low
High	Public hospital	Public Transit	Electric Utility
Low	Legal aid services	Motor Vehicle Registry	Food stamp program

The principle of generational equity

According to the principle of generational equity, the current year's taxpayers should pay only for the expenses of the current year's programs and services, and not for any expenses incurred in operating those programs or services in a prior year, or to fund the expenses a program might incur in future years. In effect, an operating deficit this year means that future years' taxpayers will pay for this year's programs (or, if the deficit is financed from a prior year's surplus, that prior year's taxpayers helped to pay for this year's programs). An operating surplus means that this year's taxpayers will help to pay for future years' programs.

In part, the generational equity principle underlies the need for an LG to have a balanced budget each year, coupled with restrictions to assure that no accounts are overspent. What the principle fails to recognize, of course, is that the revenues for many programs are not fully predictable. If they fall below the budget, and if the LG's spending restrictions are not sufficient, there will be a deficit. If they exceed the budget, and no mechanism is in place to raise the spending ceilings, there will be a surplus.

Despite having balanced annual budgets, many LGs violate the generational equity principle in two ways. First, they fail to account properly for pensions and other post-retirement benefits earned by their employees. In many EU countries, this problem is hidden from an LG's taxpayers because a portion of the LG's pension expense is funded by the central government. In the United States, by contrast, where pensions are the sole responsibility of the LG, this accounting (and audit!) failure can reach many millions of dollars in any good sized LG. Despite recently passed corrective legislation, many LGs taxpayers in the United States will be called on to fund retirement benefits that were earned over several prior decades.[4]

The second violation of the generational equity principle arises because most LGs do not depreciate their infrastructure and other fixed assets. An LG's infrastructure includes roads, bridges, tunnels, dams, and even some smaller capital items, such as a fire house. An LG also has fixed assets with somewhat shorter economic lives, such as a police cruiser. As with all fixed assets, the economic life is unknown at the time of construction or purchase. Moreover, because these assets generally have economic lives of several years, an LG has difficulty assuring that the individuals who receive their benefits pay for them in their entirety.

In part, these difficulties are the same as those that any organization – in either the private or public sector – has in selecting an economic life for a new asset. As a consequence, the failure to depreciate fixed assets is not due to the difficulty of estimating their economic lives. Rather, it is a consequence of the use of cash- or commitment-based accounting.[5] The result is that the current year's taxpayers pay for an asset that will be used by other taxpayers for several, if not many, years into the future.[6]

Some observers have argued that the generational equity issue associated with an absence of accounting for depreciation is less problematic than it might appear to be, at least for infrastructure projects and other large fixed assets. Their reasoning is that these assets ordinarily are financed with municipal bonds or other forms of long-term debt. Under this scenario, the term of the debt effectively constitutes the economic life of the asset, such that the annual principal payment on the debt is a reasonable surrogate for the asset's depreciation expense.

Thus, the argument goes, if an LG finances an infrastructure asset with a bond (or a similar long-term debt instrument), and chooses a repayment period that approximates the economic life of the asset, there is no need to incorporate depreciation into the management control system.[7] With infrastructure projects that benefit the entire community, and where no pricing units can be established, the LG need only assure that property tax and other general tax revenues are sufficient to cover the bond's debt service payments (principal and interest), in addition, of course, to the LG's other general operating expenses.

Unfortunately, a violation of the generational equity principle can occur when an asset's economic life extends well beyond (or is much shorter than) the term of the debt instrument that financed it. If the economic life is longer than the debt term, some future generations of taxpayers will benefit from an asset for which they did not pay. If the economic life is shorter than the debt term, the current generation of taxpayers will not fully pay for the cost of the asset they used.

Because of these complications, and because not all fixed assets are debt financed, movement toward the NPM paradigm requires incorporating depreciation into an LG's accounting system. Using principal payments on debt as a surrogate for depreciation is a poor substitute.

The principle of consumer equity

The principle of consumer equity holds that user fees should support a program or service when there is an easily measurable unit of output and when consumption is a matter of choice. This principle underlies the creation of what in some locales are called "enterprise funds," such as Off-Track Betting in New York City.

Between enterprise funds and programs that are supported entirely by general taxpayers (such as road maintenance or street lighting) lies a somewhat amorphous middle ground where application of the consumer-equity principle can become contentious. To illustrate the dilemma, consider the water and sewer department shown in Table 3.3.

In this situation, there has been a minor violation of the generational equity principle, since the LG's taxpayers have over-funded the €24.5 million deficit, thereby paying for €15.5 million of the services that will be received by future years' citizens. This situation could be corrected with little difficulty.

More significantly, the consumer-equity principle has been violated in several ways, most of which are more difficult to correct than the generational-equity problem. First, the department incurred a deficit prior to receiving taxpayer support, meaning that users, as a group, did not pay for the full costs of the services they received. The LG's taxpayers, who paid for their consumption directly via user fees, also paid for it *indirectly* (i.e., without regard to their consumption) via their property or other general taxes.

61

Table 3.3 *Absence of consumer equity in a water and sewer department (€000)*

	Municipal water and sewer services				
	New users	Existing users	Pre-tax surplus (deficit)	Municipality taxpayers	Total
Revenues					
Access fees	€46,700				
Usage fees		€139,000			
Total revenues	€46,700	€139,000			
Expenditures					
Operating		€67,900			
Debt service	€197,600				
Total expenditures	€197,600	€67,900			
Operating surplus (deficit)	(€150,900)	€71,100			
Grant from region	€55,300				
Surplus (deficit)	(€95,600)	€71,100	(€24,500)	€40,000	€15,500

Second, as the line just above the Surplus (Deficit) computation for new users shows, the *region*'s (as opposed to the LG's) taxpayers subsidized some of the cost of new users gaining access to the water and sewer system. One must ask what benefits accrued to the region's taxpayers from providing a €55.3 million subsidy to support the construction of water and sewer facilities in an LG where most of them do not live.

BOX 3.2 WHEN SHOULD AN LG VIOLATE THE CONSUMER EQUITY PRINCIPLE?

The use of regional funds to subsidize one or more of an LG's programs or services illustrates the importance of multiple external pressures in decision-making within LGs, a matter that was discussed in Chapter 1. Clearly, a well-managed LG will use whatever political influences it can muster to help obtain outside support for its programs. Obtaining a regional grant for the LG's water and sewer department is an excellent illustration of this tactic.

Finally, and perhaps less obviously, existing users have helped to subsidize the cost of new users gaining access to the system. This violation of the consumer-equity principle arises because there are two separate services: *access* to the water and sewer *system* and *use* of water and sewer *services*. The access fees for new users (plus the regional subsidy) did not cover the debt service costs associated with the infrastructure to which they were gaining access, resulting in a €95.6 million shortfall. At the same time, existing users (who had paid their access fees in some prior period) have paid €71.1 million more than the full cost of the department's ongoing operations.

The water and sewer department in Table 3.3 is not an anomaly. Similar situations arise regularly in the management of an LG. To address them, senior management must answer three questions about its programs and services:

1   Which should be paid exclusively by users with no taxpayer subsidies?
2   Which should be paid – in whole or in part – from property tax or other general tax revenues?
3   Which should be supported by state or regional taxpayers?

To make these questions more concrete, consider the following services, and assess whether they should be paid entirely by user fees. Alternatively, if they should be subsidized by general taxpayers, how should an LG's senior management team compute the amount of the subsidy? And, once the amount of the subsidy is determined, how should state or regional taxpayers decide on the support they should provide?

■ *Education:* Property tax revenues, sometimes a specified percentage of each property tax dollar, are used in some LGs to pay for the operating costs of the LG's school system. Sometimes state or regional aid contributes to the system's operations, meaning that taxpayers in other LGs help to pay for a given LG's school system. In addition, the use of property taxes means that families who live in the LG but have no school-age children (i.e., families receiving no educational services) help to pay for the system's costs. And it means that families with few school-age children help to pay for the educational costs of families with many school-age children.

■ *Water and sewer:* As the example in Table 3.3 demonstrates, some LGs use property tax revenues and state (or regional) aid to support a portion of the cost of running their water and sewer system. This means that all families pay a portion of the cost of the system, regardless of their consumption. It also means that those families in the LG with artesian wells and septic systems, i.e., those who use no municipal water or sewer services, help to pay the cost of water and sewer services for other residents. And the presence of state aid for new users means that people living outside the LG help to support construction of its water and sewer infrastructure.

■ *Trash pickup and disposal:* When the pickup and disposal of non-recyclable trash is paid with general tax revenues, small families subsidize large families, abstemious families subsidize wasteful families, and families who recycle subsidize those who do not.

■ *Public transportation:* When public transportation deficits are funded with property taxes, or with state (or regional) subsidies, public transit passengers do not pay the full cost of their transportation. They are subsidized by automobile drivers, cyclists, pedestrians, and shut-ins.

■ *Police protection:* When funded with property taxes, or with state (or regional) subsidies, police protection for individuals who live in high-crime neighborhoods is subsidized by individuals who live in low-crime neighborhoods. In addition, individuals who live in rural areas (where crime rates typically are low) subsidize those living in urban areas.

■ *Fire protection:* People who are safety conscious subsidize those who are careless with fire.

Positive externalities and pricing units

In many respects, an answer to whether a program or service should be subsidized by general taxpayers hinges on two factors: the presence of positive externalities and the ability to identify an output (or pricing) unit. According to this view, an LG's taxpayers should subsidize the police department, since the entire community benefits from having police protection in high-crime neighborhoods (a positive externality). In addition, using general tax revenues for funding the police department is appropriate, since it is all but impossible to develop a unit of output for pricing the service.

With a fire department, by contrast, there is an easily measurable unit of output (responding to a fire), and hence a cost and a price that can be determined relatively easily. Clearly, a positive externality exists in terms of preventing a fire's spread to other buildings, but, since the basic users of the service (those who started the fire) have a choice (use fire safely or carelessly), and since a pricing unit can be established (a response to a call), there would appear to be little reason to have the fire-extinguishing service (as opposed to the department's standby service) subsidized by general taxpayers.

The presence (or absence) of positive externalities and pricing units perhaps can be useful for arriving at a *conceptual* answer to the question of whether there should be a subsidy. But taking the next step requires an LG to address two important and related issues: the definition of the community and the amount of the subsidy. With public education, for example, the usual argument is that the LG's taxpayers should provide a subsidy because the entire community benefits from having an educated citizenry (a positive externality). But this begs the question of how to define the benefiting community. It also explains why public education in many countries is funded with *national* rather than *local* tax revenues.

With regard to the amount of the subsidy, an LG must answer two questions. First, is the department that receives the subsidy operating as efficiently as possible? Second, could the funds being used for the subsidy be put to better use for some other purpose? The first is a question of efficiency and can be answered rather easily. The second is a question of priorities and is much more difficult to answer.

64

Pricing programs and services without positive externalities

A logical extension of the above thinking is that when an output (or pricing) unit can be established, and when no positive externalities can be identified, each user or user group should pay its own way with no general taxpayer support. With water and sewer services, trash collection and disposal, public transportation, after school programs, snow removal, and a host of other municipal services there is a measurable output unit. Under these circumstances, if the LG's senior management cannot identify a positive externality that accrues to a community from the consumption of the service (or use of the program), there would appear to be no basis for taxpayer subsidies. Thus, by identifying these programs and services, and designating the departments that provide them as "profit centers" in its management control system,[8] an LG can begin to move toward the principle of consumer-equity, and, at the same time, toward a more appropriate use of its general tax revenues.

Practical barriers to effective management control

There are six practical barriers that impede good management control, and that are common to almost all LGs: (1) the lack of a control culture, (2) the presence of centralized decision making, (3) the schism between planning and control, (4) the absence of market forces, (5) the complex nature of tasks, and (6) the presence of restrictive personnel policies. Each is discussed briefly below. We discuss some of these more fully in subsequent chapters.

Lack of a control culture

Most organizations can be characterized in terms of a set of values, or a culture, that forms a framework to guide employees' behavior. Although there are three levels of organizational culture – artifacts, shared values, and basic assumptions – the key to understanding an organization's culture lies in the third level, which includes assumptions about mission, means of problem solving, organizational relationships, time, and space (Schein 2010). More specifically, basic assumptions reflect

> a pattern ... that [the organization] has learned as it solved its problems of external adaptation and internal integration, that has worked well enough to be considered valid and, therefore, to be taught to new members as the correct way to perceive, think, and feel in relation to those problems.
>
> (Schein 2010: 12)

It seems reasonable to conclude that at least some of an LG's basic assumptions will relate to management control. Indeed, it seems clear that the success of an LG's MCS relies in large part on the existence of a "control culture" that not only supports the formal system, but is so powerful that it obviates the system's need on occasion (Young 1979).

65

The control culture in most LGs suffers in at least three respects. First, LG managers frequently have limited knowledge of the ways that their management control system can assist them in furthering the LG's objectives. As a result, the control culture frequently is not supportive of either effectiveness or efficiency.

BOX 3.3   LIMITED CONTROL CULTURE

It would be possible for the manager of the department charged with snow removal or street cleaning to distinguish between cost overruns attributable to greater volume (more snow or more frequent need for street cleaning – due to, say, a parade or a student demonstration) and those due to worsened or improved efficiency (more or less time spent per kilometer plowed or cleaned). Few LGs have a control culture that encourages this sort of distinction, and hence their management control systems do not report on it.

Second, many LG managers are not encouraged to exercise good management control. Indeed, an LG's accounting system often constrains a manager's ability to shift funds when priorities change. Moreover, there frequently are no good measures of non-financial performance, and no rewards for spending less than the budget to accomplish a given set of objectives.

Third, most oversight agencies, especially legislative bodies, focus almost exclusively on adhering to budgetary line items, and, where perhaps greater sophistication exists, to remaining within programmatic spending guidelines. However, little effort ordinarily is focused on the measurement of results, or the achievement of goals, that in some way further the LG's objectives. Indeed, the culture of management control frequently collides with the political priorities set out by the LG's elected officials (Spano 2009). As a result, efficiency and effectiveness often take a back seat to the activities needed to attain citizen support in the next election.

BOX 3.4   MANAGEMENT CONTROL CULTURE VERSUS POLITICAL PRIORITIES

An LG's police cruisers may be old and in need of constant repair, such that improving efficiency would call for a capital expenditure on some new cruisers. However, until the cruisers dilapidated condition results in the police department's inability to respond to an emergency call, capital funds are more likely to be spent on, say, new playground equipment in a popular municipal park, renovations to a senior center, or the repaving of a busy thoroughfare.

In short, the culture of management control in many LGs focuses on adherence to budgetary line items and not on the accomplishment of results. It is quite logical, then, that many LG managers devote their time to abiding by norms, maintaining a narrow breadth of orientation, and adapting in only minor ways to changes in their environments.

Centralized decision making

From a somewhat broader perspective, the control culture is one element of a managerial orientation that focuses on the acquisition and maintenance of power, and that is characterized by managers who are reluctant to delegate responsibility in any meaningful way. By contrast, Alfred Chandler's (1962) review of the history of the modern corporation in the United States showed that, at a certain point, a decentralized structure was put in place to assist the organization in implementing its strategy more effectively. In each of the four major corporations that he studied, the decentralized structure came about when the company reached a size that was simply too unwieldy and complex to manage centrally. Many LGs have reached this cumbersome size and yet continue to be highly centralized.

Although it may seem counterintuitive, many large LGs no doubt could benefit from having their senior managers cease exercising close control over their subordinates' activities. Instead, for some of the same reasons that the four corporations that Chandler studied undertook steps to decentralize, managers of large LGs might consider delegating greater authority to their subordinates. If they did so, however, they also would need to begin to measure their subordinates' performance objectively, and reward them on the basis of their results and accomplishments. Unfortunately, the accounting and other information systems in many LGs are not up to the task.

Therefore, despite the apparent benefits of decentralization, many LGs give little autonomy to lower-level managers. They remain highly centralized, with a great deal of decision making lodged in the hands of only a very few senior managers, usually the city manager or general manager. These are people who are appointed by, and have a close relationship with, the LG's elected officials (such as the mayor). Yet, if we looked closely at these organizations, we quite likely would find that many of them possess characteristics that, if they were private sector entities, would have a more decentralized structure.

In many instances, what prevents senior managers of a large LG from decentralizing power and authority is a lack of trust in lower level managers, or a lack of confidence in their decision-making capabilities. Part of this problem, of course, is political – a poor decision by a lower-level manager can become highly visible to the citizenry via media coverage, and ultimately can become politically embarrassing to senior management. This can have serious repercussions when the next election takes place.

In addition, though, the absence of a market mechanism for evaluating decision-making can contribute to an unwillingness to delegate. In decentralized private sector

67

organizations, for example, division general managers interact with a market, and their performance can be assessed by the market's reactions to their decisions. By contrast, no such mechanism exists for most LGs, leading many senior managers to resist decentralization and retain centralized control. Indeed, without an objective performance-measurement mechanism, and with many decisions carefully scrutinized by the electorate and the media, decentralizing decision making is risky business.

Planning versus control

A third barrier to the movement from bureaucratic to managerial control is what might be called the seduction of planning. Clearly, it is not easy to plan. The gathering and analysis of appropriate data, the assessment of benefits and costs, the need to quantify the inherently unquantifiable, the ordering of priorities, the overlay of political realities and objectives on the quantitative analysis, the presence of funding constraints, and much more make planning extremely difficult.

But planners are not accountable for results. To verify this, one need only compare the planning document prepared, say, five years ago for any good-sized LG with the current reality. In almost all instances there will be a large gap between the goals and objectives that were stipulated in the plan and the results that actually were attained.

The gap between the plan and the reality exists because planners generally do not need to worry about whether (1) department or program managers will accomplish what is being laid out, (2) citizens will be cooperative, (3) implied cause-and-effect patterns are realistic, or (4) sufficient funding will be forthcoming. In short, the plan can be based on a wide variety of assumptions, many of which are unrealistic but do not show up as such until implementation time arrives.

Absence of market forces

As indicated above, there generally is an absence of a market mechanism between citizens receiving services and the LG providing them. The result is a need for programming decisions, budgetary procedures, performance measures, and reporting systems that not only differ from those in the private sector, but that reflect the rather large "economic distance" that can exist between an LG and its citizenry.

For example, the presence or absence of legislative (or budgetary) support for an LG's programs is quite frequently a result of factors that lie well outside of senior management's control. Legislative mandates are based on a variety of needs and concerns that are communicated by citizens to elected representatives. If these needs are communicated by sufficiently powerful constituents or lobbies, they may result in legislation that dictates performance requirements, which may not coincide with the LG's capabilities. And they may not be accompanied by sufficient budgetary resources to permit satisfactory performance. Without a market mechanism, it is difficult to determine how well the LG is performing.

BOX 3.5   DOING THE RIGHT JOB BUT MISSING THE POINT

According to one manager, "the Division of Insurance has many insurance inspectors on its payroll, but about all they ever inspect is a typewriter; this is necessary if we are to pay an experienced clerk-typist appropriately."

Task complexity

For a variety of reasons, the tasks carried out in many LGs are more complex than those in the private sector. To illustrate, consider the municipal social service agency (MSSA) illustrated in Figure 3.1. As this figure indicates, the MSSA operates along two dimensions, each of which gives rise to a different set of information needs. One is budgetary – account executives need to manage programs, each of which has a budget, classified into one of the district's appropriation accounts. The accountability here is to the legislature, which approved the budget and set spending restrictions, such that no appropriation account can have its budgeted limit exceeded. However, the legislature did not stipulate which districts or facilities were to receive the budgeted funds.

By contrast, field operations and facility managers are responsible for providing care in various settings in the district. Their accountability is to the clients and communities where services are being delivered. In effect, the account executives have budgetary responsibility but can only exercise it via the facilities that the MSSA has available in its various areas. Facility managers, on the other hand, need resources from the account executives to pay their operating expenses. Attaining a congruence among the programmatic wishes of the legislature, the needs of each district's community, and the facilities available to provide care makes the task extremely complex.

Of course, a matrix structure like this can exist in private sector organizations as well. It arises any time a task must be carried out along dual lines of authority. But it nevertheless is indicative of a complex task, and generally is considered to be the most difficult organizational form to manage. Since many private sector organizations have a difficult time managing a matrix organization, it is not hard to imagine the difficulty an LG has in doing so, especially when the performance agenda is expanded to include the goals of the legislature.

To make a structure such as this work, an LG's MCS must be able to program, budget, measure, and report along both dimensions of the matrix, and it must be able to address the needs of several constituencies. Senior management also must manage the many conflicts that can arise along the way.

The absence of a market further complicates matters. A private sector organization often uses transfer prices to manage some of the interactions in a matrix, but this works best when an outside market can be used to help determine the appropriate transfer price. The MSSA in Figure 3.1 – and many other public sector organizations

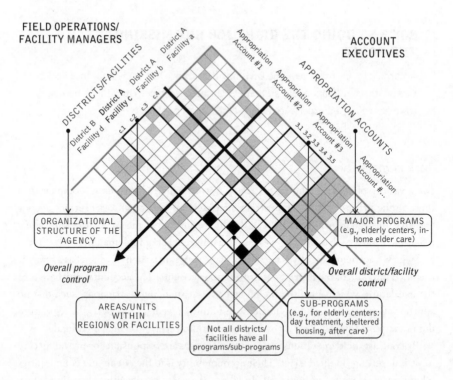

FIELD OPERATIONS/
FACILITY MANAGERS

ACCOUNT
EXECUTIVES

DISTRICTS/FACILITIES

District B
District A
District A Facility c
District A Facility b
District A Facility a
Facility d
c.1 c.2 c.3 c.4

Appropriation Account #1
Appropriation Account #2
Appropriation Account #3
Appropriation Account #...

APPROPRIATION ACCOUNTS

3.1 3.2 3.3 3.4 3.5

ORGANIZATIONAL
STRUCTURE OF THE
AGENCY

MAJOR PROGRAMS
(e.g., elderly centers, inhome elder care)

*Overall program
control*

*Overall district/facility
control*

AREAS/UNITS
WITHIN
REGIONS OR FACILITIES

Not all districts/
facilities have all
programs/sub-programs

SUB-PROGRAMS
(e.g., for elderly centers:
day treatment, sheltered
housing, after care)

Figure 3.1 *Management control structure in a municipal social services agency*
Source: Adapted from Young (2008, 121).

using a matrix – have no such outside market, and hence have considerable difficulty establishing appropriate transfer prices. We return to this issue in Chapter 4.

Personnel policies

Clearly, union regulations in the private sector pose many of the same personnel-related constraints that civil service regulations pose in an LG. Yet, LGs seem to have a more difficult time than their private sector counterparts in maintaining adequate levels of productivity and motivation among their employees. In part, this is reflective of the fact that union contracts in private sector organizations apply only to labor, not to management. By contrast, as discussed in Chapter 1, civil service coverage in many LGs can extend quite far up the managerial hierarchy, frequently including what the private sector would call "middle management."

In addition, when there is a market mechanism, and when customers can take their business elsewhere, a private sector organization requires personnel who are concerned about, and responsive to, the needs and interests of those customers. This customer focus often is lacking in an LG, which, in part, underlies the move that many LGs are making toward outsourcing (or "privatization," as it sometimes is called). The idea is not only to save money due to a contractor's experience and scale economies, but also to make the service provider more responsive to user needs.

Given that not all of an LG's services can be outsourced, however, the issue of personnel policies will always be present.[9] To address this issue, senior management must recognize that, in many LG settings, a job is a sinecure – one need only show up, not perform. Indeed, in political systems where patronage exists, neither performance *nor attendance* may be required! To say that this complicates managerial control is an understatement.

BOX 3.6 POLITICAL PATRONAGE

One large LG in the United States was well known for political patronage. To address this issue, the state engaged an audit firm. As a part of the audit, one of the firm's professional staff went unannounced to the LG's municipal hospital on a payday to physically distribute paychecks (rather than mailing them to employees as was the usual practice). He discovered that a significant percentage of the employees (much higher than illness or chance would suggest was appropriate) were not available to receive their paychecks.

Finally, in most LGs, the reward system is not designed to provide performance incentives. One receives a salary, usually with no opportunity for a bonus. High quality performance in some instances can result in a greater salary increase than one's colleagues receive, but not much. This is particularly true when the performance evaluation system is designed to minimize the number of poor performance ratings, or where, as frequently is the case, a manager is reluctant to rate an employee as a poor performer.

BOX 3.7 PERFORMANCE-RELATED PERSONNEL POLICIES

Personnel policies may represent a good starting point for LG reform. In Italy, for example, the ministry of public administration centered many of its reform efforts on personnel policies. A key element of the ministry's approach was to reward good results. It did so by stressing the idea of differentiation of performance among employees and introducing the idea that only 25 percent of employees were to be rewarded as good performers. Another 50 percent were to be designated as average, and the remaining 25 percent as substandard performers.[10]

IMPROVING THE MANAGEMENT CONTROL SYSTEM

Improving an LG's MCS requires senior management to engage in several interrelated activities, some of which are one-time and others ongoing. On a one-time basis (perhaps with periodic review), the LG's senior management team must determine which programs or departments should operate as self-sufficient entities with no (or minimal) support from general tax revenues, and which, because of either positive externalities or the absence of an output unit, should be funded with general tax revenues. An approach such as this requires careful deliberation by the LG's senior managers about positive externalities, and, when none exists, an effort to identify the appropriate output unit to use for pricing purposes. Clearly, if no output unit exists for pricing purposes (such as with street lighting), the program's or service's funding must come from general tax revenues.

Regardless of the revenue source, an LG can move toward generational equity by minimizing the surplus or deficit for each of its programs or services. However, if a realistic balanced budget for each program or service is to be developed, the accounting system will need to include depreciation for all fixed assets, regardless of how they are financed. In LGs that pay post-retirement benefits, these too will need to be accrued and included. Otherwise, senior management cannot assure the LG's citizens that they are paying for the full cost of the current year's programs and services.

To achieve self-sufficiency in departments funded with user fees, senior management needs to identify the unit of output for which a price can be established. In some instances, use of the unit is discretionary, and in others it is not. For services such as trash pickup, for instance, the user has a choice – citizens who increase their recycling or reduce their consumption can decrease the number of pounds (or kilograms) or barrels of trash that are removed. Thus, a price per unit (pound, kilogram, barrel) is appropriate, and the user can affect the total amount paid by engaging in consumption-reducing behavior.

BOX 3.8 FOSTERING CONSUMPTION-REDUCING BEHAVIOR BY FEES

Some years ago, Switzerland began to remove recyclable waste at no charge, while assessing a sizable fee for removing non-recyclable waste. As might be imagined, the amount of non-recyclable waste decreased significantly. Moreover, there were important spill-over effects, as Swiss consumers pressured manufacturers of various goods to reduce the amount of non-recyclable packaging material included with their products.

By contrast, consumption of services such as snow removal or street cleaning is not a matter of choice. Residents may not tell their city that they will plow or clean their street frontage themselves. Thus, the user fee must be part of the overall tax assessment, based on the relevant unit of output (linear feet or meters of frontage for snowplowing, for example), and assigned to a specific department for the service in question. If the department is designated as a profit center or a standard expense center (discussed in Chapter 4), the result will be greater fairness in assessing citizens for the cost of the service, and an ability to measure the department's performance more objectively.

BOX 3.9   A MINOR VIOLATION OF GENERATIONAL EQUITY

Snowplowing, and other services where the units of service are unpredictable at the beginning of a budget year, may need to violate the principle of generational equity. Some winters have relatively little snowfall, for example, such that the department might earn a surplus. In a winter with heavy snowfall, by contrast, the surplus would be used up (and there might be a need for general taxpayer support). Over a several-year period, however, the surpluses and deficits most likely would net out.

Responsibility centers as a decentralizing mechanism

One of the most difficult decisions faced by an LG's senior management is whether and how to decentralize responsibility. As discussed earlier, because decentralization is politically risky, many senior managers are reluctant to undertake it. Decentralization also is emotionally difficult, since it can lead to a feeling of a loss of control. And, finally, it is analytically tricky, since it requires designing a network of responsibility centers in which managers' responsibilities are aligned with the resources they can control (called "fairness"), and where actions to improve the performance of their responsibility centers also improve the performance of the LG overall (called "goal congruence"). Although perhaps simple sounding, this is a daunting task in both the private and public sectors. We explore this issue more fully in Chapter 4.

BOX 3.10   DECENTRALIZATION IN SWEDEN

In Sweden, many public services have been decentralized to the community level, and community agencies have a great deal of decision-making latitude.

Overall, if an LG is to decentralize successfully, its senior management team must see its role not as *giving up* control but as *restructuring* it. Nevertheless, a change such as this can be difficult for senior managers who have been accustomed to being the principal decision makers. Moreover, it is financially risky, since a poorly performing program or department could have a negative impact on the LG's overall performance. Nevertheless, senior LG managers, who wish to move away from bureaucratic control and toward managerial control must be willing to take the risk.

The need for prudence

Given the barriers that exist to shifting from bureaucratic to managerial control, and the differences that exist among an LG's programs and departments, senior management must be cautious in initiating an effort to improve the LG's MCS. Indeed, senior managers need to recognize that, in many instances, such as those where there is a matrix, their organizations do not lend themselves to neat forms of managerial control. In addition, senior managers generally are constrained both politically and financially from developing the most appropriate management control system. Finally, LGs (like most other organizations) frequently have personnel who are resistant to the development of new forms of management control and who, therefore, will not be supportive of – or may even actively resist – any initiative to change the system.

All of this suggests a need to be prudent in taking steps to improve an LG's MCS. Expectations should not be set too high, and early, simple successes should be sought before more complicated efforts are initiated. We discuss this issue more fully in Chapter 11.

SUMMARY

The discussion in this chapter has identified several changes to an LG's management control system that can help the LG's senior managers to move toward the NPM paradigm: restructured organizational units with improved definitions of responsibilities and increased managerial autonomy, an emphasis on frugal behavior so as to minimize waste, and the adoption of managerial approaches that have proven successful in the private-sector. Indeed, if it undertakes the sorts of changes discussed in this chapter in a serious and deliberate manner, an LG has the opportunity to convert the NPM paradigm from an abstract idea into an operational reality.

DISCUSSION QUESTIONS

1   Which of the general characteristics of an LG is the most serious impediment to performance measurement? Why?

2   What changes to its MCS might an LG make to move the system closer to the kind of system used in a for-profit organization? How hard will it be to make these changes?

NOTES

1 In the United States this is called "fund accounting." Similar restrictions exist in other countries but under different labels.
2 In industry, this practice has been obsolete since the nineteenth century.
3 Increases such as these can be dealt with via use of a flexible budget, which is discussed in Chapter 10.
4 In San Diego, California, for example, the city's fiscal recovery plan for 2007 included issuing $374 million in pension obligation bonds to cover its unfunded pension liabilities. In addition, $978 million went on other unfunded post-employment benefits, such as retiree healthcare costs. These two items alone represented a generational equity failure of over $1.3 billion. See City of San Diego, Fiscal Year 2007 Proposed Budget, prepared by Budget and Management Services, San Diego, CA, 2007.
5 In the United States and some other countries this problem was the consequence of a misguided accounting standard established by the Government Accounting Standards Board (GASB). The standard has since been changed, such that LGs in those countries that abide by the GASB's standards now may account for depreciation on their fixed assets without receiving a qualified audit opinion. Not all yet do.
6 For an overview and comparative international perspective of LG accounting in Belgium, China, Italy, Japan, Malaysia, Holland, New Zealand, Russia, Spain, United Kingdom, and United States, see Caperchione and Mussari (2000).
7 Under these circumstances, of course, choosing the term of the debt is equivalent to – and as difficult as – estimating the economic life of the asset for purposes of computing depreciation.
8 Designating them as profit centers means accounting for their revenues and expenses separately, and including a fair share of the municipality's overhead in the expenses of each. However, in accordance with the principle of generational equity, their goal should be to break even each year, not to earn a "profit." We discuss profit centers in Chapter 4.
9 Actually, one LG in the United States did outsource all of its services. It is too early to judge its success, however. For details see Streitfeld (2010).
10 This approach is not unusual in the private sector. It was used at General Electric Corporation some years ago. According to Jack Welch, GE's CEO at the time, "the first year was easy – there was a lot of dead wood." In subsequent years, when most of the low-performing employees had left the company, the process became increasingly difficult. Indeed, according to Welch, in the third and fourth years some managers were classifying as "substandard employees" people who were deceased! See Welch and Byrne (2001).

75

REFERENCES

Blau, M. (1955) *The Dynamics of Bureaucracy*, Chicago, Illinois: University of Chicago Press.

Borgonovi, E. and Rondo-Brovetto, P. (1988) "The Concepts of Bureaucratic and Managerial Control in Public Administration," in A.P. Kakabadse, P.R. Brovetto, and R. Holzer (eds) *Management Development and the Public Sector*, Aldershot, England: Gower Publishing Company.

Caperchione, E. and Mussari R. (eds) (2000) *Comparative Issues in Local Government Accounting*, Norwell, Massachusetts: Kluwer Academic Publishers.

Chandler, A.D. (1962) *Strategy and Structure*, Cambridge, Massachusetts: MIT Press.

Crozier, M. (1964) *The Bureaucratic Phenomenon*, Chicago, Illinois: The University of Chicago Press.

Farneti, G. (1995) *Introduzione All'economia Dell'azienda Pubblica. Il Sistema, i Principi, i Valori*, Torino, Italy: Giappichelli Editore.

Gouldner, A.W. (1954) *Patterns of Industrial Bureaucracy*, New York: Free Press.

Hood, C. (1991) "A Public Management for All Seasons?," *Public Administration*, 69(1): 3–19.

Hood, C. (1995) "The 'New Public Management' in the 1980s: Variations on a Theme," *Accounting Organization and Society*, 20(2–3): 93–109.

Koppenjan, J. and Klijn, E. (2004) *Managing Uncertainties in Networks*, London, United Kingdom: Routledge.

Kotter, J.P. and Lawrence, P.R. (1974) *Mayors in Action: 5 Approaches to Urban Governance*, New York: John Wiley and Sons.

Nolan, B.C. (ed.) (2001) *Public Sector Reform: An International Perspective*. Basingstoke, United Kingdom: Palgrave.

Osborne, D. and Gaebler T. (1992) *Reinventing Government: How the Entrepreneurial Spirit is Transforming the Public Sector*, Reading, Massachusetts: Adison Wesley.

Osborne, S.P. (ed.) (2010) *The New Public Governance? Emerging Perspectives on the Theory and Practice of Public Governance*, London: Routledge.

Parsons, T. (1960) *Structure and Process in Modern Society*, New York: Free Press.

Schein, E.H. (2010) *Organizational Culture and Leadership*, 4th edn, San Francisco: Jossey Bass Publishers.

Spano, A. (2009) "Public Value Creation and Management Control Systems," *International Journal of Public Administrations*, 32(3): 328–48.

Streitfeld, D. (2010) "A City Outsources Everything. Sky Doesn't Fall," *The New York Times*, July 19.

Weber, M. (1947) *The Theory of Social and Economic Organization*, New York: Free Press.

Welch, J. and Byrne, J.A. (2001) *Jack: Straight from the Gut*, New York: Warner Business Books.

Young, D.W. (1979) "Administrative Theory and Administrative Systems: A Synthesis Among Diverging Fields of Inquiry," *Accounting Organizations and Society*, 4(3): 235–44.

Young, D.W. (2008) *Management Control in Nonprofit Organizations*, Cambridge, Massachusetts: The Crimson Press Curriculum Center.

FURTHER READING

Two important principles in this chapter are generational equity and consumer equity. The underlying logic of both is that, when feasible, each user (or category of users) of public services should pay for the benefits it receives during the time period that it receives them. A closer consideration of consumer equity (or what sometimes is called "benefit equity") is provided by Hyman in *Public Finance: A Contemporary Application of Theory to Policy* (Dryden Press 1993). For a discussion of generational equity (or what sometimes is called "inter-generational equity") in the context of LGs, see Raimondo's *Economics of State and Local Government* (Praeger Paperback 1991). Generational equity is also discussed by Frederickson in "Can Public Officials Correctly Be Said to Have Obligations to Future Generations?" This article appeared in *Public Administration Review*, Volume 54, no. 5 (1995).

Chapter 4

The structure for management control

LEARNING OBJECTIVES

At the end of this chapter you should:

■ Be able to distinguish between a local government's (LG's) external and internal environments.

■ Know the different types of responsibility centers that can exist within an LG.

■ Be able to argue that there is a role for profit centers in an LG, including shadow profit centers.

■ Understand why LGs have difficulty finding the right balance between a program structure and a departmental structure.

KEY POINTS

■ In many LGs, the formal organizational structure consists of functional departments, such as the police department, the fire department, the recreation department, and so forth. In some LGs, however, there is more of a matrix structure.

■ In designing an LG's management control system, senior management chooses among five different types of responsibility centers: revenue centers, discretionary expense centers, standard expense centers, profit centers, and investment centers.

■ A standard expense center has its budget adjusted each period based on the actual volume and mix of its output units. This is called a flexible (or performance) budget.

- When one profit center receives goods and/or services from another and is charged for them, the charge is called a transfer price. In general, transfer prices provide a mechanism for encouraging the optimal use of resources.
- LGs exist to provide services, which frequently are organized into programs. Since the primary purpose of the classification of programs is to facilitate senior management's judgment on the allocation of resources, the program structure should correspond to the LG's principal objectives.
- To provide financial information needed by all relevant parties, the accounting system should contain an account structure that can be responsive to multiple demands. In addition to providing information to program planners, analysts, and operating managers, the account structure must provide information to senior managers, governing bodies, and resource providers.
- A major issue that an LG's senior management must address in designing the management control structure is the congruence between the personal goals of managers and professionals, and the goals of the LG itself.

An LG is affected by many forces in its *external environment*, including legal constraints, uncertain funding sources, absence of competition, and public scrutiny. These forces vary greatly among LGs. For example, one LG might have relatively certain revenues (from a stable tax base) and programs that are essentially unchanged from one year to the next (such as in a municipal school). By contrast, an LG that receives substantial financial aid from a regional or central government might have less certain sources of funding and programs whose emphases shift in accordance with the region's priorities (such as with road construction). Indeed, if it receives substantial funds from other government sources, an LG may be subject to a variety of pressures and scrutiny from legislative bodies and the general public. In these cases, the desires of the press and the public for information constitute an important management control issue.

An LG also has an *internal environment*, and senior management must give careful consideration to the fit among its elements. These elements include an authority and influence structure, a program structure, an information structure, and a variety of administrative, behavioral, and cultural factors. In a well-run LG, these elements all reinforce each other.

THE AUTHORITY AND INFLUENCE STRUCTURE

The formal organizational structure refers to the designated reporting relationships among managers and other individuals in an LG. There also is an *informal* structure that is unwritten and perhaps unintended. The informal structure encompasses a network of interpersonal relationships that has important implications for management. Because it is unwritten, however, the informal structure is difficult to identify and describe. For this reason, our focus here is on the formal structure.

Senior management weighs many considerations in determining the best formal structure. These considerations involve questions such as the most appropriate division of tasks, the activities that should be carried out by specialized staff units versus those that should be the responsibility of line managers, and the decisions that should be made at or near the top of the organization versus those that should be delegated to lower levels.

In many LGs, the formal structure consists of functional departments, such as the police department, the fire department, the recreation department, and so forth. In some LGs, however, there is more of a matrix structure. An example of this structure was shown in Figure 2.1 (Chapter 2) and Table 3.1 (Chapter 3), where several departments provided services to various programs.

Responsibility centers

As discussed briefly in Chapter 2, the formal organizational structure for management control purposes is defined in terms of responsibility centers. A responsibility center is an organizational unit headed by a manager who is in charge of its activities.

Although the type and degree of control exercised by any given responsibility center manager may be difficult to pinpoint, at some level someone in an organization has control over each resource-related decision. In some cases, control is infrequent and has long-term implications, such as the acquisition of a new fire truck, the construction of a municipal parking lot, or the commitment to a long-term building lease. In other cases, it is of shorter duration, such as the decision to sign a one-year supply contract. In still other cases, control is very short-term, such as the decision to ask employees to work overtime.

Responsibility centers versus purchasing units

A responsibility center in an LG is charged with carrying out certain aspects of the LG's strategy. In addition, there frequently are other units that are responsible for obtaining specific resources, which usually are called "purchasing units," or some similar title. This division of responsibility occurs for both logistical and bureaucratic reasons. It is logistical because purchasing units have certain skills that allow them to obtain the best price for a resource; it is bureaucratic because in most LGs, there is a need to avoid any potential conflict of interest.

BOX 4.1 RESPONSIBILITY FOR USAGE VERSUS RESPONSIBILITY FOR PURCHASING

An LG's purchasing department is responsible for buying police uniforms. It does so following certain procedures (such as to obtain at least three bids). The responsibility for the decision to purchase the uniforms is in the hands of the manager of the police department (the responsibility center), but he or she does not actually undertake the activity of making the purchase.

Types of responsibility centers

In designing an LG's management control system, senior management must decide how it wishes to decentralize financial responsibility. To do so, it chooses among five different types of responsibility centers: revenue centers, discretionary expense centers, standard expense centers, profit centers, and investment centers. These different types of responsibility centers were discussed briefly in Chapter 2. Table 4.1 lists them and the financial implications of each.

From the viewpoint of senior management, or from the perspective of an oversight body (such as a city council or a legislature), the LG is an investment center: it must obtain a satisfactory return on assets (ROA) if it is to remain financially viable. This is as true for an LG as it is for any organization where ongoing sustainability rests, in part, on the ability to replace assets as they wear out, but where, due to inflation, new assets usually cost more than those being replaced.[1] The role of senior management is to decide how best to decentralize ROA responsibility throughout the organization. As a result, in any organization except a very small one, there is a hierarchy of responsibility centers. At the lowest level, the responsibility centers are sections or other small units.

Table 4.1 Types of responsibility centers and associated responsibilities

Type of responsibility center	Responsible for
Revenue center	Revenue earned by the center
Discretionary expense center	Total expenses incurred by the center regardless of the volume of activity
Standard expense center	Expenses per unit of output, but not total expenses, incurred by the center
Profit center	Total revenues minus total expenses of the center
Investment center	Total revenues minus expenses of the center, computed as a percent of the center's assets, i.e., the center's return on assets (ROA)

At higher levels, there are departments or divisions that consist of several smaller units, and may also include staff.

The principal factor used in selecting one type of responsibility center over another is financial control. That is, senior management's goal in choosing a given type of responsibility center is to hold the center's manager accountable for those costs and revenues over which he or she can exercise a reasonable degree of control. In LGs, the most common types are discretionary expense centers and profit centers. Profit centers are used for many programs where citizens can decide whether to use the services or not, and hence where the program can earn revenue. Examples are water and sewer services, off-track betting, and municipal parking.

The distinction between discretionary and standard expense centers is important. As Table 4.1 indicates, in a discretionary expense center, the focus is on *total expenses* regardless of the volume and/or mix of activity. By contrast, in a standard expense center, the focus is on *expenses per unit of output* rather than total expenses. A standard expense center has its budget adjusted each period based on the actual volume and mix of its output units. This is called a *flexible* (or *performance*) *budget*. One finds few standard expense centers in LGs, and yet there is considerable potential for their use. Activities such as snow removal, street cleaning, and road maintenance are all potential standard expense centers.

BOX 4.2   MOVING FROM A DISCRETIONARY EXPENSE CENTER TO A STANDARD EXPENSE CENTER

A snow removal department will have some fixed costs (such as depreciation on its plowing equipment) but also some variable costs, such as gasoline, sand, and salt. It would be relatively easy to create a flexible budget for this department by basing the budget for any given month on the actual number of kilometers or miles plowed. Few LGs do this, however.

Table 4.2 shows some examples of responsibility centers in an LG. As it indicates, perhaps counter-intuitively, there is the possibility of having all five types of responsibility centers, including investment centers. It also illustrates a technique that some LGs have found useful: a profit center that computes *surrogate* (or *shadow*), revenue rather than *real* revenue. This type of profit center is appropriate for departments where there is an outside entity that engages in the same kind of activities as the LG's entity, and thus can provide a source of market prices, which sometimes are called "shadow prices."

Table 4.2 *Possible responsibility centers in a local government*

Type	Characteristics	Example
Revenue center	Department that earns revenues, and incurs minimal expenses	Tax collection department
Discretionary expense center	Department that earns no revenues but incurs expenses, and *has no easily measurable units* of service	Legal department
Standard expense center	Department that earns no revenues but incurs expenses, and *has easily measurable units* of service	Fire department
Regular profit center	Department that earns *real revenue* (via "market" prices), and incurs expenses	Tourist office reservation center
Shadow profit center	Department that earns *surrogate revenues* (via shadow prices), and incurs expenses	Vehicle repair department
Investment center	Department that earns *real revenues* (via "market" prices), incurs expenses, and uses *identifiable fixed assets*	Water and sewer department

BOX 4.3   USING SHADOW PROFIT CENTERS

Some years ago the Bureau of Motor Equipment Repair of the New York City Sanitation (trash collection) Department used the prices charged by private sector repair garages as surrogates for revenue, thereby creating a shadow-priced profit center. The resulting impact on employee behavior was dramatic. Prior to the initiation of the shadow-priced profit center, half of the 5,000 vehicles for which the Bureau was responsible were out of service on an average day, while the city was incurring some $8 million annually in driver overtime wages. Two years later, 100 percent of the vehicles were on the road and the overtime wages had been eliminated. The bureau's manager attributed much of the improvement in performance to the incentives the shadow-priced profit center created for employees to "beat" both the private repair garage prices and the "profit margins" of their colleagues in other bureau shops (transmissions, radiators, brakes, etc.) (Anthony and Young 2003).

A shadow profit center approach might be used for a wide variety of municipal programs and services, such as road maintenance, public health, recreation, and social welfare. In each of these cases, if an outside entity performs a comparable service, the LG has the ability to determine a shadow price. Of course, since the revenue in a shadow profit center is not real, it will not increase the LG's "top line." Rather, the advantage is related exclusively to improvements in the bottom line. As the above example of the Bureau of Motor Equipment Repair illustrates, however, this advantage can be dramatic.

Table 4.3 contains the responsibility center structure in a medium-sized LG, and indicates where the potential exists for shifting the focus of most of the discretionary expense centers toward either standard expense centers or some form of profit center. Note that the LG already has four profit centers (which sometimes are called "enterprise funds"), but could have many more. Indeed, of all its responsibility centers, only four need to remain as discretionary expense centers. The rest could be established as either standard expense centers or as regular or shadow profit centers.

Designing effective profit centers

To some people, the idea of profit centers in an LG seems peculiar, but the profit center idea can be an important way of facilitating management control. As such, it is not at all inconsistent to have a profit center in an LG – the term simply refers to a manager's scope of financial responsibility. If a profit center is to be effective, however, senior management must pay careful attention to several important design matters.

Record-keeping costs

Because a profit center encompasses more elements of managerial performance than an expense center, it also requires more record keeping. Clearly, the benefits of having a profit center should be greater than this extra record-keeping cost (and the cost of any other administrative activities that are required). The cost of measuring the output of most accounting departments, for example, is quite difficult, such that establishing an accounting department as a profit center probably would not be worthwhile.

Dysfunctional incentives

The competitive spirit that a profit center fosters should not have dysfunctional consequences for the LG overall. For instance, the creation of a profit center may encourage managers to place too much attention on the revenue side of the equation, or to cut expenses in a given month or year without concern for the longer-term consequences. Moreover, senior management's desired degree of cooperation of a given profit center with other responsibility centers may not occur because the profit center's manager may make decisions that add to the profit of his or her own unit but that are detrimental to other units in the organization.

Table 4.3 Departments and responsibility centers in a medium-sized municipality: potential for shifting from discretionary expense centers to another type

Existing arrangement

Discretionary expense centers		Standard expense centers	Regular profit centers	Shadow profit centers
General administration:		None	Water and sewer	None
			Recreation	
Accounting	Tax collection		Ice skating rink	
Planning office	Mail		Council on aging	
Human resources	*Depreciation*		transport	
Legal	*Pensions*			
Clerk	*Interest on debt*			
Board of assessors	*Insurance*			
Public works:				
Administration	Engineering			
Street lighting	Motor equipment			
Trash removal	repair			
Parking	Natural resources			
Building inspections	Highway			
	maintenance			
	Cemeteries			
Community safety:				
Administration	Fire services			
Police services	Animal control			
Education:				
Administration	Schools			
	Libraries			
Human services:				
Administration	Council on aging			
Veterans' services	Board of health			

Shift to standard expense and profit centers

Discretionary expense centers	Standard expense centers	Regular profit centers	Shadow profit centers
General administration	Fire services	Water and sewer	Engineering
Street lighting	Board of health	Recreation	Motor equipment repair
Police services		Ice skating rink	Natural resources
Libraries		Council on aging transport	Highway maintenance
		Trash removal	Veterans' services
		Parking	Council on aging
		Building inspections	
		Cemeteries	
		Animal control	
		Schools	

BOX 4.4 DYSFUNCTIONS IN THE USE OF RESPONSIBILITY CENTERS

A profit center manager (or even a standard or discretionary expense center manager) may be reluctant to incur overtime costs because doing so would increase the responsibility center's costs. And yet, the requested services may be badly needed by another responsibility center that could use them to increase the LG's overall surplus or reduce its deficit.

Despite the potential for dysfunctional consequences, a profit center generally is desirable if a manager has a reasonable amount of influence over the revenues and expenses of an organizational unit. In many LGs, managers who run programs, especially ones where users have a choice of how much to purchase (such as water and sewer, electricity, public transportation, or recreation), could easily have their units designated as profit centers.

Managerial autonomy

Organizations vary considerably in terms of the autonomy they give to their profit center managers. In general, although a profit center may operate almost as if it were an independent entity, its manager does not have the autonomy of a chief executive officer in a for-profit company. This is because profit centers are part of a larger organization (the LG), and their managers must abide by the LG's policies. Profit center managers rarely have the authority to initiate new programs or commit to major capital expenditures, for example, because these decisions (like others that influence overall strategy) are properly made by senior management.

Apart from these restrictions, a manager of a profit center should be able to exert reasonable influence over both the revenues and expenses of the center. This does not imply that he or she must have *complete control* over these items, for few, if any, profit center managers have such authority. However, a profit center manager should be able to exercise some degree of control over the center's volume of activity, unit variable costs, and direct fixed costs, as well as the quality of the work done. Sometimes he or she also can influence the prices charged.

Restrictions on a profit center's autonomy imposed by senior management may be communicated by formal rules or by other means. No matter how carefully the formal devices are constructed, however, informal mechanisms constitute powerful indicators of a manager's autonomy. These mechanisms include unwritten rules about, for example, the kinds of decisions that can be made independently by a profit center manager versus those that require approval of higher authority. Moreover, chief executives tend to give more autonomy to subordinates whom they know well and whose judgment they trust. As a result, despite the presence of a variety of formal devices in an LG, some profit center managers may have considerably more decision-making latitude than others.

Fairness

A profit center manager should perceive that the center's financial results fairly measure performance. This does not mean that a reported "profit" figure is completely accurate, however, or that it encompasses all aspects of performance, for no profit measure does this. The goal is to come as close as possible to such an arrangement.

Transfer prices

When one profit center receives goods and/or services from another and is charged for them, the charge is called a *transfer price*. A transfer price is used exclusively for transactions within an organization, as contrasted with an *external price*, which is used for transactions between an organization and its clients.

In general, transfer prices provide a mechanism for encouraging the optimal use of an organization's resources. This is because frequently the behavior of profit center managers (and to a lesser extent standard expense center managers) is influenced by the way the transfer prices are structured, or by the requirement that goods and services be furnished without charge under certain circumstances. For example, an internal audit organization usually provides services without charge.

In most instances, if a service is free, users are not motivated to consider its value. They tend to request as much of it as they can get without considering how much it is worth to them, or how its value compares with that of alternative services.

BOX 4.5   TRANSFER PRICES LEAD TO EFFICIENCY

An LG had a motor pool that department heads could use without charge. Senior management found that managers were requesting vehicles for trips that could have been taken less expensively and just as quickly by taxi or public transportation. When the LG started to charge departments for motor pool use, department managers gave considerable thought to the cost of alternative modes of transportation.

Because a responsibility center does not sell its services to outside customers, one might conclude that there is no reliable way to establish its transfer prices. But this is not always the case. Many service centers have counterparts in for-profit organizations. Motor pools are like taxi cabs or car rental agencies, for example. Similarly, maintenance, housekeeping, and other service centers frequently have private sector counterparts. The prices in the counterpart organizations usually can be converted rather easily to transfer prices.

Although there is no single best way to establish transfer prices, there are two basic approaches that can be used: market price and full cost.[2]

Market price: If a valid market price exists, it ordinarily is the basis for the transfer price. It may be adjusted downward to account for the profit component in prices charged by for-profit companies, or to eliminate bad debt or selling expenses that do not exist with internal transactions. Of course, valid market price information is not always available, or it may be available for some, but not all, internally provided goods and services.

A market price below the selling unit's full cost is an indication that the selling unit is operating inefficiently. If a selling unit cannot furnish products at competitive prices, or if the revenue it earns is not equal to its costs, there is an indication that something is wrong. Thus, the use of transfer prices can provide senior management with information about the efficiency (and sometimes the quality) of the goods and services being provided by the organization's selling units.

BOX 4.6   TRANSFER PRICES AS EFFICIENCY MEASURES

An LG department needed to have an electrical plug moved from one side of a wall to the other. The work was done by the LG's maintenance department, and the receiving department received a bill (via a transfer price) for about four times what the job would have cost if it had been performed by an outside contractor.

Full cost: If no valid market price exists, the transfer price ordinarily is based on the full cost of the good or service being transferred. As with market prices, some organizations exclude bad debts and selling expenses in setting a full-cost transfer price.

Arriving at the full cost for a unit of service can be tricky. In particular, if the full-cost accounting system has not been well designed, the full cost of some service units may not reflect true resource consumption. Moreover, if the full-cost approach is used, the transfer price should be based on a *standard* cost, rather than the *actual* cost incurred by the selling unit. Otherwise, the selling unit could pass on its inefficiencies to the receiving units. We discuss full cost accounting in greater detail in Chapter 7.

THE PROGRAM STRUCTURE

LGs exist to provide services, which frequently are organized into programs. Fixing responsibility for control over a program would be relatively easy if each program

(1) sold its services, (2) was staffed by personnel who worked in no other program, and (3) was run by a manager who had reasonable control over pricing, hiring, other personnel decisions, and supply purchases. Under these circumstances, each program could be designated as a profit center.

Most LGs are not organized in a way that permits such a tidy and well-defined control structure. Many operate over large geographic areas, and must consider this fact when designing their structure. In other settings, program and functional lines may become blurred. Does the director of a summer festival program have control over the number of personnel taking part in the festival or their salaries? Does the director of a program for issuing building licenses control the number of applications received, the fee per license, or the salaries of the people who work in the office?

Selecting a good program structure is not easy. Indeed, it generally is quite difficult to align responsibility with control, and to overlay an appropriate set of responsibility centers on the LG's program structure. Therefore, senior management must devote considerable time and effort to the task.

Components of a program structure

In a large LG, the program structure may consist of several layers. At the top are a few major programs, and at the bottom are a great many program *elements* – the smallest units in which information is collected in program terms. A program element is a definable activity, or a related set of activities, that the organization carries out – either directly (to accomplish the LG's objectives) or indirectly (to support other program elements).

Between programs and program elements are program categories, and, depending on how many layers are needed, program subcategories. In a relatively flat organization, there may be no need for program categories or subcategories. When this is the case, program elements can be aggregated directly into programs. In a more hierarchical organization, however, there may be several levels of program categories. Table 4.4 illustrates this complication with the simple example of programs, program categories, program subcategories, and program elements in a municipal school system.

Types of programs

In designing the program structure, senior management typically focuses its attention on mission programs and support programs. In general, the amount of resources required for support programs is roughly dependent on the size and character of the mission programs.

89

Table 4.4 *Hierarchy of programs, program categories, program subcategories, and program elements in a municipal school system*

Program	100. Formal Education
Program categories	101. Pre-elementary school education
	102. Elementary and secondary school education
	103. Post-secondary school education
	104. Special education (for exceptional students)
Program subcategories	102.1. Kindergarten
(for program category	102.2. Primary or elementary school education
102)	102.3. Secondary or high school education
	102.4 Vocational and/or trade school education
Program Elements	102.2-a. Language instruction
(for program	102.2-b. Music instruction
subcategory 102.2)	102.2-c. Art instruction
	102.2-d. Social sciences instruction

BOX 4.7   MISSION PROGRAMS VERSUS SUPPORT PROGRAMS

In a school system such as that shown in Table 4.4, mission programs would be related to instruction. Support programs would include buildings and grounds maintenance, cleaning, publications, and administration.

Ordinarily, there should be a separate support program for administration so that senior management can focus special attention on the LG's administrative activities. Senior management usually wishes to devote as much of the LG's resources as possible to mission programs, and as little as possible to administration. In the absence of special attention, however, administrative activities tend to grow. Having a support program for administration encourages senior management to direct its attention to these activities. In Table 4.3, for example, general administration would remain as a discretionary expense center, even after other types of responsibility centers had been created. Also, although not shown, it probably would be desirable to keep the administrative activities of each department (such as public works) as a separate discretionary expense center.

Program elements

Ideally, a single manager is responsible for each program element. Items for which responsibility is widely diffused, such as "postage," are not good program elements.

Table 4.5 *Line-items versus programs for a municipal public safety department (€000)*

Line item structure	Cost	Program structure	Cost
Wages and salaries	€4,232	Crime control and investigation	€2,677
Overtime	217	Traffic control	1,610
Fringe benefits	783	Correctional institutions	470
Retirement plan	720	Inspections and licenses	320
Operating supplies	216	Police training	182
Fuel	338	Police administration	680
Uniforms	68	Fire fighting	1,427
Repairs and maintenance	340	Fire prevention	86
Professional services	71	Fire training	64
Communications	226	Fire administration	236
Vehicles	482	Other protection	563
Printing and publications	61	General administration	282
Building rental	447		
Other	396		
Total	€8,597	Total	€8,597

Such items should appear not as program elements but as functional categories or expense elements in the responsibility structure. The distinction between program elements and line items is illustrated in Table 4.5. Note that the totals are the same but that the focus is quite distinct.

Management decisions about program elements cannot be carried out properly unless the elements are related to personal responsibility. An alignment of individual responsibility with specific program elements also leads to an increased sense of personal identification with programs, and thus helps to foster a greater degree of commitment among responsibility center managers.

BOX 4.8   ALIGNING INDIVIDUAL RESPONSIBILITY AND PROGRAM RESPONSIBILITY

A museum of natural history might have a program on prehistoric animals. This program might have several program elements, such as individual exhibits, gift shop items, and educational activities. Each of these is the responsibility of a manager. The program manager must coordinate the work of the managers of these different program elements.

Criteria for selecting a program structure

Since a primary purpose of programs is to facilitate senior management's judgment on the allocation of resources, the program structure should correspond to the LG's principal objectives, and it should be arranged so as to facilitate decisions having to do with the relative importance of these objectives. That is, it should focus on the LG's outputs (what it intends to achieve) rather than on its inputs (the types of resources it uses or the sources of its support). A structure that is arranged by types of resources (e.g., personnel, supplies, services) or by sources of support (e.g., property taxes, legislative appropriations, regional grants) is not a program structure.

The designation of major programs helps to clarify the LG's objectives. The development of the program structure, therefore, should correspond to those areas of activity that senior management wishes to emphasize strategically. The following questions can help to make this idea more specific:

1 Is the program structure output-oriented? Specifically, does it focus on the LG's strategic objectives and the target groups it serves or plans to serve?
2 Does the program structure assist senior management to decide whether to expand or contract a program?
3 Within a program, are there opportunities for tradeoffs; that is, are there different ways to achieve the objectives?
4 When a criticism arises that not enough (or too much) effort is being devoted to a certain activity, can the program structure provide information to address this criticism?
5 Does the program structure identify all of the important activities so that none are hidden from management's (or the public's) view?
6 Can one or more performance measure be established for each program element?

Matrix organizations

Although the program structure need not match the organization structure, there should be some person who has identifiable responsibility for each program (as well as each program category and each program element in a large LG). This need for a fit between the organizational structure and the program structure often results in a matrix organization. As discussed in Chapters 2 and 3, the matrix consists of program managers along one dimension and department managers along the other. Program managers are advocates for their programs, and are held accountable for their program's performance.

Recall that Figure 3.1 (Chapter 3) contained a matrix structure for a municipal social service agency. The task complexity discussed briefly in that chapter exists along several dimensions that affect the department's management control structure. Some of those dimensions include the following:

- The department does not generate revenues. Therefore it is an expense center. Since its budget probably cannot be changed with changes in volume during the year, it quite likely is a discretionary expense center.
- Resource allocation is along two dimensions. One is field operations and facilities (the left side of the matrix), which corresponds to the department's organizational structure. The other (the right side of the matrix) consists of the department's major programs, such as inhome elder care. The major programs correspond to appropriation accounts in the budget, and are the responsibility of "account executives" (program managers).
- Overall program control is the responsibility of the account executives, who may not spend more than the amount allotted to their appropriation accounts. However, because programs cut across all regions, and not all regions or all facilities have all programs or all subprograms, an account executive must determine the regions and facilities that can best meet the needs of their major programs and subprograms.
- Because the appropriation account budgets are fixed, account executives must be certain that increases in one region or facility are matched by decreases in others.
- Control over the activities in regions and facilities is the responsibility of the field operations and facility managers. They receive budgets from the account executives, and must adhere to them while striving to meet the objectives of the programs and subprograms that the budgets fund.
- Although the department is a discretionary expense center, its regions and facilities might be set up as standard expense centers. This is because the managers of these units have no control over the number or mix of individuals who need their services.
- With an appropriate flow of information to managers in charge of regions and facilities, such a structure can help to motivate these managers to run their operations more effectively and efficiently. In effect, each would be competing for resources from the various appropriation accounts.

THE INFORMATION STRUCTURE

Financial and non-financial information is needed for program planners and analysts, as well as for responsibility center managers. Program planners and analysts need financial information to compare a program's costs and revenues with those of similar programs, or with a program's performance in a prior period. By contrast, responsibility center managers need information on the revenues and expenses of their organizational units in order to facilitate their ability to exercise good control.

93

The program structure is designed to meet the needs of planners, analysts, and oversight agencies (such as review boards). It emphasizes the full costs of carrying out programs, and may cut across lines of operational responsibility. The organizational structure, on the other hand, is designed to meet the needs of operating managers. It must be consistent with lines of responsibility, and it emphasizes the control of costs and (sometimes) revenues.

To ensure that these differing information needs are adequately met, senior management must be certain that the design of the LG's management control system is not dominated by either planners or operating managers. Ideally, systems designers should be independent of both types of users, and should weigh equally the needs of each. Nevertheless, a financial information structure that will serve the purposes of both groups is complicated since the information needed for one purpose may differ from that needed for another. In some cases, the system designers may need to make compromises in designing the structure, but in most situations, it is possible to design a structure that serves both sets of needs.

Information for comparative purposes

Using financial information for comparative purposes can be tricky, even with a well-designed program structure. If, for example, several LGs use the same program structure for, say, schools, public works departments, and recreation departments, and if they wish to make comparisons with each other, they must take great care to assure that they all agree on the kinds of financial data they will provide. Doing so allows managers to compare data from their own programs with similar data from other organizations. Sometimes this process is called "benchmarking."

Benchmarking can be tricky, mainly because different organizations rarely view their programs in the same way. Therefore, the program structure that is used for benchmarking purposes should be quite broad, operating at a very macro level, and avoiding comparisons at the program element level.

The account structure

To provide financial information needed by all relevant parties, the accounting system should contain an account structure that can be responsive to multiple demands. In addition to providing information to program planners, analysts, and operating managers, for example, the account structure must provide information to two other groups:

■ *Senior managers and governing bodies*, who make policy decisions regarding the division of resources among programs and the relation of programs to objectives. They need information on how the organization is performing.

■ *Resource providers*, including legislative bodies, grant-making entities, taxpayers, oversight bodies, and regulatory agencies, all of whom need information about what the organization did with the resources they provided. Many resource providers and general stakeholders, particularly legislatures, often require reports prepared according to their unique specifications.

Conflicts among information needs

Since the needs of these diverse parties frequently conflict, the accounting system must strike a balance. Although a well-designed account structure should be able to reconcile most needs, the system often must make a tradeoff between different users' needs for information and the cost of collecting and processing that information.

The need for articulation

Ideally, all the accounts in the account structure make up a single, coordinated system. Technically, such a system is called an *articulated system*. Serious management control problems can arise if program accounts are not linked with responsibility accounts. When this happens, one set of reports cannot be reconciled with another, or can be reconciled only with a great deal of manual effort.

In some systems, a program structure is used for planning and budgeting purposes, but after the program has been planned and the budget approved, the structure is not rearranged according to the responsibility centers that must carry it out. Instead, a separate budget is prepared for responsibility centers, often without any relationship to the program budget. As a result, both budgeted and actual spending are recorded by responsibility centers but not by programs. Indeed, some systems fail to collect actual spending according to the same account structure used for the budget. When this happens, actual results cannot be compared to planned ones in any meaningful way.

There are two problems with systems that don't articulate. First, since the system cannot ascertain costs by program, program planners do not have the information they need to estimate future program costs. Second, without program-based costs, senior management has no adequate way to determine whether its program decisions are being implemented as planned. If senior management decides that €1 million should be spent on a certain program, such as a community day care center, it needs to know whether the responsibility center carrying out the program is doing so at the level of effort that €1 million represents. It cannot find this out unless the accounting system classifies actual spending in terms of programs.

Non-financial information

Increasingly, LGs are focusing on non-financial information in their assessment of responsibility center performance. In addition, there can be many oversight agencies –

such as central or regional governments, legislatures, auditors, inspection and regulatory bodies, judicial entities, and professional institutes – that impose a variety of non-financial performance measures on an LG. For example, in the UK, the "Best Value" program, instituted in 2000, required LGs to compute several non-financial performance measures (Talbot 2008).

ADMINISTRATIVE FACTORS

Another aspect of an LG's internal environment is the set of rules, practices, guidelines, customs, standard operating procedures, and codes of ethics that exist in any organization. For brevity, we have clustered these items together as administrative factors.

Administrative factors rarely change. Some rules, such as those set forth in manuals, are formal; others, such as understandings about acceptable behavior, are informal. Rules can relate to matters that range from the most trivial (e.g., paper clips will be issued only on the basis of a signed requisition) to the most important (e.g., capital expenditures of over €200,000 must be approved by the city council).

Types of rules and procedures

There are three categories of rules and procedures (Merchant 1985: Chapter 3):

1 *Physical control procedures:* Security guards, locked storerooms, vaults, computer passwords, video surveillance, and other physical controls are part of the internal control environment. Most of them are associated with task control, rather than with management control.
2 *Administrative control procedures:* There also are actions designed to enhance task control, such as requiring that checks for more than a specified amount be countersigned. Their enforcement frequently is the responsibility of the controller's office.
3 *Administrative rules:* These are prescribed ways of performing certain functions, such as how to use time cards or how to complete expense reports.

Some rules and procedures are only guidelines. An LG's managers are permitted (and even expected sometimes) to depart from them, either under specified circumstances or if a manager judges that departure is in the best interests of the LG overall. For example, a guideline may be that overtime is not ordinarily paid, but managers may approve overtime payments under certain circumstances, either on their own authority or after obtaining approval from their superior. Other rules are literally rules – they should never be broken. Rules that prohibit paying bribes or taking illegal drugs are examples.

Role of manuals

Much judgment is required in deciding which rules and procedures should be made formal (i.e., put in a manual), which should be guidelines, and which should be subject to managerial discretion. There are no clear cut prescriptions for making those distinctions, although there are some fairly obvious patterns. For example, bureaucratic organizations have more detailed manuals than other organizations, large organizations have more than small ones, and centralized organizations have more than decentralized ones.

It is important to keep in mind that, with the passage of time, some rules become obsolete. Manuals and other sets of rules therefore need to be re-examined periodically to ensure that they are consistent with current needs.

The motivation process and reward structure

Ideally, managers should be rewarded on the basis of actual performance compared with expected performance under the prevailing circumstances. Frequently, this ideal cannot be achieved for two basic reasons. First, the performance of a responsibility center can be influenced by many factors other than the actions of its manager. As a result, the performance of the manager usually cannot be cleanly separated from the effects of these other factors. Second, managers are supposed to achieve both long- and short-run objectives, but the management control system usually focuses primarily on the short run. This is because the system can only report what has happened; it cannot report what will happen in the future as a consequence of the manager's current actions. Thus, managers of responsibility centers and programs usually are motivated to focus on achieving short-run goals. Indeed, a lack of knowledge about how best to measure and reward a manager's performance for achieving long-term results is one of the most serious weaknesses in the management control systems of LGs.[3]

BEHAVIORAL FACTORS

Management control involves interactions among human beings. Consequently, the behavior of people in an LG is an important aspect of the internal environment. The major issue that an LG's senior management must address here is the congruence between the personal goals of managers and professionals, and the goals of the LG itself.

Personal goals

People join an organization because they believe that by doing so they can achieve one or more personal goals. Once they have joined, their decision to contribute to the work of the organization is based, in part, on their perception that their activities will help them achieve those goals.

An individual's personal goals can be expressed as needs. Some of these needs are material and can be satisfied by the money earned on the job. Others are psychological – people need to have their abilities and achievements recognized; they need social acceptance as members of a group; they need to feel a sense of personal worth; they need to feel secure; they need to be able to exercise discretion; and they need to feel good about themselves.

These personal needs can be classified as either *extrinsic* or *intrinsic*. Extrinsic needs are satisfied by the actions of others. Examples are money received from the organization and praise received from a superior. Intrinsic needs are satisfied by the opinions people have about themselves. Examples are feelings of achievement or competence, or a clear conscience.

The relative importance of these needs varies with different persons, and their relative importance for a given individual varies at different times. For example, Maslow's (1954) "hierarchy of needs" begins with most basic physical needs (food, clothing, etc.) at the bottom, and rises to "self-actualization" at the top. It is clear, though, that not all of an LG's employees will see their jobs related to the same level in Maslow's hierarchy. Indeed, it is reasonably certain many employees in an LG will not be self-actualized no matter what kind of motivation process senior management designs.

The importance that people attach to their own needs also is heavily influenced by the attitudes of their colleagues and superiors. For some people, earning a great deal of money is dominant; for others, monetary considerations are less important than serving society. A few individuals attach considerable importance to the ability to exercise discretion or to achieve results; they tend to be the leaders of the organization. Indeed, McClelland (1961) argues that there is an important relationship between the strength of the achievement needs of the leaders of an organization and the organization's success.

Individuals also are influenced by both *positive* and *negative incentives*. A positive incentive, or reward, is an outcome that is expected to result in increased need satisfaction. A negative incentive, or punishment, is the reverse. Incentives need not be monetary. Praise for a job well done can be a powerful reward. Nevertheless, many people regard monetary rewards as extremely important. In a for-profit organization, and even in some nonprofit organizations, such rewards may include a bonus based on a comparison between planned and actual results. Rarely does an LG have this option.

Jeffrey Pfeffer (1998), who has studied the impact of compensation on performance, has concluded that there is little evidence to support the idea that a firm's compensation system is as important a factor in its success as some might believe. He cites employee surveys showing that a pleasant, challenging, and empowered work place often has a greater impact on employee behavior than monetary incentives. This is an option that all LGs have, but often do not use as fully as they might. We return to this issue in Chapter 11.

Goal congruence

Since an organization cannot have a mind of its own, it cannot have goals. Organizational goals are actually the goals of the senior management team (which often includes elected officials). Although senior management wants the organization to attain these goals, they are not always congruent with the personal goals of operating managers and professionals. Because employees tend to act in their own self-interest, the achievement of organizational goals may be frustrated. Nevertheless, senior management can *influence* the personal goals of the organization's managers and professionals by using its hiring, promotion, and termination policies to select, retain, and promote individuals whose personal goals are closely aligned with the LG's goals.

This distinction between organizational and personal goals suggests that a central purpose of a management control system is to assure that the actions participants take in accordance with their perceived self-interest are also in the best interests of the LG. That is, the incentives inherent in the management control system should encourage *goal congruence*. If this condition exists, a decision that a manager regards as sound from a personal viewpoint also will be sound for the LG as a whole.

Perfect congruence between individual and organizational goals does not, and cannot, exist. For example, many individuals want as much compensation as they can get, whereas from the organization's perspective there is an upper limit to salaries. At a minimum, however, the management control system should not encourage individuals to act *against* the best interests of the LG.

BOX 4.9 ALIGNING INDIVIDUAL GOALS AND ORGANIZATIONAL GOALS

An LG has a goal of low-cost, high-quality services for its programs, but if its management control system rewards managers exclusively for reducing costs, some managers may decrease costs by reducing the quality of service. In this instance, there is an absence of goal congruence.

Given these and similar difficulties, senior management must ask two separate questions when evaluating its management control system: (1) What actions does it motivate people to take in their own perceived self-interest? (2) Are these actions in the best interest of the LG overall? If the answer to the second question is "no," there is a need to redesign the management control system.

Cooperation and conflict

Generally, the lines connecting the boxes on an organization chart imply that organizational decisions are made in a hierarchical fashion. Senior management makes a decision, which is communicated down through the organizational hierarchy, and operating managers at lower levels proceed to implement it. Clearly, this military model is not the way most LGs actually function. More generally, operating managers react to an instruction from senior management in accordance with their perception of how it affects their personal needs. In addition, interactions between and among managers also affect what actually happens.

BOX 4.10   INTERACTION OF RESPONSIBILITIES

The manager of the maintenance department may be responsible for maintenance work done in all departments, but maintenance work in one department may be slighted if there is friction between the maintenance manager and the manager of the other department.

From a broad policy perspective, for example, managers may argue about whether greater emphasis should be placed on policing the streets or providing social services. Within, say, the police department there may be disagreements about which streets need more policing than others. For these and many other reasons, there is organizational conflict.

Clearly, an organization will not achieve its objectives unless managers work together with some degree of harmony. Thus, there also must be cooperation in an organization. Without cooperation the organization will flounder, and its members will be unable to satisfy the needs that motivated them to join it in the first place.

Senior management therefore must maintain an appropriate balance between the forces that create conflict and those that create cooperation. Some conflict is both inevitable and even desirable. It results from the competition between participants for resources or power, and, within limits, it can be healthy. Conflict also arises because different managers in an LG see the world from contrasting perspectives, and believe that different actions are in the LG's best interests. For example, conflict can arise in a museum over the most appropriate exhibits, or in a school system over the most appropriate courses. To a certain extent, this sort of conflict is beneficial in that, managed appropriately, it can bring out the best ideas of an LG's members. By contrast, if undue emphasis is placed on fostering a cooperative attitude, the most able managers and professionals may be denied the opportunity to use their talents fully. Senior management must seek to foster the right balance. We return to this issue in Chapter 11.

The bureaucracy

Many observers have suggested that in LGs and other government organizations, effective management control is inhibited by the existence of the bureaucracy. In fact, bureaucracy is often used as a pejorative label for any organization that operates by complicated rules and procedures, or that is characterized by delays and avoidance of responsibility, or that treats its clients impolitely. In particular, government organizations are typically labeled as bureaucracies – with the implication that private sector organizations are not.

In fact, any large and complex organization is necessarily a bureaucracy. The classic analysis of bureaucracy is that of Max Weber, discussed briefly in Chapter 3 (Weber 1922). Weber described a bureaucratic organization as one in which the chief executive derives his authority by law or through election by an authorized body, rather than by tradition or charisma. Subordinates are responsible to the chief executive through a clearly defined hierarchy and are selected on the basis of their technical competence, rather than by election. They are promoted according to seniority or achievement, or both, and they are subject to systematic discipline and control.

The Weberian bureaucracy solves complex problems by segmenting them into a series of simpler ones, and delegating authority for solving each segment to the appropriate experts in specialized subunits. Such technical superiority, based on increased specialization, is supposed to lead to objective and impersonal decision making at the sub-unit level. Weber noted that an individual who applied personal or subjective values to policy analysis or decision making could seriously lessen the effectiveness of the organization. A bureaucracy avoids this possibility by replacing the subjective judgment of individuals with routine work tasks, and by establishing a set of rules, values, attitudes, and goals that are approved by each individual's superior.[4]

Despite the pejorative connotation, bureaucratic procedures are essential in an organization where several different units perform the same function. For example, each consular office of a country is supposed to give the same advice to a visa applicant. There would be no way of coming close to that goal without a comprehensive set of rules and regulations used by all offices. At the same time, there is occasionally a need for flexibility in enforcing the rules. As we will discuss in later chapters, an appropriate combination of consistency and flexibility can be fostered through the design of a good management control system (Young 1988).

Role of the controller

In most organizations, the controller is responsible for the operation of the management control system. It is importantly to bear in mind, however, that the controller department is a staff unit with a responsibility similar to that of a telephone company: it must assure that messages flow through the system clearly, accurately, and promptly.

It is not responsible for the content of the messages or for how managers react to them.

The controller ordinarily works with senior management to design the management control system in such a way that fairness and goal congruence are maximized. Most of this effort is associated with designing the responsibility center structure and the transfer pricing arrangements along the lines discussed earlier. The controller also works with senior management to design the four phases of the management control process. Because of the significant impact that these design choices can have on managers' and professionals' behavior, senior management should be highly involved in making the choices. In many organizations, senior management completely delegates these choices to the controller, which is a mistake since the controller typically does not have a sufficiently broad perspective of the LG and its goals.

CULTURAL FACTORS

As discussed in Chapter 3, and as we will elaborate on in Chapter 11, every organization has a culture – a climate or atmosphere in which certain attitudes are encouraged and others are discouraged (Schein 2010). Cultural norms are derived in part from tradition, in part from external influences (such as unions and societal norms), and in part from the attitude of the organization's senior managers. Cultural norms can help to explain why each of two LGs may have a similar management control system but why one has much better performance than the other.

Cultural norms are almost never written down, and attempts to do so almost always result in platitudes. Instead, they are transmitted, in part, by hiring practices and training programs. They also are conveyed by managers, professionals, and other organization members using words, deeds, and body language to indicate that some types of actions are acceptable and others are not.

Management attitude

The aspect of culture that has perhaps the most important impact on management control is the attitude of senior management. In a well-managed organization, the chief executive officer sets the tone. He or she may express this attitude in a number of ways. If performance reports typically disappear into the executive offices and no response is forthcoming, lower-level managers will soon conclude that these reports are not important. Conversely, if the CEO discusses a report at length with a manager, the signal is that the report is important.

Role of the external environment

An LG's *external* environment can affect the control climate within the organization. For example, when times are tough, people tend to take the control process more seriously than when the economy is booming. In many LGs, the cultural norms of a professional group (e.g., public health nurses, social workers, firefighters, police officers) will have a major influence on the culture of the organization itself.

In addition, in many instances, an LG is part of a wider public administration system. Sometimes this system relates to a state or a region, and sometimes to a country's central government. This broader culture will affect the relationships between political executives and senior civil servants, and it also can affect the general approach to public management. Table 4.6 shows several countries with quite different cultures, and indicates the wide variety of contextual factors that need to be considered in designing an LG's management control structure.

Some of the variations among the 68 countries in this table in terms of the different indicators of culture are as follows:

- *Power distance:* In Slovakia and Malaysia, which have a high index, the distance between superiors and subordinates is vast, whereas in Austria, which ranks the lowest among the 68 countries, subordinates are closer to superiors.
- *Individualism/collectivism:* In the United States, individualism is considered extremely important, but collectivism is more important in Guatemala.
- *Masculinity/femininity:* In Slovakia, there are rather clearly defined gender roles, whereas in Sweden there is almost no difference between the roles of men and women.
- *Uncertainty avoidance:* In Greece, with a high index, uncertainty is considered fine, but in Singapore it tends to be avoided.
- *Long-/short-term orientation:* In China, there is considerable focus on the long-term, whereas in Pakistan, a short-term orientation is more prevalent.

In essence, then, a management control system that works well in an LG of one country may be completely ineffective in the LG of another. System designers therefore must consider the overall cultural climate as they undertake their design efforts.

SUMMARY

One of the most difficult aspects of designing an LG's management control system is defining the system's structure – its network of responsibility centers. In determining what sort of responsibility center a given manager's unit will be, senior management needs to pay careful attention to the resources the manager can control. This *fairness* criterion is one of the driving forces behind responsibility center design.

Beyond this, senior management needs to consider ways to attain *goal congruence*, i.e., congruence between the personal goals of each responsibility center manger and its goals for the organization as a whole. In part, a responsibility center manager's goals

Table 4.6 *Indicators of cultures in different countries*

	Power distance		Individual/ collectivism		Masculinity/ femininity		Uncertainty avoidance		Long-/ short-term orientation	
	Index	Rank	Index	Rank	Index	Rank	Index	Rank	Index	Rank
Arab World**	80	11	38	36	52	31	68	35	n.a.	n.a.
Argentina	49	46	46	30	56	26	86	14	n.a.	n.a.
Australia	36	56	90	2	61	20	51	49	31	17
Austria	11	68	55	24	79	4	70	31	n.a.	n.a.
Bangladesh*	80	11	20	50	55	28	60	40	40	13
Belgium	65	29	75	9	54	29	94	7	n.a.	n.a.
Brazil	69	22	38	36	49	36	76	27	65	7
Bulgaria*	70	19	30	42	40	51	85	20	n.a.	n.a.
Canada	39	54	80	4	52	31	48	54	23	23
Chile	63	33	23	49	28	62	86	14	n.a.	n.a.
China*	80	11	20	50	66	11	30	62	118	1
Colombia	67	26	13	64	64	14	80	26	n.a.	n.a.
Costa Rica	35	57	15	61	21	64	86	14	n.a.	n.a.
Czech Republic*	57	40	58	23	57	23	74	30	13	27
Denmark	18	66	74	10	16	65	23	66	n.a.	n.a.
East Africa**	64	30	27	45	41	50	52	48	25	21
Ecuador	78	14	8	67	63	17	67	37	n.a.	n.a.
El Salvador	66	27	19	56	40	51	94	7	n.a.	n.a.
Estonia*	40	51	60	19	30	61	60	40	n.a.	n.a.
Finland	33	61	63	18	26	63	59	42	n.a.	n.a.
France	68	23	71	11	43	45	86	14	n.a.	n.a.
Germany	35	57	67	16	66	11	65	38	31	17
Greece	60	36	35	40	57	23	112	1	n.a.	n.a.
Guatemala	95	3	6	68	37	56	101	3	n.a.	n.a.
Hong Kong	68	23	25	48	57	23	29	64	96	2
Hungary*	46	49	80	4	88	3	82	23	50	10
India	77	16	48	28	56	26	40	58	61	8
Indonesia	78	14	14	62	46	40	48	54	n.a.	n.a.
Iran	58	38	41	33	43	45	59	42	n.a.	n.a.
Ireland	28	64	70	13	68	9	35	60	n.a.	n.a.
Israel	13	67	54	25	47	38	81	25	n.a.	n.a.
Italy	50	45	76	8	70	6	75	29	n.a.	n.a.
Jamaica	45	50	39	34	68	9	13	67	n.a.	n.a.
Japan	54	44	46	30	95	2	92	10	80	4
Luxembourg*	40	51	60	19	50	33	70	31	n.a.	n.a.
Malaysia	104	1	26	47	50	33	36	59	n.a.	n.a.
Malta*	56	42	59	22	47	38	96	5	n.a.	n.a.
Mexico	81	9	30	42	69	8	82	23	n.a.	n.a.
Morocco*	70	19	46	30	53	30	68	35	n.a.	n.a.
Netherlands	38	55	80	4	14	66	53	47	44	12
New Zealand	22	65	79	7	58	21	49	52	30	19
Norway	31	62	69	14	8	67	50	51	20	24
Pakistan	55	43	14	62	50	33	70	31	0	28
Panama	95	3	11	66	44	44	86	14	n.a.	n.a.
Peru	64	30	16	59	42	47	87	13	n.a.	n.a.

Table 4.6 Continued

	Power distance		Individual/ collectivism		Masculinity/ femininity		Uncertainty avoidance		Long-/ short-term orientation	
	Index	Rank	Index	Rank	Index	Rank	Index	Rank	Index	Rank
Philippines	94	5	32	41	64	14	44	57	19	25
Poland*	68	23	60	19	64	14	93	9	32	16
Portugal	63	33	27	45	31	60	104	2	n.a.	n.a.
Romania*	90	7	30	42	42	47	90	12	n.a.	n.a.
Russia*	93	6	39	34	36	58	95	6	n.a.	n.a.
Singapore	74	18	20	50	48	37	*8*	*68*	48	11
Slovakia*	**104**	**1**	52	26	**110**	**1**	51	49	38	14
South Africa	49	46	65	17	63	17	49	52	n.a.	n.a.
South Korea	60	36	18	57	39	54	85	20	75	6
Spain	57	40	51	27	42	47	86	14	n.a.	n.a.
Surinam*	85	8	47	29	37	56	92	10	n.a.	n.a.
Sweden	31	62	71	11	*5*	*68*	29	64	33	15
Switzerland	34	60	68	15	70	6	58	44	n.a.	n.a.
Taiwan	58	38	17	58	45	42	69	34	87	3
Thailand	64	30	20	50	34	59	64	39	56	9
Trinidad*	47	48	16	59	58	21	55	45	n.a.	n.a.
Turkey	66	27	37	38	45	42	85	20	n.a.	n.a.
United Kingdom	35	57	89	3	66	11	35	60	25	21
United States	40	51	**91**	**1**	62	19	46	56	29	20
Uruguay	61	35	36	39	38	55	100	4	n.a.	n.a.
Venezuela	81	9	12	65	73	5	76	27	n.a.	n.a.
Vietnam*	70	19	20	50	40	51	30	62	80	4
West Africa	77	16	20	50	46	40	54	46	16	26

Notes:

Power distance: The difference between the extent to which a boss can determine the behavior of a subordinate versus the extent to which a subordinate can determine the behavior of the boss.

Individualism versus collectivism: Individualism indicates a society in which the ties between individuals are loose; collectivism is a society in which people from birth onwards are integrated into strong, cohesive groups. A high index indicates greater individualism.

Masculinity versus femininity: Masculinity stands for a society in which gender roles are clearly distinct: men are supposed to be tough, assertive, and focused on material success; women are supposed to be more modest, tender, and concerned with the quality of life; with femininity gender roles overlap. A low index indicates greater masculinity.

Uncertainty avoidance: The extent to which the members of a culture feel threatened by uncertain or unknown situations. A low index indicates greater uncertainty avoidance.

Long-term versus short-term orientation: Long-term orientation stands for the fostering of virtues oriented towards future rewards (perseverance and thrift); short-term stands for the opposite.

Rank: 1 = highest rank. The highest ranking number is highlighted in **bold face type**. The lowest is highlighted in **bold italics**.

*Estimated values; **Regional estimated values: "Arab World" = Egypt, Iraq, Kuwait, Lebanon, Libya, Saudi Arabia, United Arab Emirates; "East Africa" = Ethiopia, Kenya, Tanzania, Zambia; "West Africa" = Ghana, Nigeria, Sierra Leone.

Source: Adapted from Hofstede (2011) (ranks computed by authors).

are determined by the incentives that senior management creates to reward certain forms of behavior.

Beyond these considerations, senior management also must pay close attention to the fit between programs and responsibility centers. Programs represent the operational definition of an organization's strategy, and can be broken into program categories, subcategories, and elements. Each aspect of a program must be assigned to a responsibility center, and the management control system must be designed in such a way that it can provide information on the activities of both programs and responsibility centers. This calls for a careful design of the account structure, a task that ordinarily is carried out by the accounting staff but needs considerable guidance from senior management.

Finally, senior management must constantly bear in mind that management control is fundamentally behavioral. The various control tools are effective only if they influence behavior, and they will influence behavior only if the culture of the organization is conducive. A delicate balance must be struck between cooperation and conflict so that individuals – both managers and professionals – work together toward the attainment of organizational goals and yet are able to have legitimate and healthy conflicts over the best ways to attain them.

DISCUSSION QUESTIONS

1   What traditional departments in an LG are candidates for being set up as profit centers? Why? Which should be shadow profit centers? Why?
2   Should public works be a department or a program? Why?

NOTES

1 This is a controversial point for all nonprofit organizations, but especially for LGs. To avoid the potential inconsistency with an LG needing a balanced budget each year, the budget should include a "cost of capital." For a discussion of the issues, see Young (2007).
2 There are several other approaches that can be taken, but a discussion of them is beyond the scope of this text. For details, see Solomons (1965).
3 For-profit organizations sometimes use stock options to motivate managers to think about the long-term consequences of their decisions. Some nonprofit organizations use sabbatical leaves, but it is difficult to link leave time to long-run performance.

Even so, due to legislative restrictions, an LG would find it all but impossible to implement such a policy.
4 For an argument that just the opposite takes place in a bureaucracy, see Crozier (1964).

REFERENCES

Anthony, R.N. and Young, D.W. (2003) *Management Control in Nonprofit Organizations*, 7th edn, Burr Ridge, Illinois: McGraw Hill-Irwin.

Crozier, M. (1964) *The Bureaucratic Phenomenon*, Chicago, Illlinois: University of Chicago Press.

Hofstede, G. (2011) *Geert Hofstede^{TM} Cultural Dimensions*. Available HTTP: http://www.geert-hofstede.com/hofstede_dimensions.php (accessed April 27, 2011).

McClelland, D. (1961) *The Achieving Society*, New York: Irvington Publishers.

Maslow, A.H. (1954) *Motivation and Personality*, New York: Harper & Row Publishers.

Merchant, K.A. (1985) *Control in Business Organizations*, Marshfield, Massachusetts: Pitman Publishing.

Pfeffer, J. (1998) *The Human Equation: Building Profits by Putting People First*, Boston, Massachusetts: Harvard Business School Press.

Schein, E.H. (2010) *Organizational Culture and Leadership*, 4th edn, San Francisco, California: Jossey Bass Publishers.

Solomons, D. (1965) *Divisional Performance: Measurement and Control*, Homewood, Illinois: Richard D. Irwin, Inc.

Talbot, C. (2008) "Performance Regimes – The Institutional Context of Performance Policies," *International Journal of Public Administration*, 31(14): 1,569–91.

Weber, W. (1922) *Wirtschaft und Gesellschaft*, trans. A.M. Henderson and Talcott Parsons (1947) *The Theory of Social and Economic Organization*, New York: Oxford University Press.

Young, D.W. (1988) "Management Control in the Public Sector: Overcoming the Barriers to Progress," in A.P. Kakabadse, P.R. Brovetto, and R. Holzer (eds) *Management Development and the Public Sector*, Aldershot, England: Gower Publishing Company.

Young, D.W. (2007) *Note on Financial Surpluses in Nonprofit Organizations*, Cambridge, Massachusetts: The Crimson Press Curriculum Center.

FURTHER READING

Because the organizational structure plays a pivotal role in shaping the structure for the management control system, it is essential to have a full understanding of the organizational design behind it. *Organizational Design: A Step-by-Step Approach*, by Richard

M. Burton, Gerardine DeSanctis, and Børge Obel (Cambridge University Press 2006) discusses the key aspects of organizational design for a wide variety of organizations. To understand the behavioral factors that set the context of the management control system, *Managing Human Behavior in Public and Nonprofit Organizations* by Robert B. Denhardt, Janet V. Denhardt, and Maria P. Aristigueta (Sage 2008) offers a thorough summary of organizational behavior in public-sector organizations.

Chapter 5

Programming

LEARNING OBJECTIVES

At the end of this chapter you should:

- Know how programming decisions differ from budgeting decisions.
- Be able to use the techniques of payback period, net present value, and internal rate of return to evaluate a program proposal.
- Understand the methodology for determining an appropriate discount rate for assessing net present value.
- Be able to compute a weighted cost of capital and a weighted return on assets, and incorporate risk into a program analysis.
- Understand the issues involved in quantifying the value of a human being.

KEY POINTS

- Programming is the phase of the management control process when an LG makes decisions that have a long-term impact, such as initiating a new program or purchasing a new fixed asset.
- Although there are instances where an local government's (LG's) senior management may make a programming decision without giving much formal consideration to its financial implications, well-managed LGs will use at least one of three analytical techniques to assess these implications: payback period, net present value, or internal rate of return.
- There are two errors that can result from using a discount rate that is too low (or from the failure to discount at all): (1) projects may be undertaken that are financially unfeasible, and (2) projects that are capital-intensive and long-lived will appear to be more attractive than they actually are.

- A benefit/cost approach may show that, from an economic standpoint, a proposal is outside a reasonable boundary in either direction – that it is obviously worthwhile or obviously not worth its cost.
- Assessing the value of a human life is important for projects that are intended to save lives, such as improved traffic safety or cancer screening. The cost of saving lives may be a useful way of choosing among alternative proposals even when it is not possible or feasible to measure the value of a life.
- A variety of non-quantitative considerations are part of almost every programming decision. In all instances, managers must be careful not to allow the quantitative factors to dominate the decision. They need to recognize that their judgment occasionally must override the results of the quantitative analysis.

As Chapter 2 discussed, management control systems have a structure and a process. Chapter 4 examined the management control structure and its relation to an LG's external and internal environments. With this chapter, we begin our examination of the management control process.

The management control process includes two phases that deal with planning: programming (this chapter's subject) and budgeting (the subject of Chapter 6). The former represents long-range planning; the latter focuses on short-range planning.

Programming decisions frequently involve investments in fixed assets that senior management expects will be used for several years, and that will result in some financial savings or other benefits that exceed the amount of investment. Ordinarily, the end result of the programming phase is a capital budget, and often there also are commitments to initiate some new programmatic endeavors, such as a new day care center. By contrast, the budgeting phase typically has a one-year focus and is concerned only with operating activities. The end results usually are an operating budget and a cash budget. Although this chapter focuses on programming, it is important to note that an LG's programming decisions will have an impact on both its operating and cash budgets.

It also is important to bear in mind that our focus in this chapter is on a financial (and managerial) perspective. We do not address any of a variety of political issues that frequently play pivotal roles in programming decisions; there are many texts that address these issues. We also limit our discussion in this chapter to a decision-making process that uses financial data, and do not address directly the wide variety of non-financial factors that can affect a programming decision, such as an improvement in citizen safety or quality of life.

Programming decisions that call for the purchase of a new fixed asset (such as a new library building or new police cruiser) usually rely on one or more analytical techniques that incorporate the multiyear period over which the new asset will be used.

The chapter looks at three of these techniques: payback period, net present value, and internal rate of return. Although there are instances where senior management may decide to make a capital investment without giving much formal consideration to its financial implications, many LGs use at least one of these analytical techniques in the programming phase.

Also, if an LG has begun to work with some private-sector entities as part of the move discussed in Chapter 3 toward the New Public Management paradigm, it may need to address programming proposals submitted by its vendors. As will be discussed in later chapters, if the relationship between the LG and a vendor has evolved into something approaching a partnership or alliance, this need is exacerbated, as is the resulting obligation to consider ways to help finance projects that will be undertaken by the vendor rather than the LG itself.

AN OVERVIEW OF PROGRAMMING

Programming is a key activity in implementing an LG's strategy. Because it takes place within the context of strategy, it relies on information concerning new opportunities, new or pending legislation that might affect ongoing efforts, and similar considerations. During the programming phase, senior management makes decisions of a long-term nature concerning the new programs it will undertake and the new fixed assets it will acquire.

Decisions made in the programming phase involve long-term commitments. For example, a new police cruiser may last for three to five years, sometimes longer. A new or renovated office or library may last 20 years. Thus, the programming phase of the management control process frequently looks ahead by several years. In some large LGs there is a lengthy program document that describes each program proposal in detail, estimates the resources needed to accomplish it, and calculates the expected returns.

BOX 5.1   LONG-TERM PLANNING FOR A MASS TRANSIT PROGRAM

The following was excerpted from the *2008–2012 Capital Program and 10-Year Capital Forecast* of the Toronto Transit Commission.

> Over the five-year period, 2008–2012, a total of $4,400.9 million is required for the base capital program . . . . Based on current funding assumptions, this will leave a shortfall of at least $420 million for the base program over the next 5 years . . . . This is after assuming that we will receive $481 million in long term vehicle funding from the Province and $324 million from the

Federal government for rail vehicle purchases. At the present time, neither of these amounts has been secured. All combined, this means that there is about $1.5 billion ... in basic State-of-Good-Repair work that is presently unfunded.

The 2008 capital program includes $751.6 million for the base capital program. This amount will be reduced by $54.4 million for unspecified budget reductions for a net request of $697.2 million. Based on current funding assumptions, there is enough funding available to cover this amount in 2008, with one exception – the required confirmation of funding for the streetcar fleet replacement order that is scheduled for the spring of 2008 has not yet been received from either the Provincial or Federal governments.

This places the TTC [Toronto Transit Commission] in the unusual position of having the Spadina Subway Extension largely funded and MoveOntario 2020 announced by the Province at the same time that we have up to a $1.5 billion funding shortfall in base program funding. While this report will outline plans to close this funding gap, it is not clear when we will have answers on the funding necessary for the base program.

(Toronto Transit Commission 2007)

Although programming decisions ordinarily are based on the long-term financial impact on an LG, there also are some short-term consequences. For example, the purchase of a new fixed asset will affect cash management via either the use of existing cash or the need to increase long-term debt. In this latter instance, the short-term impact on cash is mitigated, resulting in a series of annual debt service outlays (principal and interest payments) rather than the large initial cash outlay that otherwise would be necessary.

ANALYTICAL TECHNIQUES FOR CAPITAL INVESTMENT ANALYSES

A typical capital investment proposal involves an outlay of money this year so as to realize some benefits in the future. Consider, for example, a proposal to install some storm windows at a cost of $100,000, with an estimated saving in heating bills of $30,000 per year. In evaluating this proposal one must ask whether it is worth spending $100,000 now to obtain benefits of $30,000 per year in the future. There are several approaches to answering this question.

Payback period
One approach determines the number of years the benefits will have to be obtained to recover the investment. This is the payback period. It is calculated as follows for the

storm window example:

$$\text{Payback period} = \text{Initial investment} \div \text{Annual benefits}$$
$$= \$100,000 \div \$30,000 = 3.3 \text{ years}$$

If the storm windows are expected to last fewer than 3.3 years, the investment is not worthwhile. If more than 3.3 years, the storm windows will have "paid for themselves."

Present value

The payback-period approach assumes that savings in the second and third years are as valuable as savings in the first year, but this is not realistic. No rational person would give up the right to receive $30,000 now for the promise to receive $30,000 two years from now. If a person loans $30,000 to someone (other than a very good friend!) now, he or she expects to get back more than $30,000 at some time in the future. The promise of an amount to be received in the future therefore has a lower *present value* than the same amount received today. This concept is discussed more fully in Appendix 5-A.

Use of present value is important in capital budgeting. By incorporating the *time value of money* into the analysis, the present value technique recognizes that money received in the future does not have as much value as money received today. *Net present value* (NPV) is the difference between a project's estimated financial cash inflows, discounted to their value today (i.e., their *present* value), and the amount to be invested in the project. The estimated benefits often are called the project's "cash flows." The approach involves the following steps:

1 Determine the estimated annual *cash flows* (*CF*) associated with the project. These may be either increased revenues (net of increased costs) or decreased costs, but they must result exclusively from the project itself and not from any activities that would have taken place anyway.
2 Determine the estimated economic life of the investment. This is not necessarily its physical life, but rather the time period over which the cash flows will be received. The economic life may be shorter than the physical life because of obsolescence, change in demand, or other reasons.
3 Determine the net amount of the *investment* (*I*). This is the purchase price of the new asset, plus any delivery or installation costs, plus any disposal costs for the asset it is replacing (or less the salvage value of the asset being replaced).
4 Determine the required discount rate (discussed in greater detail later), and combine it with the economic life to get the *present value factor* (*PVF*).
5 Compute the proposed project's *net present value* (*NPV*) according to the formula:

$$NPV = (CF \times PVF) - I$$

6   If the NPV is greater than zero, the investment is financially feasible. That is, once we have determined a discount rate, a project that yields a NPV of zero or greater is earning that rate and therefore is acceptable from a pure financial perspective.

As discussed in Appendix 5-A, when the cash flow is identical every year, the PVF can be obtained from Table 5.2 in that appendix by combining the intersection of the year row and the percent column selected in steps 2 and 4. Present value factors for one-time cash flows can be found in Table 5.1. The (CF × PVF) portion of this equation is known as *Gross Present Value*. The *Net Present Value* is determined by deducting the investment from it.

BOX 5.2   MAKING DECISIONS USING NET PRESENT VALUE

Assume we estimate that the storm windows in the above example will last 5 years, and that our required rate of return is 8 percent. The PVF (from Table 5.2) for 8 percent over 5 years is 3.993. The analysis would look as follows:

Step 1. Annual cash flow = $30,000
Step 2. Economic life = 5 years
Step 3. Net investment amount = $100,000
Step 4. Rate of return = 8 percent
Step 5. NPV = (CF × PVF) − I
         = ($30,000 × 3.993) − $100,000
         = $119,790 − $100,000
         = $19,790
Step 6. The investment has a NPV that is greater than zero, and therefore is financially feasible.

Some complications

Several important points should be considered in undertaking an analysis of NPV. First, the above example assumed identical cash flows in each of the years, which permits us to use Table 5.2. If the cash flows were not the same in each year, we would need to calculate the term (CF × PVF) for each year separately, using Table 5.1, and then add the results together.

Second, although an analysis of this sort appears to be quite precise, we should recognize that its significant elements are only estimates and may be quite imprecise. Specifically, cash flows that are projected beyond a period of two or three years ordinarily are not very accurate, nor are the estimates of the economic lives of most investments. Thus, we should be careful about attributing too much credibility to the precision that the formula seems to provide. Because of this, many managers look for the NPV to be a *comfortable margin* above zero. Of course, what is comfortable for one manager may not be so for another.

Third, inflation is a factor. It is quite likely, for instance, that potential increases in heating rates, will cause the energy savings from the above storm window investment to be greater five years from now than they are today. If, however, we are to adjust our cash flows for the effects of inflation, we also need to adjust the required rate of return to reflect our need for a return that is at least equal to the rate of inflation. By excluding an inflation effect from both the cash flow calculations and the required rate of return, we neutralize the effect of inflation, and do not need to undertake the rather complex calculations that otherwise would be necessary.

Finally, the financial analysis is only one aspect of the decision-making process. Clearly, there are many more considerations, including strategic and political effects. Managers must be careful not to let the financial analysis dominate a decision that has political or strategic consequences that cannot be quantified easily. In these instances, a manager's judgment and "feel" for the situation may be as important as the quantitative factors. Moreover, if a project is *required* by, say, a regulatory agency, its net present value is irrelevant.

BOX 5.3 MAKING DECISIONS CONSIDERING OTHER FACTORS THAN NET PRESENT VALUE

A governmental commissioner needed to decide between two projects concerning the extension of an environmental emergency disposal plant in southern Italy. He approved the one with the lower NPV because, in his judgment, the other one would have caused difficulties in the relationship with the vendor, leading to possible service difficulties in the case of an environmental emergency.

In short, almost all capital budgeting proposals involve a wide variety of non-quantitative considerations that will influence the final decision. The use of present value or any related technique serves only to formalize the quantitative part of the analysis.

Internal rate of return

Another way of assessing the financial feasibility of a project is by its *internal (or effective) rate of return (IRR)*. The IRR method is similar to the NPV method, but instead of determining a required rate of return in advance, the analyst sets NPV equal to zero and calculates the *effective rate of return* on the investment. Proposed projects then can be ranked in terms of their rates of return.

Use of this method usually assumes identical cash flows in each year of a project's life. Given this assumption, the IRR method begins with the NPV formula:

$$NPV = (CF \times PVF) - I$$

but sets NPV equal to zero, so that:

$$CF \times PVF = I$$

or

$$PVF = I \div CF$$

Once the PVF has been calculated, it can be used in conjunction with the project's economic life to determine the IRR. This is done with Table 5.2. For instance, in the storm window example, dividing the $100,000 investment by the $30,000 annual cash flows, results in a PVF of 3.33. The figure of 3.33 can be found in the row for 5 years in Table 5.2, and lies between 15 and 16 percent. Thus the IRR for the storm window project is about 15.5 percent.

Choice of a discount rate

In any capital investment analysis, the choice of a discount rate is an important consideration, either for computing the NPV or for comparison with the IRR. The approach used by many organizations, in both the private and public sectors, begins by calculating the *weighted cost of capital* (*WCC*), followed by incorporating it into a computation of the *weighted return on assets* (*WRA*). The general approach is shown in Appendix 5-B.

Cost of equity

A tricky part of computing the WCC is selecting an interest rate for equity, which is an ongoing debate in many nonprofit organizations. Although some argue that equity funds are basically free, and therefore should be assigned a zero interest rate, most managers believe that they at least have an opportunity cost.

As mentioned briefly in Appendix 5-B, while most managers and analysts would agree on the relevance of *including* an interest rate for equity, there is considerably less agreement on how to determine the appropriate amount. One argument is that, when not needed for ongoing operations (e.g., payroll, inventory purchases, etc.), an organization's cash can be invested in stocks, bonds, or similar instruments. If some of this cash is used for a particular project, there is a reduction in the amount available for investments, and hence an opportunity cost. This opportunity cost (i.e., the rate the organization is earning on its investments) is an appropriate rate to use for equity in computing the WCC.

Weighted return on assets

If the overall return on assets (ROA) is not at least equal to the weighted cost of capital, the LG is paying more to finance its assets than it is earning on them, and therefore is atrophying. This gives rise to the need to compute a "weighted return on assets" (WRA).

The need for a WRA arises because not all assets earn a return. For example, assets like accounts (or taxes) receivable and inventory do not earn any return. It thus is necessary to determine how much property, plant, and equipment must earn if the overall ROA is to be equal to the WCC. Appendix 5-B shows how this computation can be made.

At the end of the day, if an LG is to satisfy the generational equity principle (discussed in Chapter 3) it will need to earn a surplus that gives it a return on assets that is equal to its WCC. Although earning a surplus is anathema to many LG managers, doing so avoids the need to ask future years' taxpayers to pay some portion of the "real cost" of this year's operations (Young 1982). Computing the NPV or IRR, in conjunction with a consideration of the WRA, means that a proposed project that does not meet the generational equity principle should be rejected unless there are compelling non-financial reasons to select it.

Problems associated with low discount rates

There are many instances in which LGs and other public sector organizations have analyzed capital investment proposals using discount rates that are too low. This problem is particularly important with respect to proposals for public works projects and other capital expenditures whose benefits accrue over a long period. Until fairly recently, many of these proposals either did not discount their cash flows at all, or used very low discount rates, such as the interest rate on municipal (or other government) bonds. Many analysts now agree that a government bond or loan rate is too low, and thus can result in approving projects that actually should not be undertaken.

There are two errors that can result from using a discount rate that is too low (or from the failure to discount at all). First, and most obvious, projects may be undertaken that are financially unfeasible. Second, and less obvious, projects that are capital-intensive and long-lived will appear to be more attractive than they actually are.

BOX 5.4   THE PROBLEM WITH LOW DISCOUNT RATES

In India, the mistake of using low discount rates led to the construction of large cement plants built at infrequent intervals, rather than to smaller plants built more frequently.

Incorporating risk into the analysis

Capital investment proposals are not risk free. Since they involve future cash flows, there is always the possibility that the future will not be as anticipated. This risk element needs to be incorporated into the analysis. If risk is not considered explicitly, then a very risky proposal might be evaluated in the same way as one that has a high probability of success. It also may happen that an apparent "free" capital investment may able to unexpectedly raise costs in the future.

BOX 5.5   BEWARE OF "FREE" ASSETS: THEY MAY HAVE DOWNSTREAM EXPENSES

A bronze sculpture of Pope John Paul II donated to the city of Rome by a charitable organization created a lot of complaints by citizens. These calls for the statue's removal led the mayor to hire a commission of experts to determine whether to leave it untouched, ask for changes, or put it in a less prominent location than the city's central railway station. Whatever the decision, the assertion by the head of the city's cultural heritage department that "we were happy to accept a statue that cost the city zilch" was unexpectedly incorrect (Povoledo, 25 May 2011).

There are a number of ways to incorporate risk into an analysis. With all of them, an increase in risk reduces the NPV (or IRR) of a proposal. For example, many organizations adjust their discount rate either upward or downward to account for perceived risk. The problem with this approach is that there is no easy way to establish a meaningful risk scale. Statistical techniques are available for incorporating the relative riskiness of a project, but they require analysts to estimate the probabilities of possible outcomes. This is quite difficult to accomplish.

Another approach, taken by many organizations, is to heavily discount any projected cash flows beyond some predetermined time period. They use a discount rate based on the WCC (or WRA) for all cash flows in, say, the first five years of an investment, and then use a much higher rate for all subsequent years. Some even exclude all cash flows beyond a certain number of years. In all instances, the reasoning is that the future is highly uncertain, and that the farther out the projections, the greater the uncertainty. Clearly, this approach tends to bias decisions in favor of projects with short payback periods.

Finally, in considering risk, some organizations give greater weight to projections of cost savings than to projections of additional contribution (incremental revenues less incremental costs). When a particular technological improvement, say a new piece of equipment (or even something as simple as a set of storm windows), has demonstrated its ability to produce certain cost savings in other organizations, managers reason that projections of cost savings are quite reliable. Less reliable is a projection that a certain investment will result in additional revenue (such as with a municipal parking garage). Factors such as clients' willingness to use the new service, competition, and the like will affect a new investment's return. Some organizations incorporate this risk into the analysis by using lower discount rates for projects with cost savings and higher ones for projects that are expected to yield additional contribution.

In summary, when we consider the formula:

$$NPV = (CF \times PVF) - I$$

the only element that is reasonably certain is the investment amount. Cash flow estimates and a project's economic life can be highly speculative. LGs can include adjustments for uncertainty by either shortening economic life or raising the required rate of return. Either approach requires managers and analysts to exercise considerable judgment.

BENEFIT/COST ANALYSIS

So far, we have examined one dimension of a technical analysis: making estimates of those benefits of a proposed project that can be stated in monetary terms, i.e., cash inflows, and comparing them with the investment amount. We also must recognize, however, that not all relevant factors can be expressed monetarily. This leads to the idea of a *benefit/cost analysis*. The underlying principle of a benefit/cost analysis is the obvious one – that a program (or project or asset acquisition) should not be undertaken unless its benefits exceed its costs.

Status of benefit/cost analysis

The idea of comparing the benefits of a proposed course of action with its costs has existed for many years. Proposals to build new fire stations, for example, frequently have been justified on the grounds that the benefits (reduced deaths, injuries, and property damage) exceeded the costs. In the United States, interest in benefit/cost analysis grew rapidly when the United States Department of Defense applied it to problems for which no formal analysis previously had been attempted. This idea expanded internationally, and resulted in a variety of promotional brochures, journal articles, and proposals implying that benefit/cost analysis did everything, including "taking the guesswork out of management."

BOX 5.6   A CAVALIER BENEFIT/COST ANALYSIS!

A proposal for a $275,000 research project submitted to the United States National Institute of Education promised to "address the benefit/cost question by making a macro management and policy analysis of alternate cost opportunities in elementary-secondary and post-secondary education," and to provide the results in nine months. Translated, this means that the proposer promised to use benefit/cost analysis to find the optimum amount and character of educational programs from kindergarten through college, in nine months, and all for $275,000!

For good reasons, public policy officials now question the merits of benefit/cost analyses. Nevertheless, there is no doubt that many benefit/cost analyses have produced valuable information. To assure useful results, however, decision makers need to consider two essential points:

1   A benefit/cost analysis focuses on those aspects of a proposal that can be estimated in quantitative terms. Because there is no important problem where all relevant factors can be reduced to numbers, benefit/cost analysis will never provide the complete answer. Not everything can be quantified, and no one should expect a benefit/cost analysis to do so. Analyses that claim to have quantified everything are of dubious merit.

2   To the extent that analysts can express some important factors in quantitative terms, they are better off doing so than not. This narrows the area where the decision maker must operate in the more judgment-based dimension of programming. Thus, while the need for judgment is not eliminated, it can be reduced.

Clarifying goals

The benefit in a benefit/cost analysis must be related to an organization's goals; there is no point in making a benefit/cost analysis unless all concerned agree on these goals. The purpose of benefit/cost analysis is to suggest the best alternative for reaching a goal, but the formulation of goals is largely a judgmental process. Various members of management and various staff may have different ideas of goals, and unless they reconcile their views, middle managers will find it difficult to formulate and implement appropriate proposals.

BOX 5.7   USING THE RIGHT GOALS IN A BENEFIT/COST ANALYSIS

Several years ago, an LG began to support local transportation for the disabled. Since, at that time, it subsidized local bus lines, its natural inclination was to finance the modification of buses to provide lifts that would permit easy access for wheelchairs. The extra capital and maintenance costs of such equipment turned out to be substantial, and usage was not high because disabled individuals had no way of getting from their homes to the bus stops. Consequently, the cost per passenger was high – $1,283 per trip in one study. Subsequently, transportation was provided by vans that picked up these individuals at their doors and took them directly to their destinations. This was more convenient and less expensive – between $5 and $14 per passenger trip in most cities that tried it.

A focus on the goal of transporting the disabled, rather than one of modifying existing modes of transportation, might have avoided the costly installation of passenger lifts in buses. Indeed, speculating on alternative ways of reaching the goal could have produced a more effective solution (London 1986).

Just as it is important to agree on goals, it also is important to make sure that the goals are reasonable and achievable. It is also important to ascertain that the proposed program will help to achieve them.

BOX 5.8   GOAL MISFIT

In the late 1980s, locusts threatened the crops of many African nations. International aid agencies responded with $275 million and a fleet of aircraft that helped bomb crops with millions of liters of pesticides. A few years later, a report by the United States Office of Technology Assessment (OTA) said the campaign might have been a wasted effort. The OTA concluded: "Massive insecticide spraying ... tends to be inefficient in the short term, ineffective in the medium term, and misses the roots of the problem in the longer term." Moreover, the study suggested that the justification for the entire operation might have been flawed because locusts weren't as big a threat as had been thought (Gibbons 1990).

Proposals susceptible to benefit/cost analysis

Benefit/cost analysis has two general principles: (1) management should not adopt a proposal unless its benefits exceed its costs; and (2) when there are two competing proposals, the one with the greater excess of benefits over costs is preferable. To apply these principles, we must be able to relate benefits to costs.

Economic proposals

For many proposals in an LG, an analyst can estimate both benefits and costs in monetary terms. These economic proposals are similar to capital budgeting proposals in for-profit companies. The storm window proposal discussed earlier in the chapter, or a proposal to convert a heating plant from oil to gas, involves the same type of analysis in either a for-profit organization or an LG. Problems of this type are common to all organizations, and, while important administratively, they frequently have little programmatic impact.

Conversely, for proposals that have programmatic effects, analysts may have difficulty making monetary estimates of benefits. Frequently, the benefits are elusive, and analysts cannot reliably determine them.

Alternative ways of reaching the same objective

Even if benefits cannot be quantified in monetary terms, a benefit/cost analysis may be useful in situations where there are several ways to achieve a given objective. If each alternative would achieve the objective, then management ordinarily would prefer the one with the lowest cost. This approach does not require that the objective be stated in monetary terms, or even that it be quantified. Management need not measure the degree to which each alternative meets the objective, but only make the go/no-go judgment that any of the proposed alternatives will achieve it. Of these, it seeks the least costly.

BOX 5.9 SELECTING AMONG PROPOSALS WHEN BENEFITS NEED NOT BE MEASURED

The objective of one benefit/cost analysis was to provide the optimal ground transportation for passengers arriving and departing a city by air. Analysts estimated the costs of various airport locations and associated ground transport services. Senior management chose the proposal that provided adequate service with the lowest cost. There was no need to measure the benefits of "adequate service" in monetary terms.

Equal cost programs

If competing proposals have the same cost but one produces more benefits than the other, it ordinarily is the preferred alternative. This conclusion can be reached without measuring the absolute levels of benefits. Analysts often use such an approach to determine the best mix of resources in a program.

BOX 5.10 ALTERNATIVES WHERE BENEFITS ARE DIFFICULT TO MEASURE BUT HAVE THE SAME COST

Will €1,000,000 spent to hire more teachers produce more educational benefits than €1,000,000 spent on a combination of teachers and teaching machines, or €1,000,000 on team teaching rather than individual teaching? The analysis involves estimating the amount of resources that €1,000,000 will buy and a judgment of the results that will be achieved by using this amount and mix of resources. It requires only that benefits be expressed comparatively, however, not numerically.

Different objectives

A benefit/cost comparison of proposals intended to accomplish different objectives is likely to be of little value, perhaps even worthless. For example, an analysis that attempts to compare funds to be spent for primary school education with funds to be spent for municipal street maintenance is not worthwhile. Such an analysis would require assigning monetary values to the benefits of these two programs, which is an impossible task.

On the other hand, since funds are limited, policy makers must recognize that there is an opportunity cost for any given project. While experienced managers may have an intuitive feel for these opportunity costs *within* their departments, relatively few managers have sufficient experience or skill to make such tradeoffs *across* departments, particularly when those departments have disparate goals and clientele. Nor do many managers have the *authority* to make such tradeoffs. Funds that are not used for a pollution-control program, for example, are not necessarily available for a social welfare program.

Causal connection between cost and benefits

Many benefit/cost analyses implicitly assume a causal relationship between benefits and costs, i.e., that spending X euros (or dollars, or whatever currency) produces Y benefits. Unless a causal connection actually exists, such a benefit/cost analysis is fallacious.

BOX 5.11 NON-PLAUSIBLE CONNECTION BETWEEN COST AND BENEFITS

An agency defended its job retraining program with an analysis indicating that the program would lead participants to get new jobs, which would increase their

123

lifetime earnings by €25,000 per person. Thus, the €5,000 average cost per person trained seemed well justified. However, the assertion that the proposed program would indeed generate these benefits was completely unsupported; it was strictly a guess. There was no plausible link between the amount to be spent per person and the projected results.

Benefit/cost as a way of thinking

Because of difficulties in quantifying benefits, benefit/cost analysis is feasible for only a small portion of the problems that arise in an LG. These tend to be well-structured administrative-type problems. Nevertheless, a benefit/cost *way of thinking* is useful for a great many problems. One of the characteristics of competent managers is their ability to evaluate project proposals, at least in a general way, by comparing the expected benefits with the proposed costs. They may not be able to quantify the relationship, nor do they need to do so in many instances. Nevertheless, a benefit/cost analysis can help to distinguish factors that are relevant from those that are not.

Over-reliance on the benefit/cost approach

Benefit/cost thinking can be carried to extremes. If a manager rejects all proposals that show no causal connection between costs and benefits, lower-level managers may be reluctant to submit innovative program proposals. A primary characteristic of many new, experimental – and promising – schemes is that there is no way of estimating their benefit/cost relationships in advance. Undue insistence on a rigorous benefit/cost analyses can therefore result in overly conservative proposals. The risk of failure of an innovative proposal may be high, but it frequently is worth taking that risk if an LG wishes to serve its citizens in the best way possible. Clearly, considerable judgment is required in making a decision of this sort.

Whither benefit/cost analysis

Despite its limitations, a benefit/cost *approach* to programming may be better than any alternative. It may show that a proposal is outside a reasonable boundary in either direction – that it is obviously worthwhile or obviously not worth its cost from an economic standpoint. Unfortunately, this does not guarantee either its acceptance or rejection.

BOX 5.12   ECONOMIC VALUE OF LIFE VERSUS OPPORTUNITY COST

Several studies of the effect of a 55-mile-per-hour (90 kilometer per hour) speed limit in the United States showed that the benefits might not be worth the costs. Benefits were lives saved. Costs could be measured in terms of the additional time taken to reach a destination. Even when time was valued at a low amount per hour, and lives were given a high value, the costs exceeded the benefits in most of these studies.

QUANTIFYING THE VALUE OF A HUMAN BEING

In undertaking benefit/cost analyses, LG managers frequently encounter a complication that rarely is relevant in proposals in for-profit companies: the value of a human being. This dilemma arises because some programs are designed to save or prolong human lives. Such programs include fire prevention, automobile safety, preventive health care, and drug control. In these programs, the value of a human life, or of a workday lost to accident or illness, is a relevant consideration in measuring benefits.

Analysts are often squeamish about attaching a monetary value to a human life since there is a general belief in many cultures that life is priceless. Nevertheless, such a monetary amount often facilitates the analysis of certain proposals. In a world of scarce resources, it is not possible to spend unlimited amounts to save lives in general.

There are, of course, circumstances in which society is willing to devote significant resources to saving a specific life, as when hundreds of people, supported by helicopters and various high technology devices, are brought together to hunt for a child who is lost in the woods. In most situations, however, the focus is not on saving a single life, but rather on saving the lives of a class of people (such as motorcyclists or potential cancer victims).

Analytical approaches to valuation

There are several approaches to estimating the value of a human life, all of which present difficulties. One such approach discounts the expected future earnings of the person or persons affected by the program; this discounted present value presumably represents the person's *economic value* to his or her family, or to society. A related approach subtracts the person's food, clothing, and other costs from the earnings to find the net value of his or her life.

These two approaches frequently are used in litigation involving "wrongful deaths." They are relevant to cases involving deceased persons, automobile accidents, industrial pollution, or the release of toxic chemicals.

BOX 5.13 USING INJURIES AND FATALITIES TO EVALUATE THE COST OF LIVES

In an assessment of the costs of firearm injuries, the United States General Accounting Office (GAO) reported on a study that determined the average life-time cost of a firearm injury. The costs used in the study included actual dollar amounts spent for hospital and nursing home care, physician and other medical professional services, drugs and appliances, and rehabilitation. The cost estimates also included life-years lost, plus the indirect cost associated with loss of earnings from short- and long-term disability or premature death from injury. The study concluded that the average lifetime cost of a firearm fatality was $373,520, which the GAO called "the highest of any cause of injury." Using annual figures for injuries and deaths attributable to firearms, the GAO concluded that the estimated lifetime costs for accidental shootings was close to $1 billion every year (United States General Accounting Office 1991).

Among the problems encountered in applying these approaches is the difficulty of (a) estimating the amount of future earnings and related costs, (b) choosing the relevant time period, and (c) selecting an appropriate discount rate. Perhaps more important, these approaches tend to discriminate against persons with relatively low expected lifetime earnings, such as the elderly, homemakers, school teachers, ministers, artists, and college professors.[1]

A third analytical approach computes the value of a life in terms of society's willingness to spend money to prevent deaths. One might imagine, for example, that the development and enforcement of occupational safety regulations and building codes are based on benefit/cost comparisons. This is rarely the case, however. Spending on many of these programs frequently is based on emotional arguments or political posturing, as happens, for instance, when legislators suggest that economic costs are irrelevant for questions related to human lives.

A fourth approach seeks to measure the value people place on their own lives as indicated by, say, the amount they are willing to spend on life or disability insurance, or by risk premiums they require in order to work in hazardous occupations. This implies that these individuals' decisions are based on economic considerations, but many other considerations may be involved.[2]

BOX 5.14 ASKING INDIVIDUALS TO VALUE THEIR OWN LIVES

At one time, the exposure standard for benzene was ten parts per million averaged over an eight-hour working day. At this rate, one benzene worker would die of benzene-related cancer every third year. According to the United States Occupational Safety and Health Administration (OSHA), a standard of 1 part per million would have eliminated the risk, but would have cost $100 million annually for the 30,000 workers who were exposed to benzene.

One analyst asked the following questions: Would each of the 30,000 benzene workers be willing to pay $3,333 a year (his or her share of the $100 million) to eliminate the risk? If not, would the $100 million be better spent in a highway-improvement or cancer-screening program that could save more than one life every third year? (Rhoads 1985).

Alternatives to valuation

The *cost of saving* lives may be a useful way of choosing among alternative proposals even when it is not possible or feasible to measure the *value* of a life. Specifically, the alternative that saves the most lives per currency unit spent generally is considered preferable from an economic viewpoint.

BOX 5.15   USING COST PER LIFE SAVED TO ESTABLISH PROGRAM PRIORITIES

A highway administration might use the cost-per-life-saved approach to rank the attractiveness of various highway safety alternatives. Such an analysis is limited to judging whether a particular program saves more lives per currency unit (euros, dollars, etc.) spent than other lifesaving or life-prolonging programs. It does not attempt to assign a value to a life.

Appendix 5-C illustrates an approach to benefit/cost analysis that was used by one agency in its efforts to assess the value of a human life. The commentary at the end identifies several factors that analysts might consider in making a computation such as this.

LINKS TO OTHER ORGANIZATIONAL ACTIVITIES

Beyond its role as a phase of the management control process, programming is directly or indirectly linked to several other activities of importance to an LG's senior management. Recognizing these linkages is essential if the programming phase is to be as effective as possible.

Link to strategy formulation

Programs are among the most readily observable aspects of an LG's strategy. Thus, if new programs and new capital expenditures are to remain consistent with strategy, line managers must understand the linkages between their programs and the LG's overall strategic directions. Indeed, if an LG's strategy is to evolve over time because of shifting citizen needs, senior management must find ways to monitor and manage its programs so they remain consistent with, and supportive of, the evolving strategy.

Link to culture

Programming also can be an especially important tool for managing an LG's culture in that senior management can use it to influence the basic assumptions of decision making. For example, the constraints senior management establishes on programming and the way it makes use of the "programming purse" can have a profound impact on line managers' understanding of what is acceptable and unacceptable in the organization. This, in turn, can help to either maintain or change the organization's culture (Young 2000).

Link to conflict management

Because many of the benefits of new program proposals are difficult to quantify, and because line managers tend to be quite optimistic about their program proposals, a *new program bias* tends to characterize the programming phase of the management control process. In particular, many proposals tend to overestimate financial cash flows and some may underestimate the investment amount.

Senior management typically counteracts this bias by using its staff to analyze the proposals. When this happens, there can be considerable friction between line managers and the staff. Designing a conflict management process to deal with this friction so that the final result is a tough but realistic analysis is one of the most challenging tasks senior management faces in the programming phase of the management control process.

Link to authority and influence

There is an internal political dimension to programming, which is not always well understood. For a variety of reasons, some managers may have the "ear" of senior management, or they may run units or programs that are seen as key to the LG's future, or they may simply be more articulate or more forceful than some of their colleagues. As a result, they may receive a favorable decision on a proposed project that has a much lower IRR than a project in another unit with a manger who, for one reason or another, is not seen in such a favorable light. There is not much that can be done about this; it is simply a fact of organizational life.

SUMMARY

LG's managers frequently must choose between two or more competing program proposals. When this happens, an attempt to quantify both benefits and costs usually can assist in the decision-making effort.

When two or more proposals have roughly the same benefits, the comparison is relatively easy since only costs need to be calculated. Similarly, when competing proposals have the same costs but one clearly produces more benefits than the other, the decision usually is quite easy. The decision becomes complicated when benefits and costs extend over several years (as is the case with almost all proposed new programs and capital investments), and when competing proposals have both different benefits and different costs.

When both benefits and costs can be expressed easily in monetary terms, calculating either a NPV or an IRR can facilitate a decision. When these analytical techniques are being used, the choice of a discount rate is a key decision; many relatively undesirable projects have been undertaken because analysts have used a discount rate that was too low.

Frequently, benefits and costs cannot be expressed easily in monetary terms. This happens, for example, when managers attempt to incorporate risk into the analysis, since risk is inherently difficult to measure. It also happens when managers attempt to quantify the value of a human being, and include that in the analysis. Additionally, there are a variety of other non-quantitative considerations that are part of almost every proposed program. In all instances, managers must be careful not to allow the quantitative factors to dominate the decision. They need to recognize that their judgment occasionally must override the results of the quantitative analysis.

APPENDIX 5-A THE CONCEPT OF PRESENT VALUE

The concept of present value rests on the principle that money has a time value, such that a dollar received one year from today is worth less than a dollar received today. To illustrate the concept, consider the following: *A colleague offers to pay you $1,000 one year from today. How much will you lend her today?*

Presumably, unless you were a good friend or somewhat altruistic, you would not lend your colleague $1,000 today. You could invest your $1,000, earn something on it over the course of the year, and have more than $1,000 a year from now. If, for example, you could earn 10 percent on your money, you could invest your $1,000 and

129

have $1,100 in a year. Alternatively, if you had $909, and invested it at 10 percent, you would have $1,000 a year from today.

Thus, if your colleague offers to pay you $1,000 a year from today, and you are an investor expecting a 10 percent return, you most likely would lend her only $909 today. With a 10 percent interest rate, $909 is the *present value* of $1,000 received one year hence.

Under the same circumstances as the previous question, how much would you lend your colleague if she offered to pay you $1,000 two years from today?

Here we must incorporate the concept of *compound interest*, i.e., the fact that interest is earned on interest. For example, at a 10 percent rate, $826 invested today would accumulate to roughly $1,000 in two years, as shown by the following:

Interest earned in year 1: $826 × 0.10 = $82.60
Interest earned in year 2: ($826 + $82.60) × 0.10 = $90.86
Interest earned for 2 years: $82.60 + $90.86 = $173.46
Total in hand at end of Year 2 (interest + investment): = $173.46 + $826 = $999.46

Thus, you would be willing to lend her $826.

The previous question consisted of a promise to pay a given amount two years from today with no intermediate payments. Another possibility is the situation where your colleague offers to pay you $1,000 a year from today and another $1,000 2 years from today. How much would you lend her now?

The answer requires combining the analyses in each of the above two examples. Specifically, for the $1,000 received 2 years from now, you would lend her $826, and for the $1,000 received one year from now you would lend her $909. Thus, you would lend her a total of $1,735.

Our ability to make these computations is simplified by the use of present value factor (PVF) tables. Table 5.1, "Present Value of $1," is used to determine the present value of a single payment received at some specified time in the future. For instance, we could find the answer to the first question above by looking in the column for 10 percent and the row for one year; this gives us 0.909. Multiplying 0.909 by $1,000 gives us the $909 we would lend our colleague. Similarly, if we look in the row for 2 years and multiply the entry of 0.826 by $1,000, we arrive at the answer to the second question: $826.

Table 5.2, "Present Value of $1 Received Annually for N Years," is used for even payments received over a given period. Looking at Table 5.2, we can see that the present value of 1.735 (for a payment of $1 received each year for 2 years at 10 percent) multiplied by $1,000 is $1,735. This is the amount we calculated in answering the third question above. We also can see that the 1.735 is the sum of the two amounts shown on Table 5.1 (0.909 for one year hence, and 0.826 for 2 years hence). Thus, Table 5.2 simply sums the various elements in Table 5.1 to facilitate calculations.

Table 5.1 Present value of $1 (or €1, or any other currency)

Years hence	Interest rate																			
	1%	2%	4%	6%	8%	10%	12%	14%	15%	16%	18%	20%	22%	24%	25%	26%	28%	30%
1	0.990	0.980	0.962	0.943	0.926	0.909	0.893	0.877	0.870	0.862	0.847	0.833	0.820	0.806	0.800	0.794	0.781	0.769
2	0.980	0.961	0.925	0.890	0.857	0.826	0.797	0.769	0.756	0.743	0.718	0.694	0.672	0.650	0.640	0.630	0.610	0.592
3	0.971	0.942	0.889	0.840	0.794	0.751	0.712	0.675	0.658	0.641	0.609	0.579	0.551	0.524	0.512	0.500	0.477	0.455
4	0.961	0.924	0.855	0.792	0.735	0.683	0.636	0.592	0.572	0.552	0.516	0.482	0.451	0.423	0.410	0.397	0.373	0.350
5	0.951	0.906	0.822	0.747	0.681	0.621	0.567	0.519	0.497	0.476	0.437	0.402	0.370	0.341	0.328	0.315	0.291	0.269
6	0.942	0.888	0.790	0.705	0.630	0.564	0.507	0.456	0.432	0.410	0.370	0.335	0.303	0.275	0.262	0.250	0.227	0.207
7	0.933	0.871	0.760	0.665	0.583	0.513	0.452	0.400	0.376	0.354	0.314	0.279	0.249	0.222	0.210	0.198	0.178	0.159
8	0.923	0.853	0.731	0.627	0.540	0.467	0.404	0.351	0.327	0.305	0.266	0.233	0.204	0.179	0.168	0.157	0.139	0.123
9	0.914	0.837	0.703	0.592	0.500	0.424	0.361	0.308	0.284	0.263	0.225	0.194	0.167	0.144	0.134	0.125	0.108	0.094
10	0.905	0.820	0.676	0.558	0.463	0.386	0.322	0.270	0.247	0.227	0.191	0.162	0.137	0.116	0.107	0.099	0.085	0.073
11	0.896	0.804	0.650	0.527	0.429	0.350	0.287	0.237	0.215	0.195	0.162	0.135	0.112	0.094	0.086	0.079	0.066	0.056
12	0.887	0.788	0.625	0.497	0.397	0.319	0.257	0.208	0.187	0.168	0.137	0.112	0.092	0.076	0.069	0.062	0.052	0.043
13	0.879	0.773	0.601	0.469	0.368	0.290	0.229	0.182	0.163	0.145	0.116	0.093	0.075	0.061	0.055	0.050	0.040	0.033
14	0.870	0.758	0.577	0.442	0.340	0.263	0.205	0.160	0.141	0.125	0.099	0.078	0.062	0.049	0.044	0.039	0.032	0.025
15	0.861	0.743	0.555	0.417	0.315	0.239	0.183	0.140	0.123	0.108	0.084	0.065	0.051	0.040	0.035	0.031	0.025	0.020

Table 5.2 Present value of $1 (or €1, or any other currency) received annually for N years

Years N	Interest rate																	
	1%	2%	4%	6%	8%	10%	12%	14%	15%	16%	18%	20%	22%	24%	25%	26%	28%	30%
1	0.990	0.980	0.962	0.943	0.926	0.909	0.893	0.877	0.870	0.862	0.847	0.833	0.820	0.806	0.800	0.794	0.781	0.769
2	1.970	1.941	1.887	1.833	1.783	1.735	1.690	1.646	1.626	1.605	1.565	1.527	1.492	1.456	1.440	1.424	1.391	1.361
3	2.941	2.883	2.776	2.673	2.577	2.486	2.402	2.321	2.284	2.246	2.174	2.106	2.043	1.980	1.952	1.924	1.868	1.816
4	3.902	3.807	3.631	3.465	3.312	3.169	3.038	2.913	2.856	2.798	2.690	2.588	2.494	2.403	2.362	2.321	2.241	2.166
5	4.853	4.713	4.453	4.212	3.993	3.790	3.605	3.432	3.353	3.274	3.127	2.990	2.864	2.744	2.690	2.636	2.532	2.435
6	5.795	5.601	5.243	4.917	4.623	4.354	4.112	3.888	3.785	3.684	3.497	3.325	3.167	3.019	2.952	2.886	2.759	2.642
7	6.728	6.472	6.003	5.582	5.206	4.867	4.564	4.288	4.161	4.038	3.811	3.604	3.416	3.241	3.162	3.084	2.937	2.801
8	7.651	7.325	6.734	6.209	5.746	5.334	4.968	4.639	4.488	4.343	4.077	3.837	3.620	3.420	3.330	3.241	3.076	2.924
9	8.565	8.162	7.437	6.801	6.246	5.758	5.329	4.947	4.772	4.606	4.302	4.031	3.787	3.564	3.464	3.366	3.184	3.018
10	9.470	8.982	8.113	7.359	6.709	6.144	5.651	5.217	5.019	4.833	4.493	4.193	3.924	3.680	3.571	3.465	3.269	3.091
11	10.366	9.786	8.763	7.886	7.138	6.494	5.938	5.454	5.234	5.028	4.655	4.328	4.036	3.774	3.657	3.544	3.335	3.147
12	11.253	10.574	9.388	8.383	7.535	6.813	6.195	5.662	5.421	5.196	4.792	4.440	4.128	3.850	3.726	3.606	3.387	3.190
13	12.132	11.347	9.989	8.852	7.903	7.103	6.424	5.844	5.584	5.341	4.908	4.533	4.203	3.911	3.781	3.656	3.427	3.223
14	13.002	12.105	10.566	9.294	8.243	7.366	6.629	6.004	5.725	5.466	5.007	4.611	4.265	3.960	3.825	3.695	3.459	3.248
15	13.863	12.848	11.121	9.711	8.558	7.605	6.812	6.144	5.848	5.574	5.091	4.676	4.316	4.000	3.860	3.726	3.484	3.268

APPENDIX 5-B SELECTING A DISCOUNT RATE

Selecting an appropriate discount rate requires computing a weighted cost of capital (WCC) and comparing it to a weighted return on assets (WRA). Each is discussed below, along with some of the associated complications. The balance sheet on which the computations are based is contained in Table 5.3. This is for a large nonprofit organization, rather than an LG, but there are few differences of any importance between the two.

Weighted cost of capital

The computations for the WCC are contained in the top portion of Table 5.4. The process is as follows:

1. Compute each liability's weight. For example, bonds are 0.188 or 18.8 percent of total liabilities and equity ($8,300 ÷ $44,160). If the computations are done properly, the weights will sum to 1.000 (or 100 percent).
2. Determine each liability's interest rate. For example, the bonds have an interest rate of 7 percent.
3. Multiply the interest rate by the weight in Step 1 to determine a weighted rate (0.013 or 1.3 percent for bonds).
4. Sum the weighted rates to get the WCC. Here it is 0.065 or 6.5 percent.

Table 5.3 Balance sheet for a large nonprofit organization ($000)

Assets		Liabilities and equity	
Current assets		*Current liabilities*	
Cash	$1,155	Accounts payable	$12,307
Accounts receivable	7,742	Current portion of mortgage	1,160
Inventory	10,010		13,467
Prepaid expenses	4,644	*Long-term liabilities*	
	23,551	Bonds (7%)	8,300
Non-current assets		Mortgage (9%)	5,339
Property, plant and equipment (net)	20,609		13,639
		Equity	
		Permanently restricted net assets	11,000
		Unrestricted net assets	6,054
			17,054
Total	$44,160	Total	$44,160

133

Table 5.4 Weighted cost of capital and weighted return on assets

Liabilities and equity	Amount ($000)	Weight	Rate	Weighted rate
Weighted cost of capital (WCC)				
Current liabilities				
Accounts payable	$12,307	0.279	0.00	0.000
Current portion of mortgage	1,160	0.026	0.09	0.002
Long-term liabilities				
Bonds	8,300	0.188	0.07	0.013
Mortgage	5,339	0.121	0.09	0.011
Equity				
Permanently restricted net assets	11,000	0.249	0.10^1	0.025
Unrestricted net assets	6,054	0.137	0.10^1	0.014
Total	$44,160	1.000		**0.065**
Weighted return on assets (WRA)				
Current assets				
Cash	$1,155	0.026	0.10^2	0.003
Accounts receivable	7,742	0.175	0.00	0.000
Inventory	10,010	0.227	0.00	0.000
Prepaid expenses	4,644	0.105	0.00	0.000
Non-current assets				
Property, plant, and equipment (net)	20,609	0.467	0.13	0.062
Total	$44,160	1.000		**0.065**

Notes

1 Assumed to be the organization's desired return on equity (ROE).

2 Assumed to be the return on the organization's invested cash.

Note that the interest rate used for equity was 10 percent. As Note 1 indicates, this was assumed to be the organization's desired return on equity (ROE). In many nonprofit organizations, selecting the appropriate rate is a subject of great debate.

The WCC tells us what, on average, it is costing us to finance our assets. Over time, we need to be earning at least that rate on our assets if we are to remain financially viable; otherwise, we are atrophying.

However, not all assets earn a return. Therefore, we also must compute a WRA to determine what our plant and equipment assets need to earn.

Weighted return on assets

The computations for the WRA are shown in the lower portion of Table 5.4. The process is as follows:

1   Compute each asset's weight. For example, cash is 0.026 (2.6 percent) of total assets. Again, the weights need to sum to 1.0 (100%).

2   Determine the returns of all assets except the Property, Plant and Equipment (PP&E) account. Current assets other than investments usually do not earn anything, for example. Assume, for purposes of these computations, that all cash is invested, and earns 10 percent, as indicated in Note 2.

3   Insert the WCC (here it is 6.5 percent) as the total WRA, and then determine what the weighted rate for PP&E must be to achieve it. To do so, we subtract from 6.5 the weighted return on our invested cash (plus the weighted return on any other assets, such as investments). The result here is that the weighted return on PP&E must be 6.2 percent.

4   Using the weight for PP&E from Step 1 (0.467 or 46.7 percent here), and the weighted rate from Step 3 (0.062 or 6.2 percent in this case), compute the absolute rate that is needed for PP&E projects on average. In this case, it is 0.13 (13 percent). Therefore, our PP&E assets must earn a 13 percent return if our overall ROA is to be equal to the 6.5 percent WCC. The 13 percent becomes our basic discount rate.

There are three issues to keep in mind when using this approach:

1   Some new PP&E projects will not yield the required return (13 percent here). Some plant renovations, for example, will probably lead to very little additional cash flow (although there may be some savings in utilities or in repairs and maintenance). This means that we will need to find some projects that give us greater than a 13 percent return if we are to subsidize those that do not.

2   This analysis is based on a weighted cost of capital of 6.5 percent. As we undertake additional borrowing, or as our composition of liabilities changes, our weighted cost of capital will change. This means that our required ROA also will change. As a practical matter, these changes ordinarily will be rather small.

3   To include the effects of the above changes, some organizations use a forecasted weighted cost of capital. That is, they decide (a) how much borrowing they are planning to do for the upcoming year, (b) any shift in the mix of their current liabilities, and (c) what rates they will pay for newly borrowed funds. They then use that information to compute the forecasted WCC for the upcoming year. Of course, this is only for one year in the future, and new assets will last for much longer, but it is more realistic than using an historical WCC.

APPENDIX 5-C EXAMPLE OF A PROGRAM THAT ASSESSES THE VALUE OF A HUMAN LIFE[3]

Some years ago, a task force was established to review the results of a program analysis. The task force had been asked to evaluate a series of benefit/cost analyses for nine Motor Vehicle Injury Prevention Programs, as well as eight such analyses that had been made for public health programs dealing with such diseases as arthritis, cancer, tuberculosis, and syphilis.

Mr. Harley Davidson had been given specific responsibility to evaluate the methodology and results of the benefit/cost analysis for Motor Vehicle Injury Prevention Program #4, and to recommend whether the analysis justified the proposed level of funding. Program #4 was designed to prevent accidental deaths due to head injuries of motorcycle riders through use of improved safety devices. The program comprised four phases. Each was identified separately, although all would be closely coordinated and carried out simultaneously.

1 A national education program on the use of protective headgear aimed primarily at motorcycle users. It also would include efforts to prepare operators of other motor vehicles to share the road with motorcycles.
2 A cooperative program with other national organizations and the motorcycle industry to improve protective and safety devices.
3 A coordinated effort, in conjunction with state and local health departments and medical organizations, to design programs and activities that would minimize injury and death in motorcycle accidents.
4 A surveillance activity on appropriate aspects of motorcycle accidents and injuries.

The program unit was estimated to require $8 million of funding over a five-year period (or $7.4 million when discounted at 4 percent). Table 5.5 summarizes how the proposed funds would be spent.

As Table 5.6 indicates, the benefit/cost study estimated that the program would result in saving 4,006 lives over the five-year period (no reduction in injuries was considered), resulting in a cost-per-death-averted of $1,852.

As Table 5.6 also shows, the benefits of the program, based on the lifetime earnings of the 4,006 individuals whose deaths would be averted, discounted at 3 percent, were estimated at $412.8 million. Hence, the benefit/cost ratio was 55.6 to 1. Similar computations are shown in Table 5.6 for the other programs.

Methodology

The rationale for the benefit/cost analysis such was to allow for a meaningful comparison of the changes in a given situation as a result of introducing alternative programs. To bring about this state of affairs, a measurable common denominator was used for rating program outcome and program costs. This common denominator was dollars. Granting the existence of the common denominator, there needed to be, in addition, a point on which to take a "fix" in order to support the contention that the changes had, in fact, taken place. This point established the baseline, and then shifted in relation to changes coming about via the program.

Table 5.5 *Proposed budget for program ($000)*

	Year 1	Year 2	Year 3	Year 4	Year 5	Totals
Central office staff	13	13	13	13	13	
Regional office staff	9	9	9	9	9	
State assignees	20	20	20	20	20	
Total staff and assignees	42	42	42	42	42	
Personnel costs	$504	$504	$504	$504	$504	$2,520
Non-personnel costs						
Evaluation and surveillance	$300	$300	$300	$300	$300	
State projects[1]	500	500	500	500	500	
National TV spots	60	60	60	60	60	
Educational TV series	100	100	100	100	100	
Safety films	40	40	20	20	20	
Publications	100	30	30	30	30	
Exhibits	30	30	15	15	15	
Community projects	25	25	25	25	25	
Campus projects	20	20	20	15	15	
	$1,175	$1,105	$1,070	$1,065	$1,065	$5,480
Total program costs	**$1,679**	**$1,609**	**$1,574**	**$1,569**	**$1,569**	**$8,000**

Note
1 Ten projects at $50,000 each.

In this exercise the baseline was created by assessing past rates for motor vehicle and pedestrian deaths and injuries. The assumption was made that the current level of program effort in the agency would remain constant for the five years of the program. The observed trend was then projected and applied to the anticipated population distribution for the five-year period.

Program costs and savings due to the introduction of the program were limited to the five-year period. The required common denominator was incorporated into the baseline by converting fatalities into lost earnings. Throughout this analysis, the total dollar costs and benefit for the five-year period were discounted to Year 1, the program's base year, to convert the stream of costs and benefits into its worth in the base year.

There are a number of variables that can contribute to the occurrence of a vehicular accident and its resultant injury or death. The skill of the driver, the condition of the road, the speed of the vehicle, the vehicle's condition, the failure to have or to use safety devices were just a few of many that were mentioned in the literature. What the analysts' knew about vehicular accidents was expressed in terms of these variables and, as a consequence, program formulations were generally placed in the

Table 5.6 Costs and benefits for all programs studied

Program description	Discounted program cost ($000)	Discounted program savings ($000)	Benefit/ cost ratio	Reduction in injuries	Reduction in deaths	Cost per death averted
Motor vehicle injury prevention programs:						
1 Increase seat belt use	$2,019	$2,728,374	1,351.3	1,904,000	22,930	$88
2 Use of improved restraint devices	610	681,452	1,117.1	471,600	5,811	105
3 Reduce pedestrian injury	1,061	153,110	144.3	142,700	1,650	643
4 *Increase use of protective devices by motorcyclists*	*7,419*	*412,754*	*55.6*	*—*	*4,006*	*1,852*
5 Improve driving environment	28,545	1,409,891	49.4	1,015,500	12,250	2,330
6 Reduce driver drinking	28,545	612,970	21.5	440,630	5,340	5,346
7 Improve driver licensing	6,113	22,938	3.8	23,200	442	13,830
8 Improve emergency medical services[1]	721,478	1,726,000	2.4	—	16,000	45,092
9 Improve driver training	750,550	1,287,022	1.7	665,300	8,515	88,144
Other public health programs:						
1 Arthritis	35,000	1,489,000	42.5	n.a.	n.a.	n.a.
2 Syphilis[2]	179,300	2,993,000	16.7	n.a.	11,590	15,470
3 Uterine cervix cancer[2]	118,100	1,071,000	9.1	n.a.	34,200	3,453
4 Lung cancer[2]	47,000	268,000	5.7	n.a.	7,000	6,714
5 Breast cancer	22,400	101,000	4.5	n.a.	2,396	9,349
6 Tuberculosis	130,000	573,000	4.4	n.a.	5,700	22,807
7 Head and neck cancer	7,800	9,000	1.2	n.a.	268	29,104
8 Colon-rectum cancer	7,300	4,000	0.5	n.a.	170	42,941

Notes: 1 Includes $300 million in state matching funds. This program does not reduce injury; however, it is estimated to reduce hospital bed days by 2,401,000 and work loss days by 8,180. 2 Funding shown used as basis for analysis; includes funds estimated to come from sources other than DHHS. n.a. = not available.

context of managing these variables, either singly or in combination. A program unit, as developed by the task force, usually addressed a single variable.

Two links were needed to compute the benefit/cost analysis in vehicular accidents. The first was associated with the estimate of reduction that could be realized if a given variable were addressed by a program of some sort. This link was supplied in vehicular accidents by the expertise of the task force members and recourse to studies on the particular variable in question.

The second link was associated with the effectiveness of the program proposed to bring about the estimated reduction. In vehicular accidents this was supplied by the experience with programs of the task force members and the success in the past of similar programs devoted to public health problems.

With the baseline and common denominator established, the task force was able to examine the potential payoff for a variety of program units even though these units differed with respect to such factors as cost of implementation, target group to be reached, method to be employed, and facet of the total program addressed by the proposed program. In addition, by establishing a baseline and using techniques to convert all elements of the equation to a common denominator, the task force was able to focus its energies on the alternative program units.

Estimate of benefits

In accordance with the above requirements, the benefit/cost studies of the motor vehicle injury prevention programs began with the stipulation that the baseline was the number of deaths and injuries to be expected if the level of effort remained constant. Next, an estimate was made of the number of deaths and injuries that would be avoided if the proposed program were adopted. Finally, the reduction in deaths and injuries was translated into dollar terms. These three steps, as they applied to Program Unit #4, were carried out as follows.

The baseline

The team working on the Program Unit #4 had available the information given in Table 5.7. The team estimated that the number of registered motorcycles would continue to increase at an increasing rate, and assumed that the death rate in the first year of the program would decline, even in the absence of new safety programs, to a level of 110 deaths per 100,000 registered motorcycles. Table 5.8 shows the number of motorcycle accident deaths that were expected without the safety program. (The projection for 2.9 million registered motorcycles was based on the fact that several years were expected to elapse from two years ago until Program Year #1.)

139

Table 5.7 Historical data on motorcycle registrations and fatalities

Time period	Total number of registered motorcycles	Number of deaths from motorcycle accidents	Rate of deaths per 100,000 motorcycles
Seven years ago	565,352	752	133.0
Six years ago	569,691	730	128.1
Five years ago	595,669	697	117.0
Four years ago	660,400	759	114.9
Three years ago	786,318	882	112.2
Two years ago	984,760	1,118	113.5

Table 5.8 Projected baseline case

Program year	Projected total number of registered motorcycles	Projected number of deaths from motorcycle accidents without program (based on 110 deaths per 100,000 registered motorcycles)
1	2,900,000	3,190
2	3,500,000	3,850
3	4,200,000	4,620
4	5,000,000	5,500
5	6,000,000	6,600
		23,760

Effectiveness of the program unit

Calculation of the anticipated reduction in the number of deaths resulting from the proposed program unit involved two separate estimates: (1) the effectiveness of the program in persuading motorcyclists to wear helmets and protective eye shields, and (2) the effectiveness of these devices in reducing deaths (injuries were not considered in the analysis of this program unit). The team's judgment was that the program would result in use of helmets and eye shields to the degree shown in Table 5.9.

In assessing the second factor – the effectiveness of protective devices in reducing deaths – the team relied on a study that had been conducted in an Australian local government entitled "Effect of Compulsory Safety Helmets on Motorcycle Accident Fatalities." This study reported that the number of motorcycle fatalities occurring in the Australian state of Victoria in the 2 years following the effective date of a law requiring the wearing of helmets was only 31 while the number of fatalities projected on the basis of the experience of the 2 preceding years was 62.5, for a reduction of

Table 5.9 *Estimated effectiveness of program in encouraging protective devices*

Year	Estimated percentage of motorcyclists using helmets and eye shields
1	20
2	30
3	40
4	50
5	55

Table 5.10 *Estimated reduction in deaths from proposed program*

Year	Projected number of deaths from motorcycle accidents without program	Estimated percentage reduction in deaths with program[1]	Estimated reduction in number of deaths with program
1	3,190	8	255
2	3,850	12	462
3	4,620	16	739
4	5,500	20	1,100
5	6,600	22	1,450
Total	23,760		4,006

Note

1 Example: Multiplying 20 percent from Table 5.9 by 40 percent (from the Australian study) gives 8 percent, which is the number used for Year 1 in this table.

about 50 percent. Other states, which did not have such a law, had shown a reduction of about 12 percent in the same period, a difference of 38 percent. The task force concluded that 100 percent usage of helmets and eye shields by motorcyclists would reduce the number of deaths by about 40 percent.

Multiplying the figures for projected usage of protective devices given in Table 5.9 by 40 percent gave the estimated percentage reduction in deaths. Applying these percentages to the baseline data of Table 5.8 gave the estimated reduction in number of deaths shown in Table 5.10.

Conversion to economic benefits

For the purpose of calculating the lifetime earnings lost in the event of a motorcycle fatality, the team needed to estimate the distribution of fatalities by age and sex. Five years earlier, approximately 90 percent of the victims of motorcycle accidents had

141

Table 5.11 *Estimated reduction in deaths by age and sex*

Year	Age 15–24		Age 25–34		Total
	Males	Females	Males	Females	
1	207	23	22	3	255
2	374	42	41	5	462
3	598	67	67	7	739
4	891	99	99	11	1,100
5	1,174	131	130	15	1,450
Total	3,244	362	359	41	4,006

been male and 10 percent female; about 90 percent had been in the 15–24 age group, and 10 percent in the 25–34 age group. The data were not cross classified, so the team needed to assume that the sex distribution of fatalities in each age group was the same as the overall distribution, i.e., 90:10.

Projecting these percentages into the future, the team calculated that, of the 255 fatalities that the proposed program expected to avoid in Year 1, 207 would be males between 15 and 24 (i.e., $0.9 \times 0.9 \times 255$). Combining this procedure for all categories and years resulted in the estimates of the distribution of death reductions over the five-year period shown in Table 5.11.

The final step in calculating the expected benefits of the proposed program was to assign the appropriate dollar benefits to the above estimates of decreases in deaths by age group and sex. This was done by multiplying the decrease in deaths in each sex-age group "cell" in the above exhibit by the applicable discounted lifetime earnings figure for that particular cell.

Table 5.12 shows lifetime earnings by age and sex (discounted at 3 percent) that the team used to compute the dollar benefits of reduced motorcycle accident fatalities. (Its report contained a detailed description of the methodology used in deriving these amounts.)

The number of deaths saved in each cell of Table 5.11 was multiplied by the appropriate earnings figure from Table 5.12, and then discounted at 3 percent to the base year. For example, the team estimated that, in Year 1, the lives of three females between the ages of 25 and 34 would be saved. The discounted lifetime earnings of females in this age group was found from Table 5.12 by averaging the discounted lifetime earnings for females 25–29 and 30–34, the average of $81,702 and $77,888 being $79,795. This was multiplied by three (the number of females in that group) to give a total of $239,385. Using a present value factor of one (since Year 1 was the base year), the resulting figure was $239,385. Similarly, discounted figures were obtained for each year by age group and sex; the results are shown in Table 5.13.

Thus, over the five-year program period, the team estimated that 4,006 deaths could be averted at a present-value cost of $7,419,000. The present value of the

Table 5.12 Discounted lifetime earnings by age and sex

Age	Males	Females
Under 1	$84,371	$50,842
1–4	98,986	54,636
5–9	105,836	63,494
10–14	122,933	73,719
15–19	139,729	81,929
20–24	150,536	84,152
25–29	150,512	81,702
30–34	141,356	77,888

Table 5.13 Discounted savings resulting from the program ($000)

Year	Total	Age 15–24		Age 25–34	
		Males	Females	Males	Females
1	$36,140	$30,347	$1,976	$3,578	$239
2	61,972	52,423	3,282	5,895	372
3	97,152	82,363	5,059	9,248	482
4	39,547	17,928	7,408	13,393	818
5	177,943	150,941	9,439	16,600	963
Total	$412,754	$334,002	$27,164	$48,714	$2,874

lifetime earnings of the 4,006 persons whose lives would be saved during this period was shown to be $412,754,000.

These data were summarized into the two measures of program effectiveness shown in Table 5.6: Program cost per death averted of $1,852 (7,419,000 ÷ 4,006), and a benefit/cost ratio of 55.6 ($412,754,000 ÷ $7,419,000).

Commentary

One could identify any number of potential problems with the methodology in this benefit/cost analysis that attempts to value a human life. First, and perhaps the most serious, is the implausibility of a connection between the program's costs and benefits. For example, $60,000 spent on TV spots and $1,000,000 on TV educational materials would permit ten minutes at $10,000 per minute, or 100 minutes at $1,000 per minute (with the cheapest production available). How many, if any, motorcyclists will change their behavior with this amount of persuasion? By contrast, the annual advertising budget for soft drinks runs into the hundreds of millions of dollars.

143

Second, a basic assumption here is that an appropriate measure of benefits is lifetime earnings. It is true that earnings contribute to GNP, but do they really reflect the benefit of a person to society? If so, then the cost of supporting an individual during his or her lifetime should perhaps also be considered; this would reduce the benefits substantially.

Third, another way of looking at his issue is by comparing the motorcycle program with the program for lung cancer. As shown in Table 5.6, this latter program has a benefit/cost ratio of 5.7, or only one-tenth of the benefit-cost ratio of the motorcycle program. A major reason, of course, is that lung cancer affects people later in life when they have fewer earnings years ahead of them. On the other hand, those dying of cancer often have families to support whereas those dying in motorcycle accidents often don't; the fact that their earnings are lost over a longer period of time may actually be of little social consequence.

Fourth, the use of discounting suggests that is worth more to society to prevent a death today than one ten years from now. Is that a reasonable position? Or should society be neutral among the various generations?

Finally, of course, the analysis suggests that the change lever should be education, but the agency could do what many LGs (or regions or nations) have done – propose (and presumably pass) a law that *requires* motorcyclists to use helmets. This no doubt would cost less than $8 million to implement, and quite likely would be more effective.

DISCUSSION QUESTIONS

1 How should the interest rate for "equity" be determined in an LG?
2 Should an LG attempt to determine its return on its assets? If not, why not? If so, how much should it be?
3 Is life priceless? If so, why should an LG attempt to quantify the value of a human being? If not, how should an LG go about determining its worth?

NOTES

1 Ralph Estes makes an attempt to adjust for some of these factors in *Estes®
Economic Loss Tables* (1991). He provides separate data for different education levels, different genders, whites and nonwhites, persons with and without established earnings histories, and for persons who earn the minimum wage.

2 For many years, the British Foreign Service paid a 25 percent salary supplement to employees who worked in Washington, DC. The summer heat and humidity were considered to be so severe that the supplement was deemed necessary to retain the most qualified workers (or perhaps all of the workers).

3 This appendix was adapted from the case *Disease Control Programs*, prepared by Professor Charles J. Christenson: the case is in the public domain, and may be obtained from The Crimson Press Curriculum Center (www.TheCrimsonGroup.org).

REFERENCES

Estes, R.W. (1991) *Estes Economic Loss Tables: Tables for Estimating Economic Loss in Cases of Wrongful Death and Personal Injury*, Washington, DC: A.U. Publishing.

Gibbons, A. (1990) "Overkilling the Insect Enemy," *Science*, August 10: 621.

London, A.L. (1986) "Transportation Services for the Disabled," *The GAO Review*, Spring: 21–7.

Povoledo, E. (2011) *New York Times/International Herald Tribune*, 25 May.

Rhoads, S.E. (1985) "Kind Hearts and Opportunity Costs," *Across the Board*, December: 40–7.

Toronto Transit Commission (2007) *2008–2012 Capital Program and 10-Year Capital Forecast*. Available HTTP: http://www.ttc.ca/postings/gso-comrpt/documents/report/f3405/_conv.htm (accessed July 22, 2011).

United States General Accounting Office (1991) *Accidental Shootings: Many Deaths and Injuries Caused by Firearms Could be Prevented*, Report to the Chairman, Subcommittee on Antitrust, Monopolies, and Business Rights, Committee of the Judiciary, United States Senate, Washington, DC, March.

Young, D.W. (1982) "Nonprofits Need Surplus Too," *Harvard Business Review*, 60(1): 124–31.

Young, D.W. (2000) "The Six Levers for Managing Organizational Culture," *Business Horizons*, 43(5): 19–28.

FURTHER READING

In this book we do not address any of the variety of political issues that frequently play pivotal roles in programming decisions. Therefore some readers may find it useful to have a general understanding of the interaction between politics and management. For this perspective, see the fourth chapter of *The Essential Public Manager* by Christopher Pollitt (Open University Press 2003). Net present value and its related concepts, such as the statistical analysis of risk, can be further studied in any good book on the principles of corporate finance, such as *Principles of Corporate Finance* by Richard A.

Brealey, Stewart C. Myers, and Franklin Allen (9th edn, McGraw-Hill Higher Education 2007). The use of these techniques also may be applied in programs concerning project financing in public-private partnerships. A good source, as well as an excellent reference book for the general issue of project financing, is *Project Finance in Theory and Practice* by Stefano Gatti (Academic Press 2007). For a closer examination of benefit/cost analysis, with specific reference to theoretical issues, the problem of ascribing a monetary value to various items, and the presentation of case studies, the reader might consider *Cost–Benefit Analysis*, edited by Richard Layard and Stephen Glaister (Oxford University Press 1994).

Chapter 6

Budgeting

LEARNING OBJECTIVES

At the end of this chapter you should:
- Be able to distinguish among the capital budget, the operating budget, and the cash budget.
- Understand the context for budgeting, as well as the mechanical aspects of preparing the operating budget.
- Know how a program budget differs from a line-item budget.
- Know the six generic steps that are involved in preparing the operating budget, and where budgetary "misfits" can arise.

KEY POINTS

- The operating budget represents a "fine tuning" of a local governments (LG's) programs for a given year. It incorporates the final decisions on the amounts to be spent for each program, and specifies the organizational units that are responsible for carrying out the programs.
- Because a budget is a plan against which actual results are compared, it can provide a basis for measuring the performance of each responsibility center manager.
- If the budgeting phase of the management control process is to be useful for managers at all levels in the organization, it must assist them in making a commitment to achieving some agreed-upon results. Because the "bottom

line" in an LG does not fully measure performance, these results need to be both financial and non-financial.

■ Carrying out a revenue-first policy requires (1) preparing a careful (and perhaps conservative) estimate of total revenues from all sources, including taxes, fees, grants, contracts, and third-party payments, and (2) locking in this figure such that subsequent adjustments to the budget, if needed, are restricted to reducing expenses.

■ The budgeting process generally follows a timetable that includes six steps: (1) disseminating guidelines, (2) preparing revenue budgets, (3) preparing expense budgets for profit and standard expense centers, (4) preparing expense budgets for discretionary expense centers, (5) preparing the master budget (which represents a serious commitment), and (6) preparing estimates of non-financial results.

■ The success of budgeting depends to a large extent on its fit with a variety of other organizational elements, such as the LG's cost structure, its critical success factors, its non-financial (or programmatic) objectives, and the reporting phase of its management control process.

As discussed in Chapter 5, an LG makes a variety of long-range decisions during the programming phase of the management control process. Frequently, these decisions involve investments in fixed assets that senior management expects will be used for several years, and that will result in a "payback" of some sort. Ordinarily, the result is a capital budget.

By contrast, the budgeting phase of the process typically has a one-year focus and is concerned only with operating activities. In most organizations, operating activities are assessed in two ways. First, via the *operating budget*, which is the subject of this chapter. The operating budget focuses on revenues and expenses on an accrual basis, and is used to measure the financial performance of operating managers. Second, with the *cash budget*, which analyzes cash inflows and outflows for the year, and is used by the controller's (or treasurer's) office to forecast (and manage) the organization's cash needs. As discussed in Chapter 2, because many LGs use a cash basis of accounting, they do not have separate budgets. While this lack of separation makes the budgeting phase less accurate than it might otherwise be – in terms of actual resource inputs and outputs – its need not impede an LG's use of many of the concepts discussed in this chapter.

In some LGs, other types of budgets also are used, depending largely on the types of resources involved. For example, in Italy, under what is labeled *commitment-based accounting*, an LG's budget must balance its financial inflows (which take place when an entitlement to get cash arises) and its financial outflows (which occur when an expenditure commitment is made and there is an obligation to pay). Nevertheless, the focus of this chapter is only on the operating budget. Other textbooks discuss other types of budgets (see the further reading section at the end of this chapter for some references).

The general character of operational budgeting is similar in most organizations, both for-profit and nonprofit (including LGs), but there are significant differences in emphasis. This chapter focuses on both the similarities and the differences. It looks at the operating budget through several lenses, beginning with the managerial context in which budgeting takes place, and distinguishing between the mechanical and behavioral aspects of preparing the budget. It then looks in some detail at the components of the operating budget and the steps involved in building it. It concludes with a discussion of *budgeting misfits* – areas where the budgeting phase does not work as well as it might because it does not fit well with other organizational activities.

GENERAL NATURE OF THE OPERATING BUDGET

Preparing the operating budget is an important phase in the management control process. It is during this phase that an LG sets out its plans for the upcoming year, attaches monetary amounts to its various activities and programs, and, if feasible, establishes appropriate output and performance measurement targets (discussed more fully in Chapter 9). Moreover, in many LGs the budget is used as a central aspect of measuring managerial performance, which means that the budgeting phase has *behavioral* as well as *mechanical* aspects.

Relationship between programming and budgeting

Conceptually, operational budgeting follows programming but is separate from it. Ideally, the operating budget is a "fine tuning" of an LG's programs for a given year – incorporating final decisions on the amounts to be spent for each program and specifying the organizational units (usually departments) that are responsible for carrying out each program. In some organizations, budgeting decisions are distinct from programming decisions, but in most organizations it is difficult to have a completely clean separation between the two phases. Even LGs that have a well-developed programming phase occasionally discover circumstances during the budgeting phase that require revising some programming decisions. This situation is not problematic, however, unless programming decisions get made inadvertently as part of the budgeting phase.

149

BOX 6.1 INTERMINGLING PROGRAMMING AND BUDGETING

In one LG in the United States, program proposals and the operating budget were submitted simultaneously. The operating budget contained a line item called "capital," which was $1.5 million. In other parts of the document there were capital requests for "community preservation" ($5.8 million), recreation ($75,000), municipal projects ($3.8 million), water system improvements ($1.8 million), sewer system improvements ($100,000), school projects ($952,000), and public facility projects ($2 million). These requests totaled $14.5 million. Nowhere in the document was the $13 million discrepancy explained. Moreover, there were overlaps among the categories of proposed capital projects (e.g., school roofing, flooring, and other improvements were not included in the "school projects" category). It thus was very difficult for taxpayers (and probably some of the LG's line managers) to understand the separation between programming and budgeting (Town of Lexington 2010).

Despite this overlap, it is useful to think about the two activities separately as they have different characteristics. As discussed in Chapter 5, programming proposals generally include rough estimates of the associated revenues and expenses for several years into the future. Budgeting, by contrast, requires more careful expense estimates, and usually is formulated within a ceiling of estimated available revenue.

Since a budget is a plan against which actual performance is compared, senior management must be certain that it corresponds to the LG's responsibility centers. It then provides a basis for measuring the performance of each responsibility center manager. This can be complicated because, as discussed previously, some LGs have matrix structures where several departments are responsible for different aspects of a program. In these instances, if a program earns revenue, it should be designated as a profit center. Departments can then be established as either break-even profit centers or standard expense centers, with transfer prices used to account for the program's use of each department's resources. Under this sort of arrangement, program managers and department managers must interact on a regular basis.

Two-stage budgets

In this chapter we refer to the operating budget as if there were only one, which usually is the case. In many LGs, however, there actually are two operating budgets: the legislative budget, which is essentially a request for funds, and the management budget, which is prepared after the legislature (or other oversight authority) has decided on the amount of funds to be provided. Often the two are identical, but if the funds approved by the legislative body differ from those that were requested, then a revised management budget must be prepared that abides by the approved amounts.

BOX 6.2 LEGISLATIVE BUDGET VERSUS THE MANAGEMENT BUDGET

In Italian LGs, the municipal council – which represents the LG's political power – approves the legislative budget by the end of the prior fiscal year. Then the executive committee – which represents the group of elected officials in the different sectors and departments of the LG – approves the management budget, which is transmitted to managers. During the fiscal year, managers may ask the executive committee to amend the management budget, but if these variations affect the legislative budget then a revised legislative budget must be prepared and submitted to the municipal council for approval. Additional details on these interactions are discussed in Appendix 6-A.

Our focus in this chapter is on the management budget, which corresponds to the budget prepared in a for-profit company, and which shows the amount of authorized spending for each responsibility center. Indeed, if the amount of revenue is known within reasonable limits, the management budget can be an accurate reflection of the LG's overall financial plans for the year.

Contrast with for-profit companies

Budgeting is an important part of the management control process in any organization. It is more important in an LG than in a for-profit company, however, for two reasons: cost structure and spending flexibility.

Cost structure

In a for-profit company, especially a manufacturing company, many costs are engineered. The amount of labor and the quantity of material required to produce a product are determined within close limits by design and engineering specifications. Consequently, little can be done to affect these costs during the budgeting phase. By contrast, many of an LG's costs are discretionary, and the amount to be spent can vary widely depending on management's decisions. Many of these decisions are made during the budgeting phase.

BOX 6.3 COST STRUCTURE AND DEVIATIONS FROM A STANDARD

Many municipal hospitals have developed "clinical pathways" for patients with different diagnoses or diagnosis-related groups (DRGs). A clinical pathway is like an engineered cost in that it specifies the ideal mix of resources for a "typical" patient with a given diagnosis: length of stay, lab and radiology tests, physical therapy, and so forth. However, unlike a manufacturing company, where the products of any given type are identical, all patients with a given DRG are not the same. Therefore senior management must be willing to accept some deviation from the standard. How much deviation, under what circumstances, and for what kinds of patients, are topics that must be addressed during the budgeting phase.

Spending flexibility

In a for-profit company, a budget is a fairly tentative statement of plans, and is subject to modification if the underlying conditions change. Because of shifting customer preferences, for example, volume and mix of sales can change during the year, and there is general agreement that managers need to react to such changes by making revised plans that are consistent with the overall objective of profitability.

In many LGs, conditions are more stable and predictable. In a school, for example, the number of students enrolled governs the pattern of spending for the whole year. A public school system also has a certain authorized program or set of programs for the year that it must carry out. Under these circumstances, the operating budget is a fairly accurate statement of both the activities and resources to be used. It therefore is important to prepare it carefully. Significant time – by both line managers and senior managers – should be devoted to it.

CONTEXT FOR BUDGETING

Clearly, budgeting has a mechanical aspect. Revenue forecasts must be made, the associated expenses must be estimated, and an overall budgeted surplus or deficit figure must be calculated. Many LGs also forecast a variety of non-financial performance measures during the budgeting phase, and must do so in light of the metrics that will be used to measure them.

For an LG to use the budget as a *managerial* tool, however, senior management must view it from a broader contextual perspective than just its mechanics. We look first at this contextual perspective, which has eight elements, and then use it as a basis for discussing the mechanical side of budgeting.

Element #1: the LG's environment

In many respects, an LG's environment governs much of what happens in the budgeting phase. If, for example, some programs operate in a highly regulated environment, like that of a public utility, the LG must abide by the associated regulatory constraints. If a program receives grants or other kinds of financial support from regional or national government entities, the budget must be geared, at least in part, to the needs of these outside agencies and the constraints they place on decision making. On the other hand, if a program operates in a competitive environment, as with, say, a municipal parking lot, the LG quite likely will need to use the budget to eliminate as much "slack" as possible. Sometimes all of these approaches are needed.

Element #2: the LG's strategy

An LG's strategy also will have a great deal to do with its budget. Strategy can be defined, in large part, in terms of the LG's programs, the markets where they operate, and their sources of financing. As a result, there is a great deal of room for strategic differences among LGs that are roughly the same size, and that have similar demographic and geographic features.

Element #3: senior management's values

Senior management's values will have an influence on the budget. If, for example, an LG's senior management team values a highly collegial atmosphere among its professional staff (teachers, engineers, physicians, social workers, and so forth), it quite likely will have a different set of budgeting activities from one that thinks of its professionals as "hired help." In the former instance, department managers might be expected to play an important role in formulating the budget, whereas in the latter, each would have minimal input to the budgeting phase.

Element #4: the LG's cost structure

An LG's cost structure will influence its budget largely in terms of each program's fixed and variable costs (discussed more fully in Chapter 8). For example, a day care center that has a full-time, salaried labor force will have a different cost structure from one that uses many part-time, hourly workers. Salaried labor generally can be considered a fixed cost, whereas hourly workers can be thought of as variable costs.

Element #5: critical success factors

Usually, each program in an LG will have two or three activities that are extremely important to its success. Attaining these *critical success factors* ordinarily will influence

153

the budget.[1] In many fire departments, for example, a critical success factor is average response time. Variations in this factor will have a major impact on the budget.

Managers can incorporate these factors into a spreadsheet program in such a way that "what if?" scenarios can be tested for their budgetary implications. Moreover, when spreadsheets are used, decisions made in budget meetings about reductions or increases – and their impact on critical success factors – can be incorporated into departmental budgets quickly and accurately.

Element #6: the organizational and control structure

The way an LG is structured also will influence how it goes about formulating its budget. Some LGs are organized into departments, while others have structures that are more program-based. As discussed in Chapter 4, some will have a matrix structure. These structural factors will influence how the budget is assembled and who will play a role in its formulation.

Regardless of the organizational and responsibility center structure, an important aspect of a management control system is that it holds managers accountable only for those items they can control, and not for those outside their control; earlier, we called this the "fairness criterion." Therefore, the budgeting phase must structure revenues and expenses in a way that helps program and department managers to understand their commitments. Similarly, managers need to assess their subordinates' budgets in terms of the scope of *their* responsibilities.

Element #7: programmatic goals and objectives

Some LGs specify their non-financial (or *programmatic*) goals and objectives during the budgeting phase. When these items are specified clearly, managers who are responsible for attaining them soon begin to develop relationships between their attainment and the costs associated with doing so.

Element #8: managerial commitment and communication

If a budget is to be useful as a management tool, its formulation must be more than a purely mechanical exercise, with arbitrary reductions across line items when the first pass leads to unacceptable results. Indeed, if the budgeting phase of the management control process is to be useful for managers at all levels in the organization, it must assist them in making a commitment to achieving a set of agreed-upon results. Because the "bottom line" in an LG does not fully measure performance, these results need to be both financial and non-financial. In most instances, if managers are to commit themselves to achieving the financial and non-financial aspects of the budget, they must have some degree of participation in setting the targets.

The budget also can help different departments and divisions to communicate their plans and needs to each other, and it can help managers at all levels to anticipate potential problems. This *communication element* of the budgeting phase is one of its most important benefits.

MECHANICAL ASPECTS OF BUDGETING

In all but the simplest of LGs, the operating budget is prepared in light of the decisions that senior management has made about the structure of the LG's responsibility centers. For example, profit center managers will build their budgets differently from standard expense center managers, whose budgets will differ still from those of managers who run discretionary expense centers. In general, however, the mechanical aspect of preparing the operating budget consists of three components: revenues, expenses and expenditures, and non-financial performance measures.

Revenues

The general goal of an LG is to provide as much service as it can with its available resources. In many LGs, the total amount of revenue in any given budget year is, for all practical purposes, confined within quite narrow limits. The goal in preparing the operating budget, therefore, is to decide how best to spend it. This suggests that, from the perspective of the mechanics of the budgeting phase, the first step should be to estimate revenue.

Most managers would agree that the policy of estimating revenues first, and then budgeting expenses below or equal to them, is fiscally sound. The policy also provides a bulwark against arguments, often made by highly articulate and persuasive people, that an LG should undertake some activities even though it may not be able to afford to do so.

In many LGs, application of a "revenue first" principle requires that managers make careful estimates of the funds that a state (or regional or national) legislature is likely to appropriate. It also requires estimating taxation and other revenues. In some LGs, it requires estimating the revenues to be derived from a variety of sources, ranging from the basic (such as animal licenses and parking meters) to the more significant (such as water and sewer services, recreation programs, and property taxes). In many instances, an LG's program managers do not have the authority to establish the prices associated with their units' activities. Rather, prices are decided by elected officials. Under these circumstances, revenue estimates are confined to forecasting the volume of each activity, and multiplying it by the pre-determined price.

Discipline required for a revenue-first policy

Carrying out a revenue-first policy requires considerable discipline in two respects. First, it means preparing a careful (and perhaps conservative) estimate of total revenues from all sources, including taxes, fees, grants, contracts, and third-party payments. Once this figure has been established, it is "locked in."

Second, it requires a commitment to engage in expense cutting if the first approximation to the budget indicates a deficit. The least painful course of action, of course, would be to anticipate additional sources of revenue that would eliminate the deficit, but this is a dangerous course of action. If the original revenue estimates were made carefully, all feasible sources were included. New ideas that arise subsequently may produce additional revenue, but the evidence that they will do so frequently is not strong. If the additional revenue does not materialize, a deficit will occur. The safer course of action is to take whatever steps are necessary to reduce expenses so as to bring them into balance with revenues.

BOX 6.4   CONSEQUENCES OF THE LACK OF A REVENUE-FIRST POLICY

During one fiscal year, a municipal theater budgeted its expenses first, and then compared them with estimates of earned revenue. The excess of expenses over revenue was labeled "to be raised through contributions." The sum was overly optimistic, as were estimates of earned revenue. Although monthly statements indicated unfavorable revenue variances, no corrective action was taken for several months. The result was a sizable deficit that needed to be financed from general tax revenues.

Short-run fluctuations

When there is a possibility of revenue or expense fluctuations around an average, it is appropriate to budget for the average rather than for a specific amount anticipated in a given year. In some years the actual amount will exceed the budget, and in some it will fall below it. Over time, the two should net out.

BOX 6.5   BUDGETING FOR UNPREDICTABLE FLUCTUATIONS

A budget for snow removal will never be completely accurate because weather conditions will dictate the amount of snow to be removed. An LG therefore should budget for the average amount of snow to be removed, knowing that in some years the actual amount will be below the budget and in some it will exceed the budget.

Expenses and expenditures

There are two general formats for the spending portion of the budget. The traditional format, called a *line-item budget*, focuses on expense elements, such as wages, fringe benefits, supplies, and other similar resources. The other format, called a *program budget*, was discussed in Chapter 4. It focuses on programs, program categories, and perhaps program elements. The contrast between the two for a public safety department was shown in Table 4.5.

The program budget permits decision makers to judge the appropriate amount of resources for each programmatic activity. It also permits senior management to match spending levels with planned outputs. These are important advantages of a program budget format. Nevertheless, although a program budget focuses on programs, there almost always is a listing of the various line items within each program or program element.

Link to the capital budget

If the operating budget is prepared on a cash or expenditure (rather than expense) basis, it quite likely will include amounts for equipment and other long-lived assets.[2] When this is the case, only buildings, bridges, and other major capital acquisitions will be included in the capital budget. Minor capital items, such as computers, photocopying equipment, and the like will be contained in the operating budget, even though their economic lives extend over several years. Often the magnitude of the expenditure dictates which budget is used. For example, an LG's governing body might require that any asset costing more than, say, €5,000 be included in the capital budget.

When the operating budget is prepared on a cash or expenditure basis, senior management should make a clear distinction between expenditures and expenses. Otherwise, there is a temptation to balance the operating budget by moving some items from it into the capital budget, rather than by reducing expenses.

BOX 6.6 THE FOLLY OF SHIFTING CURRENT EXPENDITURES TO THE CAPITAL BUDGET

Some years ago, officials in New York City made many maneuvers to hide the city's true operating deficit. One was to shift items from the operating budget into the capital budget, where they presumably would be financed by bonds rather than by current revenues. An extreme example was vocational education expenses, which were shifted to the capital budget on the grounds that students would reap the benefits for many years to come, and that vocational education therefore was a long-lived asset!

There also may be a temptation to sell some assets to provide the funds needed for the operating budget. In general, however, such an activity is dangerous as it constitutes a one-time solution only, and therefore only postpones to future years the need to find a more permanent solution. Phelps (1961) called this the "golden rule" of budgeting. Under this rule, assets should be sold and/or debt incurred only to provide the funds to purchase new assets, and not to provide funds for the operating budget.

Non-financial performance measures

The third component of the operating budget is information on planned targets for non-financial performance, which usually consist of process and output measures (discussed in Chapter 9). Some LGs commit themselves to specific targets for each as part of the budgeting phase.

BOX 6.7   NON-FINANCIAL PERFORMANCE MEASURES IN BUDGETING

In one public school system, principals' budgets were determined by a combination of expected enrollments and centrally mandated student-to-teacher ratios, which are process measures. The principals also committed themselves to achieving certain levels of reading scores for students completing different grades, which are output measures. Senior management believed that these "non-financial performance measures" indicated, at least in part, how well the school system was achieving its objectives.

STEPS IN FORMULATING THE OPERATING BUDGET

Although every LG formulates its operating budget somewhat differently, the process generally includes, as a minimum, the six steps discussed below. Of course within these steps there can be many activities that take place, and some LGs will have additional steps. An example of the actual budgeting phase in the Municipality of Forlì, Italy (an LG with about 110,000 inhabitants), is contained in Appendix 6-A.

Step 1: disseminating guidelines

Senior management usually begins the process by distributing a set of guidelines for managers to follow in preparing their budgets, which include dates when various documents are due. Sometimes managers are asked to submit revenue budgets before preparing the remainder of their budgets, and sometimes they are asked to submit only complete budgets.

If approved programs exist, one guideline is that the budget should be consistent with them. This does not necessarily mean that the budget should consist only of approved programs, since this can be frustrating for operating managers. Indeed, some desirable innovations may come to light if managers are permitted to propose activities that are not part of approved programs. These innovative ideas should be clearly distinguished from those in the approved programs, however, and operating managers should understand that the chances for approval of a new program during the budgeting phase are slight. Otherwise, senior management may be downgrading the programming phase of the management control process.

Senior management also must make sure that operating managers are aware of any other constraints that exist, such as a requirement that the budget be for no more than 105 percent of the prior year's budget. Constraints also can be quite detailed, such as stipulating that the budget must be consistent with: (1) planned changes in the LG's activities, (2) senior management's assumptions about wage rates and other input prices, (3) the conditions under which new employees may be recruited, (4) the number of employees who may be promoted, (5) expected productivity gains, and/or (6) services to be provided by support centers (or *staff centers*, as they sometimes are called) and the corresponding transfer prices.

In addition, there often are guidelines about the format and content of the proposed budget. These are intended to ensure that budget estimates are submitted in a fashion that both facilitates analysis and permits a comparison between actual and planned performance.

Step 2: preparing the revenue budgets

For managers of profit centers, the first step usually is to prepare a revenue budget. Doing so provides the LG with some reasonable assurance that anticipated revenues are based on market conditions. As discussed above, if expenses were estimated first, there could be a tendency to assume that revenues would be high enough to cover them, which quite likely would be unrealistic.

In preparing the revenue budget, each profit center manager in a large LG may ask the center's program managers to estimate the revenues for their programs, and then aggregate them for submission to senior management. Conversely, if the LG has a program structure, each program manager will need to prepare an estimate of the program's revenue, which then can be sent to senior management.

Sometimes revenue estimates are reviewed and evaluated by senior management's staff to assure that they are realistic in light of general economic conditions, competitive forces, service delivery capabilities, and so forth. In large, complex LGs, profit

159

center budgets often contain considerable detail on exactly what types of services will be provided, in what quantities, where, to whom, and at what prices.

Of course, in many LGs, a significant amount of revenue is derived from property or other local taxes that are not part of a profit center. Therefore, the managers in the tax-collection office also must be involved in preparing the revenue budget.

Step 3: preparing expense budgets for profit and standard expense centers

Each program's expense budget usually is constructed by beginning with the volume and mix estimates used in the revenue budget, and attaching a variable cost to each unit. The results are multiplied to give total variable costs, after which the appropriate step-function costs and fixed costs are deducted. In the case of a standard expense center, although no revenue is received, the manager still can estimate expenses by beginning with the anticipated volume and mix of its outputs. Variable, fixed, and step-function costs are discussed in Chapter 8.

BOX 6.8   PREPARING AN EXPENSE BUDGET ON THE BASIS OF COST BEHAVIOR

In a prison cafeteria, the daily total variable cost for food can be estimated by using the average variable cost per meal, multiplied by the number of meals served in a day and the anticipated number of inmates. If the variable cost is different for each meal (breakfast versus lunch and dinner), a mix factor will be needed. The resulting total can be multiplied by 365 (days in a year) to obtain the annual variable cost budget. To this total can be added the step-function costs of the cafeteria's service personnel, various nonfood supply costs, and the cafeteria's fixed costs. A similar approach could be taken in a school cafeteria.

In a welfare office, if the number of cases can be predicted, the budget for social worker salaries can be obtained by using a standard workload factor (cases per social worker) multiplied by the average salary of a social worker. If there are different levels of social workers (master in social work versus bachelor in social work, for example), a mix factor will be needed, with the possibility that each level will have a different workload factor. To this total can be added the fixed costs of the office.

Step 4: preparing expense budgets for discretionary expense centers

The manager of each discretionary expense center prepares a budget for the center's expenses. Since these expenses are unrelated to any quantifiable outputs, the budget is a fixed amount, based on assumptions about the kinds and amounts of activities that staff will need to engage in during the year. For example, if litigation is pending, the budget for legal services might be higher this year than last. Or if there are plans to undertake a major revision of the LG's management information system, the budget might be higher. Similarly, if activities that took place last year won't take place this year, the corresponding budget should be reduced.

Step 5: preparing the master (or overall) budget

The various profit center budgets are assembled to determine the forecasted contribution to standard and discretionary expense centers for the year. Standard and discretionary expense center budgets are then subtracted to give the overall surplus. This budget is then taken to the LG's governing council (board of selectmen, city council, executive committee, etc.) for approval.

If the master (or overall) budget is not approved (usually because there is a deficit or because the surplus is not sufficient, but sometimes because some flaws in forecasts are identified), it may be returned to one or more responsibility center managers for reworking. For reasons discussed earlier, profit center managers usually are not permitted to adjust their revenue forecasts. Instead, they (and sometimes standard and discretionary expense center managers) must reduce their expenses. Expense reductions in a profit or standard expense center can be achieved by lowering either fixed costs or variable costs per unit, but ordinarily not by assuming a different volume or mix of output.

Step 6: preparing estimates of non-financial results

Increasingly, as discussed previously, LGs are incorporating non-financial performance measures into their operating budgets. These results can include process measures (e.g., the amount of time needed for a restaurant inspection) and output measures (e.g., the number of secondary school graduates). When these measures are included in the operating budget, responsibility center managers must think about both what they wish to accomplish and the cost of doing so.

An illustration

Figure 6.1 shows how Steps 2–5 might be brought together for a municipal hospital operating in a DRG payment environment. As it indicates, *clinical care departments* (such as surgery and medicine), which are profit centers, forecast the number and mix of patients they will serve, classified by DRG. They multiply the totals by the price paid for each DRG to forecast revenue. They also forecast the resources they will use to treat each case, such as the average length of stay (LOS), radiology procedures, lab

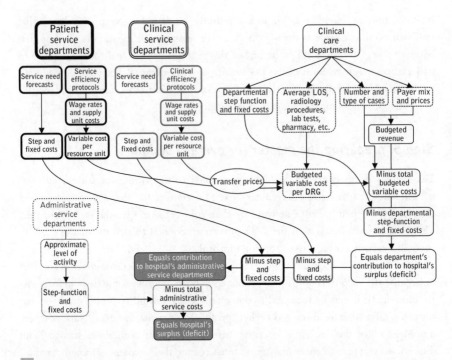

Figure 6.1 *Budgeting in a municipal hospital*

tests, and so forth. And they forecast the resources they will need from the patient service departments, such as laundry, housekeeping, medical records, and dietary.

Clinical service departments (such as radiology) and *patient service* departments (such as dietary) are treated as standard expense centers. They compute their variable costs to arrive at a transfer price for each of their services. The transfer price for each service is combined with the resources needed by the clinical care departments to treat each case, which leads to the budgeted variable cost per DRG. After a clinical care department's step-function and fixed costs are subtracted, the result is its contribution to the hospital's surplus.

From the sum of the contributions from all of the clinical care departments, the hospital next subtracts the step-function and fixed costs of its clinical service and patient service departments. The result is the contribution to the administrative service departments (which are discretionary expense centers). These expenses then are deducted to compute the hospital's surplus (or deficit).

IMPORTANT FEATURES OF THE OPERATING BUDGET

The above steps are only a rough guide to what actually happens in most LGs, and there are many variations on the general theme. Despite the specific approach an LG takes, however, there are several important features associated with preparing the operating budget:

- *The budget is taken seriously by senior management.* Senior management sets the tone for the process, and is involved in budget meetings with key managers. It does not turn the budget process over to the controller, but instead relies on the controller to assemble the information and to conduct any needed analyses.
- *The timetable remains roughly the same each year.* It is adhered to closely so that managers and others who are involved know what to expect and when.
- *Staff analyses are used as a check.* They are conducted principally by personnel in the controller's office, and are designed to verify (or contradict) forecasts by line mangers and their staff. When staff analyses contradict a forecast, neither group is allowed to dominate the decision-making process. Instead, areas of disagreement are identified, discussed, and resolved. Where corporate staff and line managers cannot resolve their differences, senior management makes the final decision.
- *There is a negotiation phase.* Line managers have an opportunity to present their case to senior management, and to defend their forecasts.
- *The final budget represents a serious commitment.* Line managers commit to achieving the budgeted financial results, usually with the stipulation that highly unusual circumstances can result in a budget revision, but nothing else. Highly unusual circumstances can include acts of nature (such as floods) or unexpected events (such as fires or prolonged strikes), or major economic downturns. Otherwise, profit center managers are expected to attain their budgeted surplus, and standard expense center managers are expected to adhere to budgeted levels of unit variable costs and total fixed costs (but not to total costs, since total costs will be affected by the volume and mix of output, which are not under their control).

RELATED BEHAVIORAL FACTORS

There are several behavioral factors that have an impact on the budgeting phase in many LGs. As they will affect different LGs in contrasting ways, and may not be relevant for some LGs at all, we discuss them only briefly below.

Expense creep

There is a tendency for support costs to creep upward. Because of this, staff analysts need to make special efforts to detect and eliminate unnecessary increases in these costs. If unit costs or ratios can be calculated, the staff can make comparisons with similar numbers in other responsibility centers or with external benchmarks. In the absence of such comparison bases, analysts can use historical ratios to help get a feel for the nature of the changes and whether they are reasonable.

This problem is particularly troublesome in responsibility centers whose output is difficult to measure (such as that of human resources or accounting departments). In these discretionary expense centers, budgetees often are motivated to acquire as many resources as they can, knowing that supervisors often find it difficult to measure the effectiveness of their resource use.

Budgetary game playing

The negotiation aspect of the budgeting phase, especially with discretionary expense centers, tends to be *zero-sum* in many LGs, with each center attempting to obtain as large a share of the fixed budget pie as possible. In instances where resources are not abundant, such an arrangement can produce a great deal of conflict and game playing.

BOX 6.9 EXAMPLES OF BUDGETARY GAME PLAYING[3]

One study of budget game playing identified five major activities: (1) understating volume estimates, (2) undeclared or understated price increases, (3) undeclared or understated cost reduction possibilities, (4) overstated expenses (such as for research), and (5) undeclared shifts in a program's client mix. A principal reason given by one manager was: "senior management just doesn't have time to check every number you put into your plans ... so one strategy is to 'pad' everything. If you're lucky, you'll still have 50 percent of your cushions after their review."

In a classic case, known as the "Washington Monument Elevator Ploy," the manager of the Washington Monument (in Washington, DC) proposed to reduce his budgeted expenses by eliminating the elevator service. He knew that doing so would arouse considerable antagonism from hundreds of thousands of visitors each year.

Some years ago, as part of a federal government financial bailout of New York City, the city's mayor was asked to reduce spending to avoid bankruptcy. He responded by dismissing 7,000 police officers and firefighters, and closing 26 fire houses. Many believe he did this to inflame public opinion against budget cuts. His ploy, in fact, had this effect, and the order to reduce expenses was reversed.

Game playing can be mitigated somewhat if there is a culture with norms that include: (1) trust between supervisors and their subordinates, (2) an assumption of competence, goodwill, and honesty on everyone's part, (3) a recognition that disagreements do not mean threats, (4) a spirit of openness and sharing of information, (5) a willingness to allow subordinates to develop their own solutions to budget-related problems, and (6) confidence in the computations and other work of staff analysts. Of course, developing a culture of this sort can be very difficult, but an attempt to do so nevertheless should be an important goal of an LG's senior management team.

Role of professionals

The attitude of professionals is a particularly important factor in many LGs. In a municipal hospital, for example, the budgetee may be a physician and the supervisor a hospital administrator. Physicians are primarily interested in maintaining or improving the quality of patient care, improving the status of the hospital as perceived by their peers, and increasing their own prestige. Their interest in the cost of care generally is secondary. By contrast, hospital administrators are primarily interested in costs, although they realize that costs must not be so low that the quality of care or the status of the hospital is impaired. Thus, the two parties weight the relevant factors quite differently.

BUDGETING MISFITS

As the above discussion has suggested, the budgeting phase is not only an integral part of an LG's management control process, but an essential ingredient in the LG's efforts to achieve its strategic goals. Moreover, the success of budgeting depends to a large extent on its fit with a variety of other organizational elements. For this reason, the failure of the budget to play a useful role in some LGs might be assessed in terms of "misfits" with these other elements.

Misfit #1: between the cost structure and the budgeting phase

A budget sometimes is not built around a program's (or department's) cost structure. For example, some programs are reimbursed (by their states, regions, or other entities) via a per-diem or per-client rate. Although the per-unit rate is designed to cover three types of costs – fixed, step-function, and variable – it ordinarily is based exclusively on volume (i.e., units of service or care provided). Since fixed costs and a portion of step-function costs are time-based (i.e., dependent on the passage of time, not on the number of units of service provided), there is a misfit between the cost structure and the reimbursement system.

The resolution of this dilemma consists of distinguishing between fixed and variable costs. Fixed costs exist because the program has committed itself to being "ready to serve," and they will exist even if no units of service are provided. The classic examples are fire departments and hospital emergency rooms. By contrast, variable costs *are* related to the volume of activity. As a result, while a program manager can be asked

165

to control variable costs *per unit*, he or she cannot be expected to control total variable costs, since they are affected by volume, which is outside the manager's control.[4]

Misfit #2: between critical success factors and the budgeting phase

As discussed earlier, most responsibility centers are able to identify one or two factors that are critical to their success. In a fire department it might be response time; in a trash removal department it might be kilograms (or pounds) picked up per day; in a social service department it might be visits per day per social worker; in snow plowing it might be centimeters (or inches) of snow plowed per hour.

Serious misfits can occur when these critical success factors are excluded from the budgeting phase. A fire department that does not include response time estimates in preparing its budget quite likely will find that it has difficulty making tradeoffs between operating costs and its overall measures of performance, such as loss of lives and property. A social service department that does not include visits per day per social worker in its budget will have a difficult time determining the staff it needs to serve its target set of clients.

BOX 6.10   BUDGET RESPONSIBILITY VERSUS COST STRUCTURE

A home health agency is reimbursed €60 per visit and has a staff of 50 nurses. Nurses make an average of six visits a day. If the average increases to 6.1 visits a day (about 1.7 percent) per nurse over the course of a year, the agency's surplus changes by €72,000. Calculations are in Table 6.1.

Table 6.1 *Sensitivity analysis for critical success factor changing*

Change in average visit per day per nurse	0.1
Number of work days in a year	240
Number of nurses	50
Revenue per visit	€60
Change in revenue (0.1 × 240 × 50 × €60)	€72,000
Change in expenses	€0
Change in surplus	€72,000

Misfit #3: between programmatic objectives and the budgeting phase

LGs that engage in program budgeting have an opportunity to be explicit about the congruence between programmatic objectives and their financial constraints. By so doing, they can address the relevant interactions during the budgeting phase, and make tradeoffs as needed. Alternatively, imbalances between financial and programmatic objectives may be resolved by default, as happens when budget cuts are necessary but managers do not have sufficient information to determine which programs are most successful in meeting the LG's overall goals.

Misfits of this sort can be corrected by revising the budgeting phase to include a component in which responsibility center managers are asked to specify programmatic objectives, and to commit themselves to their attainment in the same way that they committed themselves to the financial objectives of the budget. Generally, the problem is not a particularly easy one to solve, however, and managers often are forced to consider the budget as a financial constraint, rather than a pool of resources designed to assist them to attain some programmatic ends.

Misfit #4: between the budgeting and reporting phases

Finally, there is a possibility of a misfit between the budgeting and reporting phases of the management control process. Even if managers are prepared to take their programmatic and financial commitments seriously, the entire process is weakened, and perhaps incapacitated, if the reporting phase does not provide information that is complete (i.e., allows managers to assess the extent to which they are meeting their commitments), accurate, and timely. Yet, the reporting phase in many LGs operates with such long time lags that the information is of little managerial use when it arrives. Moreover, although an accounting technique called variance analysis (discussed in Chapter 10) has been developed to distinguish among different revenue and cost drivers, it is not always used. As a result, an LG manager may find it difficult to determine the reasons underlying a deviation between budgeted and actual performance.

BOX 6.11 IDENTIFYING THE REASONS FOR DEVIATING FROM THE BUDGET

Deviation from a snow removal budget can arise for two reasons: the quantity of snow to be removed and the efficiency of the public works department in removing it. An LG that wishes to understand the performance of its public works department needs to perform a variance analysis that distinguishes between the two. Although such an analysis is not difficult, few LGs perform it.

SUMMARY

Many aspects of budgeting in LGs are similar to those in for-profit companies. Perhaps the most important difference is on the revenue side of the budget. This difference arises because many LG programs are not revenue generating. An LG therefore must be careful to both forecast its tax revenues and other non-fee revenues accurately, and to assure itself that expenses will not exceed them. There are some exceptions to this rule, and most LGs can have a year or two where expenses exceed revenues, but those years must be balanced with years in which revenues exceed expenses. In addition, unless an LG is careful, it may have a budgeting phase that is impeded by one or more "misfits," which make it difficult for the budget to play an important role in assisting the LG to attain its strategic goals.

APPENDIX 6-A BUDGETING IN THE MUNICIPALITY OF FORLI, ITALY

The budgeting phase in the Municipality of Forlì, a medium Italian LG with about 120,000 residents and €100 million of current expenditures, is described here. Note that it closely parallels the description in the text, but has a few variations.

Forlì's budgeting phase consists of 12 steps. It also requires the involvement of a number of individuals who carry out specific activities:

1   Executive committee guidelines
2   First definition of non-financial targets
3   First definition of financial resources
4   Consolidation of non-financial targets and financial resources
5   Strategic coherence control
6A Internal job orders: Coherence control and definition of financial resources
6B Internal job orders: Negotiation between city manager and staff units
7   Financial balancing
8   Internal consistency control
9   Detailing the operating budget
10 Finalizing the operating budget
11 Final approval
12 Communication of the operating budget to managers and personnel

Step 1: executive committee's guidelines

The budgeting process begins in July of each year with the approval by the executive committee of a document that contains the guidelines that need to be followed by each responsibility center in defining its output targets and requesting financial resources.

These guidelines need to fit with the municipality's strategic plans and programs, and also with state and regional requirements.

Step 2: first definition of non-financial targets

In early September (four months before the beginning of the fiscal year), managers define their *non-financial* goals according to the strategic plan, the municipality's programs, and the executive committee's guidelines. The involved managers include both *line* responsibility centers (organizational units that deliver services to external users, such as the police department, the road maintenance department, and nursery schools) and *staff* responsibility centers (units that provide services to internal users, such as the budget office, the human resource office, and the information technology department).

Non-financial performance goals are divided into three categories: development, improvement, and maintenance. Development goals are related to a new program or service, or a radical change in the delivery approach for an existing program or service. Improvement goals are oriented toward the enhancement of a program's (or service's) efficiency or effectiveness. Maintenance goals simply repeat the previous year's levels of specific non-financial performance, which were considered to be satisfactory and therefore need only to be maintained.

Step 3: first definition of financial resources

In this step, each line center indicates the level of *financial resources* and the requests (called "job order" requests) that it expects to make to staff centers in order to accomplish its non-financial performance targets. With both improvement and maintenance targets, the line center managers use historical requests and modify them as necessary. With development targets, since no historical information is available, the line center managers need to undertake a more thorough analysis.

Step 4: consolidation of non-financial targets and financial resources

In late September, the proposed output targets are sent to the management control unit (MCU), which consolidates them into one document for the entire municipality. At the same time, the budget office combines each center's financial resource requests into a consolidated budget.

Step 5: strategic coherence control

The non-financial operating budget, which contains the consolidated non-financial performance targets proposals, is used by the MCU and the city manager to verify that operating targets agree with strategic and programmatic goals. If non-conformities arise, the MCU asks each responsibility center involved to modify its non-financial performance target proposal so that it provides a better fit with the municipality's goals. These modifications are due by the end of October.

Step 6a: internal job orders: coherence control and definition of financial resources

The MCU notifies the staff responsibility centers of all the job order requests received from line centers (from Step 3). Staff centers either verify that they are able to provide the line centers' requests, or suggest one or more options from which the line centers need to choose. At this time, staff centers make their requests for financial resources and establish their output targets for each line center.

Step 6b: internal job orders: negotiation between city manager and staff units

The city manager analyzes the operating budget (both financial and non-financial portions) of each staff unit. If the requests for financial resources are higher than the amount the municipality has available, the city manager assesses the importance of each job order depending on the priorities given to line units' goals by the strategic plan and the executive commission's guidelines.

As a result of this process, some job orders are not given financial support and therefore are eliminated. Once these decisions have been made, staff centers inform line centers of their ability to accept the job orders. If a staff center cannot fulfill a job order, the line center manager needs to decide among three options (1) drop the connected activity, (2) adjust the output goal, or (3) buy from an external contractor (assuming the center has the needed financial resources in its own budget). The revised overall operating budget, both financial and non financial, is completed by mid-November.

Step 7: financial balancing

Following receipt of the revised overall operating budget, the budget office verifies that the total requests for financial support are appropriate given the resources available from revenues. When the two are not equal, the budget office prepares a modified version of the financial operating budget, and a financial gap analysis report, where the differences between requested and available resources are explained. This information is the basis for negotiations between line responsibility center managers and the city manager.

After these negotiations have been completed, the MCU prepares the financial portion of the operating budget, and the budget office prepares a proposed budget (the legislative budget) that is in accordance with Italian law. This latter budget is a simplified version of the operating budget; it is prepared in both a program and line-item format, but does not include any reference to the municipality's responsibility centers. This budget needs to be approved by the city council before the operating budget (which includes responsibility centers) can be approved by the municipality's executive committee.

Although the two budgets have the same overall totals, there is a need for formal approval by two separate bodies, each of which has a different focus: one on programs and one on responsibility centers. This dual focus corresponds to the Italian law that requires municipalities to distinguish between the "steering power" of the city council and the "managerial power" of the executive committee. In effect, the city council focuses on the municipality's programs without regard for how they will be implemented, and the executive committee focuses on program implementation via the municipality's responsibility centers.

Step 8: internal consistency control

The MCU prepares the operating budget proposal, which contains the proposed nonfinancial targets and financial resource requests for each different unit (responsibility center). It sends the proposal to the city manager, who again analyzes the output targets for coherence and internal consistency. The city manager can combine similar goals or identify an inconsistency between or among some goals. If strategic choices or reviews of previous decisions need to be made at this point, the MCU modifies the operating budget and communicates its proposed modifications to the executive committee. Once the executive committee has signed off on the changes, the revised operating budget is sent to the various responsibility centers.

Step 9: detailing the operating budget

At this point the general structure of the budget is outlined and each responsibility center (line and staff) prepares a detailed proposal, which it sends to the MCU by 20 December. The detailed proposal includes (a) the specific actions and activities to be carried out, (b) the schedule, (c) the set of output measures, and (d) the financial resources divided by line-items and programs. The MCU combines all the proposals into one overall detailed operating budget.

Step 10: finalizing the operating budget

The MCU prepares the legislative budget, which it sends to the secretary-general for administrative auditing for review and approval. The operating budget is then sent to the executive committee for final approval.

171

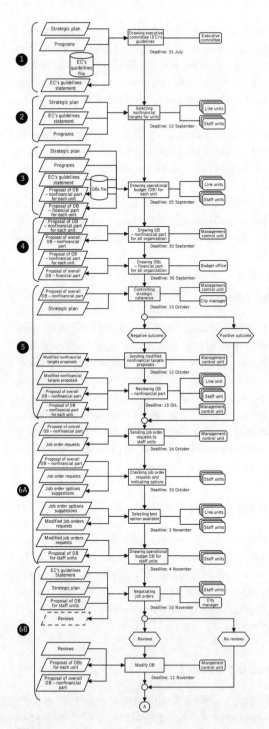

Figure 6.2 *The municipality of Forlì budgeting process*

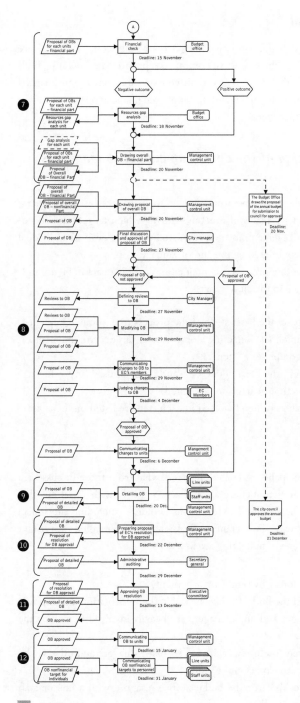

Figure 6.2 *Continued*

Step 11: final approval

A few days after the issuance of the legislative budget by the city council (but before the beginning of the fiscal year) the executive committee approves the operating budget. With this final approval, the executive committee issues the annual non-financial targets and communicates them, together with the approved financial resources, to the municipality's line and staff managers.

Step 12: communication of the operating budget to managers and personnel

The MCU communicates the final operating budget to managers by mid-January. Senior managers then conduct a series of meetings during which targets and strategic actions are presented, and each employee is entrusted with one or more individual goals. The entire process is completed by the end of January.

An overview of this budgeting process is contained in the flow chart in Figure 6.2. Three items are of importance in this flow chart.

1   The vertical lines connect the basic steps of the process (e.g., drawing up executive committee's guidelines, selecting non-financial targets for units, etc.). A group of activities comprises a "step."
2   On the left of each step, the files, documents and reports, used or produced – depending on the direction of arrows – are listed.
3   The responsibility centers (units) involved in each step are listed on the right.

Summary

The steps taken by the Municipality of Forlì differ somewhat from those discussed in the chapter, but the essential elements are all in place – clearly with variations that are needed to respond to the needs of external stakeholders (including the Italian legal system). Of perhaps greater importance, all of what the text called "important features" of the mechanical side of budgeting are in place:

■   The budget is taken seriously by senior management.
■   Although the MCU and the budget office assemble the information and conduct analyses, the city manager and line managers are heavily involved in making the major decisions.
■   The timetable is adhered to closely each year so that managers and others who are involved know what to expect and when.
■   When personnel in the MCU or the budget office disagree with a line or staff manager, neither group is allowed to dominate the decision-making process. Instead, areas of disagreement are identified, discussed, and resolved.

- There is a negotiation phase, where line managers have an opportunity to present their case to senior management, and to defend their forecasts.
- The final budget represents a serious commitment. Indeed, this commitment is taken down to individual employees and includes both output targets as well as financial responsibility.

DISCUSSION QUESTIONS

1 How should an LG prepare a budget when so much of what it is required to do (such as fire department responses) is totally unpredictable at the beginning of the year?
2 Is a "revenue first" policy realistic when so many revenues (such as parking fines and animal license fees) are completely unpredictable?
3 What is the value of a program budget?

NOTES

1 For an early discussion of critical success factors – and a framework that set the stage of much of the work that followed in this area, including the Balanced Scorecard – see Rockart (1979).
2 This is an important distinction. An "expenditure" is an outlay of cash for some purpose, such as the acquisition of a new police cruiser. At the time the expenditure takes place there is no "net outflow" of resources; the LG has simply exchanged one asset (cash) for another (the cruiser). An expense is the "using up" of a resource. Depreciation on the police cruiser is an expense, for example, as is the payment of salaries to the LG's employees.
3 These examples have been taken (with permission) from Anthony and Young (2003).
4 The classic solution to this problem is a two-part transfer price. It has been used extensively in industry (Solomons 1965) but has seen almost no application in LGs, or in the nonprofit sector in general. For a discussion of its applicability to integrated delivery systems in health care, see Young (1998).

REFERENCES

Anthony, R.N. and Young, D.W. (2003) *Management Control in Nonprofit Organizations*, 7th edn, Burr Ridge, Illinois: McGraw Hill-Irwin.

Phelps, E.S. (1961) "The Golden Rule of Capital Accumulation," *American Economic Review*, 51: 638–43.

Rockart, J.F. (1979) "Chief Executives Define Their Own Data Needs," *Harvard Business Review*, 57(2): 81–93.

Solomons, D. (1965) *Divisional Performance: Measurement and Control*, Homewood, Illinois: Richard D. Irwin, Inc.

Town of Lexington (2010) *Warrant to the 2010 Annual Town Meeting*, Lexington, Massachusetts, March 1.

Young, D. W. (1998) "Two-Part Transfer Pricing Improves IDS Financial Control," *Healthcare Financial Management*, 52(8): 56–65.

FURTHER READING

The focus of this chapter has been only on the operating budget. To have a general understanding of several related issues, such as fiscal administration, forecasting, fiscal discipline, fiscal transparency, integrity of revenue administration, performance budgeting, and capital budgeting, one might consult *Local Budgeting*, edited by Anwar Shah (World Bank Publications 2007). In addition, two books can be helpful in extending the concepts and knowledge about budgeting in LGs. *Local Government Budgeting*, by Gerasimos A. Gianakis, Clifford McCue, and Clifford P. McCue (Praeger 1999), discusses the internal resource allocation process. A critical review of theoretical and practical implications of performance budgeting, i.e., the idea of attaching financial resources to non-financial targets, is offered by Janet M. Kelly and William C. Riverbank in *Performance Budgeting for State and Local Government* (Sharpe 2010).

Chapter 7

Measuring full costs and setting prices

LEARNING OBJECTIVES

At the end of this chapter you should:

- Know how a full-cost analysis is prepared, and when it is appropriate to use it.
- Know how a local government (LG) could perform a relatively simple full-cost analysis so it could give its citizens reasonably accurate information on the way it is using resources.
- Know the distinction between Stage 1 and Stage 2 of the full-cost accounting methodology.
- Know how to use the "stepdown" method for Stage 1.
- Know the distinction between a process system and a job-order system for Stage 2.
- Understand the concept of activity-based costing (ABC).
- Know about the different potential approaches to pricing an LG's services.

KEY POINTS

- Failure to compute the full cost of a program or department can mislead citizens (and perhaps even some managers) into thinking that a particular operating unit is less costly than it is. This failure also can affect how profit centers price their services.
- Because there is a wide range of choices embedded in any organization's cost accounting system, many LG's managers simply make comparisons

over time for their own organization, knowing that the methodology has remained consistent from one year to the next.

■ The full-cost accounting methodology typically goes through two stages. In Stage 1, the accounting staff undertake several steps, at the end of which all costs reside in the LG's mission centers. During Stage 2, each mission center's costs are attached to its outputs.

■ Few LGs have developed sophisticated Stage 1 cost accounting systems, but even fewer have developed systems for the Stage 2 effort. As a result, all of these organizations, except those that operate only one program or provide only one service, have limited or – perhaps worse – incorrect, information about the full cost of their programs (including their enterprise funds).

■ In general, the smaller and more specific the pricing unit, the better. Such a unit improves senior management's knowledge of, and decisions about, cross-product subsidization, and also measures output more accurately than otherwise.

■ There are several variations from normal pricing that an LG uses when circumstances dictate: cost-plus, market-based, subsidized (for some or for all clients), and free. The latter often are called "public goods." An example is street lighting.

Measuring an LG's costs requires focusing on either full costs or differential costs. The former are used for activities such as pricing, comparative analyses, and external reporting. The latter are used in conjunction with a variety of what are called "alternative choice decisions," such as whether to outsource a particular service or activity. We discuss full-cost accounting in this chapter and differential-cost accounting in the next. This chapter is divided into two major sections. In the first, we discuss the details of full-cost accounting. In the second, recognizing that full costs are not appropriate for all pricing decisions, we address some of the complications that arise in pricing an LG's services on some basis other than full cost.

FULL-COST ACCOUNTING

Answering the question "What did it cost?" is important in many organizations, including LGs, but arriving at an answer can be much more difficult than it might first appear. Obviously, it is rather easily answered if we are discussing the purchase of inputs (supplies, labor, and so on), or even a contract with a vendor (say, for street maintenance). Calculating the full cost of a "unit" produced is also relatively easy as long as the unit can be clearly identified, and the program or department that produces it provides no other kinds of units. Complications arise when a program or department provides multiple goods and/or services, and uses different kinds and amounts of resources for each, or when, as discussed in Chapter 9, measuring units of output is tricky.

BOX 7.1   DETERMINING "UNITS" OF OUTPUT FOR DEPARTMENTS AND PROGRAMS

A police department responds to calls about domestic disputes, investigates crimes and vehicle accidents, directs traffic, monitors parking meters, and engages in a variety of other activities. It has a heterogeneous mix of services and uses different kinds and amounts of resources to provide each of them. There is no such thing as a "unit" of police service.

A town planning office provides the technical support for designing and implementing the town's roads and environmental projects. In this instance, it is difficult to determine the office's "units" of output.

In both of the examples in Box 7.1, and in many similar situations, it is relatively easy to measure the units of input – in general, an hour of time, perhaps classified by the kind of employee who spent the time. The real difficulty is measuring the units of output.

Despite these difficulties, the methodology to undertake a full-cost analysis has become much more sophisticated in many organizations – both for-profit and non-profit – over the past several decades. Unfortunately, not much of the learning has made its way into LGs. Consider the following situation: A medium-sized town has provided its citizens with the budget information contained in Table 7.1. At the town meeting, one citizen asked about the accuracy of the $1.6 million anticipated contribution from the town's enterprise funds (which, as discussed in Chapter 4, are profit centers).

It turned out that the $1.6 million was considerably overstated, and also that the budgeted education expense of $70.6 million was significantly understated. The problem lay with the $44.6 million of "shared expenses." None of these had been allocated to any of the departments or enterprise funds. The citizen noted that, since over $30 million of these expenses were employee related, they could quite easily have been allocated to the departments and enterprise funds based on the salaries being earned by their employees. It was quite easy to see, without even knowing the exact amount of the salaries, that, if the allocations were included, the enterprise fund contribution would turn negative, and the education expenses would increase. Indeed, because much of the $70 million for education no doubt was for teacher and administrative salaries, and because it comprised some 70 percent of the non-shared expenses, its total would increase by perhaps as much as 60 or 70 percent.

Table 7.1 Budget without full cost accounting ($000)

	Amounts	Totals
Revenues		
Tax levy	$120,420	
Regional aid	9,018	
Local receipts	9,957	
Revenue offsets	(1,983)	
Enterprise funds contribution*	1,629	$139,041
Expenses		
Education	$70,629	
Shared expenses**	44,625	
Municipal	26,147	
Capital	1,521	
Other	1,519	144,441
Surplus (Deficit)		$(5,400)
***Details of enterprise funds contribution**		
Revenues		$18,934
Expenses:		
Water	$7,144	
Wastewater	8,441	
Recreation	1,720	17,305
Contribution		$1,629
****Details of shared expenses**		
Employee-related:		
Contributory retirement	$3,718	
Noncontributory retirement	42	
Employee benefits	25,611	
Unemployment	199	
Workers compensation	460	$30,030
Non-employee-related:		
Property and liability insurance	586	
Uninsured losses	118	
Debt payment	3,798	
Interest on debt	727	
Temporary borrowing	145	
Reserve fund	550	
Facilities	8,671	14,595
Total shared expenses		$44,625

Uses of full-cost accounting

As the scenario in the previous section suggests, failure to compute the full cost of a program or department can mislead citizens (and perhaps even some managers) into thinking that a particular operating unit is less costly than in fact it is. This failure also can affect how profit centers price their program's services. Although cost information is not the only information that profit center managers use for pricing purposes, it nevertheless is an important ingredient.

BOX 7.2   ECONOMIC VERSUS POLITICAL DECISIONS IN SETTING FEES

Some of an LG's departments (such as recreation, waste collection and disposal, or water and sewer services) set fees or charges on the basis of their cost. If they do not have a full-cost analysis, there is no good basis for setting their prices. Sometimes, an LG's elected officials play a major role in setting prices, perhaps not relying much, if at all, on cost information. Nevertheless, a full-cost analysis can help to inform them of the financial impact of their decisions.

Comparative analyses

Many LGs can benefit from comparing their costs with those of other LGs that deliver the same sorts of services. Sometimes, central or regional governments use comparative analyses to set a standard cost per unit of service. This information is used in some countries for comparing the cost of services – such as public transportation, healthcare, education and training – among different LGs. However, as the discussion in this chapter demonstrates, there can be a variety of complexities in undertaking comparative analyses.

BOX 7.3   COMPLEXITY IN FULL-COST COMPARISON

An LG's school system is interested in comparing its cost per student with the cost per student in another LG. In making this comparison, the LG must consider issues such as average class size, the existence of specialized programs in athletics, art, music or other subjects, special services (such as career counseling), whether it wishes to include library expenses in the comparison, and the method used to calculate them (e.g., whether the library amortizes its collections and, if so, over what time period), and a variety of similar matters.

181

> A municipal hospital is interested in comparing its cost per patient with the cost per patient in a similar hospital in another LG. In making this comparison, the hospital must consider issues such as average occupancy rate, the existence of specialized programs in, say, cardiology or oncology, the provision of services (such as social work or discharge planning), whether it wishes to include outpatient costs in the comparison, and so on.

As these examples suggest, the definition of what is to be included in a full-cost calculation requires several managerial decisions. Indeed, because there is such a wide range of choices embedded in any organization's cost accounting system, LG managers ordinarily are better off if they simply make comparisons over time for their own organization, knowing that the methodology has remained consistent from one year to the next.

Despite the complications associated with inter-LG comparisons, the cost per unit of a particular LG's program or service, when compared in a sound way to that of other LGs, represents information that citizens (and others) can use to assess the program's or service's value. The comparisons often are contained in reports addressed to external stakeholders, which sometimes are called *social reports*. In some instances, small groups of LGs have collaborated in order to establish standards for benchmarking purposes (see, for example, Martin and Mikovsky 2010).

External reporting

In situations where a third party pays on the basis of cost, an LG usually must calculate its full costs according to certain guidelines. It then must submit the resulting cost report to the third party before receiving payment. Often, the principles provide for direct costs plus "an equitable share" of overhead costs. Overhead costs include items such as depreciation of buildings and equipment, facility operations and maintenance, departmental administration, and general administration.

THE FULL-COST ACCOUNTING METHODOLOGY

Conceptually, the goal of full-cost accounting is quite basic: to measure as accurately as possible the resources consumed in producing a particular good or providing a particular service. In some instances, the measurement process is quite easy. For example, an organization that produces a single, easily measured, good or service usually has little difficulty in calculating the full cost of each unit. All costs associated with the organization, and hence the good or service, can be added together.

182

These costs then can be divided by the number of units provided to arrive at a full cost per unit.

BOX 7.4 FULL-COST COMPUTATION FOR SIMPLE AND EASY-TO-MEASURE SERVICES

In a water department, computing the full cost of a cubic meter of water is relatively easy. The department can add together all of its costs for an accounting period, such as a month, and divide by the number of cubic meters of water provided during that month. Since all cubic meters are identical, this average cost figure is quite accurate. Similarly, a waste disposal department would have a reasonably accurate figure if it divided its total costs by the total metric tons of trash collected and disposed of.

By contrast, organizations that produce a variety of goods or services, each requiring different amounts of resources, will have a more difficult time determining the cost for each unit sold.

BOX 7.5 FULL-COST COMPUTATION FOR COMPLEX AND DIFFICULT-TO-MEASURE SERVICES

In a human service department that provides several different types of services (such as home-based assessments, treatment planning, outreach, education, and transportation), computing the full cost of a unit of service is more complicated than it was for a cubic meter of water. This is because each service consumes different kinds and amounts of resources. In addition, each service must receive its "fair share" of the department's overhead, which includes the department's costs for such activities as clinical supervision, training, record maintenance, and project coordination. Each service also will need to receive its "fair share" of the LG's overheads. Indeed, if the full-cost accounting effort is done properly, each unit of service will include a tiny fraction of the mayor's salary!

For LG departments with a heterogeneous mix of outputs, such as the above human service department, the full-cost accounting methodology typically goes through two stages. In Stage 1, the accounting staff undertakes several steps, at the end of which all costs reside in the LG's mission centers. During Stage 2, each mission center's costs are attached to its outputs.

BOX 7.6   MISSION CENTERS AND SERVICE CENTERS IN FULL-COST COMPUTATION

The above human service department would be considered a mission center, as would the parks department, the street maintenance department, and others that provide services directly to citizens. The mayor's office, the accounting department, the legal department, and other units that do not provide services directly to citizens would be considered as service centers. At the end of Stage 1 (discussed in detail in the next section), all service center costs will have been allocated to the LG's mission centers, such that each mission center's costs include its direct costs plus its fair share of the LG's service centers' costs.

Although an LG's accounting staff can make many of the decisions for each stage, senior management needs to take an active role in guiding the process. Otherwise the result may be a cost accounting system that fails to provide them with the kind of information, or the level of detail, they need for pricing and other decision making.

The stage 1 process

Stage 1 comprises four activities: (1) defining the LG's cost objects, (2) selecting the cost centers that will be used to collect costs, and dividing them between service centers and mission centers, (3) assigning all costs to one or more of these cost centers, and (4) allocating service center costs into mission centers.

Defining cost objects

A final cost object is the unit of output for which we wish to know the full cost. In a municipal hospital, for example, the final cost object might be an all-inclusive day of care. As such, it would include all surgical procedures, laboratory tests, radiology exams, pharmaceutical usage, and so on. When this is the case, calculating the full cost of a day of care is as simple as calculating the cost of a cubic meter of water in the above example: total costs divided by total days of care provided.

In most municipal hospitals, however, the final cost objects are more complex than an all-inclusive day of care. In some instances, for example, one cost object is a day of "routine" care (e.g., room, dietary, housekeeping, laundry, and nursing costs), with separate cost objects for other activities, such as a day of intensive care, a laboratory test, a radiological procedure, and so on. In other hospitals, the final cost object is a discharge, which includes all costs associated with the patient's entire stay (i.e., for all days of care, rather than just an average single day). Here, too, though, if we assume that all discharges use the same resources, computing the average cost per discharge would be quite easy: total costs divided by total discharges.

Complications arise only when different cost objects use resources differently. For example, most hospitals want to know the cost of a discharge according to the patient's diagnosis, or diagnosis-related group (DRG).[1] When the *final cost object* is a DRG, we must add up the unit costs of a variety of *intermediate cost objects* (which are smaller units needed to produce the final cost object).

The final cost object is used for billing payers, or for comparing the average cost of a particular DRG with the revenue the hospital receives from its payers (such as grants from regional or central governments or payments from insurance companies or health ministries). The intermediate cost objects, by contrast, are the various services, such as an X-ray or a blood test that the patient receives during a stay in the hospital.

BOX 7.7 INTERMEDIATE COST OBJECTS VERSUS FINAL COST OBJECTS

If a hospital wants to know the cost of a patient with, say, DRG 200 (the final cost object), it must add the costs of all resources provided to the patient during his or her stay (the intermediate cost objects). These include operative procedures, laboratory tests, radiological procedures, pharmaceuticals, intensive care days, routine care days, and so forth. This means that it needs to determine the cost of each intermediate cost object.

Similarly, if a public works department wants to know the cost of paving a mile (or kilometer) of roadway, it must add the costs of architectural design, engineering, paving labor, paving materials, and landscaping labor and materials. Here, too, it must compute the cost of each intermediate cost object.

When the final cost object becomes more heterogeneous than, say, a cubic meter of water or an average discharge, our focus shifts to the intermediate cost objects that were used to produce it. Different combinations of these intermediate cost objects will affect the cost of the final cost object, even though the final result (or "product") – the discharge of a patient or the paving of a mile of road – is the same. Thus, our real interest is in the cost of the intermediate cost objects.

BOX 7.8 THE VALUE OF INTERMEDIATE COST OBJECTS

The annual cost of caring for a child in a family services program (the final cost object) depends on the services the child receives (intermediate cost objects).

There are four intermediate cost objects: foster home care, psychological testing, social work counseling, and psychotherapy. A variety of costs are accumulated for each. The psychological testing center, for example, includes the costs of part-time psychologists, testing materials, and the fee the home pays to an outside organization to have the tests processed and scored. The costs in the psychological testing mission center are accumulated for the year, and are divided by the number of children tested to give a cost per child tested (this assumes that all tests are about the same). Each child who was tested has this cost added to his or her other costs to arrive at the total cost of caring for him or her for the year, which is the final cost object. Children who are not tested do not receive any costs from this mission center.

Selecting cost centers

To calculate the cost of the intermediate products, we first assign all costs to cost centers. Cost centers can be thought of as "buckets" into which an organization's costs are placed for the purpose of the Stage 1 analysis. Frequently, cost centers are identical to an LG's departments. For example, in a municipal hospital, the department of radiology might be one cost center, the social work department another, the housekeeping department a third, and so on. However, some departments are a collection of several cost centers. For example, a department of radiology might be divided into the cost centers of CT scanning, angiography, magnetic resonance imaging, and so on. If this is done, radiology will have several intermediate cost objects produced in several different cost centers.

Mission Centers versus Service Centers. An LG's cost centers are divided between mission centers and service centers. Mission centers are associated with the LG's main focus (or mission). In a typical LG, they would include public works departments, police and fire departments, recreation departments, schools, and several other entities that provide services directly to citizens.

Service centers, by contrast, accumulate the costs of activities that support the LG's mission centers. An LG's service centers might include depreciation on its buildings, interest on its debt, housekeeping, maintenance, laundry, and general administration.

Assigning costs to cost centers

After an organization's cost centers have been determined, all costs then must be assigned to either a service center or a mission center. This usually is not difficult. In most LGs, salaries can be easily identified with the department or program where a person works. So, too, can the supplies used by each department or program, as

186

well as the depreciation on the equipment (e.g., paving machines in public works or photocopiers in the controller's office).

Allocating service center costs

The full cost of a mission center includes both its assigned costs and its *fair share* of the LG's service center costs. This means that service center costs must be *allocated* to mission centers. To do so, the accounting staff must choose a *basis of allocation* for each service center that measures its use by the other cost centers as accurately as possible. For example, the allocation basis for a housekeeping service center might be square feet (or meters). We can measure the area of each cost center and divide total housekeeping costs by total square feet to get a housekeeping cost per square foot. We then multiply that rate by the number of square feet in each cost center to determine its fair share of the housekeeping center's costs.

Assignment versus allocation: It is important to distinguish between "assignment" and "allocation." Assignment precedes allocation, and serves to place costs into service centers and mission centers. By contrast, allocation distributes service center costs among mission centers.[2]

Precision of allocation bases: When selecting allocation bases, it is important to keep in mind that increased precision generally requires greater measurement efforts, giving rise to higher accounting costs. For example, not all square feet in an LG's departments are equally easy to clean. Therefore, rather than using number of square feet to allocate housekeeping costs, we might allocate them on the basis of hours spent. While hours spent is a more accurate basis, and would give us a more accurate cost figure, its use requires an ongoing compilation of the necessary data.

In summary, the more precise an allocation basis, the more accurately it captures true resource consumption. Exact measurement of resource consumption can be a time-consuming and complicated process, however, and less accurate approaches occasionally are adopted in response to time, staffing, and technical constraints.

Allocation methodology: Once we have selected an appropriate allocation basis for each service center, we must choose an allocation *methodology*. Three methods of varying complexity and accuracy are available for doing this: direct, stepdown, and reciprocal.

With the *direct* method, service center costs are allocated to mission centers only and not to other service centers. This is the simplest method of the three, and is used by many organizations. It is the least precise of the three, however, in that it excludes the cost effects associated with one service center's use of another service center.

The *stepdown* method allocates service center costs into both other service centers and mission centers. Because it allocates service centers to other service centers, as well as to mission centers, the stepdown method is more complicated than the direct method. It also is more accurate in that it includes the cost effects associated with one

187

service center's use of another. However, once a service center's costs have been allocated, it cannot receive an allocation. Thus, for a given service center, the stepdown method includes only the cost effects of its use of the service centers that precede it in the allocation sequence, and not those that follow it.

With the *reciprocal* method, all service centers make and receive allocations to and from each other, as well as to mission centers. The allocation amounts are determined by a set of simultaneous equations, which are solved on a computer. Because all service centers both make and receive allocations, the reciprocal method is the most accurate of the three, but also the most complicated to use (Young 2010).

An example using the stepdown method

Despite the greater accuracy of the reciprocal method, many organizations find that the stepdown method strikes about the right balance between accuracy and ease of use. Thus, we will use it here for illustrative purposes.

Choosing a service center sequence: When the stepdown method is used, the sequence followed in allocating the service centers can have an impact on the costs in each mission center. Conceptually, the approach to choosing a sequence is to rank service centers in order of their use by other service centers. That is, the service center that uses the other service centers the *least* is allocated *first*, and the service center that uses other service centers the *most* is allocated *last*. Clearly, considerable judgment is required to determine this sequence, and, even then, there is no such thing as the "right" sequence.

Conducting the allocations: After we have chosen the sequence for service centers, the allocation effort can begin. To illustrate, assume that a municipal children center has the three service centers and two mission centers, shown in Table 7.2. The service centers are Administration (assigned costs of €100), Housekeeping (assigned costs of €20), and Workshop Support (assigned costs of €30). The mission centers are Kindergarten (assigned costs of €1,000) and Preschool (assigned costs of €500). The children center's total costs are thus €1,650, as shown at the bottom of the Assigned Costs column.

The allocation process begins with the first service center in the sequence (here, it is Administration), which, as the note in parentheses under its *column* indicates, is allocated on the basis of number of employees (e.g., teachers in the mission centers). Each remaining cost center will receive its share of Administration costs based on its proportion of employees.

The next service center to be allocated is Housekeeping. The amount to be allocated is its assigned costs of €20 *plus* the €25 that was allocated to it from Administration. As a result a total of €45 must be allocated. As the parentheses under the Housekeeping column indicate, it is allocated to the remaining centers on the basis of square meters, such that the more space a receiving cost center has, the greater its share of Housekeeping costs.

Table 7.2 The stepdown method

	Cost centers	Assigned costs	Allocation Administration (# employees)	Housekeeping (square meters)	Workshop activities (hours)	Total
Service centers	Administration	100				
	Housekeeping	20	25			
	Workshop support	30	10	10		
Mission centers	Kindergarten	1,000	40	20	30	1,090
	Preschool	500	25	15	20	560
	Total costs	1,650	100	45	50	1,650

The final service center to be allocated is Workshop Support, which, as the table indicates, has a total of €50 to be allocated: €30 of assigned costs, plus €10 allocated from Administration, and €10 allocated from Housekeeping. It is allocated to the remaining cost centers on the basis of the hours used by each mission center.

We now can add up the costs of the two mission centers. Kindergarten has €1,000 of assigned costs, plus €40 of allocated Administration, €20 of allocated Housekeeping, and €30 of allocated Workshop Support, for a total of €1,090. The Preschool has €500 of assigned costs, plus €25 of Administration, €15 of Housekeeping, and €20 of Workshop Support, for a total of €560.

Note that our total costs of €1,650 remained the same as they were prior to allocating service center costs. However, we now have fully allocated the service center costs into the two mission centers. We did so by first allocating the Administration service center costs to the Housekeeping and Workshop Support service centers, as well as to the two mission centers, then allocating the Housekeeping service center costs (with the Administration allocation included) to Workshop Support and the two mission centers, and finally allocating Workshop Support to the two mission centers.

In summary, the full cost of a mission center includes its assigned costs, plus the costs allocated to it from the organization's service centers. The stepdown method shown in Table 7.2 is one of the formal techniques used to carry out the process.

Key aspects of the stepdown method: Several important points must be remembered when using the stepdown method:

1   Only service center costs are allocated. Mission center costs are not. Mission centers receive costs from service centers, but once a cost has been allocated to a mission center it stays there.

2   The *allocation basis* chosen for a service center attempts to measure the use of that center's resources by the other cost centers – both service centers and mission centers. For example, in a laundry, "pounds washed" frequently is used as the allocation basis. Each cost center receives a portion of the laundry center's

189

costs in accordance with its proportion of the total pounds of laundry washed. If a particular cost center had no laundry, it would not receive an allocation.

3 The amount of a service center's allocation to other cost centers depends, in part, on its position in the sequence. If it is allocated late in the sequence, it will contain some costs from service centers allocated earlier in the sequence. If it is allocated early, it will not.

4 Total costs do not change. Different allocation bases and stepdown sequences only change the distribution of total costs among the mission centers. Thus, the effect of any change in methodology is solely one of making shifts among mission centers.

The problem with poor stage 1 cost accounting

Despite the relatively easy preparation of a Stage 1 cost analysis, few LGs actually do it. As a result, they do not know the full cost of their programs and services. This is particularly problematic with services and programs that charge user fees, and when these fees are expected to cover or exceed full costs. These programs include trash collection and disposal, water and sewerage, energy provision, and parking. In these cases, if Stage 1 is not properly designed, these programs and services may be either underpriced or overpriced.

Table 7.1 illustrated the problem with the budget for a medium-sized LG in the United States.[3] As it showed, there were $44 million of "shared services" (over 30 percent of the total expense budget of $144 million). These were treated separately, and not either assigned or allocated to programs (such as education) or to "enterprise funds," i.e. those programs and services, such as water and sewerage, which are expected to cover all their costs (and perhaps earn a surplus).

As discussed earlier, of the $44 million total of shared expenses, some $30 million were employee related, suggesting that it would be rather easy to assign these expenses to mission centers by simply using a percent of payroll dollars as the assignment basis. Moreover, it should also be possible to assign the $4.5 million of debt service expenditures (principal and interest) to programs and enterprise funds based on the borrowing that was undertaken to finance their assets.[4]

If these assignments were made, only about $10 million would remain in the shared expense category. This would need to be allocated. Since almost all of it ($8.7 million) is for facilities, it should be relatively easy to allocate this amount using square feet.

If this sort of simple Stage 1 cost accounting effort were undertaken, there would be a rather dramatic change in the LG's mission center costs. For example, the direct expenses of the enterprise funds (profit centers) are about 17 percent of the total non-shared expenses ($17.3 million ÷ [$144.4 million − $44.6 million]). If the 17 percent figure were used as an estimate of their share of the employee-related expenses, they would be assigned about $5.1 million of these expenses (0.17 × $30 million). They also might receive a significant portion of the debt service payments, and at least some of the facilities allocation. However, even if we exclude their fair share of these remaining shared expenses, their $1.6 million contribution turns into a loss of about $3.5 million. Thus, it seems clear that they are under-pricing their services. Indeed, it would appear likely that raising prices in the enterprise funds, so that they operate on something close to a breakeven basis, would eliminate a significant portion of the LG's $5.4 million operating deficit.

The Stage 2 process

At the end of Stage 1, all costs reside in mission centers. Stage 1 can have some flaws, but with minimal effort, it usually can provide a reasonably accurate depiction of mission center costs. It is during Stage 2, when a mission center's costs are attached to its cost objects, that more serious difficulties can arise.

There are two approaches used to attach mission center costs to cost objects. The first is a *process system*, which is appropriate when all units of output are roughly identical. All mission center costs for a given accounting period are simply divided by the total number of units produced (which could be hours of service) to give an average cost per unit. This approach would be appropriate for the water department discussed earlier, and for other situations where all output units are roughly identical.

By contrast, a *job order system* is used when the units of output are different. Consider, for example, a repair garage for an LG's vehicles. Adding all costs for a given accounting period, and dividing them by the number of vehicles repaired to determine an average cost per repaired vehicle, would provide quite misleading information. Instead, the garage would use a job ticket, on which the time and parts associated with each repair effort would be recorded separately. The job's cost would then be determined by means of hourly wage rates, unit prices, and so on. Similar problems exist in human service agencies, special education programs, and public works departments, to name a few.

Under the above circumstances and many similar ones, an LG's cost centers (both service and mission centers) have units of output whose diversity requires a job order system. Implementing such a system requires understanding the general nature of a mission center's costs. These are shown in Table 7.3.

In a typical job order context, indirect costs (the bottom portion of Table 7.3) are "attached" to products through the use of one or more "overhead rates." The absorption process, as this effort is called, can be a little tricky, and can give misleading results on occasion. For example, when only one overhead rate is used, as frequently happens, the implicit assumption is that the unit used in that rate (e.g., direct labor hours), drives the use of all indirect costs. However, indirect costs generally arise from a more

191

Table 7.3 *Elements of full production cost*

Type of cost	Description	Examples
Direct	Costs that are unambiguously associated with a given product or service in a mission center	
Direct labor		Workers on a road repair project
		Technicians in a laboratory
Direct Materials		Books and supplies in a school
Other direct		Depreciation on a piece of equipment used for a single cost object (e.g., a truck for trash pickup)
Indirect	Costs that are unambiguously associated with the mission center where the product is produced, but that *cannot* be attached directly to a product	
Indirect Labor		Material handlers, quality inspectors, supervisors
Indirect Materials		Cleaning solvents for machines, record-keeping supplies
Other Indirect		Depreciation on the mission center's computers
Allocated service center costs	Costs that are allocated to the mission center from the organization's service centers. They are indirect with regard to both the mission center and any product or service produced in it	Housekeeping, administration, legal, accounting, and similar items

complex array of forces, such that an absorption process using a single overhead rate can give management misleading information about the full cost of a cost object. This can lead to poorly informed, and perhaps unfair, pricing decisions.

Enter activity-based costing

Activity-based costing, or ABC, is now used in many settings (both manufacturing and service) to correct for this deficiency. Designers of ABC systems use multiple "indirect cost pools," and try to design each pool so that the resources in it are as homogeneous as possible. They then identify an activity that drives the use of each pool's resources, and use it to compute the pool's overhead rate.

BOX 7.9   THE EFFECTS OF ACTIVITY DRIVERS ON ALLOCATION OF INDIRECT COSTS

An indirect cost pool in a snow removal department might be the labor and supervisory time needed to prepare the vehicles for plowing. In this case, the appropriate cost pool would be everything associated with setting up the vehicles (such as installing the plowing blades and making any needed repairs), and the appropriate unit of activity for the pool would be one setup. As a result, a unit of output (a kilometer or mile plowed in this case) in a small area or storm would get a higher share of the setup costs than one in a large area or storm.

Many nonprofit organizations (but few LGs) have developed fairly sophisticated Stage 1 cost accounting systems, but few of them (including LGs) have developed an ABC system for the Stage 2 effort. As a result, all of these organizations, except those that operate only one program or provide only one service, have limited or – perhaps worse – incorrect, information about the full cost of their units of service.

Value of ABC

In the for-profit world, ABC has led many managers to revise their thinking about the full cost of their products. It is likely that similar conclusions would be reached in an LG that undertook an ABC effort. Indeed, in an era of intense pressures for cost control, an LG that does not have an ABC system may lack essential information for decision making. If nothing else, an ABC system can help senior management to identify the nature and extent of cross-subsidization taking place among the LG's programs and services.

> ### BOX 7.10   ACTIVITY-BASED COSTING AND FUNDING MECHANISMS
>
> Many schools include in their curricula special programs for children who are nontraditional learners. Few schools know the full cost of these programs, however. They make no effort, for example, to determine how much of the school's administrative time should be attached to each child in the program. If state or regional funding is provided to assist with the cost of these programs, and if the funding is cost-based, the schools may be requesting less than is appropriate.

COMPLICATING FACTORS

In practice, the full-cost accounting effort in both Stage 1 and Stage 2 has many variations and nuances. Most of these "complicating factors," as well as the basic approach to developing a Stage 2 system using ABC, are discussed in many cost accounting texts (see Further Reading section). There are a few of these complications worth noting, however.

Assigned versus allocated costs

There are many variations in the ways that different organizations draw the line between assigned and allocated costs. For example, in calculating the cost of a town library, one LG might assign pension and other fringe benefits directly to the library, while another might assign these items to a service center and allocate them to the library. Another LG might develop a formula to assign interest on its debt directly to, say, the library, but a fourth might assign it all to a common pool (a service center). Then, as part of its Stage 1 cost accounting effort, it would allocate it to each mission center, including the library. Similarly, if electricity, heat, and other utilities are metered for each mission center, they can be assigned directly; if not, they must be assigned to a "utility" service center and then allocated to mission centers. Because of these differences in accounting practices, comparisons of indirect costs among different LGs are likely to be of little use.

Appropriateness of indirect costs

Often, the issue is not one of distinguishing between assigned and allocated costs, but of the appropriateness of a given cost item. For example, some people claim that LG's service center costs have been rising unchecked for years, and now total a significant amount of total cost (over 30 percent in Table 7.1) Some senior managers contend that such costs are needed to run the LG. At issue are two questions:

1 What kinds of service center cost increases should be allowed?
2 What kinds of efficiency standards should be used?

Imputed costs

In certain situations, imputed costs can be incorporated into an LG's cost accounting system. For example, the Dutch government developed a system of national accounting to reflect the damage done to the air, water, soil, and animal and plant life, and to account for the cost of maintaining or restoring them. Similarly, in the Ruhr Valley in Germany, polluters pay a fee to the government based on the effect of their effluents on the river's biochemical oxygen demand. The revenue derived from this fee is used to provide for water treatment.

Sweden, France, and Norway also have engaged in similar efforts, or what is now called "green accounting" (Simons 1990). In all instances, the costs are estimated (or imputed) rather than those actually incurred. A traditional cost accounting system will not include imputed costs.

PRICING

Setting prices is a tricky proposition in many organizations, but especially in LGs. Although full costs or a variety of other cost configurations can be used to assist in the effort, many LG managers have given insufficient thought to their pricing policies. In fact, many tend to regard all marketing activities (of which pricing is only one) as something to be avoided. Such an attitude can result in the LG pricing a service in a way that is unfair to some clients, or developing pricing policies that inhibit the attainment of strategic goals.

Pricing policies are important in most nonprofit organizations, including LGs, because prices (1) influence the behavior of clients, (2) provide a measure of output, and (3) influence the behavior of managers. The issues to consider differ in each of these areas.

Client behavior

The amount that a client (or third-party payer on behalf of a client) pays for a service indicates that the service is worth at least that much to the client. Indeed, the better a pricing scheme fits with clients' decision-making options, the more powerful its impact on their behavior.

195

BOX 7.11 INFLUENCING CLIENTS' BEHAVIOR BY PRICING

Residents of a city or town can be charged for water usage in at least three different ways: (1) everyone can be charged the same amount; (2) everyone can be charged a monthly or quarterly flat-rate, based on the number of water outlets in their residences; or (3) everyone can be charged individually for the water they actually consume, as measured by a meter.

In the first case, residents are not motivated to conserve water, and consumers who use little water subsidize those who use a lot. In the second case, the charge is somewhat more equitable because water usage tends to vary with the number of outlets. However, such a system does not motivate consumers to conserve water (although it may influence their decisions to add or delete bathrooms). If meters are installed, however, consumers are more likely to conserve water.

Prices that affect clients directly tend to have the greatest influence on consumption. Normally, as the price for a unit of service increases, clients consume fewer units. In some situations, however, price is a mere bookkeeping charge with no direct effect on client behavior. Some schools, for example, provide students and faculty with monetary allowances for computer and Internet usage that entitle them to a certain amount of time. These allowances may be set so high, or may be so easily supplemented, that they do not motivate thoughtful consumption of the resource.

Measure of output

Measures of output in non-monetary terms, such as the number of visitors to a community center, or the number of hours teachers spend with students, are likely to be cruder than monetary measures. If, for example, each service furnished by an LG is priced at its cost, total revenue for a period approximates the total amount of service provided during that period. Even if the prices do not measure the real value of an LG's services to individual clients or to society, the revenue-based approximation may provide useful information to managers. For example, if revenue in one year is lower than that of the previous year (after adjustments for inflation), managers have a good indication that the LG's real output has decreased.

If the quantity of service provided varies among an LG's clients, a single price will not accurately measure the variations. At one time, for example, hospital patients were charged a flat rate per day, even though the services they received varied greatly based on their illnesses. Today hospital charges vary more directly with the type and quantity of services provided. Moreover, if the unit price of a service reflects its relative magnitude, then total revenue is, in effect, a weighted measure of output, i.e., it incorporates differences in the services rendered.

Behavior of managers

If services are sold, the responsibility center that sells them frequently is established as a profit center. In general, profit center managers are motivated to think of ways to (a) render additional services (so as to increase revenue), (b) reduce costs, or (c) change prices. Under these circumstances, the manager of a profit center in an LG behaves much like a manager in a for-profit company.

NORMAL PRICING

Ideally, the price of a product or service provided by an LG is its full cost plus an appropriate margin. This is the same approach that is used in normal pricing in the for-profit sector, except that in for-profit companies the margin ordinarily is higher due to the need to provide a return to shareholders.

Rationale for normal pricing

While the basic goal of an LG is to provide services, it nevertheless must generate revenues that are at least equal to its expenses or it will encounter financial difficulties.[5] Moreover, like their for-profit counterparts, LGs need an excess of revenue over expenses to finance working capital (such as for inventories and accounts receivable) and the purchase of new or replacement fixed assets (e.g., equipment, vehicles, buildings). This latter need for a surplus is because inflation usually increases replacement costs, such that depreciation on existing assets (even if sequestered in a special fund) will not provide sufficient funds for their replacement. Finally, as many LGs have seen over the past several years, a surplus during good economic times can provide a reserve that will help the LG to weather bad times. In all instances, however, an LG needs to keep the generational equity concept in mind. That is, its senior management needs to recognize that, while small surpluses for protection against economic downturns may be appropriate, the surpluses should not be too much greater than those needed to fund working capital and fixed-asset replacement.

Approach to normal pricing

In setting a price, an LG faces three tricky issues. First, the relevant costs are not historical costs, but estimates of future costs. Making these estimates can be difficult at times, especially when the LG's environment has a great deal of uncertainty.

A second issue is whether the underlying cost analysis should include depreciation on buildings and equipment. Some people maintain that accounting for depreciation is necessary to help provide for replacement of these assets. Moreover,

197

by including depreciation as an element of cost, an LG is in keeping with generally accepted accounting standards. Of course, those LGs that use a cash-basis of accounting will not include depreciation as an item of expense, but they nevertheless could include it in a cost analysis used to set prices.

THE PRICING UNIT

In general, the smaller and more specific the pricing unit, the better. Such a unit improves senior management's knowledge of, and decisions about, cross-product subsidization, and also measures output more accurately than otherwise. By contrast, a price that includes several discrete services with different costs is not a good measure of output because it masks the actual mix of services rendered.

The practice of isolating small units of service for pricing purposes is called *unbundling*, and managers who unbundle services should be mindful of two qualifications. First, beyond a certain point, the paperwork and other costs associated with pricing tiny units of service outweigh the benefits. Some hospitals charge for individual aspirin tablets, for example, a practice that is difficult to defend.

The second qualification is that the consequences of such pricing should be consistent with the LG's overall policies and goals. This qualification extends beyond the pricing unit to matters that are much more strategic in nature. For example, the Port Authority of New York and New Jersey charges the same amount for a tunnel crossing of the Hudson River as for a crossing using the George Washington Bridge, despite a lower cost per vehicle for bridge traffic. The pricing decision is based on transportation policy, rather than on the cost of the separate services. Using a contrasting transportation policy, Boston has different toll prices for its airport tunnels.

Hospital pricing as an example of unbundling

Table 7.4 shows several approaches that could be used to price a hospital's services. Moving from Approach A to Approach D, one can see pricing practices that involve (1) an increase in record keeping, (2) a corresponding increase in the amount of output information available for senior management, and (3) a basis for charging clients that more accurately reflects the services they receive. At one extreme, for example, the hospital could charge an all-inclusive rate of, say, $2,000 per day. This practice (shown in Approach A) is advocated by some people on the grounds that patients can know in advance what their bills will be (assuming their lengths of stay can be estimated), and also because record keeping, at least for billing purposes, is simplified.

A common variation on the all-inclusive price is shown in Approach B. Here the hospital charges separately for the cost of each easily identifiable special service, but has a blanket daily charge for everything else. In fact, rather than a price per radiology film

Table 7.4 Pricing alternatives in a hospital

(A) All-inclusive rate		(B) Daily rate plus special services	
Rate, per day	$2,000	Patient care, per day	$1,000
		Operating room, per hour	500
		Pharmacy, per dosage	10
		Radiology, per film	50
		Special nurses, per hour	100
		Etc.	...

(C) Daily charge per type of service		(D) Detailed	
Medical/surgical: 1st day	$1,000	Admittance	$800
Medical/surgical: other days, per day	750	Workup, per hour	50
Maternity: 1st day	700	Medical/surgical, per day	800
Maternity: other days, per day	500	Maternity bed, per day	500
(plus special services as in B)		Bassinet, per day	200
		Nursery care, per hour	80
		Meals, per day	70
		Discharge	100
		(plus special services as in B)	

(as shown here), radiology prices, could be calculated according to a rather detailed point system that takes into account the complexity of the procedure, with each point worth a few cents. (There is, of course, some incongruity in calculating prices for certain services in terms of points worth a few cents each, while lumping other service costs into a large overall rate).

Approach C unbundles the daily charge. Different charges are made for each department, and more is charged for the first day than for subsequent days. This pricing policy accounts for the admitting and workup costs associated only with the first day of a patient's stay.

Approach D is the job-cost approach that is used in many for-profit companies. Managers of automobile repair shops, for example, cost each repair job separately. Each job is charged for the services of mechanics according to the number of hours they work on the job, as well as for each part and significant supply item required for the job's completion. The sum of these separate charges is the basis for the price the customer pays. Customers of a repair garage would not tolerate any other approach. They would not, for example, agree to pay the garage's average daily cost for repairs, regardless of the service they receive (unless, of course, they were receiving a simple, low-cost service!). Nevertheless, many LGs do not use a job-cost approach even when one could be implemented rather easily.

199

> ## BOX 7.12   JOB-COST APPROACH IN PRICING PUBLIC SERVICES
>
> In most LGs, citizens pay, via their taxes, the average cost incurred by the fire department for extinguishing a fire, even if they caused no fires or caused only a small fire. Yet, it would be rather easy to charge the person or company that caused the fire an amount that reflected the time and expenses associated with extinguishing it.

VARIATIONS FROM NORMAL PRICES

There are many situations in LGs where circumstances call for variations from the normal approach to setting prices. In some instances, these situations arise because of the requirements of third-party payers. In others, they arise because the LG wishes to distinguish between services provided as part of its main mission and those that are more peripheral. As a result, there are several areas where an LG may wish to use some approach other than normal pricing.

Cost-plus pricing

With cost-plus pricing, the purchaser of an LG's services (usually a region or state) agrees to pay full cost plus an agreed-upon increment, usually a percentage. Many government contracts are written this way, especially in the defense industry, where the argument is made that the activities needed to design and manufacture the product are so uncertain that it would be impossible to determine the cost in advance, and hence to set a reasonable price.

Although the intent of cost-plus pricing usually is to pay the full cost of the service, the definition of full cost can vary among purchasers. In particular, some purchasers define certain costs as "unallowable." These are costs that, although incurred by the LG, may not be included in the cost computation used to arrive at the payment rate. Purchasers also may specify ceilings for certain items, such as the compensation of executives or the daily amount that can be spent for travel.

Market-based pricing

LG managers may use normal prices for services that are directly (or closely) related to their organization's principal objectives, but may use market prices for peripheral services.

BOX 7.13   PRICING POLICIES RELATED TO MISSION GOALS

Many universities use normal pricing for room and board charges because students live in dormitories and eat in dining rooms as a necessary part of the educational process. By contrast, they will use market prices for space rentals to outside groups since these activities are not closely related to the main mission. Similarly, many universities use normal pricing for tuition for graduate and undergraduate programs but market rates for executive education programs.

In making pricing decisions, managers often have difficulty drawing a line between programs that are closely related to the LG's mission and those that are more peripheral. For example, market rates seem appropriate for executive education programs while their use for community education programs is much less clear.

Subsidized pricing

A subsidy exists when the price is set below full cost. Most subsidies are intended to encourage clients to use a service. For example, many public bathing beaches and other recreation facilities charge a lower price on weekdays than on weekends to encourage off-peak use.

In general, LGs use three types of subsidies: (1) for certain services, (2) for certain clients, and (3) for all clients.

Subsidizing certain services

An LG may decide to price a certain service at less than the normal price to encourage use by clients who are unable or unwilling to pay the normal price. Or, as a matter of policy, an LG may want clients to select services on some basis other than their ability to pay. Examples are public education and low-cost housing. In most circumstances, providing a service at a subsidized price is preferable to providing it for free, since a price, even if low, motivates clients to give thought to the service's value.

An LG may decide to use the same price for all services even though some cost more than others. In this case, the higher-cost services are subsidized by the lower-cost ones. Although cross-subsidization is frowned upon in some settings, there may be sound reasons for its use (see the discussion of "merit goods" in Chapter 1).

201

BOX 7.14   SUBSIDIES FOR CERTAIN SERVICES

Latin and Greek courses in a city college typically have small enrollments, result-ing in a higher faculty cost per student than in more popular courses. Because the college does not want to discourage enrollment in these courses, however, it charges the same tuition to all students. Thus, low-enrollment courses are sub-sidized by high-enrollment courses.

Most postal services subsidize rural post offices because their mission is to provide convenient mail service to everyone; this principle is rarely challenged.

Even if LG managers do not use cost as the basis for pricing, they may find it helpful to calculate the costs of subsidized services. Knowing the difference between price and full cost can help flag areas for managerial decision making. For example, if a service does not cover its full costs, managers have several possible courses of action:

- Accept the loss, recognizing that the service is sufficiently important to the LG's strategy to warrant subsidization.
- Reduce the variable costs or fixed costs directly associated with the service in an effort to have its revenue cover its costs.
- Increase volume (if the service makes a contribution, there is some breakeven volume at which full costs will be covered).
- Raise the price of the service.
- Phase out the service.

Subsidizing some clients

A client who is not charged the same amount as other clients who receive the same or comparable services is being subsidized. The usual reason for the subsidy is that the LG's objective is to provide the service to all qualified clients, even those who are unable to pay the normal price. For example, some city colleges provide subsidies to certain students in the form of scholarships and other financial aid. Some museums charge reduced prices to children.

In some instances, a class of clients is subsidized even though some members of the class have ample resources. Examples are subsidies given to disabled and elderly people for transportation, movies, restaurants, drugs, and a variety of other services. Conceptually, the subsidy should be limited to those in need, but finding a practical way to apply this concept is difficult. A "means test" usually is not feasible because it is expensive and time consuming, and, more importantly, because many people resent being classified as needy. Moreover, such a subsidy tends to be politically popular, and any attempt to eliminate or modify it would encounter considerable resistance from lobbying groups.

Subsidizing all clients

Some organizations receive contributions or appropriations intended to subsidize their services for all clients. When this happens, no client pays the normal price for services. Museums, symphony orchestras, and city universities are examples.

FREE SERVICES

Some services are provided free to clients. This sometimes happens when an LG's senior managers decide that it would be discriminatory to charge for a particular service, or when they determine that attempting to collect for a service would be unfeasible or politically untenable.

Public goods

As discussed in Chapter 1, the most important class of free services is public goods, which are services provided for the benefit of the public in general, rather than for specific users. Examples include police protection, city parks, street lighting, and traffic light maintenance. In effect, public goods are goods (and services) that simply cannot be provided through the market because (a) they are supplied to users as a group rather than to specific individuals, (b) there is no easy way to establish a pricing unit, and (c) there is no way of withholding them from users who refuse to pay for them.

BOX 7.15   PUBLIC GOODS AS INTRINSIC FREE SERVICES

Road and traffic light maintenance services are provided to all persons in an LG. Everyone receives the same services, whether they are willing to pay for them or not. There is no way of withholding the service, or creating a market that separates those who pay from those who do not. In fact, in this type of situation, rational consumers who are interested only in economics will never pay since they will get the benefit in any event (Eckstein 1967: 8).

Quasi-public goods

Many services that seem to meet the definition of public goods turn out upon analysis to be services for which prices could be charged.

203

> ## BOX 7.16   CHARGING FOR QUASI-PUBLIC GOODS?
> The classic example of a public good is a lighthouse. One ship's "consumption" of the warning light does not leave less warning light for other ships to "consume," there is no easily-established pricing unit, and there is no practical way that the lighthouse keeper could prohibit ships from consuming it. At the same time, a ship cannot refuse to consume the light. It can be argued, however, that ship owners, *as a class*, should pay for lighthouses. Then, if lighthouse costs become too high, the objections of ship owners may help bring them back in line.[6]

The lighthouse example in Box 7.16 is similar to the practice of charging users of highways for their cost via tolls or fuel-related taxes, or of charging airlines and owners of private aircraft for the cost of operating the air traffic control system. Similarly, in some countries, the airwaves are considered a quasi-public good and users are charged for them through a tax on television sets. In others, they are considered as public goods and are free.

Peripheral services

Even when some services are considered to be public goods, managers may be able to charge for certain peripheral services. For example, most LGs charge for animal licenses and municipal parking. Some public school systems charge for extracurricular programs, such as after-school athletics.

Other free services

In addition to the general class of public goods, there are other situations in which prices should not normally be charged for services. These include the following situations:

- Services are provided as a public policy, but clients cannot afford to pay for them. Examples include welfare investigations and legal aid services.
- Services are not rationed on the basis of ability to pay. Examples include elected officials, who do not charge fees for assisting constituents, even though an official's time is a valuable resource.
- A charge is politically untenable. Examples include tours of government offices. The public clamor over such a charge could be harmful to overall organizational objectives.
- Client motivation is unimportant. A nominal charge to a public park or bathing beach will not measure actual output, nor will it influence a client's decision to use the facilities. At the same time, a charge equal to full cost, would motivate

less wealthy individuals to avoid using these facilities, which may be inconsistent with public policy.

SUMMARY

A calculation of full cost is necessary for at least three reasons. First, for accountability, where the aim is to know the resources that were consumed for a specific program or service. This is especially important when a third party pays for the service on the basis of its costs or, more generally, when citizens and other stakeholders need cost information to assess value. Second, full cost information can be helpful to the LG's managers who determine the fees for different services, especially for services that are expected to be self sufficient or earn a surplus. Third, full-cost information is needed to determine the contribution that general taxpayer resources must make to those services that do not operate on a breakeven basis from user fees, or do not charge user fees.

Full-cost information also may facilitate comparisons among the costs of two or more LGs that are delivering similar services. However, such comparisons should be made with caution, as there can be many differences – all quite legitimate – in how different LGs go about their full-cost accounting efforts.

The prices that an LG charges (or decides not to charge) for its services influence the behavior of clients, provide a measure of output, and influence the behavior of managers and professional service providers. The price that is usually charged is called the "normal price." It is the sum of the full cost of a service plus an appropriate margin.

Prices charged for subsidized services are less than normal prices. Subsidized prices may be charged only for certain services, only to certain clients, or to all clients. In some instances, for sound public policy purposes, a service may be provided free of charge.

DISCUSSION QUESTIONS

1 What is the value of knowing the full cost of one of an LG's programs or departments? What can citizens do with this information?
2 How should an LG determine which programs and services should be subsidized? How should it determine the amounts of the subsidies?

NOTES

1 A DRG is a collection of several related diagnoses. There are several hundred DRGs.

2 This terminology can be confusing. *Allocation* is sometimes called *apportionment,* and vice versa. Moreover, the terms *assignment, distribution, allocation,* and *apportionment* occasionally are used interchangeably. In addition to these terminology differences, service center costs that are allocated to production centers often are called *indirect* or *overhead costs*. The context usually clarifies the meaning, but because of these terminology differences, it is important to understand the activities taking place rather than to memorize definitions of the terms.

3 As is the case in many LGs where a cash accounting system is used, this is a cash budget and not an operating budget. Yet, it is usually the only source of information available for citizens and other stakeholders, including the LG's decision makers.

4 Technically, the debt payment is an *expenditure* and not an *expense*. As discussed in Chapter 3, LGs that do not depreciate their assets (as this one apparently does not) sometimes use principal payments on their debt as a surrogate for depreciation. However, since not all assets are financed with debt, and not all debt instruments have the same term, using principal payments can be misleading. However, assigning debt service payments to cost centers based on their proportion of fixed assets would be better than not assigning them at all.

5 In recent years these difficulties have extended to the point where some LGs have filed for bankruptcy.

6 In a fascinating article, Coase (1974) describes the history of British lighthouses, showing that they, in fact, successfully charged fees from the 17th century until the present.

REFERENCES

Coase, R.E. (1974) "The Lighthouse in Economics," *Journal of Law and Economics,* 17(2): 357–76.

Eckstein, O. (1967) *Public Finance,* 2nd edn, Englewood Cliffs, New Jersey: Prentice-Hall.

Martin, L.L. and Mikovsky, L.P. (2010) "Comparative performance measurement in decentralized systems: the case of the Florida Benchmarking Consortium," *International Journal of Public Sector Performance Management,* 1(4): 376–89.

Simons, M. (1990) "Europeans Begin to Calculate the Price of Pollution," *New York Times,* December 9.

Young, D.W. (2010) *The Reciprocal Method of Cost Allocation,* Cambridge, Massachusetts: The Crimson Press Curriculum Center.

FURTHER READING

The details for developing an activity-based costing system are beyond the scope of this chapter, but might be helpful for some readers who are interested in improved cost information. For a quick overview of ABC, see D.W. Young, *Note on Activity Based Costing* (The Crimson Press Curriculum Center 2010). For a more lengthy discussion applied to a nonprofit context, see D.W. Young, *Management Control in Nonprofit Organizations*, (8th edn, The Crimson Press 2008), Chapter 3. For additional information, including a discussion in a for-profit context, see R. Cooper and R. S. Kaplan, *The Design of Cost Management Systems* (Prentice Hall 1991). Tony Proctor provides an interesting overview of pricing of public services under an economic and marketing perspective, with also a specific close examination of LGs pricing practices, in Chapter 10 of *Public Sector Marketing* (FT Press 2007).

Chapter 8

Measuring differential costs and assessing outsourcing opportunities

LEARNING OBJECTIVES

At the end of this chapter you should:

- Know when it is appropriate to use differential costs in an analysis.
- Understand the distinction among fixed, variable, step-function, and semi-variable costs.
- Be able to perform a relatively simple cost-volume-profit (CVP) analysis.
- Understand the distinction between direct and indirect costs (which typically are used in a full-cost analysis) and fixed and variable costs (which should be used in a differential-cost analysis).
- Know how to identify the level of risk inherent in an outsourcing decision, and how best to manage that risk.

KEY POINTS

- Costs can be divided between those that are relatively fixed and those that vary with changes in volume. The fixed/variable distinction can help to show how a change in the volume of activity of a particular program or service will affect its costs.
- A CVP analysis can help a local government's (LG's) management to determine the level of general taxpayer support needed for those programs and services that either do not charge fees or that have their price set below their full cost.

- A differential-cost analysis attempts to identify the behavior of an organization's costs under one or more scenarios that are related to a decision under consideration. These decisions are called alternative-choice decisions.
- The degrees of risk associated with an outsourced program or service can be assessed along three dimensions: citizen sensitivity, market competition, and switching costs.
- With high-risk outsourcing (defined as high citizen sensitivity, low market competition, and high vendor switching costs) the monitoring of a contract must be supplemented with a variety of other activities to ensure not only effectiveness, but responsiveness of the vendor to citizen needs and problems.
- Outsourcing a service does not mean excluding it from an LG's management control process. For example, the budgeting phase of the process must incorporate the contract with the vendor; otherwise the LG's budget will be incomplete. In addition, the various output measures for the outsourced services need to be an integral part of the measuring and reporting phases of the management control process.

A significant concept in cost accounting is that *different costs are used for different purposes*. The full-cost accounting principles discussed in Chapter 7 are useful for activities such as pricing, but are inappropriate for a variety of what are called "alternative choice" decisions – decisions that are made regularly in many LGs. The two principal kinds of alternative choice decisions in LGs are whether to retain or discontinue a program or service that is unprofitable on a full-cost basis (and thus requires support from general taxpayers), and whether to perform an activity in-house or outsource it.

There is nothing illegal or unethical about looking at costs differently for different purposes. Indeed, as managers' decision-making needs change, so too do the relevant costs. With full-cost accounting, for example, the goal is to determine each program's or service's direct costs plus its fair share of the LG's overhead costs. With differential-cost accounting, by contrast, the goal is to assess cost behavior, and sometimes to undertake a CVP analysis. Indeed, while the idea of profit in an LG (or any other nonprofit organization) might sound inconsistent or unethical, it is nothing of the sort (Young 2008). We discuss later how a CVP analysis can help management to determine the level of general taxpayer support needed for those programs and services that either do not charge fees or that have fee revenues below their full costs.

We have divided this chapter into two major sections. In the first, we discuss the kinds of costs analyses that typically are used for an alternative choice decision. In the second, we take up the topic of outsourcing, which has become a major issue for many LGs.

THE NATURE OF COST ANALYSIS FOR ALTERNATIVE CHOICE DECISIONS

A key question in an alternative choice analysis is "What will costs (and sometimes revenues) be under the different scenarios being considered?" That is, which costs (and revenues) will be *different*? For example, if an LG outsources an activity, some existing costs will be eliminated but some new costs will be incurred. If a fee-charging program is discontinued, some costs will be eliminated, but so will some revenues.

Assessing differential revenues ordinarily is easy, but determining how costs will change can be tricky. Indeed, using full-cost information as a basis for assessing cost behavior can lead LG managers to make decisions that are financially detrimental to their organizations.

BOX 8.1   FULL-COST INFORMATION IS NOT APPROPRIATE FOR ALTERNATIVE CHOICE DECISIONS

Assume that the full cost of educating a child in a certain public school system is $7,500 a year. This figure includes teachers' salaries, curriculum supplies and materials, a fair share of individual school overhead expenses (such as the principal's salary) and a fair share of the school system's overhead expenses (such as the school system superintendent's salary). The decision to reduce enrollment by ten students clearly would not save $75,000 (10 × $7,500), since it is unlikely that teacher salaries, individual school overhead, or school system overhead would change with a reduction of ten students.

Even the decision to close an entire school would not save $7,500 per student since it is unlikely that the school system's overhead expenses would be reduced. Moreover, if closing a given school resulted in shifting some tax revenues that had been assigned to the school system to some other use, the school system would be worse off as a result of the closing – its revenues would have declined by more than its costs.

COST BEHAVIOR

To analyze cost behavior, we need to divide costs between those that are relatively fixed and those that vary with changes in volume. This distinction between *fixed* and *variable* costs lets us see more clearly how a change in the volume of activity of a particular program or service will affect its costs. It, as well as the refinements of step-function and semi-variable costs, is shown schematically in Figure 8.1.

Fixed costs

Fixed costs are independent of the number of units that are produced. While no costs are fixed if the time period is long enough, the relevant range for fixed costs (i.e., the span of units over which they remain unchanged) generally is quite large, so they can be viewed graphically as shown in Segment A of Figure 8.1. An example of a fixed cost is building depreciation or rent. Regardless of the number of units of service provided, the amount of depreciation (or rent) will remain the same.

Step-function costs

Step-function costs are similar to fixed costs except they have much narrower relevant ranges. As such, they do not change in a smooth fashion, but are added in "lumps," or "steps." The result is that, graphically, they take the form shown in Segment B of Figure 8.1, where the dotted lines represent discontinuous jumps. A good example of a step-function cost in many organizations is supervision.

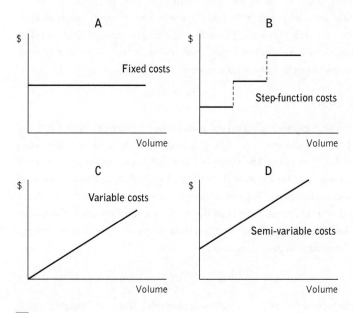

Figure 8.1 *Types of cost behavior*

BOX 8.2 EXAMPLES OF STEP-FUNCTION COSTS

In an LG's human services department, as the number of social workers and other professionals increases, supervisory personnel must be added. Since it ordinarily is difficult to add part-time supervisory help, supervisory costs will tend to behave in a step-like fashion.

In a school system or day care center, new teachers are added in step-like increments when the number of students (either in the school or in a given course) reaches a certain level.

As the number of swimming pool users increases (perhaps because the pool is open for more hours), additional lifeguards are needed; these usually are added in steps.

Variable costs

Variable costs, shown in Segment C of Figure 8.1, change in a roughly linear fashion with changes in volume, such that, as volume increases, total variable costs increase in constant proportion. The result is a straight line whose slope is determined by the amount of variable costs associated with each unit of output. In a school cafeteria, meal ingredients are variable costs – they increase in direct proportion to the number of meals served. Paving materials (e.g., gravel and asphalt) for re-grading a road are variable with respect to the length of the road. Some road projects, such as expressways, that are multilane and paved with concrete, will have relatively high variable costs per kilometer (or mile), resulting in a line that slopes upward quite steeply. Other projects, such as a two-lane rural road, will have relatively low variable costs for each kilometer, resulting in a line with a more gradual slope.

Semi-variable costs

Semi-variable costs (sometimes called mixed costs) share features of both fixed and variable costs. There is a minimum level that is fixed, and the cost line then rises linearly with increases in volume. The result is a line that begins at some level above zero, and slopes upward, as shown in Segment D of Figure 8.1. A good example of a semi-variable cost is electricity. Typically, there is some base cost each month for electrical service that an LG must incur even if it uses no electricity at all. Costs then increase in accordance with the number of kilowatt hours used. Similar cost patterns exist for other utilities such as gas and water.

Total costs

Total costs are the sum of fixed, step-function, variable, and semi-variable costs. Because cost analyses combining all four types of costs are quite complex, most analysts generally classify all costs as either fixed or variable. For semi-variable costs, an analyst can incorporate the fixed element into total fixed costs and add the variable element to the variable costs. For step-function costs, the width of the relevant range typically dictates whether the cost is added to fixed costs or incorporated into the unit-variable amount.

BOX 8.3 ANALYZING SEMI-VARIABLE AND STEP-FUNCTION COSTS

The youth center of a town has annual rent and other fixed costs of €100,000, and variable supply and material costs of €100 per client. Its annual meal costs are semi-variable. They have a fixed element (a part-time dietitian) of €14,000, and a variable component (food and beverage) of €500 per client.

In computing total costs, the center can divide its semi-variable cost item into its fixed and variable components. The result is the breakdown of costs shown in Table 8.1.

Table 8.1 *Fixed, variable, and semi-variable costs in a youth center*

Cost element	Fixed amount	Variable amount per client
Rent and other fixed	€100,000	€0
Supplies and materials	0	100
Meals	14,000	500
Total	€114,000	€600

The center also has a client:counselor ratio of 15:1. Each counselor earns €30,000 per year. The step function costs are shown in Figure 8.2.

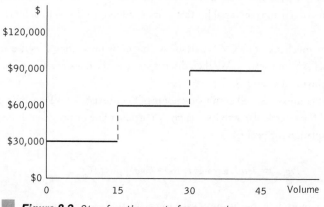

Figure 8.2 *Step-function costs for counselors*

Because counselor salaries have a relatively large relevant range, the center treats them as fixed (within their relevant range). With this simplification, total costs for an estimated 30 to 45 clients are as shown in Table 8.2.

Table 8.2 Fixed, variable, semi-variable, and step-function costs in a youth center

Cost element	Fixed amount	Variable amount per client
Rent and other fixed	€100,000	€0
Supplies and materials	0	100
Meals	14,000	500
Counselors (for 30 to 45 clients)	90,000	0
Total	€204,000	€600

Note that the fixed costs are only valid within a range of 30 to 45 clients. Above 45 clients, they jump to a higher step. Below 30 clients they drop to a lower step.

COST-VOLUME-PROFIT ANALYSIS

Once costs have been classified as either fixed or variable, we can analyze how they will vary with changes in the volume of activity. The technique commonly used for this is called *cost-volume-profit (CVP) analysis*. The intent of a CVP analysis is to determine either (a) the volume of activity needed for an organization to achieve its profit (or financial surplus) goal, (b) the price that it needs to charge to achieve that goal, or (c) the cost limits (fixed and/or variable) that it must adhere to if it is to achieve the goal.

To explain the mechanics of a CVP analysis, we begin by presenting it as it usually is conducted in a for-profit setting. We then discuss some of the considerations that are needed when applying it to an LG.

In a for-profit context (as well as in many nonprofit contexts), a CVP analysis usually is conducted for a particular activity – such as a product line or program. It begins with the basic equation for profit:

$$\text{Profit} = \text{Total Revenues (TR)} - \text{Total Costs (TC)}$$

Total revenue for most activities is quite easy to calculate. If we assume that price is represented by the letter p and volume by the letter x, then total revenue is price times volume, or:

$$TR = px$$

Total costs are somewhat more complicated. CVP analysis requires distinguishing among the four different types of cost behavior discussed earlier. Let's begin with the simplest of cases, where there are no step-function or semi-variable costs. In this instance, the formula would be quite simple:

$$Total\ costs = Fixed\ costs + Variable\ costs$$

Fixed costs can be represented by the letter a, and variable costs per unit by the letter b. Thus, total variable costs are bx, where, as before, x represents volume. The resulting cost equation is:

$$TC = a + bx$$

This means that the fundamental profit equation can be shown as:

$$Profit = px - (a + bx)$$

This equation can be represented graphically as shown in Figure 8.3. On this graph, point $x1$ is the breakeven volume – it is the point at which total revenue (px) equals total costs ($a + bx$). With volume in excess of $x1$, the organization earns a profit; below $x1$, it incurs a loss.

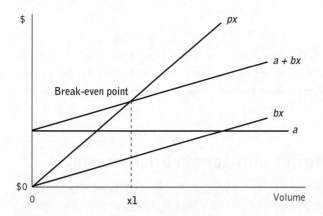

Figure 8.3 A graphic representation of a CVP analysis

BOX 8.4 COMPUTING BREAKEVEN VOLUME

The chamber of commerce of a local community publishes a monthly magazine for its members. The publication department has fixed costs of €120,000 a month, variable costs per magazine of €0.80, and it charges €2.00 per magazine. To determine breakeven volume (number of magazines per month), we can begin with the CVP formula, and substitute the known elements. We then solve for the unknown, which in this case is volume, or x.

$$Profit = px - (a + bx)$$

At breakeven, profit = 0, and, therefore, $px = a + bx$, or

$$2.00x = 120,000 + 0.80x$$
$$1.20x = 120,000$$
$$x = 100,000$$

At breakeven therefore is 100,000 magazines.

Unit contribution margin

An important aspect of CVP analysis is *unit contribution margin*. This is the contribution to fixed costs that comes about as a result of each additional unit sold, or the difference between the price and the unit-variable cost. By rearranging the terms of the CVP formula, we can see that breakeven volume is simply fixed costs divided by unit contribution margin, as follows:

$$px = a + bx$$
$$px - bx = a$$
$$x(p - b) = a$$
$$x = a \div (p - b)$$

Stated somewhat differently, price minus unit-variable cost tells us how much each unit sold contributes to the recovery of fixed costs. When this amount is divided into fixed costs, the result is the volume needed to recover all fixed costs, i.e., breakeven volume.

BOX 8.5 COMPUTING UNIT CONTRIBUTION MARGIN

The publication department of the chamber of commerce discussed above has a unit contribution margin of €1.20 (€2.00 – €0.80). Dividing this amount into its fixed costs of €120,000, gives its breakeven volume of 100,000 magazines.

Incorporating other variables into a CVP analysis

Thus far, we have been using CVP analysis to solve only for breakeven *volume*. Clearly, if we knew (a) how many units we were likely to sell, (b) our fixed costs, and (c) our unit-variable costs, we then could determine the price needed to break even. Similarly, if we were in an environment where price was given, and we knew approximately how many units we could sell at that price, we could set up either fixed costs or unit-variable costs as the unknown and solve for it.

We also could incorporate the need for a profit (or a financial surplus) into a CVP analysis simply by adding the amount of desired profit to our fixed costs. We then could calculate a "breakeven point" with the new level of "fixed costs."

BOX 8.6   INCORPORATING PROFIT INTO A CVP ANALYSIS

The chamber of commerce wants its publication department to generate a surplus of €15,000 to help fund some of the chamber's non-revenue-generating activities. To determine the number of magazines the department needs to sell to generate this surplus, we add the €15,000 surplus to the €120,000 of fixed costs, and divide the total by the unit contribution margin of €1.20, or

$$x = (€120,000 + €15,000) \div €1.20 = 112,500$$

The publication department now must sell 112,500 magazines.

CVP analysis with step-function costs

Conducting a CVP analysis with step-function costs can be a little tricky. Ideally, we would like to be able to assume that, for any given volume level, we could simply add together the step-function costs and the fixed costs to give us the total applicable fixed costs. We then could use the CVP formula. Unfortunately, since volume is the unknown in the equation, the process is not quite that simple, as the example in Box 8.7 illustrates.

BOX 8.7   INCLUDING STEP-FUNCTION COSTS IN A CVP ANALYSIS

Assume that, in addition to the €120,000 in fixed costs stipulated earlier for the chamber of commerce, the publication department has some supervisory costs. These costs behave as shown in Table 8.3.

217

Table 8.3 *Behavior of supervisory costs*

Volume (number of magazines)	Costs
0–50,000	€10,000
50,001–100,000	20,000
100,001–150,000	30,000
150,001–200,000	40,000

If we ignore the need for a surplus, we have the following equation:

$$€2.00x = (€120,000 + €10,000) + €0.80x$$

$$€1.20x = €130,000$$

$$x = 108,333$$

The problem with this solution is that, while breakeven is 108,333 magazines, the relevant range for the step-function costs was only 0–50,000 magazines. Thus, a breakeven of greater than 50,000 magazines is invalid. Only when we get to the third level do we encounter a valid solution, as follows:

$$€2.00x = (€120,000 + €30,000) + €0.80x$$

$$€1.20x = €150,000$$

$$x = 125,000$$

The conclusion we can draw from this analysis is that the incorporation of step-function costs into a CVP analysis requires a trial-and-error process to reach a valid breakeven volume.

Incorporating a local government's constraints into a CVP analysis

In many LGs, a CVP analysis can be an invaluable tool for decision-makers. For programs where clients are charged fees that were established (perhaps for political reasons, as discussed in Chapter 7) at a level below full cost, a CVP analysis can show the volume of activity that the program can provide given a certain amount of general taxpayer support (or grants from other governments entities). Alternatively, given an anticipated volume of activity and a specific amount of general support, a CVP analysis can determine the fee that the LG needs to charge. Or, if a program or service has a specific amount of general support, a CVP analysis can show the cost limits that the program or service needs to adhere to.

BOX 8.8   CVP ANALYSIS IN AN ENVIRONMENT WITH POLITICAL PRICES

The fee for use of a town's swimming pool has been set at €2.00 per person per day. The town expects that 300 people will use the pool each day of the month. The costs to run the pool comprise such items as depreciation on the equipment, chlorination of the water, salaries of the administrative staff, and electricity (all of which are fixed no matter how many people use the pool). The costs also include lifeguards (which are step-function costs). With 300 people a day using the pool, the monthly fixed and step-function costs total €23,700. The variable cost is €0.20 for the cleaning of a towel that is provided to each patron. We now can use CVP analysis to determine the required support from general tax revenues:

Revenue per month	€18,000 (€2.00 × 300 × 30 days)
Less: variable costs	€1,800 (€0.20 × 300 × 30 days)
Contribution to fixed costs	€16,200
Less: fixed costs	€23,700
Surplus (deficit)	(€7,500)

Therefore, for each month the pool is open, the support from general taxpayer revenues would need to be €7,500.

Suppose, however, that the amount of taxpayer support had been set at €3,000 a month, the manager of the swimming pool would have three options: (a) raise the fee, (b) lower costs (either fixed or variable), or (c) limit the number of patrons. CVP analysis can be used to determine the impact of each of these options by establishing the option in question as the unknown in the equation (and lowering the monthly fixed costs by the €3,000 in support). If, for example, the manager thought that the price could be increased somewhat without decreasing the number of patrons, the new price could be computed as follows:

$$px = a + bx$$
$$p = (a + bx) \div x$$
$$a = €20,700 \ (€23,700 \ \text{minus} \ €3,000 \ \text{in general support})$$
$$p = [€20,700 + (€0.20 \times 300 \times 30)] \div (300 \times 30)$$
$$p = €2.50$$

Therefore, the price per patron would need to be raised to €2.50 (of course, this assumes that a price of €2.50 would not reduce the demand to fewer than 300 patrons a day).

The swimming pool example is one of many instances of an LG program where clients are charged, but where the price is set at a level below the average full cost per unit. With public transportation, for example, the price of a single ticket usually does not cover the average cost the LG incurs in providing the ride. In several European countries, municipal kindergarten or preschools are provided to most families at fees which cover only a fraction of the expenses. The same is true for many municipal theaters and museums. There also can be on-demand services for which citizens pay no fee, such as public libraries.

When there is no fee, it is impossible to calculate a breakeven point. In cases where the fee is very low, the breakeven point may be above full capacity.

BOX 8.9   WHEN BREAKEVEN VOLUME IS ABOVE FULL CAPACITY

An LG's public transportation system has a capacity of 540,000 bus rides a month. This number is obtained by multiplying the following figures:

Number of places available per bus: 60
Number of buses available on an average day: 10
Average number of trips (between two terminus points) per bus: 30
Number of days in a month: 30

If the fare per ticket is €1.00, the maximum revenue is €540,000. If fixed cost are, say, €1.2 million (there are no variable costs per passenger), then at maximum capacity utilization, the system will incur a loss of €660,000 (€540,000–€1,200,000). Thus, at the current capacity and fare levels, it is impossible to reach breakeven.

In instances where the fee is set at a level under the variable costs, the unit contribution margin is negative, and each unit of output provided creates a larger deficit.

BOX 8.10   CVP ANALYSIS WHEN UNIT CONTRIBUTION MARGIN IS NEGATIVE

At its ancient culture museum, a municipality charged €1.50 per admission. For each admission, the museum provided a free museum guide which cost €2.00. The total fixed cost (personnel, utilities, depreciation, and allocated administrative and general costs) per month were €200,000. In this situation, each new visitor increases the museum's deficit. In a for-profit context, the business

---

(or product line) might be discontinued. However, since the municipality considered the museum to be a service with positive externalities (museum visitors patronized the town's restaurants, hotels, shops, etc.) it allowed the museum to operate at a loss.

In a situation such as this, a CVP analysis can assist the LG's senior management team to determine the amount of grants or general taxpayer support that is needed to maintain the museum's operations. For example, if the museum expects to have 10,000 visitors in a month, the amount of general taxpayer support would be €205,000 (€200,000 in fixed costs plus a negative €0.50 unit contribution margin multiplied by 10,000 visitors).

Using information from full-cost reports

Two potential problems arise when information for a differential-cost analysis is obtained from full-cost reports: cost distinctions and the behavior of allocated costs. Each of these potential problems calls for an analyst to exercise caution in obtaining and working with full-cost data.

Cost distinctions

The analysis of differential costs would be simplified if, as occasionally is assumed, all indirect (or overhead) costs are fixed and all direct costs are variable. But this is rarely the case. Table 8.4 contains examples of four different cost types and their fixed/variable, direct/indirect distinctions. Note that each of the four cells in the matrix contains a possible cost, leading to the conclusion that the direct and indirect costs in a full-cost accounting system must be analyzed individually to determine how they can be expected to behave as volume changes.

Misleading allocation bases

Although an LG's full-cost accounting system may be attempting to measure the use of service center resources as precisely as possible, there nevertheless can be many instances where a given service center's basis of allocation does not accurately reflect the actual use of its services by receiving cost centers. If, for example, a program in a mission center is discontinued, the LG may be able to reduce some of the service center costs that were allocated to the mission center in question. In most instances, however, only the variable costs in the service center (plus, perhaps, some of its step-function costs) will be reduced. The remaining costs will be reallocated to other cost centers.

Table 8.4 *Cost examples: fixed/variable versus direct/indirect in the foster home program of a human service department*

	Fixed	Variable
Direct	Supervisor's salary in the foster home program	Payments to foster parents for room and board
Indirect	A portion of the executive director's salary, which is a fixed cost, and is part of administration – a support center whose costs are allocated to the foster home program	Electric bills, which are mainly variable costs, but are part of administration – a support center whose costs are allocated to the foster home program

---

BOX 8.11   COST ALLOCATION VERSUS COST BEHAVIOR

A reduction in the number of staff in a municipal theater (a mission center) will lead to a reduction in the theater's total salaries. If the costs of the administration and general (A&G) service center are allocated on the basis of salaries, there will be a reduction in the amount of A&G allocated to the theater. It is highly unlikely, however, that there will be a corresponding reduction in the staff or other costs in the A&G service center. Thus, more A&G costs will be allocated to those mission centers that did not reduce their salaries.

The reverse may happen as well. That is, a reduction in a mission center's activity may lead to a decrease in a service center's costs, but the costs allocated to that mission center may not show the full impact.

BOX 8.12   COST BEHAVIOR VERSUS COST ALLOCATION

Consider a service center such as cleaning and maintenance (C&M), whose costs are allocated on the basis of square meters. A change in the activities in a given mission center may reduce the center's need for C&M services, which will permit the manager of the C&M service center to reduce some costs. Yet, unless the space used by the mission center is reduced, the cost report (that allocates C&M on a square-meter basis) will not show an equivalent reduction in the C&M costs allocated to that mission center. The C&M costs allocated to the mission center will fall slightly as a result of the lower C&M costs *overall*, but the reduced allocation will be much

---

less than the actual cost reductions that took place in the C&M service center. The rest of the reductions will lower the allocations to those cost centers that continue to receive the same amount of C&M services as before.

DIFFERENTIAL COSTS VERSUS FIXED AND VARIABLE COSTS

With an understanding of costs according to the nature of their behavior, and with some background in the elements of a CVP analysis, we are in a position to undertake a differential-cost analysis. A differential-cost analysis attempts to identify the behavior of an organization's costs under one or more *alternative scenarios*. These scenarios are related to the decision under consideration. To illustrate this point, consider the example contained in Box 8.13.

BOX 8.13 UNDERTAKING A DIFFERENTIAL-COSTS ANALYSIS FOR A KEEP/DROP DECISION

A city transportation agency operates two mini-vans that take senior citizens on errands and shopping trips. It charges €1.50 a kilometer for each service kilometer driven. Last year, Van 1 drove 60,000 service kilometers, and Van 2 drove 30,000 service kilometers. The variable cost per kilometer (gasoline, tires, wear and tear) for each van was €0.70. Each driver (both were part-time) was paid a salary of €15,000 per year. Rent and administration totaled €36,000, and were allocated to each van on the basis of the number of service kilometers driven. As a result, total revenues and expenses for the year were as illustrated in Table 8.5.

Table 8.5 Profit and loss for the mini-van service

Item	Van 1	Van 2	Total
Revenue	€1.50 × 60,000 = €90,000	€1.50 × 30,000 = €45,000	€135,000
Variable costs	€0.70 × 60,000 = 42,000	€0.70 × 30,000 = 21,000	63,000
Drivers	15,000	15,000	30,000
Overhead costs (rent and admin.)	24,000	12,000	36,000
Total expenses	€81,000	€48,000	€129,000
Surplus (deficit)	€9,000	(€3,000)	€6,000

To answer the question of whether the agency's financial performance would have improved if Van 2 (which lost money) had been discontinued at the beginning of the year, we must structure the data in terms of differential costs. The question is not whether Van 2 lost money on a full-cost basis (as it did), but rather the nature of its differential costs and revenues; that is, how would the transportation agency's revenues and costs have changed if Van 2 had been discontinued?

Although the data are not as good as we might like, we nevertheless can see that discontinuing Van 2 would have eliminated its revenue and its variable costs, as well as the fixed cost of the driver. From all indications, however, the overhead costs (rent and administration) would have continued (i.e., they are not differential). The result would have been a shift from a €6,000 surplus to a €3,000 deficit, as the analysis in Table 8.6 indicates.

Table 8.6 *Profit and loss for the mini-van service without van 2*

Item	Van 1
Revenue	€1.50 × 60,000 = €90,000
Variable costs	€0.70 × 60,000 = 42,000
Drivers	15,000
Overhead costs (rent and admin.)	36,000
Total expenses	€93,000
Surplus (deficit)	(€3,000)

The example in Box 8.13 illustrates several important principles.

Principle #1: full-cost information can be misleading

The kind of information available from a full-cost accounting system can produce misleading results if used for a differential-cost decision. This is due mainly to the *apparent* behavior of overhead costs when they are allocated, as contrasted with their *true* behavior. Note that the overhead allocated to Van 2 did not go away when we eliminated the vehicle; it simply was reallocated to Van 1.

Principle #2: differential costs can include both fixed and variable costs

Although initially counter-intuitive, differential costs can include both fixed and variable costs. In the city transportation agency case, the driver's salary, while a fixed cost of Van 2, was eliminated when we eliminated the van. However, as long as we operate the van, we have the fixed cost of the salary; it does not fluctuate in accordance with the number of kilometers driven (within the relevant range). But when we eliminate the van, we also eliminate this cost in its entirety (assuming that union rules or the job contract allows management to do so); thus, it is differential in terms of a decision to eliminate or retain the service.

Principle #3: assumptions are needed

Differential-cost analyses focus on the future. As such, they require an analyst to make assumptions about many factors, from unit prices to staff efficiency. For example, inflation will affect an organization's costs, and perhaps its prices. The general state of the economy along with a wide variety of other matters will affect volume. For many managers, these factors raise concerns about the reliability of a differential-cost analysis. Despite these concerns, however, since we need to make a decision, we must speculate as best we can about how costs and revenues will behave.

Principle #4: sensitivity analysis is essential

Because assumptions play an important role in a differential analysis, we must attempt to identify and document them as completely as possible, and we need to explore how changes in them would affect the conclusions of the analysis. This activity is called *sensitivity analysis*.

If we were doing a sensitivity analysis for the city transportation agency scenario, we might try to determine how many more kilometers Van 1 would need to drive for the agency to maintain its €6,000 surplus. Or, if we thought we might be able to reduce our rent and administrative costs with an elimination of Van 2, we might ask by how much they would need to fall to maintain the €6,000 surplus. For example, if, by eliminating Van 2, we could reduce these costs by €9,000, we would be indifferent. That is, with rent and administrative costs reduced to €27,000 (€36,000-€9,000), Van 1 would earn a surplus of €6,000 – the same as we were earning with both vans. As a result, any reduction in overhead beyond €9,000 that resulted from the elimination of Van 2 would favor the decision to eliminate it.

Principle #5: causality must be present

A key aspect of differential analysis is causality – for an item to be included in a differential analysis, it must be *caused* by the alternative under consideration. For example, if we assume there will be an increase in the kilometers driven by Van 1, we would need to be certain that it was *caused* by the elimination of Van 2. If Van 1 would have driven more kilometers anyway, the increased distance is irrelevant for the differential analysis. If, on the other hand, we assume that the elimination of Van 2 means that some people who would have used it now would use Van 1 instead, then the increased distance is relevant for the differential analysis. We would need to include that additional distance in computing Van 1's revenue and variable expenses under the alternative scenario.

The same is true for cost items such as rent and administration. If we were planning to decrease our administrative costs with or without Van 2, then the change is irrelevant for the differential analysis. If, by contrast, the elimination of Van 2 would allow us to decrease rent and administrative costs (such as to eliminate a portion of the rent expense), then we would need to include this decrease in the differential analysis.

Principle #6: information must be structured appropriately

An analysis of differential costs is most easily performed when the fixed and variable costs of the particular activity are analyzed separately from the allocated overhead costs. An analysis that separates costs in this way usually is structured in terms of *contribution to overhead*. The difference between a unit's revenue and its variable, semi-variable, fixed, and step-function costs is its contribution to the organization's overhead costs.

A *contribution income statement*, which is the term for this analysis, has a different format from a more traditional income statement. A typical construction is as follows:

Total revenue
Less: total variable costs
Equals: margin (for fixed and overhead costs)
Less: the program's or service's fixed costs
Equals: program's or service's contribution to the organization's overhead costs
Less: allocated overhead costs
Equals: surplus (deficit) on a full-cost basis.

Table 8.7 shows how a contribution income statement would look for the city transportation agency. As it illustrates, while Van 2 was losing money on a full-cost basis, it was contributing €9,000 to overhead. Indeed, it was the elimination of the €9,000 contribution from Van 2 that led to the shift from a €6,000 profit to an €3,000 loss.

The basic principle is that, in the short-run, it is unwise to eliminate an activity that contributes to the coverage of overhead, even if it is losing money on a full-cost basis. This is because eliminating it will reduce the total contribution to overhead costs and thus will either reduce the organization's surplus or increase its loss.

Table 8.7 *Example of a contribution income statement*

Item	Van 1	Van 2	Total
Revenue	€1.50 × 60,000 = €90,000	€1.50 × 30,000 = €45,000	€135,000
Less: Variable costs	€0.70 × 60,000 = 42,000	€0.70 × 30,000 = 21,000	63,000
Contribution to fixed expenses	€48,000	€24,000	€72,000
Less: Fixed costs (Drivers)	15,000	15,000	30,000
Contribution to overhead	€33,000	€9,000	€42,000
Less: Overhead (rent and admin.)	24,000	12,000	36,000
Surplus (Deficit)	€9,000	(€3,000)	€6,000

THE OUTSOURCING DECISION[1]

Until now, the discussion of differential costs has been in situations where an alternative choice decision involved a change in volume. This is the characteristic of most keep/drop decisions. Some types of alternative choice decisions do not involve a change in volume, however. Perhaps the most common of these is an outsourcing (sometimes called a "make/buy" or "contract out") decision. In many government entities, but elsewhere as well, the outsourcing decision involves *privatizing* the service, i.e., contracting with a private entity (either for-profit or nonprofit) to provide it.

The underlying theory of outsourcing is that by having an external vendor provide a service, an LG can take advantage of the vendor's considerable experience and economies of scale. The result will be comparable or better quality services than those provided by the LG itself, at a reduced cost to the taxpayers, while still allowing the vendor to earn a profit.

During the past three decades LGs have undertaken a wide variety of outsourcing initiatives, including such disparate activities as prison operations, animal control,[2] legal services, fire protection, trash collection, recycling, health care, snow plowing, building maintenance, bill collection, data processing, street cleaning, and street repair.

BOX 8.14 EXAMPLES OF OUTSOURCING IN LOCAL GOVERNMENTS IN THE UNITED STATES

In Indianapolis, Indiana, outsourcing reduced public employment by 40 percent over three years in fields outside of police and fire services. Butte, Montana,

---

saved $600,000 a year by contracting with a private firm to run its municipal hospital. Newark, New Jersey, used a private firm to collect about one-third of its refuse, at a reported annual saving of over $200,000. It also hired private contractors to provide services such as tree trimming, building demolition, snow plowing, and street cleaning. Farmington, New Mexico, contracted with an independent firm to run its airport control tower at a cost savings of almost $200,000 a year. Scottsdale, Arizona, the first United States city to use a private company for fire protection, boasted better than average fire response times, at less than half the cost to cities of comparable size (Martin 1986).

In Italy, extensive LG reforms that began in 1990 created an impetus toward outsourcing, such that, by 2000, some 27 percent of Italian local services were provided by privately owned companies, and 40 percent were outsourced to companies owned by the public sector (Antonioli *et al.* 2000).

Maywood, California, a small city in the United States, exemplifies what is perhaps the most dramatic illustration of outsourcing seen to date anywhere. The city outsourced everything! (Streitfeld 2010).[3]

OUTSOURCING PRINCIPLES

Unfortunately, outsourcing has not always achieved an LG's dual goals of high quality services at reduced cost. In part, this is because some LGs have not managed their vendors as well as they might have. Yet, in many instances, an external vendor needs to be managed in much the same way as the LG would manage its own department if it kept the outsourced activity in house. In this regard, although each outsourcing opportunity is unique, and must be analyzed separately to decide on the relevant costs and other matters, there are a few general principles that are pertinent to almost all such decisions.

Time period

The longer the time period involved, the more costs are differential. For example, if the alternative being considered is to outsource a single printing job rather than use in-house facilities, the only reduction in costs might be the savings in paper and ink; the machinery would remain, payment to employees probably would not be reduced, and no overhead costs would be affected. If, however, the proposal is to discontinue the in-house print shop permanently, all the direct costs associated with operating it would be saved, as well as, perhaps, some of the overhead costs that were allocated to it.

Role of depreciation

A common error in calculating differential costs for outsourcing decisions (and other alternative choice decisions) is to include depreciation on plant and equipment as a cost that would be saved if the organization used an outside contractor to provide the service. Depreciation is not a differential cost, however. Once assets have been acquired, the costs incurred to purchase them are sunk. Depreciation is simply the accounting mechanism that charges each period with the expense associated with "using up" the asset. Since the past cannot be undone, and money spent cannot be recovered, there are no cash effects associated with depreciation.

Of course, if the asset can be sold, the amount realized is a differential cash inflow associated with the outsourcing decision, but this amount is based on the asset's market value, not its book value (purchase price less accumulated depreciation). Moreover, it is a one-time cash inflow only, and thus is relevant only for the first year of outsourcing.

If the outsourcing time frame is sufficiently long, such that the acquisition of new assets would be required under the "make" option, but not under the "buy" option, then depreciation might be used as a surrogate for the costs associated with replacing the assets as they wear out. However, the replacement cost rarely will correspond to the original purchase cost. It might be lower in the case of assets whose replacement cost is falling (such as computers), or higher if the replacement cost is increasing (such as medical technology).[4]

Non-quantifiable factors

In any outsourcing decision (in fact, in any *alternative choice* decision) there are a variety of factors that cannot be quantified easily, if at all, but that can easily tip the balance in one direction or another, frequently overriding the financial analysis. This is especially true if the financial analysis indicates that all options under consideration have roughly similar cost and revenue implications.

Non-quantitative considerations typically include factors such as quality, service, delivery, and reputation of the vendor. They also may include market considerations, such as the difficulty and/or cost of switching from one vendor to another if a particular relationship does not work out to management's satisfaction. And, they can include stakeholder sensitivity. If an LG outsources a service, such as waste collection and disposal, and the service is not performed according to expectations, the citizenry generally looks to the LG, not to the private contractor, as the responsible party. Depending on the service and its importance to the community, this can have an impact on how the citizenry votes in the next election.

229

OUTSOURCING FRAMEWORKS

There are two frameworks that can assist an LG's managers to think about outsourcing issues. The first framework can be used by senior management and department heads to assess the nature of the risk in outsourcing a service. The second focuses on the activities needed to manage the vendors of high-risk outsourced services.

Framework #1: assessing outsourcing risk

Some outsourced activities are almost risk free, whereas others are highly risky. Performed badly, they can create considerable citizen dissatisfaction. At the same time, the LG may have difficulty replacing the vendor.

BOX 8.15   DIFFERENT RISK LEVELS FOR DIFFERENT OUTSOURCED ACTIVITIES

If an LG outsources the printing of a brochure for a summer youth program the quality and service goals can be stated relatively easily in the contract (e.g., turnaround time, maximum number of reworks, etc.), all of which can be monitored with little difficulty. Moreover, there is little risk to the citizenry because of poor vendor performance. Even if the vendor performs badly, the mistakes usually can be corrected before the citizenry is aware of them.

By contrast, if the municipality outsources snow removal, and the streets are not plowed within a reasonable time after a heavy snowstorm, the citizenry will be acutely aware of the problem, even if corrective measures are taken later.

In addition to snow removal, there are activities such as waste collection, water supply, street lighting, animal control, and many other services where the quality and service goals are more elusive and where the citizenry is more directly affected by a vendor's performance. To identify the nature of the risk, an LG's management needs to assess a service that is a candidate for outsourcing from three perspectives: citizen sensitivity, market competition, and switching costs. These are illustrated in Figure 8.4 and discussed in the following sections.

Citizen sensitivity

From the citizens' perspective, an LG's trash removal service clearly is more important than, say, its publications department. Citizens are concerned about the timely removal of waste and only minimally concerned, if at all, about the printing quality of a brochure. In large part, this is because they are the final clients of waste

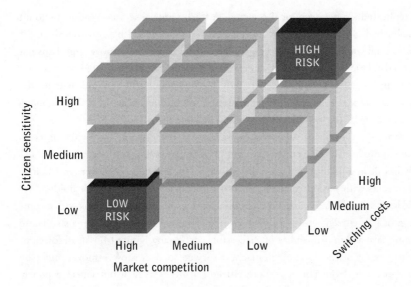

Figure 8.4 *The three dimensions of outsourcing risk assessment*
Source: Padovani and Young (2008: 220).

removal, such that, for the LG, the risk of nonperformance is much higher. As a result, any external outsourcing decision must weigh the impact of poor performance (or nonperformance) on the LG's citizenry.

Market competition

The supplier market can be characterized by its degree of competitiveness, ranging from many potential suppliers (high competition) to few or perhaps only one potential supplier. For example, there usually are many printing companies competing for an LG's publication business but there may be very few vendors offering trash removal services or nursery schools. As the number of potential vendors decreases, the ability of the LG to negotiate with them declines, as does its ability to benchmark performance.

Switching costs

Occasionally, outsourced activities are carried out with a mixture of unique resources, which cannot be transferred easily from one vendor to another. When this happens, an LG will have difficulty, and perhaps incur substantial costs, in replacing its existing vendor. For example, finding a new vendor for, say, a trash removal service or a nursery school could be quite difficult, due primarily to a variety of investments that will need

231

to be replicated if a new vendor is selected. A trash removal service vendor no doubt has established efficient routes for its vehicles, has determined how many vehicles it needs on each route due to the average volume of waste to be removed, perhaps has established relationships with certain citizens for specific kinds of waste removal, and so forth. In a nursery school, teachers have learned about children and their needs, and have established relationships with parents. In both instances, as well as in many other similar ones, the switching costs would be high.

By contrast, if a service such as snow removal is outsourced, the switching costs are likely quite low. If one vendor does not perform according to the contract, an LG usually has little difficulty replacing that vendor with another. Moreover, an LG may have contracts with several vendors to protect it from any sort of "vendor holdup."

The low-risk cube in Figure 8.4 embodies services such as publications with a combination of low citizen sensitivity, high competition, and low switching costs. These situations have a high probability of successful outsourcing without the need for careful management of the vendor. Similarly, a service such as snow removal might be in the upper left, front corner, where citizen sensitivity is high but where a poorly performing vendor can be replaced easily and quickly.

At the other end of the spectrum (high citizen sensitivity-low competition-high switching costs) are services for which outsourcing is more risky. In most of these cases, the vendor needs to be managed much like the city or town would manage its own department. Figures 8.5 and 8.6 show how several different types of services might be positioned in the cube.

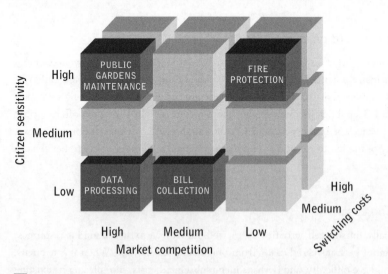

Figure 8.5 *Some examples of outsourcing risk (1)*
Source: Adapted from Padovani and Young (2008: 221).

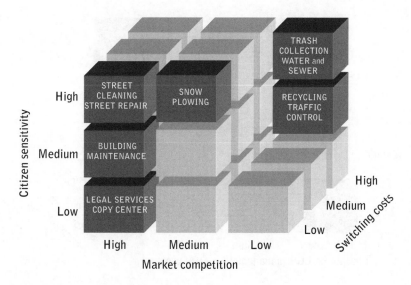

Figure 8.6 *Some examples of outsourcing risk (2)*
Source: Adapted from Padovani and Young (2008: 220).

BOX 8.16   AN EXAMPLE OF HIGH-RISK OUTSOURCING

The nature of the risk in a high-risk outsourcing strategy was seen some years ago in the United States. The state of Massachusetts had outsourced its Medicaid Management Information System, a system that mailed several hundred thousand checks each month to the state's indigent citizens. Citizen sensitivity was high, there were almost no vendors other than the one chosen that had computer systems of sufficient size and sophistication to undertake the various activities (only one of which was sending out checks). Due to a need to transfer software (or rewrite code in some instances), plus the difficulty of moving data from one vendor to the next and performing the necessary audits, the switching costs were high. When the vendor went bankrupt, the state and several hundred thousand Medicaid recipients learned quite painfully what "high risk" really meant.

Framework #2: managing high-risk outsourcing

Even though a service lies in the high-risk area of Figure 8.4, it may still have considerable potential for improving the cost-effectiveness of an LG's operations. To achieve this potential, however, the LG must manage the vendor carefully. In some cases, for example, a vendor, while abiding by the "letter" of its contract, may have made reductions in quality and features in an attempt to save costs. Other vendors may not have

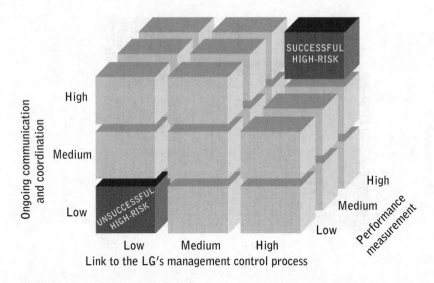

Figure 8.7 *Managing high-risk outsourcing*
Source: Adapted from Padovani and Young (2008: 242).

been responsive to citizen concerns. Still others may have attempted to raise switching costs to make it difficult for the LG to consider other vendors at the time of contract re-negotiation.

To address these sorts of problems, an LG must focus on three separate but inter-related managerial activities: performance measurement, ongoing communication and coordination, and linkages to the LG's management control process. These activities are shown schematically in Figure 8.7 and discussed in the following sections.

Performance measurement

With high-risk outsourcing, simply monitoring a contract is not enough. Rather, monitoring must be supplemented with a variety of other activities to ensure not only effectiveness, but responsiveness of the vendor to citizen needs and problems (including taking steps to ensure that problems are resolved quickly). In addition, with high-risk outsourcing, an LG must focus on exactly what it is purchasing from a vendor. In this regard, it must begin to differentiate among inputs, processes, and outputs. With traditional *regulatory contracting*, an LG specified the inputs or processes in detail.

By contrast, with *performance contracting*, an LG simply states the outputs the vendor is to provide, and allows the vendor to determine the appropriate mix and quantity of processes and inputs. For many LG managers shifting their focus in this way is difficult.

Not only do they need to develop new measurement systems, but they also must be willing to cede some of their historical control to the vendor.

Defining output: In part the difficulty of shifting to an output focus arises because the LG must define output in operational terms, and it must distinguish among outcome measures, output measures, and process measures. As will be discussed more fully in Chapter 9, an outcome measure is a broad indicator that reflects changes in societal conditions. Examples of outcome measures are reductions in the crime rate, the percentage of effluents in the air, or the suicide rate. Similarly, measures such as increases in health status, education, and housing conditions also reflect improvements in societal conditions.

Ordinarily, an outcome measure is affected by both external forces and the activities of other organizations, not just a single vendor or a single LG department. As such, it can be useful to an LG's elected officials and senior managers for strategic planning, but is not especially helpful for vendor monitoring. An example would be the outcome of "clean and safe streets," which can be affected by several LG departments, as well as the LG's citizenry.

Output measures, by contrast, define output in terms that are related to the LG's goals. They measure the services provided to citizens and are a direct result of the activities of an LG's department or the vendor to which the department has outsourced a service. Typical examples are number of passengers of an urban transport service, amount and quality of street cleaning, tons or metric tons of waste collected, and gallons or cubic meters of water distributed.

Finally, process measures refer to activities that are the department's or vendor's means to accomplish the outputs. For example, number of maintenance interventions, number of documents processed in an office, number of hours of inspections made by a department of public health, number of applications processed in a nursery school, and so forth.

Linking the measures: Prior to any outsourcing decision, an LG's senior management must undertake the very difficult analysis of how each department's outputs contribute to an improvement in the LG's outcomes. As we discuss in Chapter 9, in many instances achieving an outcome requires a coordinated effort among several different departments.

Once outcomes have been identified, the LG's senior managers must consider how each department can contribute toward progress in achieving them. To do so, the LG's senior management team must determine the relevant departments to accomplish the outcomes, set the goals for each, and specify the relevant output measures.

Once the output measures have been developed, each department can determine the activities or processes that it needs to undertake to achieve them. Each department also must select a series of process measures to assess its efficiency in achieving the desired outputs. The department then can build its budget based on these activities and processes. These are the sorts of activities that the town of Forlì was undertaking, and that were discussed in Chapter 6, Appendix 6-A.

It is at this point that the outsourcing decision becomes relevant. That is, in some instances, as it engages in its budgeting effort, a department manager may decide to consider the possibility of outsourcing an activity, presumably because outsourcing can achieve cost savings while providing comparable or improved service. However, when an activity is outsourced, the department manager must consider how to manage the vendor. At this point, the department no longer needs to be concerned with process measures. Rather, its focus is on the vendor's ability to achieve the outputs for which it is responsible, at a cost below what the department would have incurred had it undertaken the activity itself.

BOX 8.17   PROCESS VERSUS OUTPUT AND OUTCOME MEASURES IN OUTSOURCING

Consider a decision by the Department of Public Safety to outsource traffic light maintenance. The department is unconcerned with how often the vendor inspects each intersection or the efficiency of the vendor's employees in conducting the inspections (both of which are process measures). Instead, the department focuses on such output measures as the percentage of operating traffic lights, or the amount of time needed to restore a broken light. In effect, the department is purchasing "functioning traffic lights" not "maintenance" or "inspections."

At the same time, the LG needs a model that links functioning traffic lights to some of its desired outcomes, such as, say, a reduction in traffic fatalities, fewer accidents at intersections with traffic lights, a smoother flow of traffic during rush hours and hence a reduction in fuel use.

Of course, some of the above outcomes are affected by external conditions, such as weather, driving habits, use of seat belts and air bags in automobiles, and so forth. Nevertheless, all of these elements factor into the LG's, thinking about achieving a desired outcome – such as clean and safe streets. The department in charge of traffic light maintenance plays only a small part in this bigger picture.

Clearly, not all types of output measures can be in a contract. Many qualitative aspects, such as "cleanliness" in a street-cleaning contract or the quality of an out-sourced social service, can only be measured by subjective evaluation and cannot be clearly spelled out in a contract. Sometimes, surrogate measures of vendor performance can be used, such as citizen complaints about cleanliness, length of wait for assistance, and so forth, but in general some output measures simply cannot be written into a contract.

> ## BOX 8.18 PERFORMANCE MEASUREMENT IN AN OUTSOURCING CONTRACT
>
> An LG must remember not only to measure performance when it outsources a service but also to link the performance measures to appropriate motivational tools for the vendor. This lesson was learned somewhat painfully by the Metropolitan Boston Transportation Authority (MBTA) following revelations that the vendor running the commuter rail system was being paid $5 million a year in bonuses for on-time performance at the same time as the percent of on-time arrivals was declining.
>
> Part of the problem was the nature of the contract. According to one official "the current contract ... is quite complicated and [it is] hard to know how it works, unless you are a lawyer or a mathematician." Unfortunately, the contract period had two years remaining.
>
> A related problem the MBTA faced was an absence of strong market competition. Nine years earlier it had contacted 16 companies around the world about operating the commuter rail service and received three bids, one of which was disqualified on technical grounds. The MBTA also was considering bringing the operation back in house, but, if it did so, the switching costs no doubt would be very high (Murphy 2011).

Finally, unless the LG is careful, a vendor may develop a rigid focus on the output measures specified in the contract, rather than on creative thinking about how the service might be improved at no or minimal additional cost.[5] For example, it would be extremely difficult to include a focus on continuous quality improvement (CQI) in a performance contract since the associated output measures would be quite elusive. To obtain a CQI focus, an LG must rely instead on ongoing communication and coordination with its vendors.

Ongoing communication and coordination

The relationship between an LG and its vendor depends to a great extent on the nature of the contract. Sometimes, contract terms are relatively unambiguous, and, other than administrative transactions, no ongoing communication with the vendor is needed. At other times, the contract does not even attempt to define all future contingencies, especially in situations where the task to be completed is complex and evolving. Here, the relationship between the LG and the vendor may be more tightly linked, perhaps characterized by mutual trust, cooperation, and a close working relationship. The range of possibilities is shown in Figure 8.8.

To illustrate, consider the printing example discussed earlier. In a "spot-market" relationship, an LG might wish to make a one-time purchase of, say, 5,000 copies of

Figure 8.8 *Range of possible contractual relationships*
Source: Padovani and Young (2008: 228).

a brochure about a youth program. It would call several local printing companies for bids and choose the lowest-priced one, knowing that the quality would be acceptable and the delivery on time. Alternatively, the LG might have some short-term contracts with several local printing companies to meet needs such as this. If one company were unavailable, a request, to another could be made.

Another possibility is a long-term contract with a single printing company, with the idea that the company would be devoted exclusively to the LG's printing needs. This sort of contract might evolve into a strategic alliance if the LG had some uncertain printing needs in which the vendor agreed to provide services as demanded without knowing in advance exactly what kinds of requests it would receive. The contract might be a loosely worded one, calling for, say, quarterly discussions and a "settling up" of balances due.

Going even further, a joint venture might take place between an LG and a printing company where the company becomes a partner with the LG and perhaps is guaranteed a certain percentage profit each year. Finally, vertical integration would exist if the LG obtained all of its printing needs from an in-house department with no reliance on outside vendors.

Nature of the task: In assessing an outsourcing possibility, department managers must consider the nature of the task. As the task becomes higher risk, in terms of the framework shown in Figure 8.4, it is likely that a shift to the right in Figure 8.8 would be beneficial. In effect, the working relationship between the LG and the vendor becomes more important than the specific terms of the contract.

In summary, communication and coordination between the LG and its vendor has the objective of remedying problems that could cause citizen dissatisfaction. Some of these problems may be routine, and could be solved by daily contacts (phone calls, E-mails, etc.). Others, especially where the risk of citizen dissatisfaction is high, will require a close working relationship, characterized by a high level of ongoing communication and coordination between the LG and the vendor.

Linkages to the LG's management control process

Outsourcing a service does not mean that it can be excluded from an LG's management control process. Changes in the LG's strategy, for example, may mean that a vendor needs to consider new or different activities, such as a program to pick up recyclable waste, or one to synchronize traffic lights along a major artery. In addition, the budgeting phase of the LG's management control process must incorporate the contract with the vendor; otherwise the LG's budget will be incomplete.

Perhaps most importantly, the various output measures for the outsourced services need to be an integral part of the measuring and reporting phases of the management control process. As a result, the measuring and reporting phases focus on the outputs being produced by the vendor (and on the department within the LG charged with managing the vendor). Otherwise, the LG's senior management may learn too late of emerging problems.

Finally, recognizing that outsourcing is a matter of tradeoffs, and that the environment in which the tradeoffs are made is constantly evolving, an LG needs to undertake a periodic evaluation of the outsourced service. In part, this is because even the best-designed set of output measures may fail to indicate whether the citizenry is satisfied with the service as it currently is operating. Also, for any number of reasons, an outsourced activity may have moved from one cube in Figure 8.4 to another, which might call for a change in the LG's outsourcing strategy. Or, technology may have changed, such that it would be more beneficial for the LG to shift from in-house service provision to outsourcing or vice versa. Finally, it is possible that another vendor, working in another LG, has developed some considerable expertise in the outsourced activity, such that a change in vendors would improve the quality of the service, lower its cost, or both.

In general, these sorts of problems and/or opportunities will not become apparent during day-to-day operations, or even during the budgeting phase of the management control process. LG managers have much on their minds and many demands to meet. For perfectly understandable reasons, they frequently are unaware of the sorts of changes that might affect the economics of an outsourcing decision. Ordinarily, only a thorough evaluation can bring new opportunities or as-yet unseen problems to light.

SUMMARY

Differential cost accounting is appropriate when a manager wishes to know how costs will change under different alternative scenarios, such as outsourcing. In working with differential costs, managers are concerned with actual (as opposed to allocated) cost behavior. Costs can be either fixed, step-function, variable, or semi-variable, and an assessment of their behavior along these dimensions can sometimes be tricky. Because they change under different scenarios, differential costs cannot be maintained in an accounting system. Instead, an analyst must assess their behavior separately for each alternative choice decision being made.

Although differential costs provide the proper analytical focus for keep/drop and make/buy decisions, they do not dictate how the decisions themselves should be made. Indeed, a variety of strategic and other non-quantifiable factors usually enter into these decisions. These factors go beyond the financial analysis, and can create highly complex situations. Nevertheless, an adequate alternative choice analysis must incorporate as many of them as possible.

One of the most complicated – and yet most frequent – alternative choice decisions in LGs these days is whether to outsource a program or service. This decision needs to be assessed in terms of the risk that it creates for the LG, as measured along the dimensions of citizen satisfaction, market competition, and switching costs. When an LG engages in a high-risk outsourcing arrangement, it must be sure that it has good output measures, a high level of ongoing communication and cooperation with the vendor, and a full linkage of the vendor with the LG's management control process.

DISCUSSION QUESTIONS

1 Under what circumstances should an LG include a "profit" figure in a CVP analysis?
2 What criteria should an LG use to decide whether to outsource a service?
3 What measures should an LG use to assess citizen sensitivity, market competition, and switching costs?

NOTES

1 The ideas contained in this section are discussed more fully in Padovani and Young (2008) and Farneti et al. (2010).
2 For an amusing description of some of the unintended consequences of outsourcing animal control, see Crossen (2007).
3 For details go to ttp://www.nytimes.com/2010/07/20/business/20maywood.html?_r =1&scp=46&sq=DAVID%20STREITFELD&st=cse (accessed 12 May 2011).
4 If asset acquisition is a significant aspect of the decision, that is, if assets must be acquired in order to pursue the *make* option, then depreciation alone is insufficient. Instead, a technique known as *net present value* is required. This technique is discussed in Chapter 5.
5 For additional discussion of this point, see Behn and Kant (1999).

REFERENCES

Antonioli, B., Fazioli, R., and Tiraoro, L. (2000) "La Struttura dei Costi per il Servizio di Raccolta e Smaltimento dei Rifiuti in Italia: Un'analisi Econometria," *Laboratorio Servizi Pubblici Locali*, working paper no. 5, Bologna, Italy: Nomisma.

Behn, R.D. and Kant P.A. (1999) "Strategies for Avoiding the Pitfalls of Performance Contracting," *Public Productivity & Management Review*, 22(4): 470–89.

Crossen, C. (2007) "Dogs' Role in Society Evolved; Their Catcher Never Won Our Hearts," *Marketplace, The Wall Street Journal*, February 5.

Farneti, F., Padovani, E., and Young, D.W. (2010) "Governance of Outsourcing and Contractual Relationships," in S. P. Osborne, *The New Public Governance? Emerging Perspectives on the Theory and Practice of Public Governance*, London: Routledge: 255–69.

Martin, N.A. (1986) "When Public Services Go Private," *World*, May–June: 26–8.

Murphy, S.P. (2011) "MBTA Looks to Alter Rail Pact," *Boston Globe*, 17 May.

Padovani, E. and Young, D.W. (2008) "Toward a Framework for Managing High-Risk Government Outsourcing: Field Research in Three Italian Municipalities," *Journal of Public Procurement*, 8(2): 215–47.

Streitfeld, D. (2010) "A City Outsources Everything. Sky Doesn't Fall," *International Herald Tribune*, July 19.

Young, D.W. (2008) *Note on Financial Surpluses in Nonprofit Organizations*, Cambridge, Massachusetts: The Crimson Press Curriculum Center.

FURTHER READING

Outsourcing may take a variety of forms. For a useful overview of the different institutional arrangements for public service provision, the reader might benefit from *Privatization and Public-Private Partnerships* by Emanuel S. Savas (Seven Bridges Press 2000). Savas' book points out that outsourcing may have different connotations, such as contracts, franchises, and grants to private sector organizations. It also can include intergovernmental agreements and the use of vouchers. Savas also discusses the processes, methods, advantages, disadvantages, and some critical perspectives on outsourcing. He makes specific reference to outsourcing arrangements that are related to privatization. *Outsourcing State and Local Government Services: Decision-Making Strategies and Management Methods* by John A. O'Looney (Quorum Books 1998) is addressed to public managers, and provides a step-by-step approach on how to manage outsourcing. A good guidebook to government contracting and procurement is *Government Contracting: Promises and Perils* by William Sims Curry (CRC Press 2010). It describes what to do and what not to do in developing and managing government contracts so as to protect the public interest.

Chapter 9

Measuring performance

LEARNING OBJECTIVES

At the end of this chapter you should:

- Know the distinction between effectiveness and efficiency.
- Be able to distinguish among four different performance measurement dimensions in a local government (LG): inputs, processes, outputs, and outcomes, and understand the factors that complicate measurement along each of these dimensions.
- Understand how the above four dimensions can be inter-linked to improve the way an LG manages its programs and services.
- Know the general principles for implementing performance measures.
- Know about the "balanced scorecard" and how its basic elements can be used in an LG.

KEY POINTS

- Measuring performance is a tricky matter in any nonprofit, but especially in an LG where significant revenues are derived from general taxes and government grants, and hence there is no "sales revenue," as such, for many of the LG's services.
- Performance can be measured along four dimensions: inputs, processes, outputs, and outcomes. As one moves along this scale, there is an increase in the value of the information but a corresponding increase in the difficulty of obtaining reliable data.
- Output objectives ideally are stated in measurable terms, so that the corresponding output measures can be developed. When it is not feasible to

express objectives in measurable terms, as is often the case in an LG, output measures represents the closest feasible way management has to both specify the LG's objectives and measure progress toward them.

■ Properly designed, an output measure relates to an LG's success in attaining its goals. If an LG's department or program is client-oriented, its output measures should relate to what it does for its clients. Programs that render services to a class of clients, such as to alcoholics or unemployed persons, may measure their success in terms of outputs for the whole class.

■ LGs are in a unique position of being able to coordinate the outputs of several different departments toward an *outcome* that will benefit its citizenry. For example, an outcome of "clean and safe streets" would require contributions of outputs from several different departments, such as public safety, road maintenance, and trash collection.

■ It is possible to link process measures to the resources needed to carry out the processes, and hence to determine the cost of attaining certain results, and ultimately the cost of attaining the LG's outcomes. These activities can be part of the budgeting phase of the LG's management control process.

■ The balanced scorecard in for-profit organizations tracks financial results, but it also monitors progress along three other dimensions: customers, internal processes, and innovation and learning. All of these are relevant to an LG.

No single overall measure of the performance of an LG is analogous to the profit measure in a for-profit company. The goals of LGs are usually complex and often intangible, and their outputs are difficult, sometimes impossible, to measure. As a result, the performance measurement challenges faced by LGs are far greater than those faced by for-profit organizations.

In general, performance information is needed to measure *efficiency*, which is the ratio of outputs to inputs (expenses), and *effectiveness*, which is the extent to which actual outputs correspond to the LG's goals.[1] In a for-profit organization, gross margin or net income can be used to measure both efficiency and effectiveness. In an LG, no such monetary measure exists because general tax revenues do not approximate output as sales revenues do in a for-profit company. Therefore, devising ways to measure performance is especially important in an LG that wishes to be both effective and efficient.

Despite the importance of devising such substitute measures, the management control systems in many LGs tend to be deficient in this respect. This chapter looks at alternative ways to measure an LG's performance.

The problem of measuring output in non-monetary terms is not unique to LGs or even to nonprofit organizations in general. The same problem exists in responsibility centers in for-profit organizations where discretionary costs predominate (e.g., research, law, personnel). Conversely, the output of many individual activities in an LG, such as food service in a school cafeteria, vehicle maintenance, or clerical work, can be measured as easily as the corresponding activities in a for-profit entity.

BOX 9.1   MEASURING OUTPUT IN NON-MONETARY TERMS

A library estimated that it should take two minutes to re-shelve a book (including an allowance for personal time). A staff person took 4 hours to replace 100 books. The output (100 books replaced) multiplied by the standard time per book (2 minutes) gave a total expected time of 200 minutes, or 3.3 hours. This can be compared with the actual total of four hours to measure productivity. This sort of analysis could be performed in a library of any sort, whether it is part of an LG or not.

BASIC MEASUREMENT CATEGORIES

Over the past several years, there has been considerable research into ways to measure the performance of public sector organizations. Four separate performance measurement concepts have emerged from this research: inputs, processes, outputs, and outcomes.[2] Figure 9.1 shows how they are linked.

Inputs are the resources used to carry out different *processes*. They can be assessed in physical terms, such as employee hours in the tax collection office, number of trucks used for trash pickup, or square meters of low-income housing. Processes relate to a

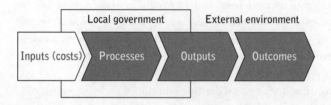

Figure 9.1 *The four concepts of performance in local government*

244

program's or a department's activities. An example of a process is the review of an application for a pre-school, or the repaving of a kilometer of roadway.

Outputs are the goods or, more often, the services that emerge from these processes and that are provided to the outside world (such as to consumers or citizens). Outputs are directly related to a program's or a department's objectives. Examples include providing a year of pre-school education, or having fewer than one pothole per kilometer of roadway.

The interaction of outputs with the environment (users, private companies, other public entities, regulators, and the population in general) generates *outcomes*. An outcome reflects the quality of life in an LG.[3] Outcomes can be useful in strategic planning in that they can help guide the decisions of elected officials and senior management about the overall directions the LG should take. Because of this, outcomes are often stated in broad terms, such as "the expectation of a healthy life, free of serious disability," or "the presence of clean and safe streets."

Clearly, few outcomes, if any, can be related to the work of a single organizational unit in an LG. In almost all instances they are affected by many different forces. The crime rate in a city can be influenced by the activities of the police department and the court system, but it is also influenced by unemployment, housing conditions, and other factors unrelated to the effectiveness of the LG. Similarly, life expectancy (or its converse, mortality) is partly influenced by the quality of health care services, but it is also affected by nutrition, environment, heredity, exercise, and other factors.

DEVELOPING APPROPRIATE MEASURES

As we discuss later in the chapter, developing appropriate measures in each of these categories can be challenging. In general, as one moves from inputs to outcomes, the challenges grow.

Input measures

The various physical inputs ordinarily are translated into costs by using wage rates, supply prices, and so forth. As discussed in Chapter 7, measuring the full cost of a cost object can be difficult at times, although it ordinarily is relatively easy to determine the cost of an individual input, such as an hour of labor, and to assign it to a cost object.

Process measures

A process measure (often called a *productivity* measure) relates to a program's or a department's activities. Ordinarily, it is *means-oriented*, rather than *ends-oriented*.

Process measures help managers gauge efficiency. Examples are the number of livestock inspected in a week, lines typed in an hour, requisitions filled in a month, or purchase orders written in a day. Since they do not measure effectiveness, however, process measures ordinarily are only remotely related to a program's or a department's objectives. Because of this, senior management must be careful not to put too much emphasis on process measures, especially if they are unrelated, or only tenuously related, to outputs.

BOX 9.2 MISLEADING PROCESS MEASURES

A city measured the performance of its building inspectors by the number of kilometers they drove each day – a process measure. As a consequence, inspectors sometimes would build up a record of performance by crisscrossing town to make inspections, rather than by designing a route that would maximize the number of inspections in a day.

Process measures are most useful in the control of lower-level responsibility centers. They are the easiest type of measure to interpret, presumably because there is a close causal relationship between them and inputs. Indeed, process measures often can be useful in constructing the relevant parts of a budget.

BOX 9.3 BUILDING A BUDGET WITH PROCESS MEASURES

In a department of public health, restaurant inspections are considered an important process measure. If each restaurant inspection (including travel time, scheduling, report-preparation time, and other factors) should take an average of 2 hours (a measure of efficiency), and there are 5,000 restaurant inspections to be made, there is a need for 10,000 inspector hours. This can be converted into the number of inspectors needed, which can be multiplied by the average inspector compensation to arrive at a budget.

Development of standards

Process measures require identifying the activities of a person or a responsibility center and developing a *unit standard*. A unit standard is the amount of time needed to complete a single activity. For instance, in the above example, a unit standard is the amount of time needed to inspect a single restaurant. When the total activity count is multiplied by the unit standard, the resulting amount can be compared with the actual time spent, and can be used to evaluate performance.

BOX 9.4   USE OF UNIT STANDARDS TO ASSESS PERFORMANCE

In the example in Box 9.3, if 3,000 restaurants were actually inspected during a given period of time, the 3,000 could be multiplied by the unit standard of 2 hours to give a total of 6,000 hours. This amount could be compared with the actual number of inspector hours used during the same period to obtain a measure of the efficiency of the inspectors. For example, if the inspectors did the job in 5,500 hours, they would be considered more efficient than anticipated. Note, however, that this says nothing about their *effectiveness* in finding restaurants that were violating the city's public health code.

In an office or clerical setting, three approaches can be used to arrive at unit standards: (1) Using time standards developed by standard-setting organizations; (2) having employees keep detailed records of the time taken to perform specific activities, and using averages of these records; and (3) having external observers record the time required to perform activities and the amount of idle time, according to a random plan of observations, and using averages of these records (this is often referred to as work sampling).

Output measures

Output measures attempt to express results in terms that are related to a department's or a program's objectives. Ideally, these objectives are stated in measurable terms so that the corresponding output measures can be developed. Properly designed, therefore, an output measure relates to a department's or a program's success in attaining its objectives. If a department or program is client-oriented, its output measures should relate to what it did for its clients. Programs that render services to a *class* of clients, such as to alcoholics or unemployed persons, may measure their success in terms of outputs for the whole class.

Although output measures usually are easier to collect and more directly tied to a specific organizational unit than outcomes, they can still pose difficulties. Indeed, it sometimes can be difficult to establish a valid cause-and-effect relationship.

BOX 9.5   OUTPUT MEASURES AND CAUSALITY

A program to rehabilitate alcoholics might measure its outputs in terms of either the percent of enrollees successfully completing the program or the rate of recidivism. While the latter is a more accurate output measure, it is complicated by three factors: (1) the choice of an appropriate time period, (2) the difficulty of identifying clients who resume drinking but do not notify the program of this fact, and (3) the influence of forces outside the program's control on an individual's decision to resume drinking.

Outcome measures

Outcomes measures attempt to reflect the impact of an LG's work on its community at large, or on the quality of life of its citizens.[4] In general, outcome measures are difficult to use properly because there ordinarily is no easily demonstrable cause-and-effect relationship between what a department or program does and the change in an outcome. Additionally, valid outcome measures are difficult to collect, and those that can be collected fairly easily are likely to be of dubious validity. Likewise, proxy indicators for outcomes, such as percentage of registered citizens voting as an indicator of citizenship, or crime and disturbance statistics as indicators of social unrest, may be collected fairly easily, but generally are of limited reliability.

BOX 9.6   LACK OF CAUSALITY IN OUTCOME MEASURES

In attempting to measure the effectiveness of its program, the Urban Corps (an inner city volunteer youth program) used measures that purported to show the change in urban residents' well being during a two-year period. Since there was no plausible way of relating the measures of residents' well being to the efforts of Urban Corps workers, the effort to measure effectiveness was of little value.

In short, outcome measures are nebulous, difficult to obtain on a current basis, little affected by a single department's or program's efforts, and much affected by external forces. As a result, they provide only a rough indication of what an LG has accomplished, and therefore are of limited use for management control purposes.

Despite the above limitations, a focus on outcomes can be useful in an LG where the work of several different departments needs to be coordinated toward a broad social goal, or outcome. If the right departments are involved, and the work is well coordinated, an LG can control many of the relevant forces (although it will not be able to control all of them). We discuss this idea later in the chapter.

COMPLICATING FACTORS

As the above discussion has suggested, performance measurement is a complicated task. There are at least three problems that LGs encounter in their efforts to do so.

Definitional problems

Productivity typically is defined as output per unit of input. The inputs (as measured by cost) in the ratio should include labor, materials, energy, equipment, and all the other resources used to achieve the output. In practice, however, productivity usually has a much narrower definition. Specifically, because labor is the critical resource in most LGs, the term usually means output per person-hour or person-year. However, an increase in output per person-hour is equivalent to an increase in productivity *only if* all input factors other than personnel remained constant.

Measurement problems

Beyond problems with definition and terminology, there also can be problems in reaching agreement on the adequacy of the measure. An important question is whether the measurement device actually gives useful information on the item in question.

BOX 9.7   ADEQUACY OF MEASURES

For many years, a program dedicated to conserving bio-diversity by protecting the lands and waters that rare species needed to survive, used two measures of success: bucks and acres. Bucks [slang for "dollars"] referred to total revenue and its annual growth rate; acres referred to land under protection. Despite growth in both measures, species extinction continued to increase at alarming rates. Even endangered species that had once lived on the land under the program's control had, over time, vanished.

As a result, the program began to develop new performance measures. The eventual result was a family of measures that addressed three areas: impact, activity, and capacity. Impact measures focused on the program's mission; activity measures focused on goals and strategies; and capacity measures were oriented toward obtaining the required resources (Sawhill and Williamson 2001). These categories are similar to outcome measures, output measures, and process measures.

249

Cause-and-effect problems

In developing process measures, management must be careful to assure itself of a cause-and-effect relationship between the processes it wants employees to undertake and its desired results. There frequently is an implicit assumption that certain processes help the organization to achieve its objectives, but this is not always the case.

BOX 9.8   EXAMPLE OF PROBLEMATIC CAUSE-AND-EFFECT RELATIONSHIPS

In an air pollution program, the change in the amount of carbon dioxide in the atmosphere is an outcome measure, while the number of inspections made of possible violators (such as drivers who ignore a weekly traffic ban) is a process measure. The implication of a causal relationship between the number of inspections made and the amount of air pollution is of dubious validity.

LINKAGES AMONG THE CATEGORIES

Despite the above problems, some LGs have had success in linking process measures to output measures, and even in suggesting a link between output measures and outcomes. For reasons discussed earlier, the linkage to outcomes usually is difficult to identify with any certainty, but the link between process and output measures is often quite feasible. Specifically, for many activities, once a program or a department has determined its objectives, management can specify the corresponding output measures, and can link those measures to the processes required to achieve them. The process measures also can be linked to the productivity of the organization's employees. Then, if objectives are not achieved, or if the cost of achieving certain objectives is higher than anticipated, the measurement system can help to pinpoint areas for investigation.

BOX 9.9   PERFORMANCE MEASUREMENT MAPPING AND MANAGEMENT CONTROL

An LG's social service department had designed a group home program for at-risk adolescent girls. In an effort to measure the program's success, the department had decided to work with each girl entering the home to determine: (a) her vocational and living goals, (b) the objectives that were related to each

---

goal, and (c) the service needs for each objective. For example, if a girl wished to become a beautician, this was established as a vocational goal. The related objectives might be obtaining a high school diploma, completing beauticians' school, improving the girl's relationships with adults, and developing her ability to manage personal finances. The associated service needs might then be ten hours per week of tutoring, tuition for beauticians' school, three hours a week of psychotherapy, and structured summer employment in a job entailing interaction with adults.

The entire structure of goals, objectives, and service needs was time phased, and progress was assessed every quarter. During the assessment, the following questions were relevant:

1 Were services delivered as anticipated and at the budgeted cost? If not, what variations took place and why?
2 Were the objectives accomplished as scheduled? If not, why not? Was it because the designated service needs were not delivered, because needed services had not been identified, or for some other reason?
3 If the objectives were accomplished, did they have the anticipated effect? If not, why?
4 Are any new objectives needed?
5 Does the girl still have the same goals, and are they realistically attainable? If not, what new goals, objectives, and service needs should be put in place?

The program aimed to develop an output measure that focused on the target population: percent of girls who achieved their goal. In addition, managers developed a number of related measures, such as percent of objectives accomplished, percent of services delivered as anticipated, and actual expenditures per girl versus the budget.

Table 9.1 is an example of how the measures were linked for a maternal and child health (MCH) program in a public health department.

Linking the measures to a budget

In some LGs, it is possible to develop a relatively strong link between output measures and process measures, and then to link the process measures to the resources (inputs) needed to carry them out. This approach can assist a program or a department to determine the cost of attaining its outputs, and ultimately can help the LG to assess the cost of attaining its outcomes.

Table 9.1 *Recommended measures for maternal and child health (MCH) in a public health agency*

Indicator (by performance measurement category)	Rationale for selecting indicator
Outcome measures	
Infant mortality rate	Widely accepted measures used by public
Low birthweight rate	health officials to measure MCH
Teenage pregnancy rate	program impacts
Rate of lead poisoning cases	
Output measures	
Number of clients authorized to be served versus number actually served by the women, infant, and children (WIC) program	Widely reported measures by MCH programs to provide an indication of MCH program long-term outputs
Projected low birthweight births prevented	
Number of inoculations for measles	
Number of clients admitted to the MCH program	Widely reported measures that provide an indication of MCH program short-term outputs
Number of clinic visits per month	
Number of prenatal and postnatal mothers contacted	
Process (efficiency) measures	
Cost per immunization	Indication of efficiency in purchasing immunizations
Cost of WIC supplements per unit	Indication of efficiency in purchasing supplements
Number of premature births/number of patients	Indication of efficiency in reducing premature births
Projected health care costs saved through routine checkups/costs of routine checkups	Indication of efficiency in reducing future healthcare costs
Input measures	
Expenditures (may be broken out by program or activity)	Measures of resources used to provide services in current and constant dollars

Source: Adapted from Carpenter (1990).

To see how such an approach might work, consider a city or town that has as one of its outcomes (selected by town councilors, the mayor, or other elected officials) the provision of clean and safe streets to its residents. It has selected two outcome measures: a reduction in the number of automobile accidents, and recognition as one of the top ten "cleanest cities" in the world on *Forbes'* list of cleanest cities.[5]

As Figure 9.2 indicates, several of the LG departments contribute to this outcome, such as public safety, road maintenance, street cleaning, and trash collection. Each department develops a set of output measures related to its contributions to achieving and maintaining the outcome of clean and safe streets. It then determines the processes that it needs to undertake to accomplish the desired outputs. Depending on the LG, different levels of managers might be involved in these different steps. Finally, each department estimates the costs of carrying out the processes, and uses the cost information to develop its annual budget request.

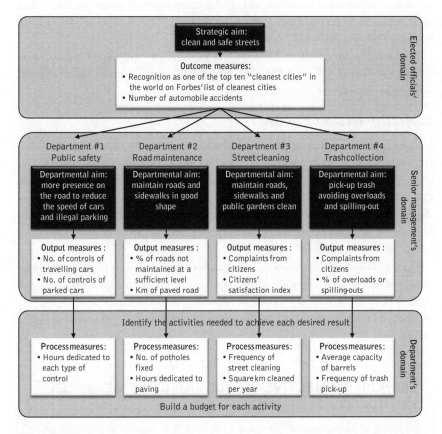

Figure 9.2 *Linking outcome measures with output measures, process measures, and budgets*

ISSUES IN SELECTING PERFORMANCE MEASURES

In selecting measures for processes, outputs, and outcomes, senior management and elected officials make several choices, each of which affects the kind of information that will be used to measure the performance of program and department managers. The choices also have an impact on how these managers and, perhaps most importantly, the LG's stakeholders (such as citizens, funders, and higher-level governments) will view its effectiveness and efficiency.

In many instances, standard-setting bodies, laws, and governmental agency rules influence the selection of performance measures. Many of these can have an impact on an LG's definition of "performance." Thus, rather than having a simple principal–agent relationship, most LGs deal with a multitude of principals who can affect or even constrain their performance.[6] The list of potential entities includes government departments, ministries, legislatures, auditors, inspection and regulatory bodies, judicial bodies, professional institutes, and, finally citizens and other service users. As a result, senior managers and elected officials often find it difficult to select performance measures that satisfy all relevant stakeholders.

In addition to these matters, LG managers must contend with several methodological issues in designing their performance measurement system. Each of these requires some tricky decision making.

Subjective versus objective

An output measure may result from the subjective judgment of a person or a group of persons, or it may be derived from data that (unless consciously manipulated) do not depend on human judgment. Of course, in many instances, a judgment made by a qualified person can be a better measure of the quality of performance than any objective measure. This is because humans incorporate the effects of circumstances and nuances of performance into their judgment. No set of objective measures can take all of these factors into account.

On the other hand, subjective judgments depend on the person making the judgment, and may be affected by his or her prejudices, attitudes, and even emotional and physical state at the time the judgment is formed. Objective measures, if properly obtained, do not have these defects. Ideally, an organization's output measures should include both.

BOX 9.10   SUBJECTIVE VERSUS OBJECTIVE MEASURES FOR QUALITY ASSESSMENT

The level of cleanliness of the water of a municipal swimming pool might be measured by asking the pool users how they rate the water quality on a scale

---

from one to ten, which is a subjective measure. Another possibility is to measure the biochemical components and the temperature of the water, which are objective measures. The latter measures require instrumentation, while the former need only personal feelings. If both measures are used, and if the objective measure says the water quality is good, but swimmers rate it low, the LG has a marketing problem. If the opposite is the case, it may have a public health problem.

Quantitative versus non-quantitative

Information in a measurement system is usually quantitative so that it can be summarized and compared. Even some subjective information can be measured quantitatively. For example, grades in schools, even though numerical, indicate the instructor's judgment as to where a student's performance is located along some scale. Similarly, although performance in figure skating contests, gymnastics, and certain other athletic events is measured by the subjective assessment of the judges, the performer is ranked along a numerical scale by each judge, and these ranks are averaged (often with one or two outliers eliminated) to give a quantitative measure.

Non-quantitative information also can be valuable in some instances, but it frequently is more useful for professionals than for supervisors or senior management. For example, most case files in a social service agency contain narrative statements of the social workers' assessments of their clients. In many instances, these statements contain judgments about the kind of progress the client is making. While the statements frequently do a good job of measuring the progress of each client, and would be valuable for a replacement social worker taking over the case, or for review with a supervisor, they ordinarily cannot be summarized and reported to management in a quantitative way. Unless senior management reviews each case file, which is an impossible task, it will have difficulty measuring client progress, and hence in measuring the agency's overall performance in meeting its goals.

Discrete versus scalar

A measure of performance may be either discrete (a "satisfactory/unsatisfactory" or "go/no-go" dichotomy), or it may be measured along a scale. For example, to measure performance of a reading program in a school, a target could be established, such as "80 percent of students should read at or above grade level on a standardized test." If the measure were discrete, any performance of 80 percent or higher would be counted as success, and any performance below 80 percent would be counted as failure. If the measure were scalar, the percentage of students reading at each grade level on a standardized test would be used as the measure of performance.

BOX 9.11   EXAMPLE OF REPLACEMENT OF DISCRETE FOR SCALAR MEASURES

Instead of measuring the date of the final adoption of its long-range plan, an LG decided to measure the completion of the different steps needed to finalize the plan. In doing so, it changed from a discrete approach to a scalar one (percentage of achievement).

In general, scalar measures are preferable to discrete ones. However, there are many situations where discrete measures are appropriate. For example, most colleges do not measure how close their applicants came to being admitted; they simply use a discrete measure: x percent of all applicants met the admission criteria.

Actual versus surrogate measures

If an actual performance measure cannot be identified, a surrogate measure may be useful, assuming it is closely related to an objective. By definition, however, a surrogate does not correspond exactly to an objective, and managers should keep this limitation in mind. Otherwise, the organization may focus too much attention on the surrogate, which may be dysfunctional. Achieving the surrogate should not be permitted to become more important than achieving the objective.

BOX 9.12   INAPPROPRIATE SURROGATE MEASURES

A city used "number of complaints" as a surrogate performance measure for the department that managed low-cost rental housing. It was later discovered that, after this measure was introduced, the department pressured tenants not to make complaints. As a result, performance, as measured by the surrogate, appeared to improve, whereas service to tenants actually had deteriorated.

A job-training program calculated its "effectiveness" by "completions." These were the mark of success; "dropouts" were the failures. When the latter appeared to be on the increase, the vendor with whom the LG had contracted began to issue "certificates of completion" every other Saturday instead of the diploma originally given at the end of six months. Immediately, the number of completions rose, and the proportion of dropouts declined. As a result, the program appeared to be successful (and its continued funding was assured).

Some employment programs measured their success by the proportion of people placed in jobs. This led to the practice known as "cream skimming:" accepting people who were temporarily unemployed but had a high probability of being placed.

The performance of a municipal hospital was measured in part by the percentage of beds occupied. Because many hospital costs are fixed, a high occupancy rate resulted in a low cost-per-patient day. A study showed that the hospital tended to keep patients longer than their clinical need for hospitalization. The result was a low cost-per-patient day, but a higher-than-necessary *total cost*.

The effectiveness of a kindergarten was measured by the number of accepted children divided by number of enrollment requests received. In any given year, the result was about 90 percent, which the kindergarten argued was an indication of a high level of effectiveness. However, the number of enrollment requests received was misleading due to the application process used by the school department. The kindergarten's capacity was 150 children, and when 170 requests had been received (from a pool of about 1,500 eligible children) the department closed the application process, thereby setting a ceiling on the denominator used to compute the percentage of acceptances.

An inappropriate surrogate output measure may cause the discontinuation of a useful program, but, more likely, it will support the continuation of a marginally useful one, with a corresponding waste of resources. Inappropriate surrogate measures also may cause departments or programs to be complacent even though they are not reaching their objectives.

Quantity versus quality

Although performance has both a quantity and a quality dimension, it usually is more feasible to measure the former. Nevertheless, the quality dimension should not be overlooked.

Frequently, the indicator chosen to measure quantity implies a quality standard. "Number of words typed per hour" usually implies that the words were typed correctly; there may even be an explicit statement of what constitutes "satisfactory," such as the requirement that the document be error-free. Similarly, the measure "number of students graduated" implies that the students met the standards of quality that are prescribed for graduation.

In some situations, judgments about quality are limited to discrete measures such as those given above: a typed document either was error-free or it was not; students either met the requirements for graduation or they did not. In these situations, it is not feasible to measure quality along a scale, and this precludes a determination of, say, whether this year's graduates received a better education than last year's.

Importance of quality

In nonprofit organizations, in general, but especially in LGs, measures of quality tend to be more important than in for-profit ones, where the market mechanism provides an automatic quality check. If a pair of shoes is shoddy, people will not buy them. The company will then have to raise quality to stay in business. If it does not, other companies will take its customers away.

Similar market mechanisms exist for some LG programs. For example, a preschool that gives poor quality education quite likely will lose students to other preschools. A museum that has poor quality exhibits will not have as many visitors as otherwise. In some instances, however, there is no such mechanism to assess consumer reaction to output. Hospital patients generally are not competent to judge the quality of their care, and, even if they are dissatisfied, they may have no viable opportunity to express their dissatisfaction. Clients of social service or public health departments, municipal courts, public safety departments, license bureaus, and other LG departments or programs cannot "vote with their feet" as customers of commercial businesses can; they have nowhere else to go. Because of the absence of market-oriented client checks on quality in LGs, it is usually worthwhile for the LG's senior management to devote considerable effort to developing quality measures. If possible, these measures should be linked to the individuals responsible for attaining them.

BOX 9.13 ATTRIBUTING PERFORMANCE MEASURES TO INDIVIDUALS

Note that the last step in the Forlì budgeting process (discussed in Chapter 6, Appendix 6-A) was to assign responsibility for achieving performance measures to individuals in each responsibility center.

Further, in some programs where a market mechanism might provide a measure of quality, an individual's personal motive for participating in the program may diverge from the program's social objective, so that personal and social measures of quality differ. For example, if a job training program neither trains nor places its clients well, unemployed people may still participate in it out of boredom, or out of hope it will assist them, or because they receive a stipend for participation. In such circumstances, unless there are adequate measures of quality, management may be misled about the value of the program's services.

Measurement of quality

Many nonprofit organizations have initiated programs in Total Quality Management (TQM) or Continuous Quality Improvement (CQI). One of the dilemmas they face with these efforts is in actually measuring quality improvements. Yet, unless management can find some way to measure quality changes in a relatively objective fashion, the claim that quality has improved will have little credibility.

There are three approaches that managers generally take to assess quality: crude measures, estimates, and surrogates. Each has advantages and disadvantages.

Crude measures of quality: The absence of quality measures may lead to an emphasis on quantity. For example, people may be pushed rapidly through an education program; or inspectors may make a large number of quick and careless building inspections; or construction jobs may be done in a quick and shoddy manner.

Thus, managers should make every effort to find acceptable quality measures, even if they are crude, and even though they may not contain the "proper" attribute of quality. In preschool programs, for example, one can measure a child's degree of literacy, social acclimation, and so forth before and after the program. In personnel training, one can ask employers to rate graduates. In construction, one can test fulfillment of construction standards. These measures may, if nothing else, serve as good motivators for the program's management and service delivery personnel.

BOX 9.14   CONSEQUENCES OF A FAILURE TO MEASURE QUALITY

In what some consider to be an infamous failure to measure quality, even crudely, Boston's "Big Dig" not only overran its original budget by several billion dollars, but, upon completion, was discovered to have water leakages that were so serious as to cause portions of the project's underground passages to be closed for repair. Then, when a portion of the ceiling in one of the underground passages collapsed and killed a motorist, a substantial section of the underground roadway was shut down for months while repairs were made. While the repairs were underway, 15 separate entities, ranging from the Massachusetts Turnpike Authority to an adhesive manufacturer, all were suing each other over the quality failures (Murphy and Allen 2007).

Estimates of quality: In the absence of objective data, *estimates* of quality may be useful. For example, in a school system, comparisons can be made between, say, the teaching assessments of the English language department in each high school, or between the current assessment and one made in the past. Similar judgments can be made about the kinds of jobs graduates hold and the kinds of organizations that employ them.

Surrogates for quality: In some LGs, surrogates for the quality of services, such as fire department response time, are important indicators. Often, objective measures of such surrogates are readily obtainable. Examples are the backlog of information requests, the number of checks returned due to error, the average time taken to process an application, and the number of applications completed within a specified number of days after their receipt. Clearly, in using surrogates, managers must be cautious to avoid some of the problems discussed earlier.

IMPLEMENTING PERFORMANCE MEASURES: SOME GENERAL PRINCIPLES

As the above discussion suggests, selecting and implementing performance measures for a management control system is a tricky task. It also is highly situational – what works for one LG may not work for another. This is certainly true if two LGs have contrasting missions, programs, and clientele.

Despite the many differences among LGs, some general principles are relevant for selecting and implementing adequate performance measures. These principles are very general – there no doubt are exceptions to each. Nevertheless, they provide some guidance to LG managers concerned with performance measurement.

Principle #1: some measure of performance is usually better than none

Valid criticisms can be made about almost any performance measure. Since no measure is perfect, there is a tendency on the part of some managers to magnify the imperfections and thus downgrade the attempt to collect and use any performance information. In most situations, a sounder approach is to take account of the imperfections and to qualify the results accordingly. In general, some performance data, however crude, are more useful to a manager than none at all.

Although there is always a possibility of inappropriate performance measures, most organizations can develop reasonable, albeit imprecise, indicators of performance. Rather than using such indicators as absolute bases for judgment, managers can use them as a basis for asking questions to determine if a problem really exists. Thus, considerable effort in finding and developing performance measures generally is worthwhile.

Inputs as a measure of outputs

Although generally less desirable than a true output measure, inputs are often better than no measure at all. For example, it may not be feasible to construct output measures for research projects. In the absence of such measures, the amount spent on a research project may provide a useful clue to output. In the extreme, if no money was spent, it is apparent that nothing was accomplished.

260

BOX 9.15 EXAMPLE OF INPUTS USED AS PROXIES FOR OUTPUTS

The New Communities Program offered assistance to private and public developers of new communities. Although funds were available, no new projects were financed for ten years. This was considered to be conclusive evidence that the program was not generating outputs.

A town council reduced the budget for all its services except social services, for which an increase of 10 percent occurred. This was considered by the LG's citizens' association to reflect a 10 percent improvement in the quantity and quality of social services.

As with other surrogates, when inputs are used as surrogates for output measures, managers must be careful to avoid undue reliance on them. An LG should continually try to develop improved performance measures.

Principle #2: compare performance measures to measures from outside sources

Many professional associations collect information from their members, and compile averages and other statistics. These statistics may provide a valuable starting point for analyzing a program's or a department's performance. In some cases, the measures reported are too detailed or not well suited to management needs, but some of the available statistics may nevertheless be useful.

Problems with comparability

When one program's performance information is being benchmarked against others, the data must be comparable. This requires that the definitions used in compiling the averages be studied carefully; the user should not rely on the brief titles given in the tables. Moreover, in using published statistics, an LG must be sure that its data are prepared according to the same definitions and ground rules as those used by the compiling organization.

BOX 9.16 SAME SUBJECT DIFFERENT MEASURES

During a benchmarking exercise, it was revealed that the number of kilometers covered by a school bus service could have different meanings. City #1 computed the distance covered by its buses during a certain time period by subtracting the number of kilometers on the odometer at the beginning of the period from the number at the end. City #2 used the theoretical distance of the bus route and multiplied by the number of days in the period that the buses operated. In City #3, an analyst computed the number of effective kilometers covered by the town's school bus routes on a day-by-day, ride-by-ride basis, which resulted in the elimination of any other routes for special services, or routes from the municipal garage to the first pick up location and back from the last drop-off location. Unless the three cities agreed on a definition of how to measure the number of kilometers driven, they had no way to make valid comparisons of the use of their school buses.

Comparability is especially important when data are reported for costs per unit of output. If an organization's definitions do not correspond to those used for both the numerator and the denominator of a ratio, the comparison is invalid. "Cost per FTE [full-time-equivalent] student" can be a valuable statistic, but there are several different ways of defining the denominator of this ratio, and innumerable ways of defining the elements of cost that make up the numerator.

Problems with reliability

Managers also should ensure that reliable data underlie the statistics. For example, if some statistics are compiled from data of dubious validity, one cannot expect to obtain valid comparative information.

Within an LG, if costs per unit of output are desired, output measures must be comparable with expense measures. In some LGs, one group develops the output measurement system, and another develops the expense reporting system. Under such circumstances, comparability is unlikely. Furthermore, if the cost-per-unit ratio is for a responsibility center, the responsibility center must be defined in the same way for measuring outputs as for measuring; this is also the case for program elements or other cost objects.

Principle #3: use measures that can be reported in a timely manner

There is no point in furnishing information after the need for it has passed. If managers need information quickly as a basis for action, the controller's staff must find a way to compile the information quickly. In this regard, the controller's office must keep in mind that, for management control purposes, a timely, but not completely accurate, performance measure may be preferable to a highly accurate but less timely one.

> ## BOX 9.17 ACCURACY VERSUS TIMELINESS
>
> Mortality from emphysema can be measured only years after the occurrence of the cause of the disease. It is less useful for control of air pollution programs than less accurate but more timely measures, such as the number of persons with eye, ear, nose, or throat irritations, the number of persons who are advised by physicians to move to another locality, or the amount of effluents in the air.

Reasons for timeliness problems

Timeliness requirements are different for different types of information, and timeliness is not necessarily equivalent to speed. Rather, it is related to when a manager needs information for taking action. In addition, the problem of timeliness often is different in an LG than in a for-profit company. There are two main reasons for the differences.

- *Lack of prompt feedback:* Performance often cannot be measured immediately after a program's efforts have taken place. The results of funds invested in a school program in September may not be measurable until the following June, for example. The effect of subsidies on the supply of low-income housing may not be measurable for two or three years after the program has been initiated due to the time needed to design and construct buildings. The full impact of park restoration programs may not be measurable for five or ten years.
- *Organizational hierarchy:* Because of the bureaucratic and political nature of many LGs, reports on a program may have to work their way through several organizational layers before they reach the appropriate decision maker. At that point, they may be too old to be of much use.

Principle #4: develop a variety of measures

There is no such thing as a general-purpose report on performance that is analogous to a general-purpose financial statement. Performance measures must be tailor-made to the needs of individual managers.

For most responsibility centers, and for an LG department or program as a whole, there are usually a few *key output measures* that are important indicators of the quality and quantity of performance. In a given situation, opinions may differ as to what these are, but it usually is worthwhile to attempt to identify them. When there are several measures, each tends to be used for a different purpose. For example, with respect to health care in a community:

1 The total cost of a health center can be used as a basis for comparison with the cost of other community services; this measures the relative emphasis given

to each service. Expressed as a cost per person in the community, this can be compared with costs per person in other communities as another expression of relative emphasis.

2 There can be a measure of the cost per visit, or per diagnosis, or per episode of illness.

3 At a lower level, information can be collected on the overall cost per-patient-day in a municipal hospital as a basis for assessing operating efficiencies. Patient-day costs for each service (medicine, surgery, pediatrics, psychiatry, and so forth) can be useful for similar reasons.

4 At a still lower level, one can measure the cost per unit of service rendered, such as cost per meal served, or cost per pound of laundry washed.

A continuum of performance measures

When several types of performance measures are used in a given organization, they tend to be arranged along a continuum, as shown in Figure 9.1. At one end are outcome measures (sometimes rough ones) that are closely related to the LG's strategic aims, as determined by senior management and elected officials. At the other end are precisely stated input measures that are used at the department, office, or program level, and that usually are only remotely related to the LG's strategic aims.

It is useful to think of performance measures in terms of this continuum for two reasons. First, higher-level performance measures generally are better indicators of the LG's or program's effectiveness than lower-level ones, which often are not closely related to goals. Second, lower-level indicators are easier to specify and quantify than higher-level indicators. This fact explains the prevalence of measures of personnel efficiency in situations where it is only marginally related to overall program goals.

The continuum also corresponds to the relative usefulness of particular types of performance indicators at various levels in the organization's hierarchy. Outcome measures (and sometimes output measures) are most useful to elected officials, senior management, governing bodies, and funding sources, whereas inputs and process measures are most useful to first-line supervisors.

BOX 9.18 MAPPING A CONTINUUM OF PERFORMANCE MEASURES

A regional air pollution control program had a wide variety of measures. It measured its own efficiency; that is, it had internal process measures, such as how fast a request was considered. At the other end of the spectrum, it had objectives for air quality in its region. The progress toward these objectives was measured by the appropriate instrumentation. There also were several measures related to the outputs of individual programs within the region.

Principle #5: don't report more information than is likely to be used

Although a variety of performance measures may be feasible, managers should not receive too much information. In part, this problem arises because there is a reluctance in many organizations to discontinue the use of certain performance measures when they no longer serve an important managerial purpose. This reluctance must be overcome if the management control system is to remain valuable and cost effective.

BOX 9.19   OBSOLETE PERFORMANCE INFORMATION

In response to a request from a manager, the Information Services Department in a city social service agency developed a report that classified clients according to race and age. This was valuable information to the manager at the time. Several years later, after that manager had left the agency, and the kinds of problems and issues the agency faced had changed, the Information Services Department continued to prepare the report, even though no one actually used it.

A similar problem also arises when performance measurement systems are being designed initially. In developing a new system, system designers have a tendency to collect a great deal of data so that there will be information available to meet everyone's desires. However, too much data swamp the system, increase its "noise level," draw attention away from important information, and lessen the credibility of the system as a whole.

Principle #6: don't give more credence to surrogates than is warranted

As discussed previously, a surrogate can be a useful *approximation* of actual output, but it never should be interpreted as a *substitute* for actual output. Its limitations must be kept in mind when developing a performance measurement system.

Principle #7: use measures that can be shared both within and outside the LG

Not only do performance measures need to be technically valid (sound, cogent, convincing, and objective) for internal and external audiences, but they also need to be legitimate (Bouckaert 1993). Legitimacy, in this context, means that, for internal management purposes, an LG must use performance measures that were not dictated by external forces such as a legislature or a regional funder.

Although external entities frequently have specific information needs, which the LG must satisfy, their needs may not meet the LG's own requirements for performance measurement. Thus, despite the frequent presence of externally derived measures, the performance measures used for internal management purposes must be derived with input from middle managers, professionals, and even lower-level employees — or at least agreed to by these people. Otherwise, the measures will have little value for internal accountability. As a result, the LG may need to operate two performance measurement systems: one for *external* accountability (that is linked to the requests of citizens, service recipients, and other resource providers) and one for *internal* management.

PERFORMANCE MEASURES FOR STRATEGIC PLANNING VERSUS FOR MANAGEMENT CONTROL

The management control system should provide performance information that is useful for both strategic planning and management control. Managers should recognize, however, that the criteria governing the performance measures used for strategic planning tend to differ from those used for management control. They do so in several ways.

Precision

For strategic planning, rough estimates of performance generally are satisfactory. For management control, the measure must be more precise (although, as indicated above, timeliness considerations sometimes outweigh the desire for precision).

Causality

For strategic planning purposes, there should be a plausible, although perhaps only tenuous, link between efforts (i.e., inputs) and the LG's performance measures. For management control purposes, the connection needs to be stronger. If performance measures are to be used in analyzing a proposal for a specific program, for example, there should be a causal connection between them and the inputs needed to achieve them. To include correlating but non-causal input and performance data in a new program analysis is not only a waste of time, but may do more harm than good, especially if it leads people to believe erroneously that such a connection exists.

BOX 9.20 MISLEADING CAUSALITIES

In one rural community, there was a high positive correlation between the number of storks observed in the spring and the number of babies born in the following winter. If health planners wished to determine the demand for maternity services, a model that used the number of storks as a predictive indicator probably would suffice. If, however, health planners wished to lower the birthrate, the systematic extermination of storks would not work. The causal factor for both storks and babies was something entirely different: the richness of spring crops. Rich crops caused the storks to come in the spring because there was plenty of food for them; the rich crops also were a cause for optimism among the farmers and their wives, resulting in higher birthrates (Normann 1975: 7–9).

The absence of a demonstrable causal connection is no reason to avoid analyzing *plausible* connections when assessing the potential impact of a certain program. When there is no causal connection, however, decisions must be based on judgments unaided by quantitative information. For example, it seems obviously desirable to spend money on a municipal court system even though no good measurement of performance is available and there is at least some evidence to suggest that some judges occasionally use bad judgment.

Responsibility

For management control purposes, performance measures must be related to the responsibility of a specific person or organization unit. For strategic planning, this is unnecessary because the LG's overall goals are decided at the senior management level, frequently with substantial input from elected officials. As a result, strategic considerations may require operating personnel to collect data for which they themselves have little or no use.

Timeliness

For management control purposes, data on processes and outputs must be available shortly after the event. For strategic planning, this is less important. For example, the crime rate of an urban area is useful for strategic planning purposes, even if the data are lagged by a year or so. On the other hand, data on police surveillance hours by neighborhood is needed within a day or two; a delay of one or two weeks would be of marginal help for taking managerial action to correct a deficiency in a particular neighborhood.

267

Cost

For both strategic planning and management control, the benefits of obtaining information about inputs and outputs must exceed the costs of obtaining it. For strategic planning, it may be possible to obtain certain data on an ad hoc or sampling basis to keep the cost low, whereas the continuous collection of the same data for management control would be prohibitively expensive.

THE BALANCED SCORECARD

One well-known approach to linking several performance measures, including some that may be useful in strategic planning, is known as the Balanced Scorecard (BSC). The BSC can help senior management translate their organization's mission and strategy into a set of performance measures.

Although the BSC in for-profit organizations tracks financial results, it also monitors progress along three other dimensions: customers, internal processes, and innovation and learning, all of which are considered to be drivers of successful financial performance (Kaplan and Norton 1992; 1993). In an LG, where successful financial performance typically means abiding by financial constraints, and is not the end goal, the other dimensions are important in and of themselves.

The designers of the BSC emphasize that the reports received by managers at all levels of the organization should contain both financial and non-financial measures. Although all responsibility centers presumably are concerned with achieving the organization's mission and strategy, each of them has a different role to play in the effort. Thus, the BSC can help a responsibility center manager to monitor his or her center's results and how they are contributing to the performance of both the center and the organization overall. Moreover, by reviewing the results of all responsibility centers, senior management can see each center's contribution to the organization's overall performance, both financially and non-financially, and can intervene when necessary to take corrective action. Additionally, since a BSC's measures are closely linked to the organization's mission, it can be a powerful tool for channeling employee energy into improved performance.

The BSC combines several elements discussed previously in this chapter. First, it includes both external and internal measures. In an LG, the external category might include not only clients, but the community, the state or region, and perhaps regulators as well, whereas the internal category comprises service-delivery processes and employees' learning and growth. Second, the BSC attempts to achieve a balance between output measures and process measures. Third, it includes both objective, easily quantified measures as well as more subjective, somewhat judgmental ones, or perhaps surrogates. Finally, it attempts to include measures that have some causal relationship with overall organizational performance and the attainment of strategic goals.

Developing and using a BSC

The BSC is based on the idea that no single measure, not even profit in the for-profit world, can capture the performance of an entire organization. At the same time, senior management would be wasting resources if it attempted to track all measurable activities and outputs. A typical BSC therefore contains a limited set of measures that focus management's attention on the key activities that the organization must do well to succeed.

Adaptating the BSC to an LG

Because profit is not the ultimate objective, some LGs have found they need to use a modified BSC structure. Robert Kaplan and David Norton, the architects of the BSC, have suggested that placing an outcome at the top of the scorecard may be appropriate. Outcomes such as a reduction in poverty or illiteracy, or improvements in the environment may provide a sufficiently broad focus that the remaining categories of the BSC can be developed to reinforce the outcome (Kaplan and Norton 2001).

BOX 9.21 APPLYING THE BSC TO AN LG: THE CITIZEN PERSPECTIVE AS FIRST PERSPECTIVE

The City of Charlotte, North Carolina, selected five themes of strategic priority: community safety, transportation, preservation of older urban neighborhoods, restructuring government, and economic development. A core project team translated these five themes into strategic objectives for a BSC. The customer (citizen) was placed at the top of the scorecard, and the team identified the elements needed to address the themes from a customer perspective. When the team moved to the other aspects of the BSC, it found that the financial, internal process, and learning and growth objectives were quite similar for all five themes (Kaplan 1998).

After deciding what to measure, an LG must set targets for each item. Doing so makes the BSC a true "scorecard" on which actual results can be compared with the targets. Management then needs to periodically re-evaluate both the target levels and the measured activities themselves to ensure that the indicators remain aligned with the LG's mission, and are responsive to changing environmental conditions.

SUMMARY

Just as the economy has many indicators of prosperity that various people interpret differently, LGs have many ways of looking at their performance. Often several performance measures, including a number of surrogates, are necessary for a valid impression of the effectiveness and/or efficiency of an LG or one of its programs. These measures exist along a spectrum from inputs (or costs) to outcomes (or the impact on the LG's quality of life).

In selecting a set of performance measures, senior management must give consideration to five separate but related matters. First, it must find measures that strike a balance between (1) subjective and objective, (2) quantitative and non-quantitative, (3) discrete and scalar, (4) actual and surrogate, and (5) quantity and quality.

Second, it must respond to seven principles concerning the implementation of performance measures: (1) the need for some measurement, (2) the ability to make comparisons, (3) the need for timely information, (4) the importance of having a variety of measures, (5) the avoidance of an excessive quantity of information reported, (6) the role of surrogates, and (7) the need to share some measures with outside organizations.

Third, management must recognize that the demands for management control purposes are quite different from those for strategic planning. It therefore must be careful to choose performance measures that are appropriate for the intended purposes.

Finally, management must consider how performance objectives can be decentralized into individual responsibility centers and how the resulting information can best be summarized and reported for review and action. In this regard, a balanced scorecard can be extremely useful.

DISCUSSION QUESTIONS

1   What is the difference between outputs and outcomes?
2   How should an LG measure the effectiveness of its programs and departments?
3   How should an LG go about assessing the tradeoff between effectiveness and efficiency?

NOTES

1 There often is some confusion about the distinction between goals and objectives. In this book, we use the term "goals" to mean something broader than "objectives."

Goals are related to an LG's strategy or what we call "outcomes." Objectives are the focus of individual programs and/or departments in an LG, and are related to what we call "outputs."

2 The literature has several slightly different conceptual models. For example, in some instances outcomes are differentiated in terms of results and impacts, and depend on the relevant time frame (short-term versus long-term outcomes). Sometimes processes are included in what we are calling outputs. Furthermore, there are differences in the use of terms, where different terms may mean the same concept (for example *activity* is sometime used as substitute for *process*) or where the same terms refer to different concepts (for example certain authors refer to results as to outputs and others call them outcomes). Obviously, it is important to understand the concept at work, rather than to attempt to memorize the terminology. For further details see Talbot (2010) and Poister (2003).

3 Young (2008) calls these social indicators. Social indicators are essentially the same as "outcomes."

4 The term *quality of life* refers to the general well-being of individuals and societies. A comprehensive list of publications on the topic and its application to different contexts and wide variety of substantive areas can be found on the International Society for Quality-of-Life Studies. Go to www.isqols.org

5 This is a periodic award given by *Forbes* magazine. For details see http://www.forbes.com/2007/04/16/worlds-cleanest-cities-biz-logistics-cx_rm_0416cleanest.html (accessed May 31, 2011).

6 This phenomenon has been called "performance shaping" or "performance regime." For a discussion, see Talbot (2010).

REFERENCES

Bouckaert, G. (1993) "Measurement and Meaningful Management," *Public Productivity and Management Review,* 17(1): 31–43.

Carpenter, V.L. (1990) "Improving Accountability: Evaluating the Performance of Public Health Agencies," *Association of Government Accountants Journal,* 39(3): 43–54.

Kaplan, R.S. (1998) "City of Charlotte," *Harvard Business School Case,* 9-199-036.

Kaplan, R.S. and Norton, D.P. (1992) "The Balanced Scorecard: Measures That Drive Performance," *Harvard Business Review,* 70(1): 71–9.

Kaplan, R.S. and Norton, D.P. (1993) "Putting the Balanced Scorecard to Work," *Harvard Business Review,* 71(5): 134–47.

Kaplan, R.S. and Norton, D.P. (2001) "Balance Without Profit," *Financial Management,* January: 23–6.

Murphy, S.A. and Allen, S. (2007) "The Big Tangle," *The Boston Globe,* 8 April.

Normann, R. (1975) *A Personal Quest for Methodology,* Stockholm, Sweden: Scandinavian Institutes for Administrative Research, SIAR Dokumentation AB, 1975.

Poister, T. H. (2003) *Measuring Performance in Public and Nonprofit Organizations,* San Francisco, California USA: Jossey-Bass.

Sawhill, J.C. and Williamson, D. (2001) "Mission Impossible: Measuring Success in Nonprofit Organizations," *Nonprofit Management and Leadership,* 11(3): 371–86.

Talbot, C. (2010) *Theories of Performance. Organizational and Service Improvement in the Public Domain*, Oxford, United Kingdom: Oxford University Press.
Young, D.W. (2008) *Management Control in Nonprofit Organization*, 8th edn, Cambridge, Massachusetts: The Crimson Press.

FURTHER READING

For an easy-to-read compendium on the theory of measuring and managing performance in the public sector, we suggest Hans de Bruijn's book *Managing Performance in the Public Sector* (Routledge 2002). *Performance Management in the Public Sector* (Wouter van Dooren, Geert Bouckaert, and John Halligan; Routledge 2010) is a more conceptual book. It positions performance in current public management debates, discusses the many definitions of "performance" and measurement, provides guidance on how to incorporate and use performance information, and explores the challenges and future directions of performance management. From a more technical point of view, Harry Hatry's well-known *Performance Measurement: Getting Results* (2nd edn, The Urban Institute Press 2007) represents one of the most popular handbooks for implementing performance measurement in public sector organizations; it presents a wide array of examples. In addition to providing a thorough examination of how to tailor performance measurement systems to support managerial activities. Theodore H. Poister's *Measuring Performance in Public and Nonprofit Organizations* (Jossey-Bass 2003) identifies implementation strategies that minimize the possible pitfalls, by offering several examples taken from the real world.

Chapter 10

Reporting and action

LEARNING OBJECTIVES

At the end of this chapter you should:

■ Understand the purpose of a set of management control reports.

■ Know how to prepare a flexible budget and undertake a reasonably simple variance analysis.

■ Know the different variances that can lead to actual results differing from budgeted ones.

■ Understand the distinction among business-like units, fixed-resource units, and fixed-job units.

■ Know the distinction between information reports and performance reports.

■ Know the criteria for a good set of management control reports.

KEY POINTS

■ In monitoring performance, managers typically rely on both quantitative and non-quantitative information. Quantitative information can be either financial or non-financial.

■ Flexible budgeting and variance analysis are techniques that have been used extensively in the private sector but have seen little application in local governments (LGs). Nevertheless, their use could improve an LG's ability to provide more cost-effective services to its citizens.

■ Some programs and departments in an LG, such as recreation, have activities that are quite similar to those in for-profit businesses. The analysis of performance in these business-like units is essentially the same as it is in a for-profit company. By contrast, other units are unlike a business in that they are not self-financing. Instead, their resources for a given year may be fixed in advance (such as for a public works department) or they may be required to do a job that is relatively fixed regardless of the amount of resources planned (such as a fire department).

■ Good control reports have three essential characteristics. They: (1) are related to personal responsibility, (2) compare actual performance to the best available standard, and (3) focus on significant information.

■ If the reporting phase of the management control process is to provide responsibility center managers with the information they need, it must meet several criteria: timeliness, hierarchy of information, relevance, accuracy, comparison with a standard, focus on significant information, and integration.

■ For a set of management control reports to be effective, action must be a priority. Unless senior management communicates its expectation that the reporting system will be used as a basis for taking action, the system will have little value.

Among other activities, managers make decisions. Ordinarily, an informed decision is better than an uninformed one. The difference, of course, is information. For this reason, the *reporting* phase of the management control process is key to an LG's successful operations.

Senior management generally reviews performance in two somewhat different ways. First, it monitors current operations on a regular basis, using a set of reports designed for this purpose, usually combined with other information. This type of review is the subject of this chapter. Second, it reviews its programs at infrequent intervals, frequently in conjunction with elected officials, using information that is developed specifically for the review. These reviews, called program evaluations, are not discussed in this text (see the Further Reading section of this chapter).

Reports concerning the performance of current operations customarily are called *management control reports* since their purpose is to aid in the management control process. The dissemination of such reports, coupled with an analysis of the information they contain, followed by the implementation of an appropriate course of action, is the final phase of the management control process.

This chapter first discusses the technical aspects of the management control reports. It focuses in particular on flexible budgeting and variance analysis – techniques that allow managers to determine in some considerable detail why actual revenues and expenses diverged from those that had been budgeted. It then looks at how the reports themselves can be structured, and how variance analysis can be combined with other information to facilitate managerial action to improve organizational performance.

TYPES OF INFORMATION

In monitoring performance, managers typically rely on both quantitative and non-quantitative information. Quantitative information can be either financial or non-financial. For example, as we will see in this chapter, flexible budgeting and variance analysis use financial information. By contrast, as discussed in Chapter 9, information on outcomes, outputs, and processes – while frequently quantitative – is not usually financial.

BOX 10.1 NON-FINANCIAL MEASURES IN MANAGEMENT CONTROL REPORTS

A school system can measure output at each school by a combination of (1) attendance figures, (2) extracurricular activity participation, (3) number of diplomas earned, (4) number of scholarships given, (5) percent of students taking a certain number of courses, (6) percent of students with an 85 percent grade average or above, and (7) standard test results. All of these are quantitative measures, but none are financial.

Quantitative information also can include non-monetary information on inputs, such as the number of employees or the number of service hours provided, which supplements the financial information on expenses. Output and input information frequently are shown on the same page as financial information, and the two types are related by reporting, say, the cost per unit of output.

Quantitative information usually is contained on reports that are prepared according to a regular schedule. The reports may arrive weekly, monthly, quarterly, or according to some other schedule that provides the information to managers in a timely way. As we discussed in Chapter 9, timely means that the information arrives soon enough to help managers make the needed decisions.

In addition to receiving these routine reports, which tend to have the same format and content month after month, managers also can receive a variety of non-routine, unsystematic, and occasionally non-quantitative information. Some information comes from trade publications, newspapers, and other outside sources. Some comes from intra-organizational communications, such as from memoranda or from managers' personal observations as they visit responsibility centers and talk with people there.

Although the routine reports serve as a useful starting point in monitoring performance, additional information obtained from these other sources is essential to understanding how an organizational unit is performing and what factors are affecting its performance. Indeed, this non-quantitative information often is more important than that contained in the routine reports.

BOX 10.2   ROUTINE REPORTS AND UNEXPECTED EVENTS

When an earthquake or major fire strikes a city, or when a tsunami or flood ravages a town, all managers in the affected LG know that the routine reports contain little information of value.

Role of the accounting staff

In many respects, the measuring and reporting phases of the management control process are where managers' needs and accountants' skills merge. Managers must be able to communicate their information needs to the accounting staff; otherwise, the accounting staff will not be able to design a measurement system that captures, analyzes, summarizes, and reports the appropriate data. At the same time, the accounting staff must recognize that they are staff, and thus need to make an effort to measure what managers think is important regardless of their personal views.

BOX 10.3   USELESS MANAGEMENT CONTROL REPORTS

The head of the accounting department of a small Italian mountain village with 2,000 inhabitants and 15 employees regularly produced what he considered to be the LG's "overall" management control report – a document that exceeded 500 pages. The report was considered "useless paperwork" in the eyes of the town's three managers, and its preparation required considerable effort by the accounting department. Despite all this, as well as the fact that no law required the report, the accounting department continued producing it year after year.

TYPES OF PROGRAMS AND DEPARTMENTS

Some programs and departments in an LG, such as recreation and municipal parking, have activities that are quite similar to those in for-profit businesses. The analysis of management performance in these *business-like* units is essentially the same as it is in a for-profit company. Other units are unlike a business in that they are not self-financing. Instead, the resources they have available for operations in a given year are fixed in advance. Public works and public health department are good examples.[1] These might be called *fixed-resource* units; they do as much as they can within the limits of the resources in their budgets. Still other units are required to do a job that is relatively fixed, regardless of the amount of resources planned; these can be called *fixed-job* units. They must do the job even if doing so means exceeding their budgets. Examples are fire departments and hospital emergency rooms.

Business-like units

A business-like unit obtains a substantial portion of its revenues from fees charged to clients, either directly or through third-party payers. These units ordinarily can exert a significant amount of influence over either the amount of revenue earned, the amount of expenses incurred, or both. Analysis of operating performance thus is similar to an analysis of the performance of a for-profit company.

BOX 10.4   EXAMPLES OF BUSINESS-LIKE UNITS

A municipal hospital cannot influence the number of individuals in its community who need hospital care, but it can – through a variety of techniques – influence the number of those individuals who seek admittance to its facility. Moreover, although management cannot directly influence physician-ordering patterns, it can have a direct effect on unit costs in terms of efficiency of personnel, average wage rates, and unit prices for supplies and materials.

A museum can engage in a wide variety of marketing activities in an attempt to increase the number of people who visit its exhibits. Choices about programming, prices, promotional activities, and the like are comparable in nature to what takes place in a for-profit company. The need for cost analysis and control are of equal significance.

Fixed-resource units

In many LG programs and departments, the amount of resources available for operations in a given year is essentially fixed, frequently based, in part, on the amount of anticipated revenues (from overall tax revenues that have been assigned to it by political bodies or from grants by regional or national entities) during the fiscal year. As indicated above, a public works department can decide which projects it will undertake once it knows its annual budget. Similarly, public school systems know their available resources, within narrow limits, as soon as the students enroll.

Fixed resource units must monitor their spending carefully to assure that it does not exceed the amount of available funds. At the same time, their success is measured by how much service they provide with these funds. In such units, spending more than the budget could portend financial difficulties, and spending too far below the budget could be the first sign of impending client dissatisfaction.

In some fixed-resource units, such as a welfare office or a job-training program, the amount of service provided is a subjective judgment rather than a measured quantity (other than clients served). When this is the case, the reporting system cannot express the output for the whole unit in quantitative terms, meaning that overall measures of effectiveness and efficiency cannot be developed. Nevertheless, there may be services where the output can be measured, and it may be possible to develop output and efficiency measures for these services. It also may be possible for managers to use quantitative information to help them determine where they need to take corrective measures.

BOX 10.5 MEASURING OUTPUTS TO TAKE ACTION IN FIXED-RESOURCE UNITS

In a job-training program, if the percent of trainees obtaining work within, say, three months of completing the program, declines over several reporting periods, this is a strong indication that some sort of corrective action is needed.

Fixed-job units

A fire department has a specific job to do: it must be ready to fight all fires that occur in its service area. Differences between its budget and actual amounts of spending may exist in either direction because of the number and/or nature of the fires that it needs to fight. Similarly, if there are many snowstorms, the budget for snowplowing may need to be exceeded. Judgments about the performance of these types of fixed-job units therefore must be in terms of how well they did whatever they were supposed to do, and whether an appropriate amount of resources was used in completing each job.

In fixed-job units, there is a tendency to ascribe differences between actual and budgeted amounts in a general way to the requirements of the job, whereas a detailed analysis may reveal inefficiencies. It is not sufficient, for example, to explain a budget overrun in the snow removal program on the grounds that the winter was severe. Analysis of the variable costs that were caused by snowstorms of varying depths may indicate that the overrun was greater than it should have been. Therefore, it is more important to consider the cost of snow removal per snowstorm, or per unit (inch or centimeter) of snow plowed, than the total snow removal cost for the year.

Indeed, in this and a variety of similar situations, an analysis of the reasons why actual results diverged from the budget is an essential management tool.

Role of responsibility centers

All three types of organizational units can use both quantitative and non-quantitative information. Because senior management usually acts by communicating with heads of responsibility centers, the information usually should be organized in terms of responsibility centers.

A fixed-resource or a fixed-job unit may be either a standard or a discretionary expense center. For example a municipal pre-school program is a fixed-resource unit. It is allotted a certain amount of resources per year based on a pre-determined (or budgeted) level of enrollments. The program is expected to control total expenses for the year at this level of activity, and therefore is treated as a discretionary expense center. By contrast, a registry office is as a fixed-job unit – it cannot refuse to register newborns, deaths, emigrants, and immigrants. Therefore, it would be treated as a standard expense center. Since its manager does not have control over volume, the expectation would be to control costs per unit (registrant).

For ease of comparison, most examples in the discussion that follows assume that the computations are being made for a single responsibility center within an LG, and that this responsibility center is either a profit center or a standard expense center. In this context, two techniques stand out as particularly relevant and important: flexible budgeting and variance analysis. Both techniques have been used extensively in for-profit organizations, and can be quite useful to LGs as well.

FLEXIBLE BUDGETING

The concept of flexible budgeting arises from the distinction between controllable and non-controllable costs. For example, standard expense center managers usually can exert considerable control over their department's fixed costs and the variable costs *per unit* of activity, but little control over the *total units* of activity. As a result, they have little control over *total* costs. The management control solution to this problem is a budget that is adjusted for volume changes prior to measuring a manager's performance. This is known as a *flexible budget*.

A flexible budget contrasts with a *fixed budget*, i.e., a budget with no variable expense component. A fixed budget typically is used in a discretionary expense center, where the manager is held responsible for spending no more than the budgeted amount each month (or other reporting period) unless there are compelling reasons to change the budget (such as a labor strike, a fire, or some similarly catastrophic event).

To develop a flexible budget, the accounting staff must divide a responsibility center's expenses into their fixed and variable components. Rather than being a fixed amount, a flexible budget is expressed as a cost formula using agreed-upon fixed expenses and agreed-upon variable expenses per unit. An expected level of volume is specified to make sure the fixed (and step-function) expenses are within the relevant range. This gives rise to the original budget.

The original budget is then "flexed" each month (or other reporting period) by applying the actual volume (and sometimes mix) of activity to the cost formula. The result is the budget against which the responsibility center manager's performance is measured. Because of this it sometimes is called a *performance budget*.

BOX 10.6   COMPARING ACTUAL COSTS WITH THE FLEXIBLE (OR PERFORMANCE) BUDGET

The manager of a large dental clinic in a city department of health estimated that 2,000 patients would need exams and cleanings each month. According to estimates each exam and cleaning would take 30 minutes of a dental hygienist's time, at an hourly rate of €20. Other costs associated with an exam and cleaning were supplies, electricity, and water, which were budgeted at €2 per cleaning. The monthly fixed costs associated with the exam and cleaning activity were €8,000. The result was the budget presented in the column "Budget" of Table 10.1.

Table 10.1 *Comparing actual costs versus flexed (or performance) budget*

	Budget	Flexible budget	Actual
Number of procedures	2,000	2,500	2,500
Hygienist cost (1/2 hour at €20/hr.)	€10	€10	
Other variable costs	2	2	
Total variable costs per procedure	€12	€12	
Total variable costs	€24,000	€30,000	
Fixed costs	€8,000	€8,000	
Total	€32,000	€38,000	€40,000
Spending variance			(€2,000)

During the reporting period, a total of 2,500 patients had an exam and cleaning, and the total costs of the clinic were €40,000. The flexible budget for the clinic would look as shown in the column "Flexible Budget" of Table 10.1. Note that, although it would appear initially there was a budget overrun of €8,000 (€32,000–€40,000), in fact only €2,000 was a "spending" overrun. The remaining €6,000 can be attributed to the volume change, which the manager could not control.

Factors other than volume

Although the flexible budget is a partial answer to the problem of aligning responsibility with control, it does not answer all the important questions. Returning to the example in Box 10.6, we might have some questions about the negative €2,000 spending variance. Among the possible explanations are: (1) a higher hygienist wage rate, (2) higher per-unit supply costs, (3) more hygienist time per procedure, (4) more supply usage per procedure, (5) usage of different kinds of supplies, and (6) higher fixed costs.

Since the answer is contained in one or more of the above factors, we need to explore the issue further. If, for example, hygienists used more time than budgeted, we would want to know why. Were there new hygienists on the job who required training and thus were slower than anticipated in exams and cleanings? Or were there some patients for whom exams and cleanings were more complex than others, resulting in more time needed to complete the procedures? Or did patients arrive late, and disrupt scheduling, slowing the hygienists down? And so on. While accounting techniques cannot answer all the above questions, the technique of variance analysis permits us to look into some of the possibilities.

VARIANCE ANALYSIS

Variance analysis is an accounting technique that permits a close examination of the difference between budgeted and actual information, and allows us to break the difference into categories that are potentially useful for managerial action. In most organizations, the difference, or *variance*, between budgeted and actual performance can be explained by five factors:

1 Volume (number of units of output)
2 Mix of units of output
3 Revenue per output unit (selling price)
4 Usage and efficiency of inputs (usage of raw materials and efficiency of labor)
5 Rates paid for inputs (such as labor wages and raw material unit costs)

Ordinarily, the variance for each factor is considered separately. There are three reasons for the separation: (1) each variance usually has a different cause, (2) different variances usually involve different managers, and (3) different variances require different types of corrective action. Thus, if responsibility for different factors has been assigned to different managers, variance analysis helps senior management to work with these managers to determine the reasons for the difference between budget and actual, and the kinds of corrective action that might be taken.

Basic techniques for calculating these variances are shown below; more complex techniques are described in cost accounting textbooks (see the Further Reading section at the end of this chapter). In many situations, computer programs are available, or can be developed easily on spreadsheet software, to perform the actual calculations.

A graphic illustration

The concept of variance analysis can most easily be illustrated graphically. Consider the example of labor costs. Total labor costs for a given employee or category of employees can be calculated using the number of hours worked and the wage rate per hour. Assume that our labor budget is $4,000, resulting from an estimate of 100 hours of work at $40 per hour. Graphically, this can be represented by a rectangle, with the vertical axis indicating the wage rate, and the horizontal axis indicating the number of hours, as specified in Figure 10.1.

Assume now that our actual labor costs for the period in question were $6,000. A typical budget report might indicate the variance showed in Table 10.2.

Although the report indicates a $2,000 negative variance, i.e., actual expenses greater than budget, it does not explain *why* the variance occurred. More specifically, in this instance, it does not tell us whether the cause was a higher wage rate than anticipated, more hours than anticipated, or some combination of the two.

If the variance were solely the result of a higher wage rate, it could be viewed as illustrated in Figure 10. 2.

If, on the other hand, it were a result solely of more hours than budgeted, it could be viewed as presented in Figure 10.3.

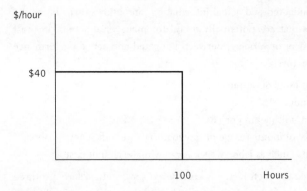

Figure 10.1 *Budgeted labor costs*

Table 10.2 *Budget report for labor costs*

Item	Budget	Actual	Variance
Labor costs	$4,000	$6,000	($2,000)

282

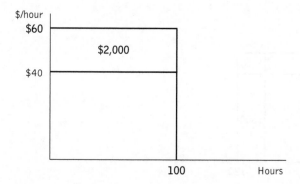

Figure 10.2 *Labor costs variance due to higher wage rate*

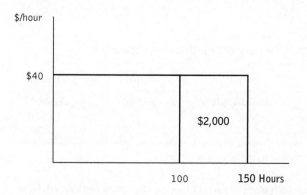

Figure 10.3 *Labor costs variance due to more hours*

Finally, if the variance were a result of a combination of both a higher wage rate and more hours, it could be depicted by several wage/hour combinations; one possibility is presented in Figure 10.4 overleaf.

The small rectangle shown on the upper right portion of the graph is a combination of the wage (or rate) variance *and* the hour (or use) variance. This variance cannot be assigned cleanly to either the higher rate or the higher use, but rather to the *combined effect* of the two. In this instance, $1,000 of the total variance can be attributed to the higher wage rate, $800 to the greater number of hours, and $200 to the combined effect.

For ease of calculation, the combined effect ordinarily is included in the rate variance (here the wage rate variance). Not only does this approach simplify the calculation and presentation of information, it also seems reasonable. Specifically, whoever is responsible for the rate variance is responsible for it for as many units as actually were used (hours in this example). This means that the $200 combination effect described above would be added to the $1,000 to give a $1,200 labor rate variance.

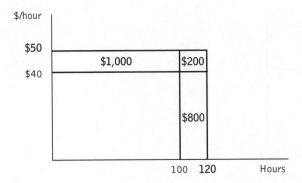

Figure 10.4 *Labor costs variance due to a combination of higher wage rate and more hours*

Table 10.3 *Budget report for labor costs with variance analysis*

Item	Budget	Actual	Variance
Labor costs	$4,000	$6,000	($2,000)
Labor rate (wage) variance			(1,200)
Use variance			(800)

Given this approach, the budget report might look as illustrated in Table 10.3.

The managerial utility of this report comes directly from the fact that in most organizations different managers are responsible for different elements of a total variance. In line with the need to align responsibility with control, it is important to designate the portion of the total variance that is attributable to each individual manager. It then becomes possible to discuss the underlying causes with these managers.

Managerial uses of variances

An important feature of variance analysis is the ability it gives senior management to link changes in revenues and expenses to managerial responsibility. It is important to emphasize, however, that a negative variance should not be used as a "club" to punish a manager. Rather, it is the first step in diagnosing the reasons why costs diverged from budget, and in exploring these reasons with the appropriate managers, so that, where possible, corrective actions can be taken to bring costs (and perhaps revenues) back in line with the budget. Similarly, as discussed below, a positive variance is not necessarily a cause for celebration. It does suggest, however, that some improvements in financial performance have been achieved that could be examined for possible transfer to other operating units.

Table 10.4 *Types of variances and controlling agents*

Variance	Controlling agent
Volume	Marketing department, senior management, other government entities, and/or the environment
Output mix	Marketing department, senior management, other government entities, and/or the environment
Selling price	Senior management, marketing department, political bodies, other government entities, and/or responsibility center managers (depending on who in the organization sets prices)
Raw material price	Purchasing department, responsibility center managers, or steward's office
Wage rate	Senior management (who negotiate union contracts); responsibility center managers (who make job offers)
Raw material usage	Responsibility center managers
Labor efficiency	Responsibility center managers
Input mix	Responsibility center managers

Variances in general

By way of summary, Table 10.4 lists each kind of variance, and identifies in a general sense the department or responsibility center manager who usually controls it. As it suggests, operating managers ordinarily do not control the volume or mix of services supplied, nor do they usually set wage rates for employees or control the prices paid for raw materials and other input items. Consequently, variance analysis permits senior management to focus attention on each individual item and the responsibility center manager who controls it.

BOX 10.7   LINKING RESPONSIBILITY TO VARIANCE ANALYSIS

The manager of a snow removal program cannot control the volume or frequency of snow, nor its nature (wet and heavy or dry and fluffy). Thus, the manager cannot control the volume or output mix variances, the prices paid for raw materials (such as sand and salt), or the wages paid to the work force (except perhaps through the use of overtime). However, the manager can control the usage of raw materials (how much sand and salt and where), the efficiency of the plow drivers (via training), and the mix of drivers (two per plow or one). Thus, the manager controls the input-mix, raw-material-usage, and labor-efficiency variances. The snow-removal program therefore could be established as a standard expense center. Doing so would result in a flexible budget for each snowstorm that could be used to measure how well the manager operated with the resources that could be controlled.

Limitations of variance analysis

It is important to remember that while variance analysis can highlight the reasons for a deviation between budgeted and actual performance, and can do so in terms of volume, rate, use, and mix, it cannot explain *why* a particular organizational unit was more or less efficient than budgeted, or *why* volume was higher or lower than anticipated. As a result, variance analysis can be a useful tool to assist managers in asking the right questions and in identifying lower-level managers to whom those questions might be addressed. However, it should be considered only as a means to assist managers to learn more about the activities of their organizations, not as a basis for punishment.

In using variance analysis for managerial action, managers need to recognize that few variances can be interpreted independently from all the others. A negative material use variance, for example, may have arisen because the purchasing department bought some raw materials of lower cost, but also lower quality (giving rise to a positive price variance). However, this positive price variance for the purchasing department may have had negative "downstream" consequences in other departments, resulting in negative use variances.

Used properly, a negative expense variance (volume, mix, price, rate, or use) can be extremely valuable, however. It can help to identify areas where operating improvements might take place, and it can allow managers to see the financial consequences of their corrective actions. But used in a club-like way it can be quite threatening, and may even lead to unproductive conflict or diminished cooperation between managers and their subordinates.

THE MANAGEMENT CONTROL REPORTS

As Chapter 2 indicated, responsibility accounting systems have both structure and process. Of particular importance in the latter area is the rhythmic flow of activities, consisting of four separate but closely related phases: programming, budgeting, measuring (and operating), and reporting. Chapters 5 and 6 discussed programming and budgeting, respectively. Chapters 7 and 8 discussed cost measurement, and Chapter 9 discussed non-financial performance measurement. We now can build on the concepts discussed in those chapters, and in the first section of this chapter, by focusing on the *reporting* phase of the management control process.

Types of reports

In all organizations – LG, nonprofit, and for-profit – managers need an ongoing flow of information to assist them in carrying out the management control function. Much of this information comes from talking with people and observing performance directly, but much also comes from formal reports. In most organizations, there are essentially two types of formal reports: information reports and performance reports. Our primary focus here is on performance reports, but to understand the distinction, we need to examine information reports briefly.

Information reports

Information reports are designed to tell management "what's going on." As such, they do not always lead to action. A manager studies these reports to detect whether something has happened that requires investigation. If nothing of significance is noted in an information report, which is often the case, the report is put aside, forwarded, or filed without action. If something strikes the reader's attention, an inquiry or other action may be initiated.

The information contained in such reports may come from the accounting system or from a variety of other sources. Information reports derived from the accounting system include income statements, balance sheets, cash flow statements, and details on such items as cash balances, the status of accounts receivable and inventories, and a list of accounts payable that are coming due.

An enumeration of non-accounting information reports could easily be quite long. Such reports might include internal information such as the number of new users. Information reports using external information might include general news summaries, legislative updates, new regulatory requirements or constraints, newsletters from trade associations, and general economic information from a variety of publications.

Performance reports

Performance reports look at three general areas: economic performance, programmatic performance, and management performance. When a conventional income statement is prepared for a program or a profit center, for example, the surplus shown on the statement is a basic measure of the unit's *economic performance*.

Programmatic performance issues were discussed in Chapter 9. In general, they relate to the non-financial results that the organization (or a responsibility center) attained during some period of time.

A *management performance* report focuses mainly on the *financial* performance of a responsibility center's manager. This report, sometimes called a *control report*, may show that the manager is doing an excellent job. Even so, an economic performance report may show that his or her responsibility center is operating at a loss, or has total costs that are higher than anticipated. Thus, action of some sort (usually at a higher level in the organization) may be required despite the manager's good performance.

287

BOX 10.8   MANAGEMENT PERFORMANCE VERSUS ECONOMIC PERFORMANCE

The manager of a department of public health may be doing a very good job of controlling the amount of time per visit, the use of medical supplies, and a variety of other factors – all of which are indicative of good performance. However, a flu outbreak may have caused the department's costs to increase. An economic performance report therefore would show that costs were higher than anticipated despite the good job being done by the manager. A flexible budget would help to distinguish between the economic and managerial performance.

In sum, apart from programmatic results, there are two quite different ways to judge the performance of a responsibility center. First, as an economic entity, in which economic considerations are dominant, and second, in terms of the financial performance of the center's manager compared to commitments made during the budgeting phase. The role of the management control reports is to assist in this latter effort.

Contents of the management control reports

Each responsibility center is expected to do its part to help the LG achieve its strategic goals (including those related to non-financial performance) given its financial resource constraints. To the extent that at least some of the expectations consist of achieving targeted revenues, controlling costs, or both, they are set forth in the responsibility center's budget. An important purpose of the control reports is to communicate how well the LG's responsibility center managers performed in comparison with the budget.

Prepared properly and taken seriously, the budget is a valid statement of expected financial performance. The control report simply calculates the difference between it and actual financial performance. Assuming no change in quality or service, positive differences represent good performance, and negative differences represent poor performance. Because, such labels are valid only if there has been no change in the circumstances that were assumed when the budget was prepared, there also usually is a need to examine the reasons why actual performance differed from the budget.

The purpose of a control report, then, is to compare actual performance with what performance should have been considering the actual circumstances. If inflation was greater than expected, if volume was down for uncontrollable reasons, or if any of a number of other circumstances altered the original assumptions, a negative variance does not necessarily represent poor performance.

Key characteristics of good performance reports

Good control reports have three essential characteristics. They: (1) are related to personal responsibility, (2) compare actual performance to the best available standard, and (3) focus on significant information. Let's examine these characteristics in light of the sample set of reports shown in Table 10.5, which is an example of the way information might be structured in a human service agency. (There are more programs than the three shown here, but these are sufficient for illustrative purposes.)

Relationship to personal responsibility

Because the focus is on the controllable costs in each responsibility center, many control reports show only these costs. (Some also show non-controllable costs, but as a separate category for information purposes only.) To facilitate analysis and appropriate action, the controllable costs in this human service agency are classified by program, as shown in the Level 1 report of Table 10.5. On this report, controllable overhead is reported separately from direct costs, but non-controllable costs are excluded. Note that, in terms of direct costs for the year to date (YTD), the Maternal and Infant Nutrition program is performing $2,590,000 worse than budgeted (assuming the computations have been made properly, there is no need to see the budget to know this).

The Level 2 report shows direct costs for each program, broken down by cost element. Direct costs include not only direct labor, but also supplies, materials, and contract services. Note that the total on this report is the same $2,590,000 shown on the Level 1 report, and that $620,000 of it is for the nutritionists.

On the Level 3 report, the direct labor cost for each job category, such as nutritionists, is divided into direct-contact time and non-contact time in order to facilitate the analysis of the activities of employees and the associated costs. Efficiency and rate variances are calculated for direct-contact time. Non-contact time is divided into categories that are meaningful for the supervisor. Note that the $620,000 negative variance for nutritionists is divided between a positive $90,000 for direct contact time, and a negative $710,000 for non-contact time.

Finally, on the Level 4 report, the costs and variances for direct-contact time are broken down by region. This allows responsibility to be decentralized to a very low level in the organization – in this instance, a regional supervisor of nutritionists. Note that the $90,000 positive variance is the sum of a negative $425,000 rate variance and a positive $515,000 efficiency variance. As it indicates, all three regions had negative rate variances that were offset by positive efficiency variances.

As the arrows indicate, each report shows the total of the report above it in the hierarchy, but breaks the total down into items that are useful for the designated report reader. The YTD negative variance of $2,590,000 for Maternal and Infant Nutrition in the Level 1 report, for example, is the total in the Level 2 report, but in this report it is

289

Table 10.5 *Reporting hierarchy for human service agency ($000)*

Level 1 report: program summary (for agency director)

	Actual results		Under (over) budget	
	June	*YTD*	*June*	*YTD*
Direct costs				
Senior citizen services	21.110	120.030	–315	35
Maternal and infant nutrition	*24.525*	*147.280*	*–710*	*–2.590* ◄
Early childhood screening	11.235	70.570	–125	–210
Total	56.870	337.880	–1.150	–2.765
Controllable overhead	27.120	161.970	320	1.130
Total expenses	83.990	499.850	–830	–1.635

Level 2 report: maternal and infant nutrition program (for program manager)

	June	*YTD*	*June*	*YTD*
Direct labor				
Counselors	5.340	35.845	–625	–1.380
Nutritionists	*3.310*	*19.605*	*–30*	*–620* ◄
Physicians	3.115	18.085	90	–135
Supplies and materials				
Food and beverages	5.740	33.635	–65	–640
Stationery	1.865	9.795	–175	825
Contract services				
Computer expense	3.195	18.015	210	35
Housekeeping	1.960	12.300	–115	–675
Total expenses	24.525	147.280	–710	–2.590 ◄

Level 3 report: nutritionists (for nutrition supervisor)

	June	*YTD*	*June*	*YTD*
Efficiency variance			*–115*	*515* ◄
Rate variance			*–150*	*–425* ◄
Direct-contact time cost	*2.18*	*12.524*	*–265*	*90* ◄
Non-contact time cost				
Meetings	420	1.916	180	91
Community/collateral work	284	1.748	–75	–530
Professional development	115	808	–121	–384
Administrative activities	60	721	160	–82
Sick and vacation time	244	1.888	91	195
Total non-contact time cost	1.123	7.081	235	–710
Total direct labor cost	3.310	19.605	–30	–620 ◄

Level 4 report: regional summary of nutritionists (for regional manager)

	June	*YTD*	*June*	*YTD*
Direct contact time cost				
Region 1	750	4.140	–85	27
Region 2	795	3.890	–70	30
Region 3	642	4.494	–110	33
Total	2.187	12.524	–265	90 ◄
Efficiency variances				
Region 1			–15	120
Region 2			–25	155
Region 3			–75	240
Total			–115	515 ◄
Rate variances				
Region 1			–70	–93
Region 2			–65	–120
Region 3			–15	–212
Total			–150	–425 ◄

divided into its separate elements, one of which is a negative $620,000 for nutritionists. This $620,000 is the same as the total in the Level 3 report, but the Level 3 report divides it into meaningful line items, one of which is a positive $90,000 of direct-contact time cost (of which a positive $515,000 is efficiency and a negative $425,000 is rate). Finally, the Level 4 report divides the positive $90,000 direct-contact time among the three regions. It also divides both the efficiency and rate variances among the three regions.

In summary, reporting on management performance requires that (1) costs (and sometimes revenues) be classified by responsibility center (e.g., Maternal and Infant Nutrition, Early Childhood Screening), (2) costs (and revenues) within each center be classified as to whether they are controllable or non-controllable, and (3) controllable costs be broken down into sufficient detail to provide a useful basis for analysis and action. If it is not possible to give a positive answer to the question "Is there any conceivable action the responsibility manager could take on the basis of this report?" the report is a candidate for either revision or elimination.

CRITERIA FOR AN ACTION ORIENTATION

In summary, once appropriate data have been collected and the necessary variances have been calculated, the results must be structured and presented so that managers receive information they can use as a basis for action. If the reporting phase of the management control process is to provide responsibility center managers with the information they need, it must satisfy several criteria.

Timeliness

As discussed in Chapter 9, timely does not necessarily mean that the information must arrive quickly, but rather appropriately with respect to the managerial action that may be necessary. In some instances, monthly reports that arrive within a few days of the end of each month may be necessary; in others, it may be acceptable for the monthly reports to arrive within a week or two after the end of the month. Similarly, daily, weekly, quarterly, or annual reports may be necessary, and each will have an appropriate time lag between the effective date of the information it contains and the date managers need to receive it if they are to use it as a basis for taking action.

Hierarchy of information

Information must be available in various levels of aggregation, from summarized to detailed. Not all managers at all levels in the organization will need to have the same level of detail, and information on small units ordinarily will appear at a lower level in the hierarchy so it does not impede the reading of more summarized information. As Table 10.5 illustrates, a good reporting system has several levels of detail:

- A *highly summarized level*, used by senior management only, generally to review program performance.

- A *breakdown by sections or departments within a program*, used primarily by section or department managers in that program but available to senior management for reference.
- A *breakdown by activities within a section or department*, used primarily by managers of those activities, but also available to section or department managers for reference purposes.
- A *detailed listing of both personnel and supplies*, used for in-depth reference; this level comprises the building blocks for all the previous levels (and also is used for both the financial accounting and full cost accounting systems).

Obviously the levels of detail must be tailored to each organization's needs. For small LGs, where management is intimately aware of the activities, a highly summarized level and a detail level may be all that is needed. As potential problems are identified, they can be discussed with the individuals involved, using detail information, as necessary, to answer questions. For larger LGs, all four (or even more) levels may be needed.

Selection of the levels

Several factors are central to a decision about the appropriate number of levels of the reports and their content: (1) the managerial time associated with using the reports, (2) the kinds of actions that can be taken based on the information, (3) the amount of decision-making latitude given to individuals at different levels of the organization, and (4) the cost of preparing the reports.[2] A careful weighing of these factors is essential to the design of an effective set of reports.

Relevance and accuracy

A good set of reports is characterized by the presence of relevant and accurate information. Although *accurate* needs no elaboration, *relevant* is more slippery. Many reporting systems offer a great deal of information that is of marginal or no use to managers receiving the reports, and yet certain crucial information is missing entirely. A good example is YTD information, which generally is of some use to a manager but often is not included in a set of management reports. By contrast, if a program has a highly seasonal pattern of operations (such as snow removal), YTD information may be of little use unless adjusted for seasonality.

Unit cost information also may be of little use. If a manager has no control over volume, then total unit cost information (which includes both fixed and variable costs) is of almost no value, and might be quite misleading. The relevant information is either controllable or variable cost per unit, which presumably is not affected by volume and therefore includes costs that can be controlled by the manager.

On the other hand, unit cost information can be useful for benchmarking purposes or for abiding by legal requirements (such as when a grant to the LG includes a requirement that certain unit cost ceilings not be exceeded). However, even when this is the case, managers may wish to divide the total unit cost into its fixed and variable elements in order to enhance their ability to exercise good cost control.

Comparison with a standard

The existence of variances in Table 10.5 means there must have been a standard against which actual performance was compared. A report that contains only information on actual results is virtually useless for control purposes. To be useful, control reports must compare actual performance with a standard. There are three types of standards that can be used for this purpose: budgeted, historical, and external.

Budgeted standards

If carefully prepared, a budget is the best standard. It takes into account the conditions that were expected to exist in the budget year. Although budgeted amounts are not shown in Table 10.5, it is clear that they exist since there are columns labeled "Under (over) budget." It would be a relatively easy matter to include the budgeted amounts, but they are not necessary. Some managers may wish to see them, however, in which case the accounting staff can include them on the reports.

Historical standards

Some organizations compare current performance with past performance. Results for the second quarter of a given year, for example, could be compared with those for the first quarter of the same year or with the second quarter of the previous year. Ordinarily, an historical standard is not as good as a well-prepared budget for at least two reasons: (1) conditions in the current period are probably different from those in a prior period, and (2) performance in the prior period may not have represented good performance.

Despite these limitations, historical data are better than the data in a poorly prepared budged. Since they are drawn from the accounting records, they are not influenced by the persuasive arguments that sometimes affect the budget numbers. Furthermore, if an organization's environment is relatively stable from one year to the next (as it is for many LGs), an historical standard (assuming it represented good performance) may be as good as a budget.

External standards

The standard for analyzing performance in a given responsibility center could be the average performance in similar responsibility centers in the same organization or in similar organizations. Unfortunately, in practice, similar conditions rarely exist. A program's size, demographic and social environment, labor market, supply market, and a variety of other factors all affect its performance in some way. Senior management must decide if these conditions are sufficiently different to invalidate any sort of meaningful comparison.

Many industry associations compile and distribute information about changes in the general environment of their member institutions, and provide current data on average costs and other statistics. Senior managers can use these data for comparative analyses that may provide helpful indicators of whether the organization is drifting out of line with its peers. Of course, senior management must be certain that the comparisons are valid.

BOX 10.9 MISLEADING COMPARISONS

Some state governments in the United States publish data on cost per mile of highway maintenance. However, some states use "trunk-line miles" (i.e., linear miles of main highways), while others adjust the miles for the number of lanes. Still others use "equivalent trunk-line miles." Without an agreed-upon set of definitions, managers find it difficult to use the data for comparison purposes.

Once definitional difficulties are resolved, comparative measures can be quite useful for control in situations involving a large number of moderately small, discrete, and independent entities, with similar clientele, operations, and cost structures. Examples include daycare centers, urban schools, suburban schools, municipal hospitals, and inner-city job placement programs. In these cases, measures of similar aspects of performance (such as student-to-teacher ratios, cost of instruction, cost of supervisory personnel, or cost of maintenance) may be valid indicators of *relative performance* even in the absence of an absolute performance measure.

Focus on significant information

The problem of designing reports is, in part, one of deciding on the right type of information to give to managers at various levels. Clearly, whenever feasible, managers should be given all the information they request. At the same time, to swamp managers with more information than they can assimilate is not helpful. Indeed, experiments have shown that if *information overload* exists, there is a tendency for a manager to disregard the entire reporting mechanism.

As a result, the controller should assure that line managers are receiving only the information they need. Periodic discussions with them to ascertain what information is being used for what purposes can facilitate this process. A similar review process should take place at the senior management level as well.

Definition of significant

What is significant for one manager may not be significant for another. In general, significant items are those that can make a difference in the way a manager makes decisions. There is no way to specify exactly what such items are as they vary depending on both the situation and the backgrounds and wishes of the individual managers. Nevertheless, it is possible to make some generalizations:

■ The significance of an item is not necessarily proportional to its size. In particular, certain discretionary cost items, such as travel, or dues and subscriptions, may be significant to many individuals, especially professionals, even though the totals are comparatively small.

■ Minor items should be aggregated. For example, costs of heating, air conditioning, and electricity can be reported as "utilities." Reporting a long list of cost items, many of which are relatively minor, can tend to obscure the few relatively significant items.

■ The higher the management level using a report, the more aggregated the information should be. Table 10.5 illustrates this point – each level contains less detail than the level below it.

■ Managers ordinarily do not care about the calculations (assuming they are accurate!). As indicated earlier, for example, the report in Table 10.5 does not show the budgeted amounts, but only the difference between actual and budget. Similarly, variances calculations also are omitted.

Key indicators

In most responsibility centers, there are a few factors that must be watched closely. These *key results* or *key success factors* (or, sometimes, *danger signals*) often can signal the possibility of upcoming problems.

BOX 10.10   EXAMPLE OF KEY INDICATORS

The director of a mental health clinic stated that, in order to know how well the clinic was doing financially, she only needed to focus on three items: (1) billed hours (i.e., the number of hours spent with clients), (2) accounts receivable as a percent of monthly billings (an indication of how promptly clients were paying their bills), and (3) the ratio of expenses to revenues.

Integration

Ordinarily, control reports should be an integrated package. Reports for lower-level responsibility centers should be consistent with, and easily related to, summary reports prepared for higher-level responsibility centers. The report shown in

295

Table 10.5 has this characteristic. As a result, senior and line managers can drill down very deeply into the organization's activities, if they wish to do so, in order to learn about the underlying reasons for a variance. This, in turn, can help them to plan and implement any needed corrective actions.

Behavioral factors

For a set of management control reports to be effective, action must be a priority. It is not sufficient to simply prepare and distribute reports. Unless senior management communicates its expectation that the reporting system will be used as a basis for taking action, the system will have little value.

Senior management can take any number of steps to communicate its intent, including holding regular meetings to discuss the reports, requiring follow-up memos from middle managers, or making telephone calls and participating in hallway conversations. Conversely, if senior management ignores the reports, line managers probably will do so also.

MEASURING AND REPORTING NON-FINANCIAL INFORMATION

As discussed in Chapter 9, in addition to reporting on financial performance, the management control process in an LG must measure and report on non-financial performance. Indeed, managers must constantly bear in mind the fact that the objectives of an LG extend beyond the satisfaction of annual financial targets to encompass a wide variety of non-financial (or programmatic) objectives. These objectives tend to fall into four general categories: (1) improving the quality of the LG's services, (2) avoiding unneeded services, (3) improving citizen satisfaction, and (4) fostering improved job satisfaction and performance for the organization's professional staff and others. When these sorts of non-financial objectives are important to the LG's strategy, the reporting phase of the management control process must accommodate them.

The actual reporting mechanism an organization uses is less important than recognizing that one consequence of developing and measuring non-financial results is a need to provide reports on these results to the appropriate managers. To the extent feasible, these reports should be integrated so that managers can determine the resources being consumed in the attainment of various non-financial results. And, as discussed in Chapter 9, a non-financial reporting system also must provide accurate, timely, and useful information to the appropriate managers.

TECHNICAL CRITERIA FOR CONTROL REPORTS

In addition to the basic characteristics discussed above concerning their content, control reports also must satisfy certain technical criteria. While the satisfaction of these criteria is largely the controller's responsibility, senior management needs to be aware of the criteria so it can guide the controller in the design effort, and so that it can recognize potential problems when they arise.

The control period

The period of time covered by a report should be the shortest period in which management can usefully take action and in which significant changes in performance are likely. If a serious situation develops, management needs to know immediately; otherwise, difficulties may occur.

Of particular importance is the fact that key indicators usually need to be reported separately from revenues, expenses, and variances. They also tend to be distributed more frequently than financial information so as to facilitate timely intervention.

BOX 10.11   TIMELINESS OF KEY INDICATORS

The principal of a junior high school received a report that showed the cumulative number of days of absence in the school year for each student. Since there was a strong correlation between attendance and performance, and since ten days of absences meant that a student needed to repeat a school year, a growing number of absences for any given student was an important danger signal. The only action needed was for the principal to express concern to the student when they saw each other. The fact that the principal knew – and the student knew that the principal knew – provided the proper motivation. To be useful, the report needed to be prepared on a daily basis.

Bases for comparison

A control report should compare actual amounts with budgeted ones for the same time period. Unless revenues and expenses flow evenly during a fiscal year, the budgeted amounts for, say, a monthly report should not be obtained by taking one-twelfth of the annual budget. Rather, separate monthly budgets should be constructed by estimating the portion of the annual budget that is applicable to each month. Otherwise, the comparison will have little value.

Clarity

A control report is a communication device, and it is not doing its job unless it communicates its intended message clearly. This is much easier said than done, however. The individuals who design reports need to spend considerable amount of time carefully choosing terminology that conveys the intended meaning, and arranging the numbers in a way that emphasizes the important relationships.

Clarity may also be enhanced if the variances are expressed as percentages of budget as well as absolute amounts. A percentage gives a quick impression of the relative importance of the variance, and can call attention to important relationships. Occasionally, depending on the audience, even greater clarity can be achieved by using graphs and narrative explanations.

If a narrative explanation is used, it ordinarily needs to go beyond simply restating what a report already says. Rather, it needs to describe the reasons underlying a variance or other items of importance. On the other hand, because many elected officials of LGs are professionals or community leaders, often without a strong background in accounting or finance, narrative explanations, even though restating what the report says, can be helpful in drawing their attention to important items.

BOX 10.12   CLARITY AS A KEY PRINCIPLE

In an LG community center, each month's financial report began with a brief summary of the revenue that had been derived from each of the activities that had taken place that month, and any unusual or unanticipated expenses. The report also computed total revenue and total expenses as percentages of the annual budgeted amounts, and compared those percentages to the percent of the fiscal year that had elapsed. This approach allowed many members of the city council to know what was happening financially without the need to spend a lot of time examining the details. Because there was little seasonality, if the percentages were on track, there was no need to spend a great deal of time discussing the underlying revenue and expense items.

Rounding

To help a manager focus on significant information, the accounting staff should round the numbers in control reports rather than calculate them to the last penny. Most managers care little about cents; some, depending on the magnitude of the budget, may not care about the last thousand dollars (or other currency units). In general, the amount of rounding depends on the size of the responsibility center, combined with what makes most sense for its manager.

As a rule of thumb, most control reports do not need financial amounts reported with more than three or four digits, although decimal points might be used to make a column easier to understand or add. An amount of $433,876 might just as easily be reported for control purposes as $433.9, with the report headed "Dollar Amounts in Thousands" or "$000."

Benefit/cost

A reporting system, like anything else, should not cost more than it is worth. Unfortunately, there are great difficulties in applying this obvious statement to practical situations. For one thing, it is difficult to measure the cost of a given report. This is partly because most preparation costs are joint costs for several reports, and partly because the real cost includes not only the preparation cost but also the opportunity cost of the time that managers spend reading reports when they might be doing something else.

Because of the difficulty in assessing the benefit/cost ratio of reports, it is worthwhile reviewing an organization's management control reports periodically, and eliminating those that no longer are needed. Useless reports are not uncommon, and frequently exist because a problem area that no longer exists created a need for a report at an earlier time. A report structure, like a tree, is often healthier if it is pruned regularly.

USE OF CONTROL REPORTS

If control reports are to have any value, they must be used; that is, managers must treat them as important resources. In this regard, an issue that frequently arises concerns the value of a comparison between expected and actual performance after the performance already has taken place. Since the work has been completed, and the past cannot be changed, of what value is such a report? There are two answers to this question.

First, if managers know their performance is being measured and evaluated, there is some tendency to attempt to influence the results so as to obtain a good report. Assuming the reporting system is fair – i.e., it has been designed so that a good managerial action (one that benefits the LG) will be reflected accordingly on the control reports – managers ordinarily will tend to act in ways that benefit both their responsibility centers and the LG overall.

Second, although the past cannot be changed, analysis of it can be helpful. Among other things, such an analysis can help to identify ways that performance can be improved in the future. Specifically, designed properly, a set of control reports can help managers to take whatever corrective action appears to be appropriate. Clearly, an important aspect of this process is the involvement of the managers' superior, who can praise, constructively criticize, or otherwise suggest ways to improve performance. In this regard, the use of control reports involves three separate steps.

Step 1: review and identification

A good control report will highlight areas that could benefit from investigation. An investigation sometimes, although not always, may come about because of a significant

299

negative variance between budgeted and actual performance. However, large unfavorable variances are not necessarily a reason for investigation, nor are large favorable variances a reason for complacency. Good managers will interpret the information on a control report in light of their knowledge about conditions in the responsibility center and their intuitive feel for what is right.

BOX 10.13   INFORMAL VERSUS FORMAL KNOWLEDGE

If a manager has learned from conversations and personal observation that, because of personnel shortages, there was a need for considerable overtime (and therefore payment of overtime wage rates) in a particular responsibility center, there is little need to investigate the causes of a large wage rate variance. On the other hand, a large favorable price variance in purchasing for, say, paving supplies for a school parking lot, may indicate that low quality supplies were purchased, and problems may arise later on when the supplies are used.

Absence of surprises

Some managers argue that an essential characteristic of a good management control system is that the reports contain no surprises. These managers expect their subordinates to inform them when significant events occur so that appropriate action can be taken immediately. Then, when the control report subsequently arrives, the manager is not surprised by a particular variance since the factors leading up to it were known, and he or she is confident that corrective action is underway.

The exception principle

Problem identification is facilitated if the control system uses the exception principle. According to this principle, a good control report helps a manager to focus on those limited number of items that, if "out of control," will have a negative impact on performance.

Obviously, no control system can make this sort of distinction perfectly. Sometimes, as mentioned above, a large positive variance can be as much of a red flag as a large, negative one. Sometimes a negligible variance masks underlying factors that a manager needs to address. For example, in Table 10.5, the positive $90,000 variance in direct-contact time cost was the result of a relatively large negative wage rate variance ($425,000) and a slightly larger positive efficiency variance ($525,000).

The exception principle is tricky to apply in practice because it requires a definition of "out of control," which often is a matter of judgment. Nevertheless, a good set of control reports will at least attempt to highlight problem areas so as to save managers as much time as possible in the process of review and problem identification.

Engineered and discretionary costs

In reviewing a set of control reports, a manager must distinguish between engineered and discretionary costs. In general, managers are looking for engineered costs to be at or below the standard (consistent, of course, with quality and safety standards). Discretionary costs, on the other hand, are somewhat more complicated since optimal performance frequently consists of spending the amount agreed upon in the budget. Spending too little may be as problematic as spending too much.

BOX 10.14   SHORT-RUN VERSUS LONG-RUN EFFECTS IN DISCRETIONARY COST DECISIONS

To reduce expenses, a manager in a public works department could easily cut back on vehicle maintenance. Similarly, the manager of the information services department could turn down or delay responding to requests for changes to the LG's web page. Senior management could cancel a project to investigate the feasibility of outsourcing an activity. All of these actions result in lower discretionary costs during the current budget year, but they may not be in the best long-run interest of the LG.

Limitation of the standard

No standard is perfect. Sometimes, standards are derived in ways that are not methodologically sound. And, even if a standard cost is carefully prepared, it may not accurately estimate what the costs should have been under the particular set of circumstances a manager faced during a given reporting period.

In short, managers should exercise caution in using variances as indicators of performance. A variance may come about because of a combination of causes, some of which were controllable and some not. At best, a good variance analysis provides the starting point for evaluating performance and discovering the underlying causes of deviations from the budget. Therefore, in deciding what action to take, managers should use not only the control reports, but also whatever information they have obtained through other channels, as well as their judgment regarding areas that need attention.

Step 2: investigation

Ordinarily, an investigation includes a *conversation* between a responsibility center manager and one or more superiors or subordinates. The superior typically probes to determine whether corrective action of some sort is needed or underway. Frequently, it turns out that special circumstances gave rise to the variance; that is, the assumptions that underlay the budget did not hold. If these changes were not controllable by the subordinate, there is little that can be done. Certainly there is no cause to criticize the subordinate. This does not mean that corrective action cannot be taken, however, but rather that corrective action may need to be taken at some level above the subordinate's.

It also is possible that the variance resulted from a random occurrence that is unlikely to be repeated, such as an equipment breakdown or a strike. In this case, about all that can be done is to accept the variance and assume that it will not recur.

Finally, it is possible that the variance came about from performance that needs to be modified. In this case, the superior needs to determine the underlying causes of the deviation from budget, and assist the subordinate to take corrective action to reverse the trend.

Step 3: action

Usually, if a meeting between a superior and a subordinate revolves around one or more specific variances, the result is a planned course of action. If a variance is negative, the two individuals may agree on the steps that must be taken to remedy the situation. If a favorable variance is the result of good performance, praise is appropriate.

In all respects, it is important for superiors to weigh the tradeoffs between current performance and the long-run interests of the organization. An inherent weakness of management control systems is that they tend to focus on short- rather than long-run performance. They measure current revenues and expenses, for example, rather than the impact that current actions will have on the organization's future financial health, or the quality of its services. Thus, if too much emphasis is placed on short-term financial results as they are depicted in the management control reports, the LG's long-run non-financial performance may be affected.

SUMMARY

Performance reports, as distinct from information reports, typically address three types of performance: economic, programmatic, and managerial. Most of this chapter focused on managerial performance, which is the subject of the management control reports.

Good management control reports have three essential characteristics: (1) they are related to personal responsibility, which typically calls for several levels of detail; (2) they compare actual performance to a standard, usually the budget; and (3) they focus on significant information, which frequently includes key indicators (many of which are non-financial in nature). By focusing on key indicators, managers may see a problem developing, and can take action to address it before it becomes serious.

Good management control reports also must satisfy certain technical criteria. They must (1) cover a period of time that facilitates management action; (2) be timely enough to allow a manager's actions to have an effect; (3) clarify important relationships, which frequently requires using graphs and narrative explanations, and rounding numbers; (4) consist of an integrated package in which the reports of lower-level responsibility centers are consistent with and easily relatable to the reports for higher-level responsibility centers; and (5) be worth more than they cost.

A good set of management control reports functions as a feedback mechanism that guides managers in identifying and investigating areas for possible action. To do this, the reports should function on the exception principle, which can help managers to focus their attention on a few areas where investigation, and perhaps action, is required. In so doing, managers need to bear in mind that a standard, no matter how carefully prepared, may not be an accurate depiction of what the costs or revenues should have been under actual circumstances. Therefore, variances should be used with caution – they are a means to guide a manager's investigation and subsequent action, but not necessarily a reason for criticism.

DISCUSSION QUESTIONS

1   What is the point of preparing a flexible budget when it is simply a description of what should have happened in the past?
2   How should an LG measure the performance of its fixed-resource units? Its fixed-job units?
3   Why is it that most LGs do not have better performance reports?

NOTES

1   As discussed in Chapter 4, many fixed resource units could be set up as shadow profit centers, or as standard expense centers, in order to gain a better understanding of how they have managed the resources under their control.
2   It is important to note that most of the cost of a set of reports is in their initial design (and subsequent modifications). Generally, on a monthly (or more frequent) basis, since the accounting building blocks are already present, the preparation effort is minimal.

303

FURTHER READING

This chapter has focused on how managers should monitor current operations. Another type of reporting concerns the in-depth evaluations of programs that management carries out in conjunction with elected officials. A good starting point to delve into this matter is *Program Evaluation: Forms and Approaches* by John M. Owen (3rd edn, Allen and Unwin 2006), a book that offers a practical introduction to evaluation for beginners and practitioners, and includes examples from health, education, welfare, community, and other settings in both the public and private sectors. The many approaches to program evaluation, including process evaluations, continuous monitoring of program performance, and ad hoc studies of past and present programs can be found in *Handbook of Practical Program Evaluation* by Joseph S. Wholey, Harry P. Hatry, and Kathryn E. Newcomer (3rd edn, Jossey-Bass 2010). One key to the reporting phase of the management control process is the choice of which variances to compute and use, and how to structure the management control reports. Readers can find additional information about variance analysis in *Cost Accounting; A Managerial Emphasis* by C.T. Horngren, S. M. Datar, and M. Rajan (14th edn, Prentice Hall 2012). Some thinking about how to present information that "tells a story" can be found in *The Visual Display of Quantitative Information* by E. R. Tufte (2nd edn, The Graphics Press 2001).

Chapter 11

The organizational context for a local government's management control system

LEARNING OBJECTIVES

At the end of this chapter you should:

- Know the 20 characteristics of a local government (LG) that is performing in accordance with the concepts and approaches to management control that we have discussed in previous chapters.
- Understand the six cross-functional processes that related to the management control process.
- Know the kinds of questions to ask about each of the cross-functional processes, and be able to assess the linkages among them.
- Appreciate the difficulty of managing a change effort, and have a sense of the steps needed for a successful effort.

KEY POINTS

- The management control process is one of seven cross-functional processes that must be integrated and managed in concert if an LG is to achieve its goals. The other processes are strategy formulation, authority and influence, cultural maintenance, motivation, conflict management, and client management.
- The motivation process is an area where many LG managers often think they have little flexibility due to civil service or union restrictions. However,

non-financial compensation can play an important role, and it often can
have a greater impact on employee behavior than monetary incentives.

■ To achieve the sort of coordinated processes needed for successful
performance, an LG's senior management team must engage in some
important leadership activities. In particular, it must take eight steps if it is
to make changes to the management control system: (1) establish a sense
of urgency, (2) form a powerful guiding coalition, (3) create a vision,
(4) communicate the vision, (5) empower others to act on the vision,
(6) plan and create short-term wins, (7) consolidate improvements and
produce still more change, (8) institutionalize the new approaches.

Chapter 1 provided a geographical context for management control systems in
LGs, and discussed some of the characteristics of LGs that affect their management
control systems. Chapter 2 then provided an overview of management control systems, positioning management control between strategy formulation and task control.
It also briefly discussed the structure and process of a management control system. Chapter 3 then discussed the many barriers that can and often do exist to
implementing a good management control system in an LG.

The next several chapters were somewhat technical. Chapter 4 looked at the structure of a management control system, and argued that there are many opportunities
for LGs to use profit centers, even though the term may seem inconsistent with an
LG's mission. Chapter 5 addressed some of the tricky issues that an LG faces in making programming decisions, such as computing present value and valuing a human life.
Chapter 6 discussed the operating budget, and argued that an LG's budget could be
built with "cost drivers," rather than with line items, as has been done traditionally in
most LGs. In many instances, this would lead to a program budget.

Chapters 7 and 8 were especially technical, focusing on the measurement of costs,
an activity that few LGs have undertaken in a serious manner. These chapters distinguished between full-cost accounting and differential cost accounting. Chapter 7 also
addressed the tricky topic of pricing when a service's price must be based on something other than full cost. And, in addition to discussing differential costs, Chapter 8
looked at outsourcing, a topic of considerable interest to many LGs, and one that
relies, in part, on an analysis of differential costs.

Chapter 9 examined the difficult task an LG faces in measuring its non-financial
performance, especially in relating its inputs (costs), processes, and outputs to a set
of outcomes. Chapter 10 concluded the technical material with an explanation of
the concepts of flexible budgeting and variance analysis, and an illustration of how
reporting in an LG could have more of an action orientation than it has in most settings.

The value of Chapters 4 through 10 – and the concepts that form the basis of a good management control system – is in their applicability to real-world situations and problems. The ultimate goal for an LG's senior management team is to develop a management control system that facilitates improved organizational performance. Doing so requires assessing how the management control system fits into the LG's broader organizational context.

To examine the question of fit, we begin this chapter with a brief summary of the key characteristics of a good management control system. The management control process is then positioned as one of seven cross-functional processes that exist in any organization, including an LG. We then place considerable emphasis on the motivation process, one of the more difficult activities facing senior management in an LG.

Finally, the chapter looks at some issues involved in implementing a new management control system, or in modifying an existing one. It is fine to know what one wants, but getting from "here" to "there" can be, and generally is, tricky. This section of the chapter provides some thoughts about how to manage the change effort.

CHARACTERISTICS OF A GOOD MANAGEMENT CONTROL SYSTEM

Most of the previous chapters had in mind an LG of moderate size (say 100,000 residents or more) that has reasonable financial and statutory autonomy. Smaller LGs can operate successfully with a less sophisticated management control system than the chapters have described, although they no doubt will find some of the basic concepts helpful. Similarly, an LG that is financially or statutorily constrained in some way may need to compromise on some of the points below. Nevertheless, an LG that is performing in accordance with the concepts and approaches to management control that we have discussed in previous chapters displays (or will be attempting to move toward) several characteristics:

1 It has a strong governing body. Some members of this body spend considerable time examining program and budget proposals before they are submitted to the full body. Members of the governing body also analyze formal reports on performance, as well as communications from citizens and others on how well the LG is performing.

2 In performing its functions, the governing body is careful not to infringe on the prerogatives of management. Rather, it ensures that management has full authority to execute policies, and it supports their decisions. The governing body also attempts to ensure that senior management's compensation is appropriate.

3 Department and program managers have the authority to use their judgment in running their responsibility centers and in accomplishing results. However, because of the importance of spending taxpayer resources appropriately, they

may be required to operate within somewhat closer budgetary and other constraints than is customary in for-profit organizations, and even in some private nonprofit organizations.[1]

4 The management control system contains two principal account classifications, one in terms of programs and the other in terms of responsibility centers. This frequently results in a matrix-like structure.

5 The management control accounts are part of the organization's overall accounting system, which ordinarily includes a full-cost accounting system. While the full-cost accounting system and the management control system draw information from the same sources, the two are not co-mingled.

6 Costs, expenses, and revenues are accounted for by using an accrual system, rather than the more traditional cash or modified-cash system.[2]

7 Except in circumstances involving public goods whose outputs cannot be easily measured (e.g., police protection, street lighting, green spaces), the LG charges its clients for the services they receive. In this way, it generates a monetary measure of the quantity of its outputs, and it motivates department and program managers to be concerned about the cost and quality of the services their units provide.

8 When it charges clients for services, the pricing unit is as specific as feasible so as to provide a good measure of the quantity of services rendered, and therefore a good basis for decisions on resource allocation.

9 Senior management's selection of responsibility centers is based on its assessment of the resources a manager can control. The goal is to hold each manager responsible only for those resources over which he or she exerts a reasonable amount of control.

10 In this regard profit centers are used whenever feasible, even though the idea of a profit center in an LG seems contradictory. In all instances, senior management is seeking *goal congruence*, such that a decision that is "good" for a given responsibility center also is good for the LG overall. This may mean using other types of responsibility centers (e.g., standard expense centers, or discretionary expense centers) for some activities.

11 Where feasible, support units that provide intra-LG services (e.g., maintenance, housekeeping) are set up as zero-surplus profit centers. Under these circumstances, senior management makes sure that there is an appropriate set of transfer prices to facilitate the control process. The transfer prices are used in lieu of allocations for determining a responsibility center's support costs.

12 The LG has a programming phase in its management control process that has a twofold purpose. First, it is used to generate ideas for new programs, analyze them, reach decisions on them, and decide how to incorporate the accepted ones into ongoing operations. Second, it is used to make decisions about the acquisition of new fixed assets.

13 Programming decisions include a financial analysis that considers the time value of money, with future cash flows discounted using a rate that is based in part on the LG's weighted cost of capital and its weighted return on assets. The financial analysis does not dominate the decision-making process, but is an important ingredient in it.

14 Budgeting is viewed as an important part of the management control process. The annual operating budget is derived from the approved programs, and responsibility for carrying out the programs is assigned to individual responsibility centers. Budgets include both financial and non-financial measures of performance.

15 Senior management devotes considerable attention to developing satisfactory process, output, and outcome measures. It recognizes that although many of these measures may be of limited validity, they are better than nothing. As a result, there is a constant search for new, more valid, measures that are appropriate for both internal and external stakeholders.

16 Despite the fact that many people, especially professionals, dislike the idea of accountability, which is associated with the measurement of processes and outputs (and, occasionally, outcomes), senior management proceeds with such measurements. All levels of management, including senior management and governing bodies, as well as external stakeholders (such as citizens, regional governments, and grant-making agencies) are involved in monitoring performance.

17 The reporting phase of the management control process helps to assure that actual spending is kept within budgetary limits. At the same time, the organization has a procedure for revising the budget, or allowing deviations from it, should unusual circumstances require doing so.

18 Reports sent to responsibility center managers are (a) made available in a timely way, (b) designed so as to highlight significant information, and (c) structured so that managers can "drill down" to increasingly detailed information. Where appropriate, variances between planned and actual revenues and expenses are isolated by cause: price, volume, mix, rate, and efficiency.

19 Senior management holds meetings with immediate subordinates to discuss results, variances, and planned corrective actions. It expects them to hold similar meetings with their subordinates, and so on down the line.

20 Senior management undertakes systematic evaluations of the organization's programs. These evaluations are conducted at infrequent intervals, perhaps every five years for each program, but each program receives such an evaluation periodically.[3]

21 Senior management assures itself that the management control process fits with, supports, and is supported by, a variety of other organizational activities, including its own management style, the organization's culture, and a motivation system that rewards responsibility managers for good performance.

THE MANAGEMENT CONTROL CONTEXT

Given these criteria, the management control process can now be put into a some-what broader context than we have used to date. Specifically, the management control process is part of – and is influenced by – several other organizational activities, which we call "cross-functional processes." One such activity is strategy formula-tion, since, as discussed in Chapter 2, an LG's strategy influences its financial and programmatic goals. Another activity is conflict management, since it occasionally is the case that organizational (as distinct from interpersonal) conflict can arise con-cerning matters such as the best programs to adopt, the best approaches to use for client management, or the best programmatic objectives to pursue. A third activ-ity relates to the ways that the LG's senior management uses compensation packages and other mechanisms to motivate its employees in an attempt to encourage good performance.

Beyond these three activities, senior management uses recruitment, training, promotion, and severance in an effort to maintain the LG's culture. It also gives con-siderable thought to how authority and influence flow within the LG (which includes designing the management control structure), and to how that affects the way clients are "managed" in those programs that deal directly with citizens.

Overall, there is a need to attain a *fit* among these various activities. To attain this fit, senior management must address a wide variety of matters. It must, for exam-ple, assure itself that the programming phase of the management control process is leading to programs that support the full range of services needed to achieve the LG's strategy. Similarly, it must design a motivation process that encourages profes-sionals and managers in the LG to propose new programmatic endeavors, or, more generally, to act in the best interest of the LG overall. At the same time, some of the decisions that senior management makes in strategy formulation will depend on the kind of information it receives from the reporting phase of the management control process.

These cross-functional processes are shown in Figure 11.1. As this figure indicates, beyond assuring that the LG has a well-designed management control process, senior management needs to make sure that there is:

- A *strategy-formulation* process that addresses the LG's environment, including reg-ulatory and competitive forces (for its profit centers), and decides on a direction and a set of desired outcomes.
- An *authority and influence* process that has an appropriate network of responsibility centers, and that fosters collaborative decision making when necessary.
- A *motivation* process that provides appropriate incentives, and that rewards people for behavior that is in the LG's best interest.
- A set of *conflict management* processes that addresses the many differences of opinion that can arise in the course of attempting to achieve the LG's strategy.

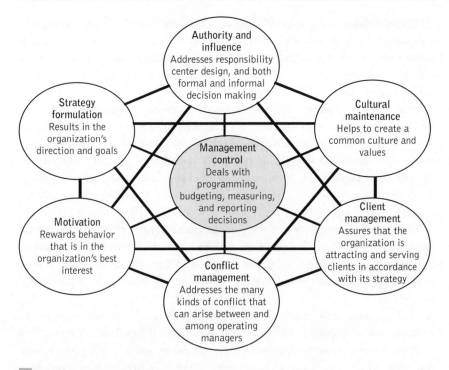

Figure 11.1 *Cross-functional process in a local government*

Source: Adapted from Young (2009).

- A *client management* process that helps the LG to determine what services its citizens need, and to provide those services at appropriate times, in appropriate locales, with appropriate quality, and, where feasible, at appropriate prices.
- A *cultural maintenance* process that helps to create a set of common values and assumptions that underlie decision making in the LG.

In addition, as the lines in Figure 11.1 indicate, the various processes must be linked to and reinforce one another. As such, they collectively help to assure the LG that its citizens are receiving appropriate, timely, coordinated, and cost-effective services.

THE NEED FOR SENIOR MANAGEMENT LEADERSHIP

To achieve the sort of coordinated processes depicted in Figure 11.1, an LG's senior management team must engage in some important leadership activities. This can be tricky in that the topic of leadership is often misunderstood – in both the academic and practical circles of management.

One of the most widely acknowledged authorities on leadership is John Kotter, who argues that "true leadership is an elusive quality, and too often we confuse management duties and personal style with leadership, or even mistake unworthy leaders for the real thing" (Kotter 1999). In his view, true leaders are able to make use of power, influence, dependence, and strategies for change.

Jeffrey Pfeffer, another well-known authority on the topic, agrees with Kotter on the importance of power and influence as essential qualities of a good leader. He argues that "The big problem facing managers and their organizations today is one of implementation – how to get things done in a timely and effective way." According to him "[p]roblems of implementation are really issues of how to influence behavior, change the course of events, overcome resistance, and get people to do things they would not otherwise do" (Pfeffer 1994).

Pfeffer also identifies some of the personal characteristics of an effective leader, including such attributes as "flexibility, stamina, and a high tolerance for conflict." But he goes on to argue that leaders also need to have formal authority, control of resources, and access to information if they are to assure their organizations' success.

In effect, then, leadership is a combination of personal characteristics and formal organizational arrangements that allow managers to get things done in the way they want them done. Sometimes, personal style is a factor, but so too is perseverance. And, from all accounts, a leader's effectiveness depends, in large measure, on the way he or she uses what in this chapter we call "cross-functional processes."

Viewing their organizations in the way depicted in Figure 11.1 is extremely important for an LG's senior managers. Many believe they are highly constrained in their ability to exercise leadership, but in fact they have more tools available to them than they may think. To see how some of these tools can work, Box 11.1 looks at several examples from outside the LG world.[4]

BOX 11.1   EXAMPLES OF LEADERSHIP IN PRACTICE

As CEO of Disney Corporation, Michael Eisner did not dictate the kinds of stories to be broadcast by ABC's news division, but he exerted considerable power through his use of one or more of the seven cross-functional processes (other than authority and influence). For example, the division's managers knew that Eisner had the power to allocate resources to them, and to advance or impede their careers. They thus tended to select artistic and journalistic content that reflected Disney's tradition of family values (Scheinin 1995; Antonucci 1995). In effect, Eisner was using the programming and budgeting phases of the management control process, as well as the motivation process, both to exert his influence on decision making and to manage the organization's culture.

Senior management at the Polo Ralph Lauren distribution center in Greensboro, North Carolina, decided to let employees determine for themselves when to take their breaks and lunch hours. Productivity increased by 20 percent.

Management of Dana Corporation, an automotive parts maker, allowed employees to spend $500 for an efficiency improvement project without authorization. More than 80 percent of the improvements were made without the plant manager's knowledge.

Bar-Nunn Transportation of Granger, Iowa, provided employees with two monthly publications: a newsletter and a cassette tape with industry and company news, music, information on company benefits, and personalized messages such birthday greetings. Shortly after starting this program, employee turnover decreased by 35 percent.

The manager of a Holiday Inn with a low (67 percent) occupancy rate began to communicate the rate to the hotel's employees every day. Within 18 months, the rate had gone up to 85 percent.

Medical Health Outsourcing emphasized freedom and flexibility for its employees. Its CEO "doesn't really care how or when her employees get their work done, but if they don't meet their goals and their deadlines, they've got some explaining to do." On the other hand, "if they get their work done by Thursday, they can take Friday off and go to the beach" (Fenn 2000).

THE MOTIVATION PROCESS

Most of the examples in Box 11.1 relate to the motivation process, an area where many LG managers often think they have little flexibility due to civil service or union restrictions. Yet, as the examples indicate, non-financial compensation can play an important role. Indeed, as discussed in Chapter 4, Jeffrey Pfeffer emphasized that an organization's compensation system was relatively *unimportant* to its success. He did not disagree with the importance of compensation, but he cited employee surveys showing that a pleasant, challenging, and empowered workplace could have a greater impact on employee behavior than monetary incentives (Pfeffer 1998).

Leonard and Swap made a parallel argument, emphasizing the importance of employees' passion for work that can lead them to lose the distinction between work and play. They gave examples of 3M (where R&D employees were allowed to use 15 percent of their time to pursue any project they wanted) and Hewlett-Packard (where R&D employees could set aside 10 percent of their time to work on new project ideas). As a result, they argued, both 3M and Hewlett-Packard were among the most innovative companies in the world (Leonard and Swap 1999). Google, another highly innovative company, expects its professional employees to spend 20 percent of their time working on an idea that might turn into a profitable product.

Similarly, Blanchard and Johnson identify "one minute praising" and "one minute reprimanding." They discuss the importance of rewarding the right behavior of employees, giving them feedback, and discouraging undesirable behavior. They make the point that if managers tell employees what is expected of them, praise them for little accomplishments, and set increasingly high standards for rewards, the employees will feel appreciated. They also will learn that they can get more rewards by doing more productive work. Gradually they will learn what their responsibilities are without trying to figure out the whole picture on their own (Blanchard and Johnson 1982).

The link between the motivation process and the authority and influence process

In considering the motivation process, an LG's senior management team needs to focus on a fit among (1) employee personalities, (2) the six other cross-functional processes, and (3) the organization's external environment – citizens, competitors (for services provided by profit centers), regulators, lenders, and other stakeholders. For example, a hierarchical authority and influence process – with many controls on decision making and highly structured ways of organizing employee behavior – is appropriate when the external environment is relatively certain, when employees prefer dependent authority relationships, and when they have a relatively low tolerance for ambiguity. By contrast, a more collegial authority and influence process – with few controls on decisions and relatively unstructured ways of organizing employee behavior – is appropriate for an uncertain external environment, where employees prefer considerable autonomy, and where they have a high tolerance for ambiguity.

BOX 11.2 FITTING MOTIVATION AND AUTHORITY AND INFLUENCE

Motivation for workers on a road repair project (with a strong hierarchical authority and influence process) might be tied to work standards, with extra compensation linked to increased productivity. By contrast, motivation for social workers or teachers, both of whom have a more collegial authority and influence process, might be related to collaboration and the sharing of ideas, with peer recognition seen as more important than financial rewards.

In all cases, the motivation process, especially when aligned with the authority and influence process, constitutes an important activity to help an LG achieve its strategy.

However, as the examples in the previous boxes illustrate, there is no single "right" motivation process that will work in all LGs under all conditions.

Conceptual foundations of the motivation process

The idea that there is no one right motivation process is deeply rooted in psychological theories of human behavior, many of which are relevant to an LG's senior managers considering the design of an appropriate motivation process. As discussed in Chapter 4, Maslow's "hierarchy of needs" begins with most basic physical needs (food, clothing, etc.) at the bottom, and rises to "self-actualization" at the top (Maslow 1954). However, few, if any, motivation processes will be able to self-actualize all employees.

Maslow's concept of a hierarchy of needs is supported by Douglas McGregor's notion of Theory X and Theory Y – two contrasting assumptions about what motivates employee behavior (McGregor 1960). Managers who believe in Theory X think that employees are motivated only by their basic needs and not by a desire to contribute to the organization's success. By contrast, managers who believe in Theory Y see employees as motivated by "higher-order growth needs." In fact, looking at McGregor's dichotomy in conjunction with Maslow's hierarchy suggests at least the *possibility* that some employees are motivated by basic needs, whereas others – those who have moved up Maslow's hierarchy, perhaps because they have reached positions of greater responsibility in the organization – have more lofty aspirations. Certainly, this would seem to be what Frederick Herzberg had in mind in his classic article on motivation, when he suggested that some employees need a KITA ("kick in the pants") and others need job enrichment (Herzberg 2003).

Clearly, people are far more complex than some of these bifurcated theories would suggest. For example, as David McClelland (1962) argued, most employees (indeed, most *people*) have some combination of three motives: achievement (the need to seek tasks that will provide a sense of accomplishment), power (the need to be in charge of and influence others), and affiliation (the need to have social and interpersonal relationships). An ideal motivation process would target each employee's mix of these three motives, and align itself with them – a challenging task in any organization, but no more so in an LG than elsewhere.

Overarching concepts

In light of these various theories, it is not surprising that so much has been written about the topic of motivation. Yet, most managers would agree that there is no theory or combination of theories that can be used to eliminate the difficult task of designing an appropriate motivation process for an LG's employees. Nevertheless, out of all this literature, three basic concepts emerge that can be of use to senior managers who are

315

designing (or redesigning) their LG's motivation process:

■   *Concept #1: There are two basic sources of rewards: extrinsic and intrinsic.* Other than financial rewards, extrinsic rewards can include praise, recognition, gold watches, employee-of-the-month parking places, and a variety of other non-financial items. Intrinsic rewards, by contrast, are derived from within employees themselves, and relate to how well they believe they performed a task or set of tasks. A good motivation process will incorporate both sources.

■   *Concept #2: Employees need feedback.* Regardless of the set of rewards and recognition activities that senior management uses, it needs to find ways to provide employees with feedback on their performance. Feedback allows employees to satisfy any one of several needs, such as relating rewards to the effort they expended, or comparing rewards to an external standard of some sort.

■   *Concept #3: Procedural justice is important.* Employees need to believe that a fair process was used to determine the distribution of rewards among them, and that their compensation is an appropriate reflection of their contributions to the organization.

In addition to the above three concepts, a fourth also appears to be important, although it is rarely discussed in the organizational literature, and then only in a tangential way: *the motivation process must fit with an LG's other cross-functional processes.* Without this sort of fit, it is likely that senior management will be sending mixed messages to employees, or that a lack of *goal congruence* will arise. Recall that, when there is goal congruence, an employee behaving in accordance with his or her own best interests – as defined by the motivation process – is also behaving in the LG's best interests.[5]

Link to strategy formulation

In terms of the LG's best interests, senior management needs to recognize that the design of the motivation process depends to a great extent on the LG's strategy and the nature of its other cross-functional processes. Indeed, regardless of where one comes out on the issue of contingent compensation, intrinsic rewards, feedback, procedural justice, and the like, it is important to try to find a link between the motivation process and the LG's strategy.

Many nonprofit organizations, but especially LGs, have difficulty finding this link.[6] Some nonprofits outside the public sector have sought it by encouraging entrepreneurial behavior and providing supplemental resources to successful managers. An LG could easily do this for its profit centers, and perhaps even for some of its standard expense centers.

■ **316**

BOX 11.3   ENCOURAGING ENTREPRENEURIAL BEHAVIOR

The City of Phoenix, Arizona used a "gainsharing" approach. It had a suggestion program that encouraged employees to submit ideas that promoted cost savings or measurable improvements in productivity, product quality, employee morale, or safety, and it paid cash awards of up to $2,500. The Phoenix system received several national awards (Nelson 1997).

As discussed in Chapter 4, the manager of the Bureau of Motor Equipment Repair of the New York City Sanitation (trash collection) Department created pseudo profit centers by using outside garage prices as "revenue." This manager also faced a variety of union-related constraints on productivity, but by creating teams of mechanics, using shadow prices to compare each team's productivity to the cost of a similar repair job in a private garage, and making it a "game" to beat the private sector garages, the manager was able to achieve a dramatic increase in the department's productivity.

ATTAINING A FIT

Beyond designing an effective motivation process, an LG's senior management team needs to think about a fit among all seven cross-functional processes. This is especially important in an LG that has created profit centers along the lines discussed in Chapter 4. This is not a fit that it is likely to get right on the first try. Instead, senior management will need to experiment with various approaches and make adjustments when necessary. In this regard, there are several issues that senior management must consider within each of the seven processes.

Strategy formulation

In many respects the strategy formulation process is at the center of an LG's activities. This process, which can be quite rigorous and systematic or, alternatively, can operate very informally and haphazardly, is how senior management examines the LG's environment, assesses the kinds of signals it is sending, compares this information with the LG's strengths and weaknesses, incorporates the LG's cultural values and its own personal values into the analysis, and decides on a strategic direction.

This part of the strategy formulation process is sometimes called a SWOT analysis (for strengths, weaknesses, opportunities, and threats). One of its most difficult aspects is assessing the nature of the environmental signals. How, for example, does senior management learn what regional or national legislation is being drafted that could affect its operations? How does it gain a full understanding of citizen needs, ascertain the kinds of external resources (such as grants or contracts) that are available to support its efforts, and determine what services are available from other sources?

Many LGs solicit environmental information from their line managers and professionals. Thus, if senior management supports them, both groups can be a rather unique source of information about the environment. Line managers and professionals frequently know about citizens' concerns with the LG services, new service needs, industry trends, and the like. These individuals can be extremely valuable in "processing" this information and deciding what is important.

Authority and influence

Profit center managers ordinarily have greater (and different) authority than expense center managers. Indeed, because they have bottom line responsibility, profit center managers generally have considerably more influence than other managers. In this regard, a key role for senior management is to select an appropriate type of responsibility center for each organizational unit and to determine a corresponding transfer pricing arrangement. These are tasks that senior management frequently delegates to the controller's office, but, unfortunately, the controller usually does not have enough information to carry them out appropriately. Thus, senior management must remain intimately involved, and perhaps even lead the effort.

Cultural maintenance

Although organizational culture has been a popular topic in the management literature for several years, relatively little has been written about the process of maintaining (or modifying) it. Organizational culture is important in that it constitutes one of two ways to encourage line managers, professionals, and other employees to do what is necessary for the LG's success. Specifically, if people in an LG believe in and subscribe to the culture, they are much more likely to make decisions that are consistent with and supportive of the LG's strategy without the need for intervention by superiors in their decision-making activities. A well-understood culture can also influence the nature of the conflict management process in that conflicts can be resolved more effectively if everyone involved has the same general understanding of what is important for the LG and its citizens/clients.

Clearly, an LG senior manager cannot ask his or her executive assistant to have a new culture in place in time for Monday's staff meeting. Thus, while a cultural change cannot be accomplished overnight, culture nevertheless can be managed through a careful use of the various cross-functional processes (Young 2000).

318

Client management

In organizations other than LGs, the client management process is undergoing the closest thing to a revolution of any of the seven process. One important shift is the fusion of marketing and operations – two traditionally separate functions that now are linked in many organizations. In addition, the client management process is influenced in important ways by the Internet, new information technologies, mass customization, total quality management, re-engineering, and a variety of other activities that have inundated the management literature during the past several decades.

The presence of these trends suggests that, in LGs as elsewhere, the client management process must fit with several other cross-functional processes. For example, since client management involves a number of decisions, made by a variety of individuals within the LG, frequently including citizens/clients themselves, senior management must assure itself that appropriate conflict management processes are in place. Similarly, it is likely that the reporting phase of the management control process will need to undergo constant revisions in an effort to provide line managers, professionals, and others, as well as senior management, with timely information on the effectiveness and efficiency of the client management process. Unfortunately, the accounting departments of many LGs do not welcome change with open arms, and many tend to resist the development of new kinds of reports. Thus, senior management leadership will be essential if the needed changes are to be made.

Conflict management

Many senior managers attempt to eliminate conflict, or at least resolve it as quickly as possible so that department and program managers can get on with the LG's "real" business. However, some senior managers have found that conflict frequently can be quite beneficial. One of the advantages of conflict is that, properly managed, it allows important concerns to surface and be addressed. As such, it constitutes a powerful cross-functional process.

Although it can be powerful, conflict also can be detrimental to an LG if it is not managed properly. Among other difficulties, unresolved conflict can result in different members of the LG carrying out contradictory activities with respect to a given client or program.

Despite its potential advantages, the conflict management process has received relatively scant attention in the management literature. Yet, based on the idea that conflict provides information about the LG's environment that otherwise would not be available, some successful senior managers actually have developed mechanisms to *generate* it. To do so, however, these managers also have instilled a culture that not only permits, but embraces, different points of view on a wide variety of matters.

319

BOX 11.4   GENERATING IDEAS FROM CONFLICT MANAGEMENT

Michael Eisner, while Chairman and CEO of the Disney Corporation, was asked, "How do you create the environment for supportive conflict?" His response included the following:

> We're entertaining people, so we should have an energized culture ... that kind of culture doesn't just happen – you have to make it happen. That's one of the reasons we started doing our own internal "gong show" back in the 1970s. It started as a concept where, once a week, we'd invite everybody to come to a conference room, and anyone could offer up an idea or two and, right on the spot, people would react. We loved the idea of big, unruly, disruptive meetings ... *The Little Mermaid* came out of a gong show, and so did *Pocahontas*. Lots of ideas came out of those meetings.

> Another way we get creative juices going and ideas flowing is with "charettes." These are meetings with our architects and theme park designers. I love them because they are so brutally honest. Because everybody has a different opinion about color and style and size and look and landscaping and all the rest, these meetings take on an event stature. Eventually resolution arrives, but not before every possible idea is put on the table ... There is no pecking order. All of a sudden it gets really creative. You may have a ten-hour meeting, but it's during the last half hour that the best ideas come out. Everybody starts driving each other crazy with ideas, and then somebody says something and it all comes together (Wetlaufer 2000).

Motivation

As discussed above, the motivation process is an essential ingredient in an LG's success. Moreover, if it is well-designed, it will encourage profit center managers to think long term as well as short term. In general, however, profit center managers tend to think short term, and senior management leadership is needed to encourage them to extend their thinking beyond the current budget year.

BOX 11.5   LONG- VERSUS SHORT-TERM PERSPECTIVE

A public works manager needs to be concerned about both the daily removal and disposal of trash, but he or she also needs to be thinking about the longer-run efficiency and cost of the department, such as whether removal and disposal should be done by the LG's own employees or outsourced, or whether a new kind of recycling program should be initiated.

Management control

As discussed in Chapters 5 through 10, programming, budgeting, measuring, and reporting are essential activities for an LG that wishes to provide cost-effective and high-quality services to its citizens. But the management control process cannot take place in a vacuum. As we have discussed, if it is to be successful, it must be carried out in concert with the other six cross-functional processes shown in Figure 11.1.

A list of the kinds of questions senior management needs to ask itself in conjunction with each of these cross-functional processes is contained in Table 11.1. As this list indicates, senior management must continually take action on several related fronts: planning, organizational, and informational.

MANAGING THE CHANGE EFFORT

It's one thing to want it, but quite another to get it. If senior management wishes to make some changes to its management control system, how does it go about the change effort? John Kotter (1995), a leading authority on change management, has described eight steps that a manager or management team must take:

1   Establish a sense of urgency
2   Form a powerful guiding coalition
3   Create a vision
4   Communicate the vision
5   Empower others to act on the vision
6   Plan and create short-term wins
7   Consolidate improvements and produce still more change
8   Institutionalize new approaches

Although these steps may seem evident and intuitive, Kotter's article discussing them contains the ominous subtitle "why transformation efforts fail," suggesting that change efforts frequently are unsuccessful. His article is required reading for any senior management team considering modifications to its management control system.

Resistance to the change effort

It is highly likely that some (perhaps many) people in an LG will resist senior management's efforts to implement a change in the management control system. How senior management deals with these individuals is, in part, style-based. For example, some senior managers will embrace the resistors and attempt to work with them, while others will attempt to ride roughshod over them. Regardless of its style, however, the

Table 11.1 *Questions concerning cross-functional processes*

Cross-functional processes	Questions
Strategy-formulation	What sorts of analyses are carried out, by whom?
	Are decisions made with sufficient senior management involvement, or are they a result of individual groups acting independently?
Client management	How do citizens use the LG's programs?
	■ How does a citizen (client) initially come into contact with a program?
	■ What decisions are made about how a client will (or will not) be served? Who makes those decisions?
	■ What decisions are made concerning a client leaving a program? By whom?
	Are services delivered at the best site and by the most appropriate person(s)?
Cultural maintenance	What are the LG's principal values, i.e., what does it see as its relatively unchanging criteria that guide decision making?
	How do the LG's programs fit with these values?
	How are the values reinforced and maintained through activities such as recruitment, training, promotion, and severance?
Authority and influence	What kinds of responsibility centers have been overlaid on the LG's organizational structure? Do they satisfy the fairness and goal congruence criteria?
	Does the flow of authority and influence foster collaborative decision making where appropriate?
	What formal mechanisms exist for professionals (e.g., social workers) to influence decision making? Do these help the LG move toward its strategy?
Motivation	How are people rewarded for doing good work?
	Is there is an incentive compensation system? If so, is it part of the budget formulation process?
	How deeply into the LG does the incentive-compensation system extend? Does it cover the professional staff, for example?

Table 11.1 *Continued*

Cross-functional processes	Questions
Conflict management	Where are the potential sources of conflict within the LG? Who typically is involved?
	How is this conflict managed, i.e., what sorts of formal mechanisms are in place (such as permanent or ad hoc committees) to manage it?
Management control programming	How and by whom are decisions made to begin new programs? To change or drop existing programs?
	Does the process lead to programs that reflect and reinforce the LG's strategy?
Budgeting	Who participates in formulating the LG's annual budget? What is the timetable?
	How does the budget relate to programs?
	What kinds of "drivers" are used to build the budget?
	Have transfer prices been established? If so, are responsibility center managers allowed to purchase from outside the system if they think a transfer price is too high? If not, how is the pricing problem addressed?
Financial measuring and reporting	Are fixed and variable costs measured for different mixes of clients in the LG's programs, and are variances computed?
	What other financial information is reported to managers?
	Are managers held responsible for the resources they control?
	Do the reports help managers to assess their financial performance against the budget?
	Do senior managers meet with middle managers to discuss the actions that will be taken on the basis of the reports? Do middle managers do the same with their subordinates? And so on down the line?
Programmatic measuring and reporting	How are programmatic results measured (such as for quality, client satisfaction, etc.)?
	How do programmatic and financial measurement and reporting relate to each other?
	What are the LG's key success factors, and how are these incorporated into the reports? Are these results linked to the motivation process?

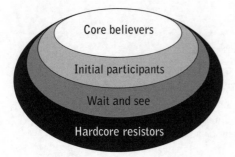

■ *Figure 11.2* *Categories of commitment to change*

Source: Adapted from an exhibit prepared by Professor Martin Charns, Boston University, School of Public Health.

senior management team must recognize that line managers' and others' commitment to the change effort can be classified into one of four categories identified by Martin Charns, and shown in Figure 11.2.

Generally, when senior management forms a "powerful guiding coalition" (Step 2 of Kotter's eight Steps), it chooses the coalition's membership from among the core believers and perhaps the initial participants. That is, the change effort begins with the inner circle and moves to the outer one.

There is no clear consensus on how to deal with hardcore resistors. On the one hand, they may fear that the changes, once implemented, will have a negative impact on their careers, income, power in the organization, or something else of a personal nature. Under those circumstances, any attempt to involve them may be futile, and the best course of action might be to encourage them to seek employment elsewhere. On the other hand, hardcore resistors may be resisting the change for good reasons, and their views might be important – perhaps even constructive – contributions to the change effort. When this appears to be the case, a manager may try to bring them into the effort early on, either as members of task forces focused on specific issues, or as sources of concern.

There are six basic methods to deal with resistance to change: education, communication, participation, support, negotiation, and coercion (Kotter and Schlesinger 1979). Each of these is appropriate under certain circumstances, and each has some advantages and disadvantages. Sometimes, for example, education and/or communication can be effective in making people aware of why the change is underway. At other times, asking people to participate or become involved in the effort can be useful. Sometimes, people simply need to be supported in "embracing" the change, and sometimes negotiation may be needed to secure their support. At the extreme, there may be a need for a much heavier hand, which might involve coercion.

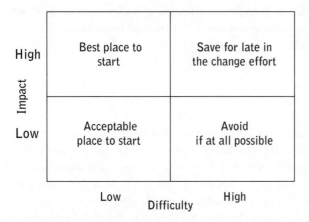

Figure 11.3 *Impact versus difficulty*

Source: Prepared by Professor Martin Charns, Boston University School of Public Health.

Short-term wins

It is easy to say that senior management should plan and create some short-term wins (Kotter's Step 6), but it is much more difficult to determine in advance what those might be. To assist with this selection effort, Martin Charns has developed the matrix shown in Figure 11.3.

Clearly, to create some short-term wins, senior management should start in the column of low difficulty, preferably in the high-impact quadrant. For example, in one successful change effort, senior management chose as its first task the goal of making sure that all the clocks in the facility were running on time, an easy and seemingly low impact item. Yet, because unreliable clocks were a source of considerable employee complaints, the task actually had a high impact on morale. As a result, subsequent tasks were much easier to carry out.

Despite how obvious this seems, many change efforts nevertheless begin in the lower right quadrant of Figure 11.3! In a school of management, for example, where a new dean was attempting to strengthen the school's reputation in the business and academic communities, one of his first efforts was to attempt to eliminate tenure. Well over a year of time, scores of meetings, two full faculty assemblies and votes, and many reams of paper were consumed in the effort. Meanwhile, the school continued to languish in the bottom quartile of the top 100 management schools.

Consolidating and moving forward

In most organizations, the hardcore resistors cannot be left out of the effort indefinitely. Sooner or later they either must be brought into the effort or encouraged to leave the organization. Assuming the former takes place, one or more of the above six methods can be used by senior management as it consolidates and moves forward (Step 7 in the Kotter Model).

SUMMARY

Designing and implementing a new management control system is a complex undertaking. Revising an existing system may be even more difficult, as people have grown accustomed to it, including all of its flaws. In both instances, there is bound to be resistance, due in part to the uncertainty about the consequences of the change, and in part to the fact that, other than a salary increase, few people like change.

The design (or redesign) effort is further complicated by the fact that the management control system does not exist in isolation – it is part of a much larger organizational whole, and senior management needs to see it in that context. The management control system cannot be divorced from strategy formulation, for example, as it must help to provide relevant information to senior management in thinking about strategy, while, at the same time, it must report on movement toward the strategy. Nor can it be divorced from the LG's motivation process. Indeed, if people are not rewarded for good performance, they likely will have little incentive to worry about accomplishing the organization's goals. The management control process is also linked to authority, conflict, and culture, and, ultimately, to an LG's success (or lack thereof) in serving its citizens in accordance with its strategy.

DISCUSSION QUESTIONS

1   Which of the six activities that constitute the broader context in which a management control system operates is the most difficult to manage? Why?

2   If an LG wants to implement some changes to its management control system, where should it start? Where can it expect to encounter the most resistance?

3   What, besides monetary compensation, motivates the employees of an LG to do a better job?

NOTES

1 These constraints sometimes are called "non-mission-based values." They result from the need of all government entities, not just LGs, to provide both equity

and transparency. For additional discussion, see Piotrowski and Rosenbloom (2002).

2 For the definitions of different accounting methods and a comparative analysis of them, see Christiaens *et al.* (2010).

3 In some LGs, program evaluations tend to take place shortly before (or shortly after) an election.

4 Unless otherwise indicated, these examples all come from Nelson (1997).

5 A lack of goal congruence is perhaps most vividly demonstrated in the classic article by Kerr (1975).

6 For a discussion of this idea, see Mirvis and Hackett (1983).

REFERENCES

Antonucci, M. (1995) "Even Mega-Media Corporations Must Bow to Consumer Demands," *San Jose Mercury News*, August 5.

Blanchard, K.H. and Johnson, S. (1982) *The One-Minute Manager*, New York: William Morrow & Co.

Christiaens, J., Reyniers, B., and Rolle, C. (2010) "Impact of IPSAS on Reforming Governmental Financial Information Systems: A Comparative Study," *International Review of Administrative Sciences*, 76(3): 537–54.

Fenn, D. (2000) "Personnel Best," *Inc.*, February: 75–83.

Herzberg, F. (2003) "One More Time: How Do You Motivate Employees?," *Harvard Business Review* 81(1): 87–96.

Kerr, S. (1975) "On the Folly of Rewarding 'A' While Hoping for 'B,'" *Academy of Management Journal*, 18(4): 769–83.

Kotter, J.P. (1995) "Leading Change: Why Transformation Efforts Fail," *Harvard Business Review*, 73(2): 59–67.

Kotter, J.P. (1999) *What Leaders Really Do*, Boston, Massachusetts: Harvard Business School Press.

Kotter, J.P. and Schlesinger, L.A. (1979) "Choosing Strategies for Change," *Harvard Business Review*, 57(2): 106–14.

Leonard, D. and Swap, L. (1999) *When Sparks Fly: Igniting Creativity in Groups*, Boston, Massachusetts: Harvard Business School Press.

McClelland, D.C. (1962) "Business Drives and National Achievement," *Harvard Business Review*, 40(4): 99–112.

McGregor, D. (1960) *The Human Side of Enterprise*, New York: McGraw-Hill.

Maslow, A.H. (1954) *Motivation and Personality*, New York: Harper & Row Publishers.

Mirvis, P.H. and Hackett, E.J. (1983) "Work and Work Force Characteristics in the Nonprofit Sector," *Monthly Labor Review*, 106(4): 3–12.

Nelson, B. (1997) *1001 Ways to Energize Employees*, New York: Workman Publishing.

Pfeffer, J. (1994) *Managing with Power: Politics and Influence in Organizations*, Boston, Massachusetts: Harvard Business School Press.

Pfeffer, J. (1998) *The Human Equation: Building Profits by Putting People First*, Boston, Massachusetts: Harvard Business School Press.

Piotrowski, S.J. and Rosenbloom, D.H. (2002) "Non Mission-based Values in Results-oriented Public Management: The Case of Freedom of Information," *Public Administration Review*, 62: 643–57.

Scheinin, R. (1995) "Welcome to Disneyworld," *San Jose Mercury News*, August 5.

Wetlaufer, S. (2000) "Common Sense and Conflict: An Interview with Disney's Michael Eisner," *Harvard Business Review*, 78(1): 115–24.

Young, D.W. (2000) "The Six Levers for Managing Organizational Culture," *Business Horizons*, 43(5): 19–28.

FURTHER READING

Readers interested in an especially useful coverage of the topic of leadership may wish to order a paperback anthology entitled *HBR's Ten Must Reads on Leadership* (Harvard Business Press 2011). The book contains ten of the *Harvard Business Review's* most influential articles on the topic. For a discussion of leadership and related issues – such as change strategies, thinking strategically, and strategic management in the public services – one can refer to *Strategic Leadership in the Public Services* by Paul Joyce (Routledge 2011). As has been argued in this chapter, the implementation or transformation of a management control system requires a change effort. Kerry Brown and Stephen P. Osborne discuss the skills necessary to understand, manage and sustain change and innovation in public service organizations in their book *Managing Change and Innovation in Public Service Organizations* (Routledge 2005).

Index

accounting systems 37–8
accrual accounting 37, 308
activity-based costing 193–4
actual costs 43, 88, 280
actual performance, measures of 256–7
administrative rules and procedures 96–7
alternative choice analysis 210; and cost
    behavior 210–14; and full-cost
    accounting 210
appropriation accounts 67, 69, 93
authority and influence structures 79–88,
    307–8, 310; and profit centers 318

balanced scorecard (BSC) 268–70
behavioral management 97–9
benefit/cost analysis 119–25
Blanchard, K.H. 314
Borgonovi, E. 57
breakeven volumes 202, 215–18, 220
budgetary games 164–5
budgeting 148–50; behavioral influences
    on 163–5; and cost drivers 167,
    306; deviation from 167; elements
    of 152–5; and flexible budgets 82,
    279–81; and for-profit companies
    151–2; in Forlì 168–75, 236; and
    management control processes 49,
    309; mechanical aspects of 155–8;
    non-financial measures used in 158
budgeting misfits 149, 165–7
bureaucracy and bureaucratic control 57,
    74, 101
business-like units 277

capital budgets 110, 113, 115, 122, 148,
    157–8
capital investment analysis techniques
    112–19; cash flows 113–14; cost of
    equity 116; discount rates 113,
    116–19, 133–5; gross present value
    114; internal rate of return 115–18,
    129; net present value (NPV)
    113–16, 129; payback period
    112–13; present value 113–15,

129–32; and risk 118–19; weighted
    cost of capital (WCC) 116, 133–4;
    weighted return on assets (WRA)
    116–17, 134–5
capital investments 111–12, 116–18, 129
cash accounting systems 37, 52
cash budgets 110, 148
cash flows 113–14
centralized decision-making 67–8
Chandler, A. 67
change management 321–6
Charns, M. 324–5
citizen sensitivity 209, 230–3
civil service 23–4, 27; management
    control and 70, 313
client management 310–11, 319, 322
collectivism 103–5
commitment-based accounting 148–9
comparative analysis 181–2
competition 25, 79, 100, 119, 309;
    market forms of 230–3, 237, 240
conflict management 310–11, 318–20
consumer equity 58, 61–4
continuous quality improvement 237, 258
contribution income statements 226
contribution to overhead 226
control culture 65–7
controller's role 101–2
cost allocation 194; and cost behavior
    222–3; direct method 187; reciprocal
    method 188; stepdown method
    187–90
cost assignment 187, 194
cost behavior 210–14; and cost allocation
    222–3
cost/benefit analysis 119–25
cost centers 186–8
cost distinctions 221
cost drivers 167, 306
cost of equity 116
cost information 38–40, 181, 205, 253,
    292; see also full costs
cost objects 39, 184, 191, 262; definition
    of 184–6

329

strategic planning 33–4, 52; and
    performance measurement 266–8
strategy-formulation process 310; and
    motivation 316–21; and SWOT
    analysis 317
subjective performance measures 254–5
subsidized pricing 201–3
support centers 45
support programs 90
surrogate performance measures 256–7,
    259
Swap, L. 313–14
switching costs 231–3
SWOT analysis 317

task complexity 69–70
task control 34, 52
Theory X and *Theory Y,* 315
3M (company) 313–14
time orientation 103
timeliness 266; and accuracy 263;
    and performance measurement 267;
    and reporting 274, 291
total costs 212–15

total quality management 258
trade unions 23–4, 27, 313
transfer prices 87–8; as efficiency
    measures 88
two-stage budgets 150–1

uncertainty avoidance 103
unit contribution margin 216, 220–1
United States Department of Defense 119

variable costs 40, 212, 215; and
    differential costs 223–7
variance analysis 281–6, 306

Weber, M. 57, 101
weighted cost of capital (WCC) 116–18,
    133–4
weighted return on assets (WRA) 116–18,
    134–5

Young, D. 48, 231–3, 238, 311

zero-surplus profit centers 308